FINANCE, DEVELOPMENT, AND THE IMF

Finance, Development, and the IMF

James M. Boughton and Domenico Lombardi (Editors)

OXFORD
UNIVERSITY PRESS

Great Clarendon Street, Oxford OX2 6DP

Oxford University Press is a department of the University of Oxford.
It furthers the University's objective of excellence in research, scholarship,
and education by publishing worldwide in

Oxford New York

Auckland Cape Town Dar es Salaam Hong Kong Karachi
Kuala Lumpur Madrid Melbourne Mexico City Nairobi
New Delhi Shanghai Taipei Toronto

With offices in

Argentina Austria Brazil Chile Czech Republic France Greece
Guatemala Hungary Italy Japan Poland Portugal Singapore
South Korea Switzerland Thailand Turkey Ukraine Vietnam

Oxford is a registered trade mark of Oxford University Press
in the UK and in certain other countries

Published in the United States
by Oxford University Press Inc., New York

© Oxford University Press 2009

The moral rights of the authors have been asserted
Database right Oxford University Press (maker)

First published 2009

British Library Cataloguing in Publication Data

Data available

Library of Congress Cataloging in Publication Data

Data available

Typeset by SPI Publisher Services, Pondicherry, India
Printed in Great Britain
on acid-free paper by the
MPG Books Group, Bodmin and King's Lynn

ISBN 978–0–19–923986–3

1 3 5 7 9 10 8 6 4 2

Foreword by Michel Camdessus

More than many multilateral institutions, the IMF, its mandate, its role, and its record are frequently at the center of international debates. Views expressed are in a permanent pendulum swinging between a narrowly focused mandate, based on a literal interpretation of its "monetary character" and—particularly at times of emergencies—the convenience of taking advantage of the high professionalism of its staff, of its experience and *savoir faire*, for relying on it to lead the international response to unexpected challenges.

Its role in supporting the economic progress of the low-income countries has been part of these controversies. There are frequent calls, particularly from the civil society, inviting the Fund "to do more for the poor". They contrast with the warning of my former colleagues from the Treasuries or the Central Banks, against what they suspected to be an excessive attention lent to poverty issues. In certain quarters, I have heard opinions expressed with no particular ambiguity; this was the case of a very high representative of a leading country recommending me, a few days after my election "to work with the G10, leave the poor under the umbrella of the World Bank . . . and play golf". I must confess that, during my thirteen years tenure at the IMF, I failed to find time to initiate myself to that sport or to understand why people question the responsibility of the IMF to help the poorest countries. Are not they its members?

Certainly poor countries need assistance from development agencies such as the World Bank and the African Development Bank. Those institutions have unique skills, and they have a mandate to offer grants and long-term support for economic and social development. But that support is not a substitute for what the IMF has to offer. The governments of poor countries may also need to strengthen their own economic policies so that they can use that aid effectively for the good of their people. They may need to stabilize the economy after a natural disaster, an armed conflict, or other shock. And they need to develop their financial, economic, and statistical capacity to prepare themselves for further development. Many of these actions are related to balance of payments and monetary issues for which the Fund has a unique role to play. To ignore that responsibility would be inexcusable. I am happy to see that if the controversy has not ended, the commitment of the Fund itself remains—and I hope will continue to be—unquestionable.

The only real question, the only real debate, concerns how best to strengthen the IMF so that it can serve its low-income members most effectively. I believe that the Fund should have more resources to lend on concessional terms, but I understand why others believe differently. On conditionality, views can reasonably differ on how best to work with countries whose economies exhibit deep-seated problems, on how to ensure that IMF-supported programs truly reflect the countries' priorities and that governments are genuinely committed to carry out reforms. On its governance, as low-income countries make for an important share of the IMF membership, they should have enough voice in the institution to make it unquestionably responsive to their needs. These are but a few of the many issues which need to be clarified. The contribution to it of this new book could be of major importance.

James Boughton, who has spent more than 25 years at the IMF, as economist and historian, and Domenico Lombardi, who has advised both the Fund and the World Bank and has proven his scholarship at Oxford University and the Brookings Institution, have done a masterful job of assembling a wide range of interdisciplinary articles on the key poverty-related issues facing the IMF today. Because they have not shied away from controversy, they have produced a book that should provoke a lively discussion. If it does, the cooperative nature of the IMF, the difficulties of its tasks, and the importance of its cooperation with the World Bank and of its dialogue with all the stakeholders in finance and development will be better understood by both supporters and critics. This is the safest way of contributing to its future and to the sustainable human development of its member countries.

Contents

Part III. IMF Policies and Financing in Low-Income Countries

Contents

Abbreviations

CFA	African Financial Community
CFF	Compensatory Financing Facility
CPIA	Country Policy and Institutional Assessment
DSF	Debt Sustainability Framework
ECA	export credit agency
EFF	Extended Fund Facility
EME	Emerging Market Economy
EPCA	Emergency Post-Conflict Assistance
ESAF	Enhanced Structural Adjustment Facility
ESF	Exogenous Shocks Facility
FSAP	Financial Sector Assessment Program
FSSA	Financial Sector Stability Assessments
GFSR	Global Financial Stability Report
HIPC	Heavily Indebted Poor Country (Initiative)
ICOR	incremental capital output ratio
IDA	International Development Association
IEO	Independent Evaluation Office
IFI	International Financial Institution
IMFC	International Monetary and Finance Committee
IO	international organization
JMAP	Joint Management Action Plan
LIC	low-income country
LTEF	Long Term Expenditure Framework
MDG	Millennium Development Goal
MDRI	Multilateral Debt Relief Initiative
MTEF	Medium Term Expenditure Framework
MTS	Medium Term Strategy
NGO	nongovernmental organization
ODA	official development assistance

PFP	Policy Framework Paper
PRGF	Poverty Reduction and Growth Facility
PRS	Poverty Reduction Strategy
PRSP	Poverty Reduction Strategy Paper
PSI	Policy Support Instrument
PSIA	poverty and social impact analysis
QFRG	Quota Formula Review Group
ROSCs	Reports on the Observance of Standards and Codes
SAF	Structural Adjustment Facility
SDR	Special Drawing Right
SFF	Supplemental Financing Facility
SMP	Staff-Monitored Program
SRF	Supplemental Reserve Facility
SSA	sub-Saharan Africa
TA	technical assistance
UNCTAD	United Nations Conference on Trade and Development
UNECLA	United Nations Economic Commission for Latin America
WEO	World Economic Outlook

Part I

Introduction

1

The Role of the IMF in Low-Income Countries

James M. Boughton (IMF) and Domenico Lombardi
(Oxford University and Brookings Institution)

I. Introduction

In recent years, a large portion of the work of the International Monetary Fund has focused on stabilizing the economies of low-income countries (LICs) and creating conditions conducive to poverty reduction and sustainable economic growth. Most of the IMF's borrowers in the past decade have been countries that are poor enough to qualify for concessional loans and that receive most of their external capital from official creditors and donors rather than through international capital markets. As many of these countries have had severe difficulties servicing external debts—even debts with long maturities and very low interest rates—the IMF has initiated and participated in a series of debt-relief and debt-reduction operations since the mid-1990s.

Even though the Fund's interactions with LICs concentrate on issues of macroeconomics and financial stability—the same issues that predominate in its work with other member countries—the effects of these interactions reverberate much more widely. Each IMF-supported policy program with an LIC has the potential to raise the country's development prospects and lift its people out of extreme poverty. Success is far from assured, however. Only if a program is well designed to meet the needs of a country at an early stage of economic development (and possibly also political development), and only if the country is capable of implementing, and prepared to implement, the program will it have any real chance of succeeding. These are daunting requirements, and it should not be surprising to find that many IMF-supported programs in LICs have failed to achieve their objectives.

Such challenges are not confined to LICs. Some 70 percent of the world's people who live in extreme poverty inhabit countries with average per capita incomes that are above the cutoff level for concessional assistance programs. Thus, the IMF cannot ignore the consequences of its actions for development and poverty reduction even when it is advising or lending to a relatively advanced middle-income country.

In view of these challenges, it is natural to ask what role, if any, the IMF should have in the effort of the international community to help LICs develop and to assist in lifting vast numbers of people around the world out of abject poverty. Should it confine itself to helping middle-income countries cope with financial instability? Views on this question differ dramatically, and considerable debate has arisen among academics, policymakers, and advocates from nongovernmental organizations (NGOs). The debate has gained momentum since the adoption of the Millennium Development Goals (MDGs) by the international community in 2000. While the MDG campaign is led by the United Nations, with key operational roles for the World Bank and other multilateral development agencies, the IMF has been assigned important responsibilities to help determine what policies participating countries must adopt in order to achieve their goals. For its part, the IMF has officially and repeatedly reaffirmed its commitment to being fully engaged with its poorer members and with poverty issues more generally.

The bulk of the literature on the IMF's role in poverty alleviation derives from the theory of development economics. Both theoretically and empirically, this economic literature has examined whether the IMF's approach to macroeconomic stability and financial soundness contributes to, or is at least consistent with, sustained economic development. Separately, some political scientists have examined whether the IMF has the right structure, system of governance, and mandate to be effective in this domain.

This book aims to pull these strands together and extend them in order to present a more comprehensive picture of what the IMF can and does do in LICs. It adopts an interdisciplinary approach that brings together economists, economic historians, and political scientists who have studied and written about the IMF extensively and from a variety of professional perspectives. A few of these scholars work, or have worked, in the IMF; others are academics with a strong understanding of the institution and of what reforms are feasible, as well as desirable. This breadth of experience yields a rich and diverse perspective that further builds on the interdisciplinary approach.

This volume is organized thematically in four sections. Following this introduction, the next section explores the history and the nature of the role of the IMF in low-income countries; the third investigates IMF policies and financing in low-income countries; and the fourth analyzes the role of low-income member countries in the IMF's own governance.

While the authors of these chapters come from a wide range of backgrounds and academic disciplines, they all start with an appreciation of the importance of the Fund's work in this domain. Some are highly critical of the Fund's record; some give more emphasis to the successes and the progress that has been achieved. In selecting the papers and editing this volume, we have aimed to build up a comprehensive analysis without imposing uniform conclusions. Each reader will find points with which to agree and points that are more challenging. If the cumulative effect is to move the debate forward and clarify the key issues, the book will have met its goal.

II. History and nature of the role of the IMF in low-income countries

The second section of the volume lays the groundwork for the chapters that follow by tracing the historical evolution of thinking about the IMF's role in low-income countries, as well as how that role has been implemented. In the first essay, Harold James analyzes the conceptions of the IMF's role with respect to LICs as they have developed since the time of the Bretton Woods conference in 1944. The participants in that historic event hoped to create a universal economic and financial order with generally applicable solutions to the problems of the world. Although Article I of the IMF's Articles of Agreement states, as one of the objectives of the newly born institution, "the development of the productive resources of all members," the role that the IMF would in fact play in low-income countries was a peripheral concern of the founding members. Indeed, that dealing with the economies of poor countries represented a separate problem would become clear only in the following decades, when LICs joined the IMF's membership following their achievement of independence. James discusses how the Fund was then drawn into much broader discussions of development issues that went beyond simple short-term balance of payments problems and revealed the multidimensional nature of the challenges faced by this segment of its membership—ultimately launching a debate that is still ongoing.

Picking up this history from a different perspective, James Boughton's contribution provides further evidence of the complexity of the issues faced by the IMF in a discussion of its several attempts to tailor lending instruments to the needs of low-income economies. As LICs' membership within the IMF grew, Boughton argues, it became evident that the standard facilities offered by the IMF for short-run stabilization purposes were ill-suited to help those economies with protracted balance of payments deficits with their origin in deep-seated structural problems. As the IMF gathered experience with low-income economies, the institution learned that unless these countries "owned" the objectives and conditions associated with a given IMF program, that program was unlikely to succeed. This long learning process, Boughton argues, resulted in 1999 in the design of the Poverty Reduction and Growth Facility (PRGF), which now constitutes the Fund's main concessional lending arm for low-income member countries.

In a second essay, Boughton turns from the past to the present to suggest an integrating framework for thinking about how the IMF can assist its member countries across the full spectrum of financial development. As a universal institution with 185 member countries, the IMF is the cornerstone of the international financial system, with the purpose of fostering sound macroeconomic policies to help its members succeed in implementing their growth strategies. Given the intrinsically dynamic nature of the world economy, countries cannot be expected to remain permanently within taxonomies that label them "LICs," "pre-emerging economies," and the like. Rather, as countries grow, they will move up the development ladder—although occasionally they may also bounce back. The IMF, in addition to serving as a standby lender to all of its member countries, including the most advanced economies, provides macroeconomic advice that is bound to be relevant to member countries, regardless of their stage of development. In the case of a low-income country, Boughton posits that the IMF's advice may enable the country to achieve macroeconomic stabilization in the context of—and in support of—a longer-run development strategy aimed at economic growth and poverty reduction.

Building on the previous chapters' historical analysis, Domenico Lombardi outlines the rationale for the engagement of the IMF with low-income member countries in the final essay of the volume's second part. This chapter investigates the political economy foundations of the IMF's role in LICs, analyzes the broad nature of the IMF's current activities vis-à-vis low-income members, and assesses the effectiveness of these activities. In assisting low-income members, Lombardi argues, the IMF leverages on its ability to serve as a financial institution, an information provider, and a commitment device by offering a range of activities that are bundled together, such as policy advice, lending, and capacity building. Low-income countries potentially stand to benefit greatly from these activities, but closer scrutiny of how such activities are carried out clearly points to some challenges that the institution will have to manage carefully if it wishes to succeed.

III. IMF policies and financing in low-income countries

The third section offers an analysis of IMF policies and the role of its lending programs for low-income members. In the first contribution to this section, Graham Bird and Dane Rowlands provide a theoretical as well as empirical foundation for understanding what IMF policy aims ought to be when the Fund engages with a low-income country. For any poor country, they argue, there will be an optimal blend of external financing, short-run stabilization, and longer-term economic reform. As reliance on any one of these components on its own will be inadequate, the key question is how the IMF can help low-income countries discover and implement such a blend. At a time when aid flows are declining, the principal test facing the IMF is whether it can organize additional external financing either directly—through its own lending facilities—or by catalyzing others to lend so as to relax, as far as possible, the external financing constraint. In contrast, if aid flows are rising and the constraints imposed by external financing are being relaxed, the IMF should ensure that additional financial resources are used to maximum benefit. Bird and Rowlands conclude that, in the current setting, the IMF should be playing more of a facilitator than a financier role. It could still retain a lending role, however, by providing rapid-response finance designed to protect agreed-upon policy strategies from unforeseen short-term contingencies.

Turning from lending to policy formulation, David Bevan's essay reviews recent policy innovations in the IMF's toolkit and argues that the Fund has an important role to play by providing policy formulation in support of low-income countries, as well as enhanced macroeconomic monitoring as an input to donor decisions. In making this argument, he uncovers a tension between the Fund's lending arm and the goal of supporting LICs in their progress along a path of growth and poverty reduction: the latter requires taking a long-term view of the nature of the Fund's engagement with LICs, but such a view sits uncomfortably with the Fund's lending activities, which are mostly designed to provide balance of payments support. Bevan argues that the IMF would be more likely to provide a disinterested judgment of member countries' circumstances if it were not financially committed, just as an auditor who does not need to have a financial interest in a company for its statements to be credible. In this context, the recent introduction of an unfunded arrangement, the Policy Support Instrument (PSI), is an interesting development. The PSI adds flexibility to the Fund's toolkit and provides for a path whereby a low-income member that has benefited from a PRGF arrangement may progress to an unfunded program with formal conditionality—that is, to the PSI—to a phase of intensive surveillance before finally ending up with just the statutory Article IV consultations that the Fund conducts with all of its members.

Timothy Lane's essay investigates the theoretical foundations of the IMF's signaling, or facilitator, role that underpins, but is not limited to, the PSI. The IMF provides a "seal of approval" for the economic policies of a country through the use of an on-track IMF financial arrangement as a trigger for aid and the associated financing gap as an indication of a country's financing needs. Lane uses a simple model of delegated monitoring to illustrate the idea that a financial arrangement can function as an incentive mechanism for the IMF to monitor policies, ensuring that they are sufficiently sound that aid can be used effectively. In this framework, the amount of financing provided by the

IMF ought to be dictated not by a country's financing needs, but by the need to give the IMF a stake in the country's macroeconomic policies sufficient to create an incentive for it to provide a thorough and candid policy assessment. After critically reviewing the assumptions that underpin the signaling role of IMF financial arrangements, Lane argues that a shift to programs providing little or (as with the PSI) no financing implies a fundamental change in that signaling role. This change heightens the importance of strengthening the IMF's mandate to provide a candid assessment of whether a country's macroeconomic policies are consistent with its broader objectives for growth and poverty reduction. No financing on the part of the IMF would necessarily be required to underpin such an assessment.

The remaining three essays in the third section shift from a theoretical approach to a more empirical assessment of the IMF's performance with its low-income member countries. The IMF has provided support to low-income countries through various initiatives aimed at relieving their economies from the burden of excessive debt. While scholars have looked into specific aspects of such initiatives, no study has investigated the broader role of the IMF in providing debt relief to poor economies and how this fits its responsibility vis-à-vis low-income member countries. Graham Bird and Robert Powell trace the evolution of poor countries' external debt problems and the various policy initiatives that have been pursued to alleviate and eventually eradicate them. They focus in particular on how the measures designed to deal with poor countries' debt problems have evolved in the last two decades through the Enhanced Heavily Indebted Poor Countries (HIPC) Initiative and the Multilateral Debt Relief Initiative (MDRI). The authors then appraise various aspects of debt relief operations, including their additionality. By estimating a model of aid allocation on a sample of sub-Saharan economies, they find that, on average, debt relief under the HIPC Initiative has been additional for the country involved. However, aggregate net aid transfers to sub-Saharan economies (including non-HIPCs) declined, consistent with the claim that the additionality to countries benefiting from debt relief was at the expense of those not receiving it.

The essay that follows offers an insider's view of IMF interaction with LICs. Drawing on a recent evaluation that she led in the IMF's Independent Evaluation Office (IEO), Joanne Salop reviews the role of the IMF in aid in low-income countries from 1999 to 2005. This review encompasses the first six years of the PRGF, which aimed to establish a new relationship between the Fund and its low-income members. As this new facility was intended to build on the country-led Poverty Reduction Strategy process, it was thought that PRGF-supported programs would involve more direct measures for accelerating poverty reduction and growth and for identifying the associated financing requirements. Salop finds tensions, however, in how different branches of the institution have interpreted the IMF's overall institutional role vis-à-vis low-income countries. She finds a lack of consensus and clarity regarding this role within the Fund, despite the PRGF having been approved and endorsed by its Executive Board. A similar disconnect has emerged in the way different stakeholders have received the IEO's evaluation findings, with each group claiming that the evaluation validates its long-standing concerns about the role of the IMF in low-income countries.

In a final consideration of IMF effectiveness with its low-income members, Patrick Conway's chapter assesses whether a country's participation in an IMF-supported program has any independent and significant effect on income inequality. His analysis builds on the apparent association of increasing inequality in a wide sample of developing countries with more frequent and widespread participation in IMF arrangements. In presenting an empirical analysis of the determinants of income distribution in a sample of 108 developing countries over the period 1988 to 1998, he concludes that the majority of variation in income inequality is cross-country in nature. This component of income inequality, in fact, depends primarily upon the development characteristics of the countries, not on participation in IMF programs. Conway also finds that cumulative past participation in IMF programs is, on average, associated with an adjustment toward greater income equality rather than inequality.

IV. The role of low-income member countries in the governance of the IMF

The book's final section elaborates on the role of low-income member countries within the governance framework of the IMF, on the assumption that if the institution is to discharge an effective role in support of its low-income members, the latter need to share the decisions that will affect them. In the first essay of this section, Ngaire Woods argues that the governance of the institution affects its responsiveness in terms of generating relevant programs and instruments that could be enhanced if the end users could voice their concern and if, in addition, others within the organization had an incentive to listen. Better representation of low-income countries could also improve IMF performance by making its policies more effective. If low-income countries were fully in a position to own the policies generated from within the institution thanks to better representation in its governance bodies, then the IMF's engagement in those countries would be more successful. Finally, governance affects the IMF's impact in LICs through the organization's accountability: as the IMF's Executive Board sets the priorities and oversees the implementation of its policies, players across the organization have an incentive to meet the desiderata of those members of the Board who can most powerfully affect their careers and direction of work. If low-income countries have little role in the Board, the risk is that policies designed for this segment of the membership will be constantly underserved by a system that skews accountability toward meeting the preferences of other, more powerful groups.

Scholars and policymakers have long since concluded that the terms of LIC membership in IMF governance ought to be reformed. Bessma Momani reviews the current debate on IMF reform from the perspective of low-income member countries. She argues that the debate is mainly prompted by the desire of the Fund's more powerful members to regain the trust of emerging-market countries, which have over time gradually disengaged from the institution, through a package of measures designed to appeal more to them than to other segments of the membership. In fact, the centrality of the quotas issue in the current debate is likely to benefit the fast-growing emerging-market economies more than low-income ones. Momani maintains that low-income members would gain from a reform addressing substantive policy issues about the efficacy, the application, and the fundamentals of IMF advice. This type of reform has, however, been sidelined in the current debate. As a result, even after the current reform proposals have been fully implemented, they would likely lead to few substantive changes in the responsiveness of the IMF's policies to low-income countries. What is needed, Momani posits, is a bottom-up reorganization of IMF operators—the staff—that grows out of the reexamination of Fund recruitment and organizational design, with the goal of bringing in more staff members who are attuned to the political circumstances of low-income countries and skilled in providing implementable advice.

The final chapter, by Abbas Mirakhor and Iqbal Zaidi, considers the broader role of developing countries in the institution, arguing that for the IMF to play an important role in global governance, it is essential to enhance the organization's credibility as an international cooperative institution. The authors set out the principal issues to be resolved in formulating a proposal for quotas and voice reform that could command broad support. Mirakhor and Zaidi argue that Rawls's theory of justice provides an appropriate method for guiding the debate on IMF reform while suggesting a more fundamental review than is implied in the current discussions. The current emphasis on quota formulas and basic votes should, they maintain, be seen within the wider and more holistic approach of making IMF governance more democratic. In this setting, low-income countries should have an adequate opportunity to participate in the governance of an institution that spends a growing and considerable amount of its resources on their economies.

V. Concluding observations

As these essays were being written, the IMF was undertaking an internal stocktaking of its role in the world, the focus of its work, its relations with its 185 member countries, and its own governance. That "strategic review" was prompted by the cumulative effect of many changes in the world economy: the emergence of large imbalances in world trade, a strong growth in private-sector cross-border financial transactions, rapid and sustained growth in some developing countries while others remained stagnant, and a universal commitment by the world's political leaders to reduce extreme poverty and meet the Millennium Development Goals. It was clear to all that any international financial institution that failed to respond to these changes would soon lose its relevance and its ability to help its members.

Much of the public discussion of these issues was focused on the "emerging market" countries that were growing rapidly and enjoying access to increasing amounts of capital from private-sector creditors and investors. In that context, the question was how could the IMF reform itself so as to be ready to help if one or more of those countries were to suffer a major financial crisis. More generally, in a world awash in liquidity, would the IMF still be needed?

Those questions certainly are central to the core work of the IMF as a financial institution, and the global financial crisis that struck in 2008 provided strong affirmation of its importance. But those who look ahead even further, to a future in which today's emerging markets will graduate from even episodic dependence on official financing, just as most of today's advanced economies already have, see a different and more persistent issue. As markets in today's low-income countries begin to emerge, as they start to gain some access to private capital, what kind of institutional response will be required to spare them from the pitfalls that others have faced in the recent past? If called upon, will the IMF be ready with an adequate response, or will new institutions arise instead? As a first step toward answering these questions, we offer the following essays.

Part II

History and Nature of the Role of the IMF in Low-Income Countries

2

Bretton Woods and the Debate about Development

Harold James (Princeton University)

I. Introduction

The participants of the United Nations Monetary and Financial Conference at Bretton Woods in July 1944 hoped to create a universal financial and economic order, with generally applicable solutions to the problems of the world. But within a few years a very different vision emerged, according to which there were two very different kinds of economy, one developed and one underdeveloped, with very different sorts of problems that consequently required very different sorts of solution. This debate, which began in the early 1960s, has lasted until today, with positions staked out that have been remarkably long-lived. The fact of this debate—and the policy failures associated with it—obliged the IMF and the World Bank to begin to rethink issues concerned with the design of the international order and their own role within it.

In particular, the IMF worked out a technical and analytical device for the achievement of stabilization, but its operation was limited by what was at that time usually described as a failure or absence of political will in member countries. The debate about reform and its effectiveness anticipated many modern discussions over the association between policy reform and financial crisis: and especially the paradox that the unpleasant and contractionary medicine taken as a response to a crisis can (but need not) have much more promising long-term effects because of the way it shifts the political economy of the policy framework.

II. Bretton Woods

The conference of Bretton Woods, held in the last phase of a great world war, had—perhaps not surprisingly—concerned itself only rather peripherally with development issues. Although Article I of the Fund's Articles of Agreement stated an objective of "the development of the productive resources of all members," development finance had not been a major concern of the great powers who shaped the Bretton Woods order in the highly peculiar circumstances of 1944. The conference had avoided any attempt to distinguish between groups of members, and its participants ruled out an additional phrase suggested by the Indian delegation as part of the second "purpose of the Fund" set out in that Article: "to assist in the fuller utilisation of the resources of economically under-developed countries."[1]

Indeed it only became clear later that there was a specific problem about "development." It was only in the course of the first postwar decades that the "developing world" began to define itself politically and economically. Politically, the new definition came about as a result of the breakup of colonial regimes and the advent of independence. Within a short space of time, international institutions gained a large number of new members, and a new sort of political presence. From 1960 to 1963, the membership of the IMF rose from 68 to 101. Economically, states now regarded themselves as "developing," or in the more usual expressions of the 1950s and 1960s as "underdeveloped" or "less developed." Development would be an important part of the assertion of national independence: it meant evolving a material basis that would eliminate economic dependence, and also satisfy the new demands and expectations of citizens. The new states searched for a particular economic strategy appropriate to their particular political condition. Their answer often lay in a partial disengagement from the world economy, and a reluctance to accept the IMF Article VIII goal of currency convertibility, or to see any substantial advantages in trade liberalization. The great movement of trade and currency liberalization, which reached a climax in the early 1960s in the developed world, thus left many poorer countries untouched.

Explaining why is not easy; and indeed the reasons clearly varied considerably from country to country. In general, some mixture of the following arguments led states to look for a separate path of development.

(1) The most obvious reason belongs to the realm of ideas and was the consequence of the application of what proved to be an inappropriate theory of development. According to a widely prevalent approach, development required a radical relative reduction of the agricultural and commodity producing sectors, which could only be achieved through the manipulation of prices and the creation of a different price structure from that prevailing on the world market. Thus a development strategy required the fostering of substitutes for previously imported manufactured products. The apparent success of the Soviet model of development reinforced this theoretical preference.[2] Most

---

[1] Gold (1979; 478) and Narasimham (1984; 9).
[2] Krueger (1993; 39).

development strategies envisaged a powerful role for the state in overcoming barriers to development and in planning growth.

(2) Another explanation is concerned with the domestic sociology of politics. The bias against agriculture, which was almost always presented as a necessary kick-start of development and as an essential part of any successful modernization strategy, was initiated by urban elites, and as it proceeded built up its own urban vested interest, with a substantial political leverage. Again, the result was to emphasize the state's role in development.

(3) A final explanation concerns the international financial and economic order. Some features of the international system posed a deterrent to would-be participant countries, and threw them back onto particular and national development trajectories. The highly restricted international availability of private capital in the 1950s and 1960s, and then again in the 1980s and 1990s, meant that only a very limited number of countries had good access to capital markets. Sharply fluctuating commodity prices, especially in the first half of the 1950s, and then again in the 1980s and 1990s, meant that export earnings looked volatile and undependable. Such uncertainties heightened fears of external influence and dependence and a revival of imperialism in a new guise.

In most cases, these motives for separate or autarkic development overlapped and reinforced one another. Ideas (in this case about development) not only affect the way interest groups put their demands forward but also actually may move such organizations to form in the first place. Ideas, however, are not born in a vacuum. The existence of problems in the international order encourages people to formulate theories to explain why such problems exist.

How easy would it have been to reverse these attitudes and policies? A rethinking would only be possible as a consequence of the perception that something had gone wrong. Frequently this only arises in the case of an acute crisis. But by that time the problem may be so deeply entrenched that it is impossible easily to solve. In some cases, where a large internal market and a dynamic entrepreneurial culture existed, import-substitution growth could be sustained at very high rates for a relatively long time period. The most striking example is to be found in the "Brazilian miracle" of the 1930s or again in the late 1960s and 1970s, which encouraged many other Latin American countries to embark on the same course. In such cases, little rethinking even appeared to be necessary.

Could these problems have been tackled by a more forthcoming or better-organized international system? The World Bank, the General Agreement on Tariffs and Trade (GATT), and the IMF tried to make access to the system easier, but their efforts were by no means always successful.

The World Bank tried to make up through its loans for the very sluggish private capital market of the early postwar years, or to spur the private sector into international lending by giving guarantees; but it would never be a perfect substitute for a private market, with its larger capacities and its ability to make a wide range of choices and assessments. For the moment, and for most countries, there was little external private-sector investment available. Even in the 1990s and 2000s, after decades of very active international capital markets, most poor countries had little access, and the big flows occurred to just a handful of borrowers. In addition, in regard to its own operations, the World Bank was limited to lending for public-sector projects.

The GATT initially was restricted largely to industrial countries. As it became more universal in the course of the 1960s (by the beginning of 1971 it had 77 members), it also attempted to adapt more to the particular needs of developing countries. Article 18 of the original charter allowed developing countries to withdraw concessions on customs duties, and also to give subsidies, if these measures were needed in order to establish new industries that would increase production and raise living standards; they could also take exceptional measures to protect their balance of payments. For their part, industrial countries under Article 37 had committed themselves to reduce or eliminate barriers to the exports of less developed countries. But when it came to putting these principles into practice, the European countries that were members of the European Economic Community (EEC) were unable to agree to a plan to remove restrictions contrary to the GATT; and the GATT instead formulated in 1965 a much vaguer and less substantive Part IV of the Agreement (which became Articles 37 to 39 and diluted the previous commitment).[3] In all the most important areas of trade for poorer countries—in agriculture, steel, and textiles—industrial countries in fact evolved restrictive and sometimes discriminatory trade practices. It was only after the replacement of the GATT by the WTO in 1995 that significant efforts were made to bring agriculture and textiles back into the multilateral trade regime, and the issue of agricultural subsidies by industrial countries has still not been adequately solved. As a result, some commentators began to speak of a " 'conspiracy' of noncompliance."[4]

The IMF's task was initially defined at Bretton Woods as the provision of short-term balance of payments support. This assumed a great significance in connecting economies with the world system. In the absence of available capital imports, balance of payments difficulties could prove an insuperable obstacle to integration. More fundamentally, analyzing the origins of balance of payments problems could provide a tool for diagnosing more wide-ranging economic difficulties. The balance of payments acted as a fever thermometer. Deficits might indicate the presence of wrong exchange rates or disincentives to export. The practical difficulty involved in responding to the diagnostic tool with short-term support was that, to continue the analogy, it might only

---

[3] van Meerhaeghe (1971; 113–14).
[4] Low (1993; 26).

provisionally lower the temperature without curing the sickness. In many cases, the short-term support in practice became a very protracted involvement that was quite counter to the original concept of the Fund at the time of Bretton Woods, and has been the subject of a great deal of criticism.

III. The clash of ideas

The first reason for the separation of many economies from the international system derived from the widespread conviction that an alternative set of economic rules or even a different logic applied to developing countries.[5] The differences concerned the appropriate degree of exposure to the international economy and the desirability of domestic financial stability. (These issues were linked, in that the adoption of convertibility and fixed parities would necessarily limit the possibilities for fiscal experimentation or inflationism.) A difference in understanding about the operation of the international economy, and the associated conviction that the other side was acting out of a fundamentally political logic, profoundly handicapped the IMF in its relations with many developing country members. In order to become more influential, it would have had to demonstrate the validity of an economic approach as much as provide financial resources. Many influential analysts, however, believed that poorer countries would be damaged by exposure to the international system, that emerging manufactures would be destroyed, and that the export of a limited number of commodities would create an intolerable dependence. Access to capital flows would be difficult or impossible.

The tyranny of the past played a part in creating these beliefs. They appeared as lessons of history, and especially of the prewar era. There was, it was thought, a general need for protection. In the environment of the 1930s, the adoption of tariffs and quotas had made sense as an insulation against the spread of deflation.[6] And before that, the relatively open international financial system had transmitted financial shocks too easily. This was a preventative argument for intervention in trade, but there was also, it appeared, a powerful developmental case. In this view, trade measures could be used as a way of engineering a transformation of the economic structure. Countries interpreted the interwar experience as showing that, after an initial postwar boom, commodity prices were likely to weaken. In general, a commitment to agricultural production was thought to mean an obstacle to development, and the best hope for advance lay in moving underemployed people and resources out of agriculture as rapidly as possible. Multiple exchange rates had been an aspect of Nazi economic and trade policy in the 1930s that the United States had

---

[5] For a critique see Haberler (1961) and Bauer (1972).
[6] See Lewis (1949; 59–60).

found deeply objectionable.[7] But they had also been seen, particularly in Latin America, as a way of managing trade so as to promote import substitution and thus promote industrialization, as well as of raising revenue to pay off foreign debt and thus avoiding default. In short, lessons drawn about how to adapt to the dismal world of the 1930s were frequently much more compelling than the high hopes of Bretton Woods that there might be created a better world.

The practical experiences of the interwar period were systematized as an economic theory that explained why primary producing countries would inevitably experience a secular decline in their terms of trade. The historical record, as well as assumptions about the propensity of developed countries to buy foodstuffs and raw materials as incomes rose, led Hans Singer and Raúl Prebisch to claim that the demand for manufactured goods would rise more quickly than for primary products and that differences in demand would be reflected in the evolution of relative prices.[8] The policy conclusion derived from this economic reasoning was that only by shifting substantial resources into the production of manufactured goods could developing countries escape a permanent poverty trap. The theory of the long-run decline of commodity terms of trade provided the intellectual underpinning for the politics of import substitution and for "export pessimism," a view frequently associated with the United Nations Economic Commission for Latin America (UNECLA). Exports, according to the doctrine, could rarely be an adequate motor for development. Integration into an international economy would damage an initially uncompetitive industrial sector, which, however, held out the only hope for breaking out of the traps of poverty and underdevelopment. The sustained weakness of commodity prices in the 1980s and 1990s (after big spikes in the 1970s) seemed to provide a powerful empirical basis for the UNECLA position.

Some analysts went further than Singer and Prebisch and asserted that the entire process of development was a political struggle. According to this view, developed countries, in order to be able to appropriate for themselves a greater share of the world's resources, had used the theory of neoclassical economics as an ideological instrument. Their insistence on comparative advantage and the mutuality of gains from trade constituted a duplicitous and hypocritical masking of their own exploitative interests. Import substitution strategies, on the other hand, might provide an economic basis for the assertion of sovereignty and political independence, as well as self-enrichment, by developing countries. If this analysis were valid, the demand for speedy balance of payments adjustment looked like another weapon of developed countries to hold down developing countries below their optimum growth path.

The "structural approach" derived further support from the problem of commodity price volatility. Economists looked at a historical record in which these

---

[7] See Ellis (1941).
[8] Singer (1949); Prebisch (1959).

prices moved much more than those of manufactured products. Sudden and unanticipated drops in the prices of major exports would induce both immediate balance of payments problems and rising fiscal deficits as governments tried to compensate the losses of politically powerful producers. Adjustment programs in these circumstances would force subsidized prices to rise, marginal industries would suffer from the application of credit restrictions, and the exchange rate would fall: all of these responses would injure powerful groups who would challenge the goal of monetary stabilization. In these circumstances, the adjust-ment program could not affect the basic problem of commodity price instability, but would only make more damaging the consequences and repercussions. Serious remedial action would need to deal with the international issues of commodity prices and commodity trading.

The policy implication involved the conclusion that devaluations should be avoided and that the external economy should be managed through exchange control often with the use of multiple exchange rates (different exchange rates for different categories of product in a licensed trading system). These were a common phenomenon of the 1950s, in every Latin American economy, but also in countries as diverse as France, the Benelux countries, Israel, the Philippines, and Yugoslavia (which with about 200 different exchange rates had probably the world's most complicated system). In 1958, 36 out of 58 members of the IMF operated such multiple rates. Such exchange control allowed countries to run higher rates of inflation without increasing imports. A substantial further difference in views about economic management con-cerned the appropriate level of inflation and an assessment of the economic consequences of inflation. The advocates of a protected national development saw fewer dangers in inflation.

In the experience of Europe, the United States, and some parts of Asia (especially India and Japan), inflation had been a legacy of wartime finance and was associated with major price distortions and in consequence irrational and misguided investment undertakings. A return to balanced economic development, in which price signals could be used as a basis for investment decisions, required a reduction of inflation rates through fiscal discipline and appropriate monetary policy. But Latin America had not been so directly affected by wartime finance and as a result developed a much more relaxed attitude to inflation. Investment often occurred, especially since the 1930s, under state direction. When a boost in investment was required in order to set the economy on the appropriate course of development, state expenditure would necessarily expand.

Inflation was thus seen as a product of "structural" political and economic forces that led to budget deficits and credit expansion. It would be misguided to intervene in this network of social pressures, and the cost would be economic and political collapse. Inflation acted not as an incentive to misallocation, but rather as a stimulus to development, which might remove obstacles such as labor immobility, disguised unemployment, or production bottlenecks.[9] Nor were Latin American economists alone in proposing such an interpretation. They derived a substantial amount of support from economists in Western countries who told them that "a case could be made for making inflation an instrument of policy, rather than the control of inflation an object of policy."[10] Adjustment programs thus were seen as bearing no long-run benefits at all but only imposing the short-run costs of production lost and opportunities forgone. The result was a theory—and a political practice—that has been termed "economic populism": "an approach to economics that emphasizes growth and income distribution and deemphasizes the risks of inflation and deficit finance, external constraints, and the reaction of economic agents to aggressive nonmarket policies."[11]

In 1959 the Secretary-General of the United Nations, Dag Hammarskjöld, appeared to endorse this populist and pro-inflationary view when he asked rhetorically: "Are we not, perhaps, rather inclined to solve the conflict between stability and growth too exclusively in favor of stability, to the detriment of the vigor and dynamism so characteristic of the world economy during the first post-war decade? . . . The issue cannot be sidestepped by simple resort to global measures of fiscal and monetary control, without serious risk that the economy may lose all forward momentum."[12]

By contrast, the IMF in particular seemed to numerous hostile observers intent on applying the narrowly anti-inflationary and fiscal view of the 1920s League of Nations when it came to the discussion of currency stabilization. Per Jacobsson, who became Managing Director of the IMF in 1956, after having been the chief economist at the Bank for International Settlements, looked to many like the embodiment of the continuity. In the 1959 Annual Report the IMF stated its approach in the following way: "Notwithstanding the realization that is now fairly general that sound economic development is not compatible with the distortions that rapid or chronic inflation always creates, a number of the less developed countries have had great difficulty in abating or slowing down the rate of inflation . . . The temporary deterioration of the standard of living, which in such circumstances [a stabilization program following a period of low saving] is inevitable, may be interpreted by some sections of the public as an indication of the failure of the program, and give rise to claims for prompt upward adjustments in wages and salaries and for more liberal credit terms, which, if granted, will again generate inflationary

---

[9] Furtado (1963; 252–3).

[10] Bruton (1961; 57).

[11] Dornbusch and Edwards (1991; 9).

[12] United Nations Economic and Social Council on the World Economic Situation, Press Release ECOSOC/1168, July 6, 1959.

pressures."[13] The 1962 Annual Report concluded: "Experience shows that, if prices rise fast enough to initiate a wage–price spiral or to undermine confidence in the real value of assets denominated in money (e.g., savings deposits), economic growth will be discouraged."[14]

Inflation in this picture encouraged the misallocation of investment. According to the IMF view, inventories would become irrationally large, as money could no longer be relied on as a store of liquidity. Funds would be channeled into luxury housing, and, as the exchange value fell, into foreign assets, despite attempts that governments might make to control capital flight. Inflation would deter foreign investment; and the fall of the exchange rate would stimulate excessive import substitution.[15] In the light of these arguments, the best approach to stabilization lay in a shock therapy, since a rapid action stood a greater chance of breaking inflationary expectations, while "an attempt to slow down inflation will take a long time to be effective and its final result will be uncertain."[16]

This was precisely the claim that at the time most development economists found objectionable. They saw inflation as a desirable source of investment funds. Fighting it would reduce investment and the capacity for growth. If inflationary options could only be followed away from the international economic system—then the sacrifice was not a great one. In face of the argument that stabilization would create a more rational investment climate and attract foreign inflows, they did not need to be complete cynics to see that those resources might not in reality be so easily available at moments when there was a great demand for resources. As the economist Richard Cooper pointed out in 1968, "it is a perverse characteristic of international capital that it fails to move when it is most needed."[17]

The intellectual consensus around the particular discipline of development economics only really broke down in the late 1970s and 1980s, despite the activity of isolated critics of the development orthodoxy such as Peter Bauer. The first and most important blow came with the recognition that attempts to foster inward-oriented development distorted the economic structure and created opportunities for rent-seeking as favored sectors used the help of state protection and thus imposed high costs on the rest of the economy. In practice, this interpretation focused on the bad political economy of conventional development economics, in which the harmful long-term effects of the political economy of inflation formed a crucial element.

---

[13] IMF Annual Report (1959; 70, 73).
[14] IMF Annual Report (1962; 42).
[15] Wai (1959) and Dorrance (1963).
[16] Dorrance (1963; 30).
[17] Cooper (1968; 90).

IV. The sociology of politics

As the alternative or unorthodox mercantilistic ideas about development came to be applied in practice, they evolved their own political momentum. Once programs for import substitution were under way, they created social groups with a vested interest in their continuation, who saw greater openness as only bringing losses for them. Industrialization created urban centers with apparently higher wages and conditions of work than prevailed in the countryside. These were the beneficiaries of the inflation regime. The towns then exercised a powerful pull on the rural labor force. The new businessmen and workers were well placed to press governments for further concessions to their particular interests.

The initial impetus toward import substitution and the distortion of the domestic terms of trade against agriculture (the traditional beneficiary of state policy in many colonial states as well as in Latin America) created a powerful and well-paid urban working class and a strong interest in import-substitution industrialization. An overvalued exchange rate (which made agricultural exports less profitable and allowed cheap imports for specifically targeted groups) was frequently used to transfer income away from traditional agricultural producers.[18] The exchange rate became a vehicle for forcing social change. The penalization of agriculture, and a de facto subsidization of urban consumers, led as an unintended consequence to the creation of greater rural poverty and to increased disparities of income and wealth. Those countries that applied import substitution most systematically as a result developed far more inegalitarian societies. In general, there was a remarkable contrast in this respect between import-substituting Latin American countries, and East Asian societies, which largely abandoned this strategy as early as the beginning of the 1960s. But it was only after the major shift of the 1980s in the priorities of development economics that South Korea became widely regarded as a highly attractive model of development, which might be imitated not just in Asia but in Latin America or Africa.

In the years immediately following independence, governments assumed that only a strong industrial performance could create an escape from poverty, dependence, and underdevelopment. At least two sets of prices were manipulated and thus distorted: the rate of interest and prices of agricultural goods. The distortions created a deliberate bias toward import-competing activities and the capital goods sector.

A critical price that determines savings and investment behavior is the interest rate. Holding interest at low levels was widely thought by development economists to promote higher levels of investment. The inflationary consequences of uncontrolled monetary policy, however, meant that real rates

---

[18] Kafka (1961; 21).

were often highly negative, and also very volatile. This price distortion produced a misallocation of resources as (approved) investment projects were too cheap. It also dissuaded investors from holding financial assets. For sub-Saharan Africa, the average real interest rate as calculated by the World Bank in the 1980s was –11 percent, with much higher negative levels in a few countries (Ghana and Zambia).[19] Subsidized credit brought credit rationing, directed toward the creation of a heavy industrial sector in accordance with the theories held by policymakers. Negative interest rates also turn the control of credit into a major source of economic and political power, since allocating loans in effect means distributing subsidies. The emergence of corruption and the disintegration of public morality are a rational, and perhaps an inevitable, consequence of this sort of distortion.

Industrialization programs were further almost always supported by a deliberate manipulation of the domestic price structure. Internally, the terms of trade were to be turned against agriculture, in order to assist industrial accumulation, whatever might be the level of prevailing world prices. This in turn required controls to separate domestic prices from those on world markets. Marketing boards often functioned to buy up agricultural products at low prices.[20]

Conceptually, these attempts did not differ from the strategies adopted simultaneously in many Latin American and some Asian countries. In the African case, they had a generally more destructive influence simply because the size of the agricultural sector at the outset was much larger and also because the policies were more extreme. Unfortunately, from the point of view of the planners, and regrettably for the course of development, most of the population worked in agriculture. As most of the very poor lived in rural areas, anti-agriculture policies accentuated income inequality and social injustice.

As the industrialization strategy gained pace, it created its own political momentum. It produced a powerful intellectual and political elite that supported it, and that drew benefits from it. The strategy also produced another beneficiary: a small and usually relatively well-paid working class. Both of these groups, based as they were in cities, had a strong grip on the political process. One survey concluded that "even in the poorer countries, however, urban popular classes are likely to be more active politically than both the rural poor and the poorest fringes of urban society."[21] The industrial groups were determined to preserve their positions and believed that alternative policies, with a more balanced development, would mean a return to colonial-style subordination. This view was articulated particularly forcefully by academics

---

[19] World Bank (1993; 206).
[20] See Bates (1981).
[21] Nelson (1992; 244).

and also by those in government bureaucracies who found in the spending associated with industrialization plans "the golden gateway to fortune."[22] By the end of the 1970s, this mechanism had produced widespread fiscal crisis. On the one hand was the inability of the state in most poor countries to raise additional revenues, while on the other the expanding government patronage systems expanded with a dynamic and logic of their own. This development was the fundamental cause of the decline in savings discussed earlier. High levels of inflation that resulted from fiscal problems also made it politically more difficult to abandon subsidies and price distortions. Attempts to move in such a direction frequently provoked mass discontent.

At the end of the 1970s, as a result of the obvious failures of industry-focused development, the old view came under a sustained intellectual and practical challenge. Academic studies pointed out the high costs of protection.[23] In 1979, a World Conference on Agrarian Reform and Rural Development adopted a "program of Action" under which targets for agricultural reform were to be integrated in an overall development strategy. Also in 1979, the Brandt Commission Report recognized that "food must be a priority."[24] But, in practice, the industrial emphasis had long since acquired its own momentum and, in the interstices of decision making, found convinced and unshakable advocates in many countries.

Though in every case, the industrial policy collapsed in the course of the 1970s at the latest, its intellectual underpinning still remains attractive at least to some commentators, and those who challenge it are frequently assumed to have sinister motives. It is still possible to observe among some commentators the fear that the IMF is "a *recolonizing instrument* which would not allow the indigenous entrepreneurs to make the critical choices that would propel the economy to self-sustained growth."[25] Some African academics argue that "both the World Bank and the IMF implicitly or explicitly endorse the coloni-ally imposed role of primary production by Third World countries on the bogus basis of comparative advantage . . . Africa has, with the massive collapse of commodity markets, reached the limits of export-oriented primary produc-tion."[26] Such erroneous assertions were, and unfortunately still are, used to support the continuation of industrialization based on a protected economy.

In many poor countries, external economic policy had in fact been subor-dinated to the distorted logic of induced industrialization. The exchange rate played a crucial part in the development of the industrial strategy. Here was yet another manipulated price. The combination of a high exchange rate with import licensing and restriction allowed an easy way of setting the domestic

---

[22] Schatz (1984; 55) and Sandbrook (1993; 30).
[23] The two most important works were Krueger (1978) and Bhagwati (1978).
[24] Independent Commission on International Development Issues (1980; 92).
[25] Bangura (1987; 106).
[26] Onimode (1989; 26, 33).

terms of trade. It could be justified as a policy by the need to import basic products needed for industrialization, and sometimes also foodstuffs, at reduced prices. By determining who could obtain foreign exchange to import (at cheap prices) and what they could import, governments could program the direction of development. Such control also gave the controllers an obvious but critical political instrument. One commentator has described foreign exchange as the "lifeblood of the new political class" in new states;[27] but it would be a mistake to assume that the groups interested in an overvalued exchange rate were just domestic elites. In many cases, major foreign investors also defended the practice because it lowered the apparent cost of their investments.

The political importance of the preferential allocation of exchange to favored projects naturally altered the economics of development. Provided with cheaper inputs, projects that would not otherwise have made economic sense appeared attractive. They began to seem economically as well as politically rational and rewarding. The more politically prestigious a project became, the more it was allowed to cost; and, at the same time, the less it appeared to cost because of the distortions created by artificially high exchange rates. As a result, it would be less likely to be allowed to fail; and the industrial sectors accumulated examples of factories that were actually adding negative value (where, at international prices, the factors of production are worth more than the product).

The industrialization strategy had often evolved as a response to the failure of an external trade regime dependent on a limited number of products and extremely vulnerable to external shocks. Shocks were often treated not as an opportunity to re-examine policy but rather as an unanticipated setback, which called for further isolation from the international economy. This attitude shaped the approach to debt management. Countries believed that they should borrow after a commodity price collapse in order to avoid adjustment; while, on the other hand, commodity price booms were rarely used as an opportunity for consolidation and reduction of external debt. Commodity price changes thus had an asymmetric effect, in which price falls meant a greater need to borrow, but price rises also provided a justification for continued borrowing. Each price change, either way, required more financing. Movements of commodity prices in this way encouraged the incurring of higher levels of debt. A world economy in which fluctuations became more pronounced as a result helped to destabilize many commodity producers and drove them to adopt increasingly unsustainable policies.

In the 1960s it was impossible to detect any signs of the relatively poor performance of sub-Saharan Africa compared with a "developing country average." But in the period after the collapse of the classical Bretton Woods

---

[27] Callaghy (1990; 259).

system, each of the major shocks to the world economy caused a further divergence. The oil price rise of the 1970s, the second oil shock and the world depression at the beginning of the 1980s, and then the debt crisis: in each case, most sub-Saharan African countries found adjustment hard and painful. The debt crisis and the need to service debt helped to produce a further obstacle in the mid-1980s. In order to service debt, countries needed to increase exports; but the increased supply on inelastic markets produced a dramatic and very damaging price decline of major commodities: cocoa, coffee, copper. The belief that economic problems were related to the flawed development of the international system increased the propensity to turn inward, and to look for autonomous sources of development.

The social inequality that was associated with bad development strategies helped to produce increased political instability, strained democratic systems, and increased the likelihood of coups. Political instability in turn had economic effects: it encouraged the constant formulation of "new" or different approaches. In this way, it played a part in the process that produced rapidly alternating policies and economic performance and that helped to reduce the overall long-term rate of growth.

Perhaps the most dramatic early example of this process was Argentina, where the case for the import-substituting strategy had been clearly enunciated by Prebisch, and a practical application had been implemented already earlier, in the 1930s, and then more dramatically immediately after the Second World War by the Peronist regime. After 1958, governments took an opposite tack and attempted to liberalize, decontrol, and integrate into the world economy with the support of IMF programs. The German currency reform and liberalization of 1948 and the Spanish reforms of 1959 were used as an explicit model; and the new course was supported through an IMF stand-by arrangement. "We must achieve", Arturo Frondizi explained, "an Argentine miracle; we must show that we too are capable of transforming despair into hope and the ruins of defeat into great victories." Alvaro Carlos Alsogaray, who in June 1959 became Minister of Labor and the Economy, was an explicit admirer of Ludwig Erhard. Alsogaray believed that German-style liberalization with a single exchange rate and a control of the money supply exercised only through changes in banks' reserve requirements would produce the Argentine *Wirtschaftswunder*. In the particular circumstances of Argentina, such reforms would attract foreign capital. Roberto Alemann, who in 1959 was Under-Secretary in the Finance Ministry, later made this argument into a general theory of development, in which domestic liberalization provided new incentives for international capital inflows: "International cooperation leading to the elimination of restrictions on trade and on international long-term lending, as well as to the amelioration of the stimulus given by developed countries to investments in their own economies, should be explored, in order to re-establish a vigorous flow of genuine long-term private capital."[28] In Argentina, however, the attempted stabilization quickly collapsed, and the country began a cycle of reform, failure, and the reassertion of traditional populist policy priorities. The consequent extreme instability produced very sharp economic fluctuations and a very poor overall growth performance.

V. Managing the international financial system

In the 1950s, countries described at the time as "underdeveloped" grew quickly, but their growth rates were similar to, rather than markedly higher than, those of industrial countries. They appeared to have missed the process of "catching up" implicit in the notion of development. The widespread character of development did nothing to discourage the thought that the potential for growth might be greater outside the world economic system.

In addition, decadal or other long-term average figures on growth miss one of the most important features of postwar development: its uneven or irregular character in most developing countries, and the fact that as a consequence it was punctuated by frequent crises which included balance of payments crises. At the same time as some economists in developed countries were speaking of the demise of the business cycle, outside the industrial world there could be no doubt that growth rates were very volatile. The responsibility, however, lay, according to most observers, not in endogenous cyclical factors but rather in constraints imposed by the international system. Intensive growth spurts led to the emergence of balance of payments problems and the need to adjust by slowing down. The dislocations caused by joining the world economic system were most directly reflected in the external balance.

The IMF, as an institution immediately concerned with the management of payments, found itself gradually drawn into a much wider discussion of development issues. As a result, it began to function as a kind of doorkeeper to the international financial system, and quickly came to find itself dealing with issues much broader than simple short-term balance of payments problems. In particular, it necessarily faced the following questions posed by the theorists of development:

(1) Does development necessarily result in current account deficits, as a consequence of the need to import raw materials and capital goods?

(2) Does development necessarily result in fiscal deficits, as the state supplies saving that cannot be provided by an inadequate private sector? The first two hypotheses, as expounded by Hollis Chenery, became known as theory of the "two gaps" (the payments and savings gaps).[29]

---

[28] Díaz-Alejandro (1965; 146); IMF Annual Meetings (1961; 45).
[29] Chenery and Strout (1966).

(3) How should the gaps be financed? In particular, are private inflows of investment capital appropriate, or does the long time frame implied by the process of development rule out any involvement of private capital except on conditions in which it is given a substantial measure of control? And would that control be politically unacceptable by bringing a limitation of national sovereignty, which had just been obtained in many countries with great sacrifice and was passionately defended?

(4) If the capital flows were to be regulated by international government action, equally troubling questions would arise. How could recipient countries avoid the intrusion of political calculations or inappropriate economic conditions (such as donors' insistence that aid be tied to the purchases of their own national products)?

(5) All these issues were logically connected in a highly politicized web. Supposing that private flows only come if they are shown a green light by official capital flows and that official flows are made conditional on the establishment of policies under the supervision of international institutions to encourage long-term and stable inflows of private funds? Or supposing that the answers given by multilateral institutions to short-term balance of payments problems are associated with recommendations designed to produce long-term solutions in which private and official flows play an important part? In these cases, dependence seemed to be reimposed, as a result of economic interconnectedness, and the promise and goal of political independence might be undermined.

Such linkages create some of the most painful political problems arising out of the development process. Discussion of the balance of payments as a constraint on development exposed some fundamental problems. If advice from the outside comes differently from different sources, it looks inconsistent. On the other hand, if it emphasizes the linkages between different elements of a reform strategy, it looks too well coordinated and too intrusive. If the same sorts of conditions are set for assistance by multilateral institutions, industrial countries, and private lenders, they create the suspicion that there is some sinister "external interest" aimed at the subversion of national priorities. If advice from the outside is to be effective, or even if it is to be implemented at all, it needs to be accepted by national governments and civil servants. It is most useless when imposed by external authority and most useful when it comes as the result of a common search for a solution to a problem that represents a general concern. The likelihood of a long-term success is greatest when a common framework for analysis is established, and in this way the suspicions that attend on external advice are dispelled.

From the beginning, one of the major functions of the IMF had been concerned with the transmission of ideas. An international institution can play a major part in national decision making not so much by intervention from the outside or even through financial support (though this was frequently crucial in the implementation of new economic strategies), but by bolstering the position of reformers in the bureaucratic structure, usually in the finance ministry or the central bank. The best way of doing this was to supply accurate information about world economic developments and helpful ideas. This side of the IMF's activities acquired some new institutional dimensions in the 1960s. In 1964, the IMF Institute was created as a training institution; also in 1964, the Central Banking Service was launched, offering advice mostly to African countries. In 1969, the Bureau of Statistics began to provide technical assistance to help member countries to improve data collection and establish or extend central bank bulletins.

Already earlier, in the 1950s, IMF missions had developed into one of the most obvious ways in which the institution expressed its views to the outside world. The mission was usually composed of a relatively small team (initially four to six people) with representatives of the IMF area departments involved (these had been created in 1953), as well as of departments with a particular concern (Exchange Restrictions, Central Banking, or Fiscal Affairs). This team negotiated on the basis of an internal briefing paper agreed in advance through consultation and discussion in the Fund, and on its return produced a report for the Fund management that would then be the subject of an Executive Board discussion. This was a way not only of investigating the external economic problems and difficulties of member countries, but also of establishing conditions on which financial assistance could be given, and of transmitting views and suggestions between the member countries and the Fund.

Even an agreement and a shared intellectual analysis is sometimes not enough. Often, high short-term costs of adjustment are required in order to achieve the long-term benefits of the confidence established by the common outlook and vision. But when these costs are too great, they can also exercise a lasting and damaging effect on confidence and on the credibility of the political and administrative leadership. In order to be credible, policies require a certain commitment on the part of governments that there will be no sudden and dramatic reversal. Where growth produces instability, and political change leads to international upheavals, it is hard to establish commitment and credibility. This in turn makes the formulation of an appropriate policy more difficult and leads to an orientation toward the short term.

What are the chances of establishing a common, universal framework that will increase the chances of stability? Every country has its own individual problems, complex and peculiar. International orders depend on the creation of universal rules and principles: such was the great truth of Bretton Woods. But treating countries according to general rules may look harsh and inflexible in the light of the remorseless individuality of the suffering and sorrows of mankind. Such questions became acute as the general principles established at Bretton Woods began to shape not just the re-establishment of European currency convertibility, but in the late 1950s also the discussion of liberalization in the rest of the world economy. Providing answers to the dilemma of how to reconcile a universal institutional framework with the need to deal with the specificity of particular problems in individual countries provided a continual challenge to the system established at Bretton Woods.

Almost every non-Western country had a deep-seated and quite justifiable suspicion of imperialism and its legacy. In some cases, anti-imperialism strengthened the initial appeal of international multilateral economic institutions. Particularly in the early 1960s, as many African states became independent, they found working with the IMF and the World Bank an effective way of shaking off the patronizing advice of finance ministries and central banks from the former imperial powers. The Bank of England, for instance, systematically resisted attempts to set up new central banks and preferred to advise on the operation of currency boards or more limited types of monetary authority.[30] The creation of central banks required, as a result, the technical assistance of the IMF.

In other cases, however, anti-imperialism soured the relations of poorer states toward the international financial system and international financial institutions. Many states believed, rightly, that there was a close involvement of the United States in many Fund and World Bank programs. Where American political power was believed to be a problem and a threat and where that perception generated a nationalist response, the role of the Bretton Woods institutions almost inevitably became highly problematic. A great deal of the IMF's activity relating to non-industrial countries took place in the western hemisphere; but this is where the attractions and the suspicions of US power were at their greatest. The US government, which historically had been very closely involved in Latin American affairs, felt vulnerable to the criticism that much of its aid to the hemisphere was being wasted or frittered away. It began to make some aid programs dependent on reaching an agreement with the IMF, which would guarantee the pursuit of sound policy, and might encourage also the involvement of private capital. Thus Peru concluded in February 1954 a $12.5 million stand-by arrangement with the IMF, borrowed from the US government, and simultaneously established a substantial credit line with the Chase National Bank of New York. But such linkages created suspicions in many Latin Americans about the politics surrounding IMF involvement and recommendations. The influential Brazilian economist Celso Furtado, for instance, claimed that the IMF was a "premature" international creation, which "operated primarily as a U.S. serving control instrument over the economic and financial policies of other countries, especially the so-called under-developed countries."[31]

[30] For currency boards, see especially Tignor (1998) and Hanke and Schuler (1994).
[31] Furtado (1978; 6).

At the same time, a growing international consensus insisted that growth was a natural, desirable, and steady long-term process. Academic observers insisted that the "tricks of growth are not all that difficult; they may seem so, at moments of frustration and confusion in transitional societies."[32]

International unease about the limited success of development strategies resulted in new initiatives to remove "obstacles," establish "preconditions," and encourage faster "growth." The United Nations declared the 1960s to be the "development decade." The World Bank had already successfully used its relatively modest capital as a basis for a great expansion of lending using borrowed funds. Eugene R. Black (President 1949–62), a former Vice President of the Chase National Bank, had a very solid reputation in the financial community and set about using the guaranteed capital of the World Bank as a basis for financial intermediation. The Bank with its government-guaranteed capital could borrow from private sources on very favorable terms and raised money in the 1950s substantially on the abundant US capital markets. In the 1960s, as the US payments position deteriorated, it then turned to European (chiefly German) and then Japanese and Saudi Arabian markets for funds. The Bank, in effect, stepped in where markets were nervous because of inadequate information, and educated lenders as well as helping its borrowers. It played in this way a major role in the development of international capital markets, whose operation had been curtailed and whose confidence had been profoundly shaken during the interwar world economic crisis. The World Bank now encouraged markets to respond to the need for world financial flows, an encouragement particularly needed in circumstances when banks were nervous and hesitant about their foreign exposure.

These operations were conducted at market rates and allowed borrowers access to funds that they would have otherwise been unable to obtain. But there was also a need for funding for projects where the return would not be as immediately visible, at least in financial terms. Particularly in the case of very poor countries, borrowing on commercial terms was out of the question. After a long debate, the World Bank in 1960 created the International Development Association (IDA) as a "soft loan" institution, with "a more benign personality than the Bank."[33] It was financed through subscriptions (called "replenishments") from the richer member countries and gave credits with a substantial grant element for more "social" objects than the Bank, with its insistence on commercial returns, could provide.

In practice, the World Bank in the 1950s and 1960s had developed into a major development agency. It also encouraged emulation. In 1958, the European Development Fund was set up, for development aid, most of which went to francophone Africa, as well as the European Investment Bank, which supported

---

[32] Rostow (1971; 166).
[33] Mason and Asher (1973; 397).

projects for regional development within the EEC. Much later, in 1990, another European institution was added, the European Bank for Reconstruction and Development, to assist economic restructuring in Central and Eastern Europe. In 1959, an Inter-American Development Bank was established. The African Development Bank began operations in 1964, to provide a "concrete contribution to the human drive against backwardness"; but soon complained bitterly that the World Bank was taking away the better projects.[34] The more successful Asian Development Bank, which started in 1966, was the outcome of a number of Japanese initiatives going back to the 1950s, and was modeled very directly on the World Bank. One of the principal attractions of the newly created regional banks was to attract more resources than could be made available by the Bretton Woods institutions. They were both "a tribute and a rebuke" to the World Bank: a tribute in that their operating principle was based on the same model, but a rebuke in that they reflected a feeling that the World Bank loans were insufficient and that the Bank was not sufficiently sympathetic to ambitions for regional integration.[35]

VI. Approaching the international system

At Bretton Woods, few had anticipated that poorer countries might borrow. In the optimistic environment of the late 1950s, some policymakers began to assume that countries could solve their balance of payments difficulties relatively easily and that as a result the door to the international financial system would readily swing open, as capital markets became wider and more experienced. Only a limited amount of initial assistance would be required. The reality was much more problematic. The existence of balance of payments problems in poor countries involved the Fund in a whole range of development problems and led to an overlap and potential clashes with the World Bank and to a discussion of the relationship of the Bank to private capital flows. As long as the Fund had been largely inactive the ambiguities inherent in the delimitations of spheres of activity in Bretton Woods remained unproblematical;[36] with greater Fund activity it was bound to become clear that short-term balance of payments problems did not constitute a logically distinct problem and could not be treated as such. The IMF thus became a gatekeeper standing between poor countries and the possibility of external financial support.

In the aftermath of the 1956 political crisis of Suez and the resulting need of the United Kingdom and France for balance of payments assistance, IMF activities expanded quite dramatically with regard also to other countries.[37]

---

[34] African Development Bank Report (1964–65; 1).
[35] Mason and Asher (1973; 578).
[36] Polak (1994).
[37] See Boughton (2000a) and (2000b).

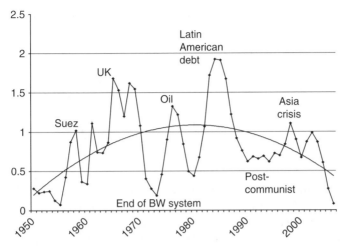

Figure 2.1 The History of IMF Lending: IMF Drawings as Proportion of World Exports 1948–2006

Source: IMF

Total drawings rose substantially even apart from the major resources devoted to France or the United Kingdom: from $27.5 million in 1955 to $131.5 million in 1956 ($692.6 million if the United Kingdom is included) and $977.1 million in 1957, but then falling again to $337.9 million in 1958 and $179.8 million in 1959. In fact, measured as a share of world trade, drawings on the IMF were at their highest ever in the decade that followed 1956, with the brief exception of the 1980s Latin American debt crisis (Figure 2.1). Most of the assistance involved developing countries.

The new expansion of activity frightened many observers, and especially many Americans. The Fund appeared to hostile observers as being sucked into long-term lending, or into areas that commercial banks would not touch. The IMF's new Managing Director, Per Jacobsson, told Jean Monnet that the United States was concerned that the exhaustion of quotas would be followed by a demand for a quota increase and that almost every one except the Americans (who could veto it because of the Articles' requirement of special majorities) was in favor of such an increase.[38] The conservative University of Chicago economist Melchior Palyi took the opportunity to restate the bitter accusations he had already made during the debate over the ratification of the Bretton Woods Agreements. Now he said that he feared a sudden burst of

---

[38] Jacobsson (1958).

profligacy on the part of the Bretton Woods institutions: "The ineffectuality of both... and the very limited aid they provide have caused so much criticism among debtor countries as to make their survival questionable—or the deterioration of their credit standards a virtual certainty (which is what is happening since the Suez crisis)."[39] Again, this kind of case was made again and again from the political right, especially in the United States, as part of an argument against the involvement of the Bretton Woods institutions: this was the point made in the 1980s on the op-ed pages of the *Wall Street Journal* in the discussion of the Latin American debt crisis, or by Milton Friedman in 1997–8 in discussing the Asian financial crisis.

The work of the IMF in this initial period of activism was based on the hope that developing countries would soon participate in the general movement that was so evident in Europe away from inflation, exchange controls, and multiple rates and toward liberalization and the growth of international trade. Per Jacobsson in particular embraced this activity with a missionary's enthusiasm and energy. The campaign against multiple exchange rates produced major successes, and after 1956 a movement toward unified, but often floating, rates began, with Bolivia, Chile, and Iran leading the way. In 1957 an IMF Executive Board memorandum encouraged the process of simplification of exchange rate regimes. But financial resources were also required in the transition. Jacobsson realized that it would need a substantial financial commitment. In 1957, for instance, when India encountered an acute balance of payments crisis, Jacobsson became enmeshed in a struggle for a very large Indian stand-by arrangement. Eventually, the amount of the support was scaled down from the $200 million proposed by Jacobsson to $72.5 million at the insistence of the United States.

Fund programs, it was believed, would create a new incentive structure to encourage stabilization, and stabilization would encourage long-term capital inflows. The purpose of systematic intervention by the IMF was to compensate for temporary falloffs in the long-term movement of capital. Per Jacobsson set out this view most explicitly during the Annual Meetings of 1961: "Insofar as such development is financed by long-term foreign capital, the actual use of these resources will normally be reflected in a deficit in the current account of the balance of payments. Provided that the other elements of the balance of payments are in equilibrium, this current account deficit would be matched by the external financing, and there would then be no overall deficit." Where this was not the case, Fund financing over a three- to five-year period would "provide the time needed for the appropriate measures to take effect, and thus to relate the long-term development to the available long-term finance."[40] Maintaining the five-year limit on the availability of Fund resources was a

---

[39] Palyi (1958; 91).
[40] IMF Annual Meetings (1961; 19–20).

crucial element in the Fund's mission to deal with short-term balance of payments problems by the provision of revolving credits. Longer-term credit would be supplied for specific projects by the World Bank or by private capital. The Fund should not, however, become too closely involved with the activities of the private banks, and international institutions should not try directly to give information to the markets. This issue arose particularly dramatically in the case of Argentina, when, after an apparently successful stabilization attempt, foreign banks requested that the IMF take a direct part in debt rescheduling and restructuring.

European banks in particular were quite nervous about any new overseas lending. They had little recent experience with overseas lending except in financing some commercial activity. Argentina had only just reached an agreement providing for the multilateralization of payments and nondiscrimination in trade with Europe, as well as for the consolidation and repayment of debts over a ten-year period (the Act of Paris, May 30, 1956, which created an initially loose institutional mechanism, known as the Paris Club, for renegotiating official debt). In 1959 some European banks concluded a syndicated $70 million Argentine credit. But before they would be willing to go farther, they sought the involvement of international institutions in order to supply an additional measure of security. First they appealed to the IMF to act as a trustee for loans to developing countries. One European banker explained to Per Jacobsson that the banks wanted "a certain amount of moral support, which, under certain circumstances, might become very important particularly if there should be a change of government in Argentina." European banks did not have the extensive machinery of the US government to follow the economic and monetary policies of non-European states and also did not have the experience of New York banks in Latin America. Jacobsson refused to allow the IMF to be used in this way: "Where what I would call 'parallel' credit arrangements . . . have been made by the Fund, and other international organizations, other countries, or private banks, each party considering the extension of credit should make its own decision on whether or not to make its funds available, and on what terms." The Fund needed to retain the confidence of its members that all its decisions on drawings were "impartially arrived at on the basis of its own practices and policies, and influenced only by the appropriate technical considerations."[41] In order to be effective, the Fund had to dissociate itself from both commercial and political calculations, and establish its identity as a reservoir of economic skill. By the 1980s, however, in the context of the resolution of the Latin American debt crisis, Fund programs became a part of deals under which bank lending was resumed.

Apart from institutional and financial assistance, countries required an appropriate intellectual and theoretical framework with which to interpret

[41] James (1996; 139–40).

and analyze their economies, including the international aspects. In the course of the 1950s, the IMF developed an approach that linked balance of payments issues to monetary and fiscal behavior. The major breakthrough came as a result of a mixture of theoretical and practical work by Polak. Traditionally Keynesian analysis had neglected the external sector. In an article written with William H. White in 1955, Polak took a traditional Keynesian model but widened it so as to examine the money supply as influenced by the foreign balance.[42] In the same year, Polak headed an IMF mission to Mexico, which worked very closely with the Bank of Mexico to invent a technique for ensuring external stability and avoiding a new devaluation of the peso. The result was a practical formula: the money supply should expand at a rate not faster than growth of real GNP. In Polak's report, he set out a way of estimating the amount of money that could "safely" be created over a four-year period, based on estimates of output and of the increase of foreign exchange reserves and loans to the government. On the basis of these estimates, the amount of credit available to the private sector could be calculated and compared to the credit that would be created by the application of different marginal reserve requirements for banks.

This model evolved as a practical matter of consensus between the Fund mission, the central bank, and private bankers in Mexico. Its most fundamental policy implication concerned credit creation, or the interaction of the central bank with the banking system. Bankers were willing to accept the high marginal reserve requirements imposed by the Bank of Mexico because they too wished to avoid the uncertainty that would result from a new balance of payments crisis and a new devaluation. In 1957 Polak gave a formal and systematic statement of the new approach, which started with the observation of the "embarrassing inability" of analysts to make forecasts of the effect of monetary expansion on the balance of payments.[43] Polak's model provided, on the basis of estimates of capital movements, exports, and domestic credit creation ("the ultimate variable"), a basis for predicting the development of income, money, and imports. The paper was concerned with two levels of analysis. Theoretically, it showed how the behavior of the Keynesian multiplier was affected by an open economy, in which exports offered the possibility of income gains. Second, the discussion consistently paid attention to practical issues and problems, and in particular to the puzzle of why a country with increased exports does not continue to show payments surpluses in subsequent years. The critical concept was domestic credit expansion.

Polak came to the conclusion that in the absence of domestic credit expansion an increase in exports would lead to an equivalent increase in national income, an increase in the rate of imports, and an increase in the quantity of money. He then investigated the effects on the model of a long-run increase in

---

[42] Polak and White (1955).   [43] Polak (1957).

credit expansion. This would produce the same increase in money income and money stock as would have been produced by an equivalent increase in exports, and also would lead to an increase in the rate of reserves equivalent to the increase in credit expansion. It would, however, have a very different effect on reserve behavior: the rate of reserve loss would approach the rate of credit expansion, and the loss of reserves would be equivalent to the total credit expansion that had taken place minus the increase in the quantity of money.

The argument contained important implications for monetary and trade policies. In particular, Polak had demonstrated that an increase in exports would only lead to a short-term improvement in the balance of payments and that import restrictions could not correct a balance of payments deficit in the long term. (The initially favorable effect would disappear once the income effect was realized, and increased incomes led to increased demands for imports.) Countries could control the behavior of their reserves through monetary policy, and the behavior of domestic credit expansion. This was also a rather practical model, in that it required for its application a knowledge of trade behavior and of domestic credit expansion, but did not require national income calculations (which would have been much harder to make in countries with only rudimentary statistical services). The model was later extended to encompass capital flows and to be applied to the problems of industrial countries. It was a crucial step in the development of the theory of international finance and of the integration of Keynesian and monetary economics. Without such a framework for analysis, Jacobsson's insistence on monetary stability as a fundamental part of a liberalization strategy would have been purely rhetorical and practically ineffective.

Too often, unfortunately, the incentives provided by international institutions for the integration of their members in the international system and the economic analysis produced results that were disappointing in practice. A study of 36 trade reforms carried out in the 1950s and 1960s in developing countries showed that only 15 of the reforms were fully sustained.[44] After the 1980s, the empirical evidence of how trade opening produced major growth effects became more and more powerfully convincing.[45] But the political phenomenon of "reform fatigue" or backsliding remained quite powerful, especially in Latin America.[46] In many countries the economic pendulum constantly swung periodically and quite violently between enthusiastic acceptance of programs, slippage, negotiated modification, rejection, rapid growth following abandonment of the program, increased inflation and

---

[44] Papageorgiou, Choksi, and Michaely (1990).
[45] See especially Sachs and Warner (1995), Edwards (1998), Winters (2004), and Winters and Baldwin (2005).
[46] See Lora, Panizza, and Quispe-Agnola (2004).

balance of payments difficulties, stagnation, and then eventually the elaboration of a newly agreed package. The attractions of an alternative theory of development to that involved in what became known as the "Washington consensus" provided a constant siren song, an inducement to break with rather than cooperate in the international system.

VII. More than balance of payments

By the mid-1960s a substantial and vociferous criticism had emerged in member countries, in newspapers, and among academics of the IMF's approach to stabilization. The London *Economist* had written in 1961 that the Fund's stabilization programs in Latin America had been so harsh that Per Jacobsson might be described as "Mr. Khrushchev's secret weapon." "There is little sense of shared purpose between the fund and the governments it is helping; instead, Latin American economists see the strict orthodoxy of the fund's tenets as a challenge to them to find ways of outwitting the lawgiver." The article concluded that "it is feared that if restrictive monetary policies are adopted without social safeguards, the countries run the risk of serious social eruption."[47]

In November 1962, in the middle of protracted and difficult negotiations for an IMF stand-by arrangement, Brazil introduced in the United Nations General Assembly a resolution calling for a thorough empirical and analytical study of inflation and its effects in "under-developed countries," and which implicitly condemned the IMF for ignoring the structural factors that had led to sustained inflation. In its original form, the resolution claimed that "inflation in under-developed countries is often aggravated by the process of urbanization and by the incorporation into the market economy of populations previously living in a subsistence economy, thus requiring difficult structural adjustments and creating additional pressures on the available supply of goods and services." The resolution gained the additional support of Bolivia, Hungary, and Tunisia (though with the terminologically interesting difference that it now referred to the problems of "developing countries").[48]

In 1963 an internal IMF staff memorandum concluded that it was "not too strong to say that the Colombian case tends to support many of the recent criticisms of [Fund] stabilization programs."[49] In 1966 the World Bank prepared a draft paper that argued that the balance of payments difficulties caused by development constituted a long-term and not simply a transitory phenomenon, with the result that short-term stabilizations necessarily imposed an

---

[47] *Economist* (1961; 329).

[48] UN General Assembly, 17th Session, Draft Resolution November 2, 1962; and Resolution 1830, December 18, 1962 ("Inflation and Economic Development").

[49] IMF Archives (1963).

excessive cost. The paper included bitterly critical passages arguing that long-term confidence in developing countries had often been undermined by frequent exchange rate changes, that the IMF's approach had had the effect of discouraging savings, and that "a certain amount of inflation seems to be unavoidable in the development process, in which hitherto unemployed or underemployed resources have to be more fully utilized." In conclusion, the authors recommended an urgent reconsideration of the IMF's approach to the performance of developing countries.[50]

In some cases, most notably India in 1965–6, the World Bank seemed to be taking over some of the functions of the Fund by default, as a result of the inadequate financial capacity of the Fund in dealing with large-scale problems. In India, 1965 and 1966 were years of catastrophic rice and wheat harvests following monsoon failures, as well as massive dislocation as a result of the 1965 war with Pakistan and the temporary suspension of work by the consortium established in the 1950s with World Bank and donor countries' participation. These crises indicated a deep-seated problem, but also required the much more conventional and limited solution of an IMF stand-by arrangement (of $200 million), a devaluation of 36 percent (largely at the suggestion of the World Bank), and $900 million provided by the consortium after pressure from the Bank. The 1966 World Bank India package, though dressed up as project lending, in practice amounted to support in a balance of payments crisis. During the discussion in the Bank's Executive Board, one Director complained that "we are doing here the job of the Monetary Fund, which has the responsibility of financing short-term balance-of-payments deficits. The Bank has no such responsibility."[51]

The increasing overlap between the activities of the Bretton Woods twins in the course of the early 1960s required some institutional or bureaucratic response. After a lengthy discussion between the Bank and the Fund, the two eventually reached an agreement in 1966 about procedures and cooperation, intended to reduce the frictions between the two institutions. According to this concordat, the Fund had primary responsibility for exchange rates and restrictive systems, adjustment of temporary balance of payments disequilibria, and financial stabilization. The Bank would deal with development programs and the evaluation of projects. The concordat also recognized the reality of the overlap, although its attempt to deal with it remained rather on the level of pious sentiment. Neither institution would ignore any aspect of the " 'structure and progress' of member countries."[52] In other words, monetary stabilization and growth-oriented structural policies should not be considered in isolation from each other: though in practice, the balancing of stability and growth

[50] IMF Archives (1966).
[51] Mason and Asher (1973; 285–6).
[52] Mason and Asher (1973; 551).

remained a contentious issue, not just in developing countries. Each successive round of financial crises in low-income countries raised new issues and required some reworking of the concordat. After a dramatic clash over assistance to Argentina in the aftermath of the Latin American debt crisis, in 1989 the Bank agreed to limit adjustment lending to countries having concurrent stabilization programs with the Fund; and there was a formal agreement for the regular meeting of senior Fund and Bank staff.[53] Again, after the East Asian crisis of 1997–8, which seemed to bring the Fund heavily into the area of microeconomic conditionality, a new delineation of responsibilities was needed.

The criticisms directed against Fund programs that had emerged in the course of repeated turf wars with the Bank could not be dealt with simply by the piecemeal tinkering accompanied by high-level diplomacy that essentially had characterized in particular Per Jacobsson's distinctive and initially very promising approach to creating a single world economy. The attention of analysts turned to the structure of the world economy as a whole. These debates were inevitably reflected in discussion, of the role of the Bretton Woods institutions, as well as in internal debates. During the course of the 1960s, two major problems stood out in the policy debate and provided conceptual red herrings that would weave in and out of discussions for the subsequent decades: the volatility of export earnings and the problem of reserve inadequacy. Both these issues became the subject of discussion, investigation, and reform initiatives both within and outside the Fund.

VIII. The first red herring: commodities

The diagnosis of Prebisch and the UNECLA school placed the long-run deterioration of commodity prices at the center of its diagnosis, and it consequently became tempting to believe that some alleviative measure to deal with commodity pricing might help the cause of development.

A major demand of commodity producers reflected the experience of the volatility of the 1950s: first the Korean war boom, and then the collapse of prices. One of the most obvious problems lay in the way balance of payments difficulties emerged out of large and unanticipated fluctuations in export earnings that resulted from dependence on commodities. An important element of the initial Keynes proposals for an international bank had been concerned with the problem of commodity prices. Could not the volatility of the commodity market be reduced? The most radical solution involved intervention in price setting. The stabilization of commodity prices was a major goal when developing countries in 1964 created the United Nations Conference on Trade and Development

[53] Polak (1994).

(UNCTAD). But, in practice, for the first nine years of its existence—until a commodity boom in the early 1970s created very different economic and also political conditions—UNCTAD produced no major initiatives on commodity prices. A less dramatic approach involved creating a support mechanism for countries that suffered from the effects of fluctuations, so that the vagaries of prices would not disrupt the process of development. In 1963 the IMF established a facility for the compensatory financing of export fluctuations, which was extended in 1966. Under this initiative, funds were made available if exports over the previous twelve-month period had fallen short of the estimated medium-term level of exports defined as a moving five-year average. Brazil in 1963, with a $60 million borrowing was the first country to make use of this side of the new approach.

In 1967, at the Annual Meetings of the World Bank and the IMF in Rio de Janeiro, France and 14 African members of the franc zone submitted a resolution calling for the stabilization of commodity prices. A report produced in 1969 as a result of the Rio meetings recommended temporary financing of buffer stocks, and the first use was made in 1971 to fund a stock of tin maintained under the Fourth International Tin Agreement.[54] But this initiative was overshadowed by the currency instability of the early 1970s and the dramatic development of the oil price in 1973.

IX. The second red herring: reserves

The most far-ranging initiatives concerned with development involved the creation of new reserve assets as part of an overall strategy. Balance of payments crises in developing countries had been particularly severe and especially disruptive. Would the most economically efficient solution not lie in a channeling of reserves created to deal with the international liquidity issue to developing countries? This discussion proceeded in parallel with an increased concern in the 1960s with the general issue of international liquidity. One vision of what eventually became the SDR (Special Drawing Right) saw an important role for what came to be called the "link" with development, on the grounds that the effects of a liquidity shortage in dealing with short-term balance of payments problems were felt most acutely outside the developed world.

Some of the early practical and academic suggestions for liquidity creation contained a quite explicit link. In 1958 Sir Maxwell Stamp proposed a scheme under which the IMF would create liquidity by issuing certificates that would be given to an aid-coordinating agency and used to purchase products from industrial countries. In 1962, Stamp gave this idea a more explicitly British

---

[54] See Garritsen de Vries (1976; Vol. I; 269 ff).

twist by adding that the spending of the developing countries should take place specifically in those developed countries which, like Britain at that time, could be held to be suffering from an underemployment of resources. In 1960, Robert Triffin's scheme for monetary reform included the issue of certificates by the IMF that would be used to purchase World Bank bonds or equivalent securities. In 1966, Tibor Scitovsky proposed that reserves should be created for the purchase of goods by developing countries from developed countries with balance of payments deficits and underemployed resources.[55]

In establishing the SDR, the IMF groped for a way of reconciling the interests of developed and developing countries. The many failures to sustain heroic efforts at domestic stabilization, the idealistic discussions of the "development decade" in the early 1960s, and the resentments and disappointments engendered in the immediate aftermath of colonial imperialism, all had created the impression that there existed a difference of interest between two groups of countries. In the late 1960s, the political complexities grew. Clearly articulated distinctions and differences based on conceptions of national interest emerged in the debates about changes in the international monetary system between developed countries. The behavior of the major industrial countries, and in particular of the two reserve centers, seemed to spur others to consider the international order as the playground of national and power interests.

When the SDR was eventually launched, and the first issue of SDRs made in 1969, there were only rather oblique references to the concept of the "link." The SDR had been created as a response to a perception that there was an international shortage of liquidity. The major evidence that there was indeed such a shortage came from the prevalence of balance of payments problems, as well as the ever-increasing share of foreign exchange (largely US dollars) in official reserve holdings. "The main indications of reserve inadequacy in these years (after 1965) lie in the increased reliance on restrictions on international transactions and the increased recourse to international financial assistance, bilateral and multilateral, for the purpose of meeting payments deficits and sustaining reserves."[56] The problems of development were used here to explain the SDR creation, but SDRs were kept within the universalistic framework provided in the original legal framework of the Articles of Agreement before the First (SDR) Amendment. There was as a result no reference in the Articles to any theory of a "link."

But this debate continued through every international financial crisis. The "link" provided a key plank in the demands of developing countries in the 1970s, via the forum of the United Nations, for a New International Economic Order. It formed a significant part of the recommendations of the Brandt report. The G-24 in 1985 in the aftermath of the Latin American debt crisis

---

[55] See Cline (1976).
[56] Garritsen de Vries (1976; Vol. II; 254).

advised that a link of the SDR to development would help meet resource constraints but would also "reduce the pressures on the industrial countries to accommodate an improvement in the current account balances of developing countries."[57] The development of capital markets and the extensive accumulation of reserves by emerging market economies more recently have made liquidity concerns less central to debates about the international monetary order, but there are still demands for a preferential allocation of SDRs for poorer countries, or to be used as part of an exercise in debt relief.

X. Conclusion: the preconditions of policy reform

In retrospect, both of the attempts to alter the system in the 1960s, by attempting to control commodity prices through such schemes as buffer stocks, or by using international reserves as an instrument of development aid, appear misguided. One of the most important insights of the classical economic tradition—it was formulated by Adam Smith and Sir James Steuart—is that every country is a "developing" country in that its economic structure is constantly undergoing change. If this is true, then the problems of development should be treated less as peculiar difficulties with their own separate logic, than as general economic issues. It would be more promising to reduce the extent of dependence on particular exports through the development of a broader range of export products (including manufactures) than to engage in the construction of elaborate support schemes. It would be better to open more economies more rapidly to international capital flows than to make use of the very small amount of external assistance that might have been provided under any conceivable version of the "link." But these changes would require a revolution both in economic thought and in international financial institutions and capital markets that by and large had not yet occurred. In the absence of such a revolution, and in the face of the pressing problems of poverty and inequality, it was hard to argue that even the palliatives should not be tried.

A number of lessons can be learned from the cases of successful adjustment. They apply more to the general policy environment than specifically to the design of programs by international financial institutions. Learning these lessons may draw the international financial institutions into ever more complicated and problematical tasks concerned with the management of micro policy. But the risk of not using these results of experience is that the programs may replicate the hardship involved in successful adjustment without producing long-term benefits.

---

[57] G-24 (1985).

First, for political economy reasons, it is hard to reform without an external impetus. The reforms required to move a country onto a graduation trajectory may be home-grown or may be imported or developed by domestic actors as an alternative to the IMF. An example of the latter is the case of the "Chicago boys" (trained by the University of Chicago's Arnold Harberger, who later wrote about the phenomenon) who engineered Chile's miracle in the late 1970s, or the "Berkeley mafia" in Indonesia in the late 1960s. Advice from the outside need of course not always be good advice, and foreign advisers such as the former Nazi German economics minister Hjalmar Schacht gave very bad advice to Indonesia in the early 1960s, as well as to Egypt, Iraq, and Syria. It is attractive to see the IMF as an outside agent that can shift policy debates within a country, but to do this requires reform ideas as well as financial support. The financial support was often in practice a vehicle for transmitting the ideas in a complex political economy.

The IMF has played a special role because its traditional emphasis on fiscal stabilization and anti-inflation policies is particularly directed against the political economy logic that produced unbalanced fiscal dynamics in many developing countries. Debates about fiscal and monetary stabilization become particularly important in crisis situations, when outside institutions can be used to produce outcomes that many domestic actors recognize as desirable, but which are blocked by institutional and political dynamics. If the transformation takes place following a crisis, the necessary reforms instituted once the country has hit rock bottom may be promoted by domestic players or by the IMF through the conditionality that accompanies its lending.

Second, and also for political economy reasons, the process of adapting economic structures can never just be accomplished by the diktat of a technocratic elite. Such a top-down approach is likely to provoke widespread discontent. It courts the risk of a sudden reversal of policy. Indeed, in 1959, in an interview in Spain, Per Jacobsson made exactly this point: "I must emphasize that such programs can only succeed if there is the will to succeed in the countries themselves. The Fund has always found people in these countries who know very well what is to be done. The Fund does not impose conditions on countries; they themselves freely have come to the conclusion that the measures they arrange to take—even when they are sometimes harsh—are in the best interests of their own countries."[58]

Adjustment frequently increases the resources available to a large number of people; devaluations, for instance, often bring benefits to the ill-organized rural majority. In this way, the consequences of adjustment are frequently actually anti-elitist, helping majorities against powerfully organized special interests.

---

[58] IMF Archives (1959).

Greater social cohesion can help to make more bearable the strains inevitably created by the transition. Targeted interventions to reduce poverty and prevent starvation are an important part of the effort to increase the resilience and the adaptability of societies. One feature of many low-income countries that stands out in a statistical cross-country analysis (and that contrasts remarkably with the experience of many of the outward-oriented rapidly growing economies in Asia) is the prevalence of extremes of income disparity.[59] Tackling this through the extension of education, by the provision of greater opportunities, and through the guarantees of a rule of law is an important social precondition for effective economic performance. And economic performance, in turn, is justified and in the longer run only sustainable if it accords with the demands of justice. The process of building confidence needs to take place on several planes simultaneously; and in that case, each achievement will reinforce the others. For instance, in terms of credit relations, better performance at a local level will help to keep capital in the country and reverse capital flight, and this serves as a signal of strength to the international market.

The most common form of more recent criticism of Fund and Bank programs is not so much they are too harsh or restrictive, but rather that programs are worked out by Western-educated political elites in association with international civil servants who are likely to be unfamiliar with local cultures and insensitive to the local environment. In short, desirable macro-reforms may not deal adequately with the issue of how to secure reform on the micro level, so that there is a more adequate response to an improved macroeconomic environment.[60] This is both a more realistic and appropriate critique than the older one, and one much more difficult to deal with. How should programs and policy recommendations best be attuned to the circumstances of daily life?

All societies can benefit from the exchange of the products of different sorts of human skill—not just within countries, but also across national barriers. But for that exchange to occur smoothly requires the operation of a sophisticated system of credit and trust that also reaches across frontiers. International institutions can and should facilitate the operation of that system: but when they are forced by circumstance to attempt to make themselves into a substitute for the system as a whole the results cannot be expected to be satisfactory. Often this chapter has described developments in terms of a vicious cycle. This cycle needs to be arrested and reversed. Reforming domestic economies and building a functioning international financial system are not two logically disparate tasks, but rather part of the same endeavor. Such reforms often take place in the context of a crisis, which can be seen as giving the best setting for a reform that takes countries back into a globally integrated economy. Crises

---

[59] World Bank (1993; 29–32).
[60] Sandbrook (1993; 49–50, 139–40).

may be cathartic in the kind of shock that they administer. But crises are unpleasant and the institutions associated with their management necessarily take on considerable political opprobrium.

XI. References

African Development Bank, 1966, *African Development Bank Report 1964–65* (Abidjan: African Development Bank).

Bangura, Yusuf, 1987, "IMF/World Bank Conditionality and Nigeria's Structural Adjustment Programme," in Kjell J. Havnevik (editor), *The IMF and the World Bank in Africa: Conditionality, Impact and Alternatives* (Uppsala: Scandinavian Institute of African Studies).

Bates, Robert H., 1981, *Markets and States in Tropical Africa: The Political Basis of Agricultural Policies* (Berkeley: University of California Press).

Bauer, Peter, 1972, *Dissent on Development: Studies and Debates in Development Economics* (Cambridge, MA: Harvard University Press).

Bhagwati, Jagdish, 1978, *Anatomy and Consequences of Exchange Control Regimes* (New York: NBER).

Boughton, James, 2000a, "From Suez to Tequila: The IMF as Crisis Manager," *Economic Journal 110*.

—— 2000b, "Northwest of Suez: The 1956 Crisis and the IMF," *IMF Staff Papers, 48/3*.

Bruton, Henry J., 1961, *Inflation in a Growing Economy* (Bombay: Bombay University Press).

Callaghy, Thomas M., 1990, "Lost Between State and Market: The Politics of Economic Adjustment in Ghana, Zambia and Nigeria," in Joan M. Nelson (editor), *Economic Crisis and Policy Choice: The Politics of Adjustment in the Third World* (Princeton, NJ: Princeton University Press).

Chenery, H.B. and A.M. Strout, 1966, "Economic Assistance and Economic Development," *American Economic Review, 56*.

Cline, William R., 1976, *International Monetary Reform and the Developing Countries* (Washington, DC: Brookings Institution).

Cooper, Richard N., 1968, *The Economics of Interdependence* (New York: McGraw-Hill).

Díaz-Alejandro, Carlos F., 1965, *Exchange-Rate Devaluation in a Semi-Industrialized Country: The Experience of Argentina* (Cambridge, MA: MIT Press).

Dornbusch, Rudiger and Sebastian Edwards, 1991, "The Macroeconomics of Populism," in Rudiger Dornbusch and Sebastian Edwards (editors), *The Macroeconomics of Populism in Latin America* (Chicago: University of Chicago Press).

Dorrance, Graeme S., 1963, "The Effect of Inflation on Economic Development," *IMF Staff Papers, 10*.

Economist, April 22, 1961, "To Balance or Not".

Edwards, Sebastian, 1998, "Openness, Productivity and Growth: What Do We Really Know?" *Economic Journal, 108*.

Ellis, Howard S., 1941, *Exchange Control in Central Europe* (Cambridge, MA: Harvard University Press).

Furtado, Celso, 1963, *The Economic Growth of Brazil: A Survey from Colonial to Modern Times*, translated by Ricardo W. de Aguiar and Eric C. Drysdale (Berkeley: University of California Press).

—— 1978, "Post-National Capitalism," *Latin American Research Unit Studies, 2/2*.

G-24, 1985, "The Functioning and Improvement of the International Monetary System."

Garritsen de Vries, Margaret, 1976, *The International Monetary Fund 1966–1971: The System Under Stress* (Washington, DC: International Monetary Fund).

Gold, Joseph, 1979, "Uniformity as a Legal Principle of the Fund," in Joseph Gold (editor), *Legal and Instutitional Aspects of the International Monetary System, Selected Essays Vol. I* (Washington, DC: International Monetary Fund).

Haberler, Gottfried, 1961, "Terms of Trade and Economic Development," in Howard S. Ellis (editor), *Economic Development for Latin America* (New York: St. Martin's Press).

Hanke, Steve and Kurt Schuler, 1994, *Currency Boards for Developing Countries: A Handbook* (San Francisco: ICS Press).

IMF Archives, 1959, CF C/Spain/810, June 23, television interview.

IMF Annual Report 1959.

IMF Annual Meetings, 1961, Proceedings.

IMF Annual Report, 1962.

IMF Archives, 1963, CF C/Colombia/420, January 7, memorandum.

IMF Archives, 1966, CF B640, IBRD, The Evaluation of Economic Performance in Developing Countries, June 1.

Independent Commission on International Development Issues, 1980, *North–South: A Programme for Survival* (Cambridge, MA: MIT Press).

Jacobsson, Per, 1958, Diary, University of Basel.

James, Harold, 1996, *International Monetary Cooperation Since Bretton Woods* (New York: Oxford University Press).

Kafka, Alexander, 1961, "Theoretical Interpretation," in Howard S. Ellis (editor), *Economic Development for Latin America* (New York: St. Martin's Press).

Krueger, Anne O., 1978, *Liberation Attempts and Consequences* (New York: NBER).

—— 1993, *Political Economy of Policy Reform in Developing Countries* (Cambridge, MA: MIT Press).

Lewis, W. Arthur, 1949, *Economic Survey 1919–1939* (London: Allen & Unwin).

Lora, Eduardo, Ugo Panizza and Myriam Quispe-Agnola, 2004, "Reform Fatigue: Symptoms, Reasons, Implications," *Federal Reserve Bank of Atlanta Economic Review*.

Low, Patrick, 1993, *Trading Free: The GATT and U.S. Trade Policy* (New York: Twentieth Century Fund).

Mason, Edward S. and Robert E. Asher, 1973, *The World Bank Since Bretton Woods* (Washington, DC: Brookings Institution).

Narasimham, M., 1984, *Bretton Woods: Forty Years On* (Bombay: Forum of Free Enterprise).

Nelson, Joan M., 1992, "Poverty, Equity and the Politics of Adjustment," in Stephan Haggard and Robert R. Kaufman (editors), *The Politics of Economic Adjustment: International Constraints, Distributive Conflicts and the State* (Princeton, NJ: Princeton University Press).

Onimode, Bade, 1989, "IMF and World Bank Programmes in Africa," in Bade Onimode (editor), *The IMF, the World Bank and the African Debt Vol. I: The Economic Impact* (London: Institute for African Alternatives and Zed Books).

Palyi, Melchior, 1958, *Managed Money at the Crossroads: The European Experience* (Notre Dame, IN: University of Notre Dame Press).

Papageorgiou, Demetrios, Armeane M. Choksi and Michael Michaely, 1990, *Liberalizing Foreign Trade in Developing Countries: The Lessons of Experience* (Washington, DC: World Bank).

Polak, Jacques J., 1957, "Monetary Analysis of Income Formation and Payments Problems," *IMF Staff Papers, 6*.

—— 1994, *The World Bank and the International Monetary Fund: A Changing Relationship* (Washington, DC: Brookings Institution).

—— and W.H. White, 1955, "The Effect of Income Expansion on the Quantity of Money," *IMF Staff Papers, 4*.

Prebisch, Raúl, 1959, "Commercial Policy in Underdeveloped Countries," *American Economic Review: Papers and Proceedings, 49*.

Rostow, W.W., 1971, *The Stages of Economic Growth: A Non-Communist Manifesto* (Cambridge, UK: Cambridge University Press).

Sachs, Jeffrey and Andrew M. Warner, 1995, "Economic Convergence and Economic Policies," *Brookings Papers in Economic Activity, 1*.

Sandbrook, Richard, 1993, *The Politics of Africa's Recovery* (Cambridge, UK: Cambridge University Press).

Schatz, Sayre P., 1984, "Pirate Capitalism and the Inert Economy of Nigeria," *Journal of Modern African Studies, 22/1*.

Singer, Hans, 1949, "Economic Progress in Under-Developed Countries," *Social Research, 16*.

Tignor, Robert L., 1998, *Capitalism and Nationalism at the End of Empire: State and Business in Decolonizing Egypt, Nigeria, and Kenya, 1945–1963* (Princeton, NJ: Princeton University Press).

United Nations Economic and Social Council on the World Economic Situation, Press Release ECOSOC/1168, July 6, 1959.

UN General Assembly, 17th Session, Draft Resolution November 2, 1962; and Resolution 1830, December 18, 1962 ("Inflation and Economic Development").

van Meerhaeghe, M.A.G., 1971, *International Economic Institutions* (London: Longman).

Wai, U Tun, 1959, "The Relation between Inflation and Economic Development: A Statistical Inductive Study," *IMF Staff Papers, 7*.

Winters, L. Alan, 2004, "Trade Liberalization and Economic Performance: An Overview," *Economic Journal, 114*.

—— and Robert E. Baldwin, 2005, *Challenges to Globalization: Analyzing the Economics* (Chicago: University of Chicago Press).

World Bank, 1993, *The East Asian Miracle: Economic Growth and Public Policy* (New York: Oxford University Press).

3

Lending to and for the Poor: How the IMF's Role Has Evolved

James M. Boughton (IMF)

I. Introduction

The first country ever to ask for a loan from the IMF was one of the poorest. In April 1947, the government of Ethiopia represented that it faced a deficit in its balance of payments, and it asked to borrow $900,000. The IMF turned down the request on the grounds that the money was not really needed for balance of payments purposes, but rather for development, which was not the purpose of the Fund. Half a century later, when Ethiopia asked for a loan commitment of $127 million in October 1996, the country's still-underdeveloped economic condition was accepted by the IMF as the primary source of a chronic balance of payments problem. How and why did IMF policy evolve from a sharp dichotomy between finance and development to one where—for the least developed countries—the two were seen as unavoidably linked?

This evolution took place gradually, in large and small and uneven steps. The transformation resulted from a combination of five interrelated forces: changes in the nature of the Fund and its membership, as it grew from an association of 40 countries in 1946 to a nearly universal institution with more than 180 members in the 1990s; changes in the world economy, as the number of financially mature countries rose slowly but dramatically; changes in economic theory, especially about the nature of development; changes in IMF leadership, as a succession of Managing Directors brought new ideas and priorities to the fore; and changes in external pressures on the IMF, resulting in large part from the growing influence of civil society in world politics.

As the IMF grew over the past 60 years, the portion of its membership that would now be considered low-income—low enough to qualify for financial assistance on concessional terms—also grew, especially in the first two decades (Figure 3.1). From 11 percent at the outset, it rose to 40 percent by the

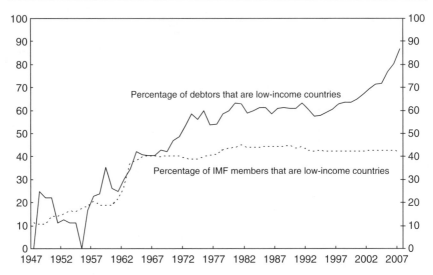

Figure 3.1 Low-Income Countries in the IMF (in percent)
Source: IMF Fund Accounts

mid-1960s and has remained just over that level ever since. As a share of borrowing countries, of course, the rise has been much stronger. Around one-sixth of the borrowing countries in the 1950s were low-income countries (LICs). That ratio passed 50 percent in 1972, and LICs have been in the majority every year since then. In 2006–7, as loan demand from LICs continued unabated while demand from middle-income developing countries waned, more than 80 percent of LICs were indebted to the IMF, and more than 80 percent of all indebted countries were LICs.

LICs have always faced four large hurdles when seeking to borrow from the IMF.

First is the question of whether they can afford to take on the debt; whether they have the economic capacity to pay interest and to repay the loans when they come due. The IMF was established as a cooperative fund, with a limited amount of money to lend for limited periods of time. Lacking a funding source or a mandate for granting development aid, it could not continue to function if its lending became a back-door substitute for grants.

Second is the question of whether they have temporary balance of payments problems, separable from their needs for development finance. If not, then even if they have the capacity to repay the Fund, they will require a continual rollover of loans in order to derive any lasting benefit.

Third is the question of whether they have the will, the administrative capacity, and the political backing to carry out the economic policies that will correct the underlying causes of their payments imbalances. While this issue is central to any country's request to borrow from the IMF, it is an especially high hurdle for those at a very early stage of development.

Fourth is the question of whether the government has the will to direct the proceeds toward poverty reduction, infrastructure development, and the country's other basic needs rather than toward preserving officials' own hold on political power. This last issue—whether IMF lending is really helping the poor—was largely ignored in the early years of the Fund on the grounds that it was a matter of domestic politics rather than international policy, but it has become a central concern in more recent times.

II. Lending to the poor

When the IMF began lending in 1947, most of its members were countries that were struggling to resume normal international trading and financial relationships after the disruptions of the Depression and Second World War. Only five of the original members were countries that now would be considered LICs. That number began to grow in the late 1950s and early 1960s, as newly independent countries applied for membership as one element of an entry into the community of nations. In response, the IMF began looking for ways to solve what was then thought to be the central problem: many of the poorer countries had payments deficits, not because of their own weak policies, but because of adverse conditions in the world economy.

The first significant step toward accommodating the special needs of the poor was made in 1963, with the establishment of the Compensatory Financing Facility (CFF) within the IMF. The impetus for setting up this new lending window was that many of the Fund's less developed members were heavily dependent on revenues from exporting primary commodities. The markets for those commodities, both agricultural and mineral, were and are volatile, for a variety of reasons mostly beyond the control or influence of the exporting countries. To help them cope with the effects of temporary declines on the balance of payments, the Fund set up the CFF so that members could borrow up to specified limits without having to develop detailed programs of economic policy adjustments and without reducing their eligibility to borrow for other purposes.

Use of the CFF was not restricted to less developed countries or to those exporting primary commodities, but it was designed specifically for them, and they became its main customers. More generally, the establishment of the CFF epitomized a shift in tactics and mindset at the IMF that facilitated lending to the poor. Overall, lending to LICs tripled in four years, from $243 million in 1963 to $723 million in 1967 (Figure 3.2).

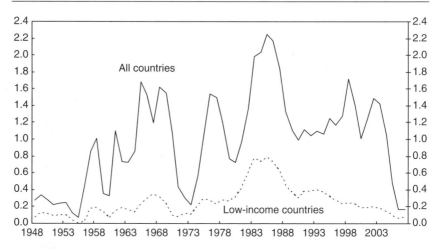

Figure 3.2 Outstanding Use of IMF Credit: 1948–2007 (in percent of total world exports)
Notes: Includes loans from PRGF and other administered accounts. End data are for September.
Source: IMF Fund Accounts

The idea behind the CFF was that countries suffering from external shocks might not need to adjust policies in order to cope, as long as the shocks were temporary and not a result of the country's own bad policies. That idea was carried forward in the 1970s with the establishment of the Oil Facility. Also known as the Witteveen Facility, after H. Johannes Witteveen, the Fund's Managing Director who championed it, it offered loans almost automatically to fuel-importing countries after the large increases in oil prices. For 25 countries that were deemed to be particularly hard hit by the increased cost of oil imports and to have the most difficulty servicing external debts, the IMF set up the Oil Facility Subsidy Account with contributions from donor countries. Use of that account reduced the interest rate on Oil Facility loans by five percentage points below market rates.

More directly and broadly aimed at LICs was the Trust Fund, established in 1976 to provide longer-term (ten-year) loans at very low interest rates (0.5 percent) and without the usual requirements for policy adjustments. The IMF's Articles of Agreement specify that the Fund must treat all of its members alike, which means that any two members facing similar circumstances must receive equal treatment. That provision prohibits the Fund from using its general financial resources to lend only to LICs or to subsidize loans to them but not to others. The Trust Fund therefore was financed separately through the sale of one-sixth of the IMF's stock of gold and investing the lion's share of the profits in a separate administered account. Through the Trust Fund, the IMF lent $3.3 billion to 55 LICs from 1977 through 1980.

None of these innovations—the CFF, the Oil Facility, or the Trust Fund—was particularly successful at helping LICs escape from chronic external financing deficits. Part of the problem was simply the scale of the financing gaps faced by these countries, which in many countries were far in excess of the loans that the IMF could make. More fundamentally, the problem was that the shortfalls turned out not to be temporary and to be aggravated by policy weaknesses. The sharp jump in world oil prices in 1973–4, originally thought to be a temporary consequence of war in the Middle East and the new-found economic clout of a cartel of oil exporters, turned out to be a shift toward a new equilibrium in the global market for oil. The end of a boom in the markets for a wide range of primary commodities in the mid-1970s, originally thought to be part of a recurring cycle, turned out to be the resumption of a long downward slide in commodity prices relative to manufactured goods, a slide that actually accelerated in the following decade. By providing low-conditionality loans to the countries adversely affected by these developments, the IMF inadvertently helped delay the policy adjustments that LICs in particular needed to make.

A second type of innovation ultimately turned out to be more successful, but it took a while to hone the strategy. In 1974, the IMF established the Extended Fund Facility (EFF) to make larger and longer-term loans to member countries. To qualify, borrowers were supposed to prepare a structural reform and investment program aimed at putting the economy on a sustainable growth path. Once the Fund approved that plan, normally after consultation with the World Bank, it could approve a three-year sequence of loans, with disbursements phased and conditional on the authorities carrying out both macroeconomic stabilization measures and the investment program. These loans could be repaid over ten years with a seven-year grace period, rather than the three- to five-year repayment on conventional stand-by arrangements.

EFF loans were available to all member countries and were paid out from the Fund's general resources. To make enough money available for the longer maturities, the IMF borrowed more than $10 billion from a group of 14 member countries and central banks to fund a Supplemental Financing Facility (SFF). The Fund paid market interest rates on these borrowings, and it charged the same high rates on SFF-funded loans. To make those loans more affordable to LICs, the IMF also established a subsidy account financed by donations and loans. That account was used to subsidize interest payments for LICs, bringing them closer to the Fund's regular rate of charge. From 1982 to 1985, LICs received $530 million in subsidies on SFF-funded loans.[1]

At the beginning of the 1980s, LICs constituted 44 percent of the Fund's membership, and around 60 percent of its borrowers. The Fund's Managing Director from 1978 to 1986, Jacques de Larosière, was eager to provide more

---

[1] For background and details on these developments, see de Vries (1985), pp. 545–57, and Boughton (2001), pp. 642–4.

help to this group of countries, and he urged the staff to make a strong effort to negotiate loans to LICs. In 1979, the IMF adopted new guidelines for its policy conditions on stand-by arrangements. Aimed primarily at formalizing and standardizing the Fund's conditionality, the new guidelines also helped enable lending to countries with limited administrative capacity by restricting policy conditions on stand-by arrangements to macroeconomics. The Fund could advise countries to reform structural and social policies, but it was not supposed to require such reforms as a condition for its ordinary lending. The new guidelines made that restriction explicit.

The initial outcome of de Larosière's push was that more of the IMF's lending was conditional, in the form of stand-by and EFF arrangements rather than CFF, Oil Facility, or Trust Fund loans. But the conditions in many cases were not strict enough or appropriate enough to solve the real causes of the borrowers' payments deficits. Moreover, domestic ownership of the reform agenda was lacking, partly because the Fund was still learning how to tailor its advice on structural reforms to countries' circumstances and partly because country officials were not yet ready to embrace market-oriented reforms. Several LICs were unable to repay these loans and fell into protracted arrears to the Fund. Others became prolonged borrowers, as the IMF repeatedly approved new arrangements as a way to roll over existing credits that could not be immediately repaid.

The next evolutionary step came in 1985, with the establishment of the Structural Adjustment Facility (SAF). The Trust Fund loans that the IMF had made in the late 1970s were now being repaid, and the question arose as to what should be done with the proceeds. At the suggestion of the minister of finance of India, V.P. Singh, the Fund's ministerial governing body then known as the Interim Committee decided that the money should be reinvested in a new fund dedicated to the benefit of LICs. Unlike the Trust Fund, this new facility would make conditional loans, but the policy conditions would be less strict than on conventional stand-by arrangements. Like the Trust Fund, SAF loans would be highly concessional and have ten-year maturities.

As the SAF began operating in 1986, it quickly became apparent that it had two serious limitations. First, it was too small, with just $2.3 billion to lend and 60 LICs eligible to draw on it. SAF loans were limited to less than 50 percent of the borrower's quota, which was insufficient to make a real difference for many countries. Second, the conditionality was too weak. The facility was designed to make loans readily available, but that aspect meant that necessary policy adjustments were likely to be delayed.

When Michel Camdessus became Managing Director in 1987, he set out to remedy these two problems. First, he proposed to triple the resources of the SAF by obtaining additional grants and loans from a wide range of member countries. Second, drawings on this enlarged facility—the Enhanced Structural Adjustment Facility (ESAF)—would be subject to more detailed policy conditions, essentially similar to the conditionality on EFF arrangements. The ESAF began lending in 1988, and it appeared that the IMF finally had found the right combination of easy financial terms and tough policy conditions. Whether the Fund's structural conditionality would be appropriate to the needs of these borrowers remained to be seen.

While the ESAF did succeed in mitigating the shortcomings of the SAF, two broader problems soon emerged.

First, even with the availability of multilateral credit on highly concessional terms, many LICs were accumulating more external debt than they could afford to service or repay. Part of the problem was that bilateral aid from donor countries was often provided in the form of loans, not grants, and the burden of servicing that debt just kept growing. The major donor countries acknowledged the difficulty around the same time as the ESAF was established, and they began offering debt relief to the poorest countries through a series of increasingly generous packages. That effort culminated in 1996 with the announcement of the "Lyon terms," under which heavily indebted LICs implementing strong economic policies could have up to 80 percent of the present value of their bilateral debts written off. That same year, the IMF and the World Bank joined the debt reduction effort for the first time by establishing the Heavily Indebted Poor Countries (HIPC) Initiative. The IMF's part in the initiative was to provide grants—the first time in its history the institution had made grants to its member countries—to be used to repay outstanding balances owed to the Fund.

HIPC grants, which were equivalent to partial debt write-offs, were financed by donor contributions, and later by off-market gold transactions by the IMF. The grants were calibrated to reduce the overall outstanding debts of eligible HIPCs, after allowing for World Bank and bilateral debt relief, to a level that the debtors could service without undermining their development needs. Over the next decade, this initiative provided or committed more than $2 billion in relief on IMF debts to 30 HIPCs. In 2005, the HIPC Initiative was supplemented by the Multilateral Debt Relief Initiative (MDRI), which provides total debt relief for the poorest countries and for those HIPCs that have already qualified for and received partial relief under the earlier program. MDRI relief on IMF debts totaled around $3 billion in the first two years.

Second, many LICs initially lacked the administrative capacity to develop comprehensive policy reform packages on their own. To qualify for ESAF loans and for corresponding loans from the World Bank, country authorities were required to prepare a Policy Framework Paper (PFP) setting out a strategy for reducing poverty, stabilizing the government's finances and balancing its international payments, and reaching a sustainable path of economic growth. In practice, the staffs of the Bank and the Fund usually thought it necessary to prepare detailed drafts in Washington before negotiating final versions in the field.

The role of Bank and Fund staff in preparing PFPs led to widespread resentment, perceptions that policies were being dictated from abroad, and to an undercutting of national processes of policy formation. Even the name of the Fund's facility, with its emphasis on "structural adjustment," came to symbolize for many the imposition of outside ideas. Accordingly, in 1999 the IMF scrapped both the ESAF and its PFP process and replaced them with a new program called the Poverty Reduction and Growth Facility (PRGF). To qualify for PRGF loans, the authorities would have to prepare a Poverty Reduction Strategy Paper (PRSP). To avert the fate of the PFP, the rules of the new facility specified that the PRSP had to be prepared domestically with an appropriate degree of participation by local citizen groups. In 2006, the IMF eased the rules a bit by creating an Exogenous Shocks Facility within the PRGF. Countries applying to borrow under this facility are required to prepare only a shorter-term program of macroeconomic policies to adjust to a temporary external shock.

III. Lending for the poor

The IMF's traditional stance in all of its lending until the late 1970s was that the only real concern was achieving financial stability in the framework of an open exchange regime. As long as the borrower was adopting macroeconomic and financial policies that were internally consistent, stable, not designed to gain an unfair advantage over other countries, and not—in the words of the Fund's Articles of Agreement—"destructive of national or international prosperity," then the structural details of those policies were, in principle, left to the discretion of the country authorities. If the government needed to reduce its fiscal deficit, then the means to do so—whether to raise taxes or cut spending, and which taxes or spending categories—was up to the authorities to decide.

When most of the IMF's borrowers were fairly advanced economies with open and well functioning domestic political systems, this hands-off approach was usually appropriate. As the clientele shifted more to less developed countries, it became less reliable, and the staff found it increasingly difficult to adhere to it. Its weaknesses suddenly became clear in 1977, with the outbreak of "bread riots" in Egypt.[2]

In January 1977, the Egyptian authorities were negotiating terms for a possible stand-by arrangement with a team of IMF staff. The Fund was insisting that the government find a way to cut the deficit in the forthcoming budget. In the midst of these negotiations, the government suddenly announced publicly that it faced a budget crisis and would have to cut subsidies on a

---

[2] For more on this and the following developments, see Bernstein and Boughton (1993).

number of basic goods such as flour. Since those cuts would have raised prices by up to 50 percent for many goods that were especially important for low-income consumers, the announcement was met with massive and violent demonstrations throughout Egypt. Only after scores of people died did the government withdraw the plan and go back to the negotiating table. With help from the Fund, the authorities then devised a new budget with much more gradual reductions in subsidies. In April, the IMF approved a stand-by arrangement to help finance it.

For the next ten years, the Fund continued to maintain an essentially neutral stance on the composition of budget cuts, but it became increasingly difficult to do so consistently in cases where the authorities found it expedient to slash subsidies or services for the poor while maintaining programs for the more well-connected groups that were their main base of political support. In 1984, for example, deadly riots broke out in the Dominican Republic after the government announced policy changes as part of an IMF-supported reform program that would force large price increases for food and imported fuel. As in the Egyptian case, rioters' anger was directed as much at the Fund as at the government, as the authorities' perceived indifference was seen as the illegitimate spawn of the influence of the outside agency.

By the late 1980s, the IMF was shifting toward a pro-poor stance in its policy advice to LICs, and it was beginning to defend itself more openly against allegations that it was responsible when governments tried to tighten policies without protecting the interests of the poor. A major breakthrough came in 1989, after the president of Venezuela, Carlos Andrés Pérez, publicly blamed the Fund for imposing austerity, an act that again resulted in large-scale rioting. In response, Camdessus wrote an open letter to Pérez, insisting that it was the "prerogative of sovereign states to decide themselves what measures are required for recovery, however unpleasant those measures may be," but also that the needs of the poor should be adequately safeguarded in any adjustment program.

Camdessus' approach required striking a very delicate balance between ignoring the social consequences of financial adjustment and meddling in countries' internal affairs to try to get more satisfactory outcomes. As a cooperative institution, the IMF does not have the luxury of choosing to lend only to countries that develop strong economic programs on their own. If it insists that borrowers undertake structural reforms that promote the interests of the poor over other groups, then it has to inject itself into the policymaking process. If it insists on staying out of that process, then it has to accept that the social consequences of adjustment might not be acceptable by international standards.

The 1980s also ushered in a general disaffection with the idea that economic growth was necessarily beneficial across all economic strata in a country. The possibility of immiserating growth was a well-established component of development economics, but it had not played a major role in the debate about the efficacy of the IMF policy toolkit until the Fund started lending frequently to very poor countries. On close examination, it is easy to see that macroeconomic stability can be achieved in ways that either promote or retard the reduction of extreme poverty, but that issue was usually treated as a second-order problem that was outside the mandate or expertise of the IMF.

The Fund staff began studying the distributional consequences of adjustment programs in the late 1970s. Two key early studies were papers by Jitendra Borpujari (1980, 1985) and Omotunde Johnson and Joanne Salop (1980). Borpujari's analysis showed the limitations of standard macroeconomic policy prescriptions in countries with a shortage in the availability of goods to meet basic consumer needs. Johnson and Salop examined conditions under which a tightening of financial policies would have favorable or unfavorable effects on the distribution of income, determined largely by the country's structure of production. They showed that in a country such as Bolivia, where large numbers of rural poor families produced agricultural and other basic products for domestic consumption, conventional adjustment strategies could easily reduce the portion of national income accruing to the poor. Later staff studies, such as that by Charles Sisson (1986), explored ways to fine-tune the Fund's policy advice, particularly with regard to fiscal policies, so as to mitigate these adverse effects.

As the staff gradually began to develop some expertise in distributional economics, the Executive Board discussed these findings on several occasions, starting in 1985. The outcome of those discussions was not a call to shift direction or introduce a new model of economic adjustment and development, simply because no viable alternative existed. Nor was the Board prepared to have the Fund take responsibility for improving member countries' social policies. The compromise that emerged from these meetings was an understanding that the IMF would continue to develop more expertise on the distributional consequences of adjustment programs and would advise and assist borrowers (and other member countries, in the context of regular surveillance consultations) on how to protect the poor from the short-term costs of adjustment. It would not, however, impose conditions on its stand-by arrangements related to structural policies, including those affecting the distribution of income.

That injunction against structural conditionality was never formally overturned, but it was gradually eroded in the 1990s. The main force driving this change was the requirement that SAF and ESAF lending support members' programs as expressed in a PFP and that the PFP set out a program of structural reforms as well as macroeconomic stabilization. To make SAF and ESAF lending effective, the Fund devised a number of procedures linking disbursements to implementation of the policy framework, notably in the form of structural benchmarks. As a natural extension, when lending through EFF or even ordinary stand-by arrangements to countries embarking on structural reform programs, the Fund had increasingly broader recourse to these benchmarks and in some cases began specifying structural performance criteria.[3]

As the Fund's involvement in structural reforms deepened, the institution endeavored to broaden and deepen its interactions and cooperation with other multilateral agencies. The World Bank was the primary partner, of course, and collaboration with the regional development banks for Africa, Asia, and Latin America was also important on an ongoing basis. A 1988 agreement between the Managing Director of the IMF and the President of the World Bank, in a document that came to be known as the Concordat, helped codify how that relationship should work and set a benchmark for the Fund's interaction with other agencies. The essence of the agreement was that the Fund's core mandate covered macroeconomics, while the World Bank had primary responsibility for the design and oversight of structural policies. The difficulty was in defining the border between those two fields, and the boundary line therefore was left unspecified.[4]

Three later developments helped greatly to clarify the Fund's role, especially with regard to structural policies affecting the alleviation of poverty in developing countries.

The first development, discussed above, was the replacement of the PFP with the PRSP process in 1999. In contrast to the PFP, countries' PRSPs were to have a specific focus on poverty reduction rather than a more general focus on structural economic reforms.

Second was the adoption by the United Nations in 2000 of the Millennium Development Goals (MDGs), which set quantifiable goals for the reduction of extreme poverty and for basic development needs such as the reduction of infant mortality, the provision of clean water supplies, and the universalization of primary education. Two years later, the UN's adoption of the Monterrey Consensus gave the IMF a specific role in the MDG campaign, to advise countries on the policy requirements for making sufficient progress and to monitor the implementation of those policies.[5]

The third, with still broader implications, was the adoption of new conditionality guidelines in 2002.[6] Those guidelines, which applied to all Fund-supported programs, specified that structural conditions were to be employed

---

[3] The distinction between a benchmark and a performance criterion is that the latter is a formal requirement for a drawing or disbursement under a Fund-supported lending arrangement. Failure to meet a performance criterion makes the country ineligible for the next drawing unless the Executive Board grants a waiver. A benchmark is examined as one element of a program review, but failure to meet it does not necessarily preclude a positive completion of the review.

[4] See Boughton (2001), pp. 995–1005.

[5] For an overview, see IMF and World Bank (2004).

[6] See "Guidelines on Conditionality," September 25, 2002. Available on the internet at <http://www.imf.org/External/np/pdr/cond/2002/eng/guid/092302.htm>.

only if they were critical to the achievement of the macroeconomic goals of the program or were necessary to safeguard the use of the Fund's resources. In the case of PRGF-supported programs, legitimate macroeconomic goals included poverty reduction, since that was a central purpose of the facility. The intent was not to eliminate structural conditionality, but to ensure that its use was restricted to situations where it was needed to ensure that the Fund and the country were working together to reduce poverty and put the economy on a sustainable path of economic growth.

IV. Concluding observations

The focus of this chapter has been on the IMF's lending to poor countries and on ways that it has tried to target some of that lending towards supporting countries' poverty reduction efforts. Lending, of course, is not the Fund's only function. The Fund conducts surveillance with each of its member countries and provides technical assistance on request. Surveillance consultations with LICs focus on poverty reduction and progress toward achieving the MDGs as well as on macroeconomics. Technical assistance, often provided in conjunction with Fund-supported reform programs, might include advice on how to reorient fiscal operations so as to accommodate development aid more effectively or to avoid crowding out necessary social spending. In recent years, these activities have been supplemented by the establishment of regional training centers for officials in developing countries and by the introduction of a "policy support instrument" as a way of formalizing the Fund's policy advice in a program context for countries that do not need IMF financial support for balance of payments purposes.

As for lending, the net result of the various innovations described in Section II has been to create a fund within the Fund, dedicated to LICs. It has its own financing sources and its own rules for eligibility, designed to provide grants and low-cost, long-term loans to countries at the very early stages of economic development. With more than $12 billion in assets, this fund is a significant contribution to the provision of official financial assistance to LICs. Its major importance, however, is that it seats the IMF at the cornerstone of the system of official assistance. The intent is to identify those countries that are pursuing sound macroeconomic policies and implementing appropriate structural reforms, so that other multilateral and bilateral creditors and donors can direct their own aid efforts effectively.

The gatekeeper function of IMF lending to LICs is, however, not without controversy. Are the Fund's standards appropriate, or are they biased toward the prevailing ideology of major creditor countries and ill-suited to the circumstances of the least developed? Is the IMF, with its expertise in macroeconomics, the right institution to judge whether very poor countries have the right structural policies and qualify for development assistance? Since IMF lending to LICs is small relative to the development assistance provided by other agencies, is it wise for development agencies to rely on IMF judgments? Those questions have become important themes in the modern debate about the future of the IMF and plans for its reform and are the subject of other chapters in this book.

V. References

Bernstein, Boris, and James M. Boughton, 1993, "Adjusting to Development: The IMF and the Poor," IMF Paper on Policy Analysis and Assessment (PPAA/93/4). Washington: International Monetary Fund.

Borpujari, Jitendra G., 1980, "Toward a Basic Needs Approach to Economic Development with Financial Stability," IMF Departmental Memorandum (DM/80/16). Washington: International Monetary Fund.

—— 1985, "Savings Generation and Financial Programming in a Basic Need Constrained Developing Economy," in Armin Gutowski, A.A. Arnaúdo, and Hans-Eckart Scharrer (Editors), *Financing Problems of Developing Countries*, pp. 59–82. New York: St. Martin's Press.

Boughton, James M., 2001, *Silent Revolution: The International Monetary Fund, 1979–1989*. Washington: International Monetary Fund.

de Vries, Margaret Garritsen, 1985, *The International Monetary Fund 1972–1978: Cooperation on Trial*. Washington: International Monetary Fund.

International Monetary Fund and World Bank, 2004, *Global Monitoring Report 2004: Policies and Actions for Achieving the Millennium Development Goals and Related Outcomes*. Washington: The World Bank. Available on the internet at <http://siteresources.worldbank.org/INTGLOBALMONITORING/Resources/GMR_2004.pdf>.

Johnson, Omotunde, and Joanne Salop, 1980, "Distributional Aspects of Stabilization Programs in Developing Countries," *IMF Staff Papers*, Vol. 27 (March), pp. 1–23.

Sisson, Charles A., 1986, "Fund-Supported Programs and Income Distribution in LDCs," *Finance and Development*, Vol. 23 (March), pp. 33–6.

4

The Case for a Universal Financial Institution

James M. Boughton (IMF)

> "The issue is not whether the Fund should take an interest in poverty, but whether it should continue working, and working better, with its poorest member countries. The answer to that is yes: as a universal institution, we have to stay involved with all our members."
>
> Stanley Fischer (2001)

The appropriateness of the IMF's role in low-income countries (LICs) is best analyzed in the context of its broader role in the world economy. Should the IMF be engaged in advising and lending to LICs? If so, should that role differ from its engagement with more advanced economies?

When the Soviet Union disintegrated in 1991 and all of the newly emergent countries joined the membership of the International Monetary Fund, the IMF almost overnight became a nearly universal financial institution. Today it has 185 member countries, just 7 fewer than the United Nations. In contrast, Citibank—the world's most globally engaged private financial institution—is active in about 100 countries. As Stanley Fischer (then the First Deputy Managing Director of the IMF) indicated in his farewell address to the IMF's Executive Board (quoted above), the distinction is not trivial.

Universalism is not only a question of membership. Several official international agencies now have universal, or near-universal, membership, including the United Nations and many of its specialized agencies as well as both the IMF and the World Bank (but not yet the World Trade Organization). Having a very broad and inclusive membership is obviously a necessary condition, but it is not sufficient. More fundamentally, it is a question of focus. The World Bank lends only to developing countries: to middle-income countries through its original body, the International Bank for Reconstruction and Development, and to low-income countries through its concessional-lending arm, the International Development Association (World Bank, 2007). In contrast, any one of the 185 member countries—Uganda or the United States—can borrow from the IMF: the only financial institution in the world with this universal approach to lending.

A broad implication of this fact is that the IMF is designed to function as a cooperative, or a club of peers. In principle, each member country might be a creditor part of the time and a borrower at other times. Since the early years of the IMF (which started lending in 1947), this revolving-fund aspect has been important. Canada, Denmark, France, Italy, and the United Kingdom are all countries that are now financial and industrial powers but that in the past cycled between being creditors and debtors of the IMF. Even Japan and the United States had stand-by arrangements in the early years. And this distinguishing feature of the Fund has not vanished. More recently, China, the Czech Republic, Estonia, Korea, and Russia have been borrowers for a time and are now creditors. Over the past 28 years (1980–2007), some 47 countries have switched between being net financial contributors to the IMF and being debtors, *and back*, at least once.

Universal lending by the IMF is an adjunct to the even more comprehensive use of surveillance. The Fund is the only financial institution that conducts routine (annual) consultations with all countries. These consultations focus primarily on macroeconomic policies but also cover related issues such as the soundness of the financial sector and the country's adherence to a variety of internationally accepted standards and codes. When and if a member country applies to borrow from the Fund, the knowledge that the staff has gained through these consultations, and the policy advice that it has given, make a useful starting point for discussion of lending terms and policy conditions. More generally, the consultations are a platform for the Fund to develop and disseminate a comprehensive and consistent policy framework covering all regions and economies.

I. The evolution of the IMF and its membership

The predominant perception of the IMF today is rather different from this universal model of uniform treatment of member countries.[1] For the most part, the Fund today is thought to be an institution with a sizeable number of member countries that have had persistent creditor positions for at least the past two decades, an even larger (but now dwindling) number of members with persistent debtor positions, and a small middle group that might move from one side to the other. The seven largest industrial countries, which constitute themselves as the Group of Seven for financial discussions, are often used as a metaphor for the larger group of creditor countries. Hence

---

[1] For an earlier, related, treatment of this subject, see Boughton (2005).

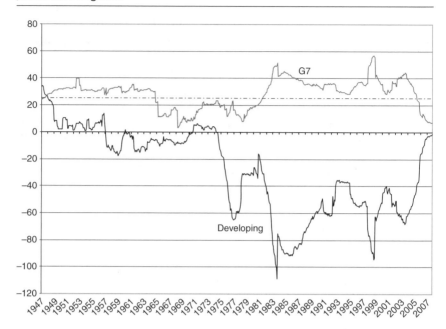

Figure 4.1 G7 and Developing Countries: Net Financial Position in the IMF, 1947–2007 (in percent of quota)

Note: Net position = 100% - line.

Source: IMF, International Financial Statistics

the popular image of the Fund is illustrated by Figure 4.1, which shows how a large debit position by developing countries in the aggregate has been financed in large part by the corresponding credit positions of the G7. While this pattern is evident to some extent in the first half of the chart (1947 through the 1970s), it is especially striking in the more recent period.

The dotted line at +25 percent in this and the following diagram normally marks the boundary between making a standard financial contribution to the Fund as a condition of membership and being an active creditor. A contribution of approximately 25 percent of quota is the standard quota subscription for each member country. A country with no outstanding net transactions other than its subscription will have a net credit position at that level.[2] As a corollary, a zero position means that the member has withdrawn its own subscription and is

---

[2] The net financial position shown in the diagram is equal to one minus the Fund's holdings of the country's currency in percent of quota. When a country joins the Fund, it is required to deposit 22.7% of its quota in Special Drawing Rights (SDRs) or in strong currencies that the Fund is currently using in lending operations. The balance is credited in the member's own currency. Subscriptions for subsequent increases in quotas are paid 25 percent in strong currencies or SDRs, the balance in the member's currency. Consequently, a country that has had no transactions with the Fund other than its quota subscriptions would have a net

neither contributing to the Fund nor borrowing from it. When the IMF lends to a country, it normally uses currencies contributed by members with strong finances and credits those countries with an additional claim. Countries with net claims greater than 25 percent of quota are thereby the creditors of the Fund.[3]

From 1965 through mid-1981, when some G7 countries had outstanding debts to the Fund, the group's aggregate net creditor position fell below the 25 percent threshold (bottoming out at 3.2% in June 1968). For most of the Fund's history, however, the G7 has had an aggregate creditor position.

The devil being in the details, it is worth taking a closer look at the IMF's financial relations with a few individual countries (Figure 4.2). The top two panels illustrate how two G7 countries—the United Kingdom and Italy—had recourse to IMF financing in the past. The United Kingdom had five separate episodes as a debtor—and had a debtor position for more than half of the time—before ascending to an apparently permanent position as a financial contributor or creditor in 1980. Note, however, that the United Kingdom has had a significant *creditor* position only in the early 1980s and since 1997. In contrast, Italy has been a creditor for most of its time as an IMF member, but it too borrowed fairly large sums in the 1970s.

Next, as an illustration of how this cycle of fortune is continuing in more recent periods, consider the case of the Republic of Korea (middle left panel). Korea spent its first two decades in the IMF as a contributor, then borrowed heavily for a decade or so. By the end of the 1980s, Korea appeared—like the United Kingdom—to have become a permanent creditor. In an implicit recognition of that new, stronger, status, the OECD accepted Korea as a member in 1996, and the IMF reclassified Korea alongside countries such as Japan as an "advanced economy" rather than alongside China and others as a developing country. Then came the financial crisis of 1997, and Korea briefly became the Fund's largest debtor, with a debit position of nearly 17 times its quota in 1998. By 2001, however, Korea had repaid all of its debts to the IMF and had regained its creditor position.

The next two panels demonstrate that developing countries also may cycle in and out of debtor status as they try to advance economically along a bumpy path. Israel has had four distinct episodes as a debtor and currently has a sizeable creditor position.[4] Indonesia cycled regularly between debtor and contributor or creditor positions over more than four decades prior to the

---

creditor position close to 25% of quota, but the exact percentage would depend on the length of membership and on how the country's quota has evolved. Here, 25 percent is used uniformly for simplicity. Since 1978, each member has the right to withdraw all or any part of its hard-currency payment, even permanently, without penalty or cost except for the interest forgone on the balance.

[3] This description applies only when outstanding loans are large enough to require the net use of creditors' currencies. Starting in 2005, the repayment of several large IMF loans and a lull in new lending reduced all creditors' positions well below the 25 percent threshold.

[4] In 1997, the IMF reclassified Israel from a developing country to an advanced economy.

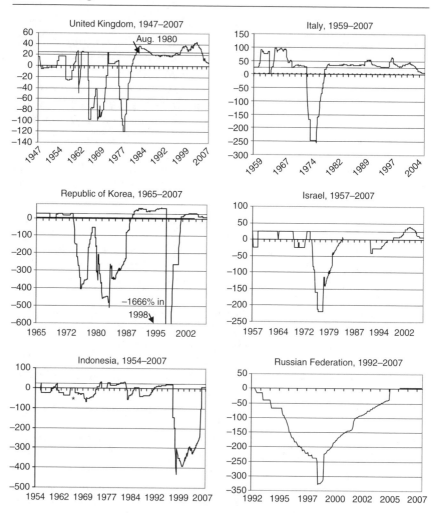

* withdrew from membership, August 1965 to February 1967

Figure 4.2 Selected Countries: Net Financial Position in the IMF, through 2007 (in percent of quota)

Source: See Figure 4.1

crisis of 1997–8. Although neither of these examples may be considered typical of the experience of developing countries, neither are they isolated examples. As of 2007, 74 of the 155 members classified as developing countries had a positive financial position in the Fund, and 21 of those were creditors.

To complete the picture, the last panel in Figure 4.2 shows the brief history of Russia's financial relations with the IMF, starting in 1992 when Russia became a member. As Russia struggled with its initial transition toward establishing a market economy, it borrowed heavily for the first six years and then (following the financial crisis of 1998) began repaying. At the end of January 2005, Russia completed all of its repayments ahead of schedule and brought its debtor position to a close. Two months later, the IMF added Russia to the list of countries whose currencies were to be used in lending operations. And Russia is not alone. In all, 6 of the 28 countries recently classified as "transition" have become creditors of the IMF, and 13 others have repaid all their debts.

Focusing on the aggregate picture rather than on the demands and needs of individual countries can lead one to question the relevance of the universal-institution model and even the very rationale for an institution such as the IMF. High-income countries, as a rule, no longer borrow from the Fund.[5] Low-income countries do, but what they need most is long-term development aid, not shorter-term stabilization assistance. Middle-income countries usually borrow only in response to a financial crisis, in which case crisis resolution may require sums that are quite large in relation to the IMF's resources. In any case, what middle-income countries would benefit from most—and can usually obtain except during crisis periods—is private rather than official capital.

The logic of this aggregate and static view of the world led the Meltzer Commission to recommend to the US Congress that IMF lending should be limited to short-term lending to "solvent emerging economies" (Meltzer, 2000, p. 41), a phrase intended to exclude most low-income countries as well as middle-income countries that are in severe crisis. Countries that lack access to private credit markets and that need long-term financing on concessional terms would, under their proposal, generally be shunted over to the World Bank, regional development banks, and bilateral donors. Similarly, but from a quite different ideological perspective, Oxfam International also has argued for a smaller IMF role in low-income countries, based on an essentially static view of the world. Their 2003 report criticized the IMF for aiming to help poor countries graduate from aid dependence to a more reliable access to private-sector financing. In Oxfam's view, this goal "is simply not realistic for many poor countries" (p. 6) and therefore should not underpin the Fund's assistance.[6] From a political science perspective, Kapur and Naím (2005) argue that

[5] Aside from Korea, the last stand-by arrangements with industrial countries were in 1977 (Italy and the United Kingdom) and 1978 (Spain). In a few cases in the 1980s, industrial countries did draw on the Fund in other ways: Australia (from the Buffer Stock Financing Facility, in 1982), Iceland (from the Compensatory Financing Facility, also in 1982), and Denmark (a reserve tranche drawing, in 1987).

[6] The Oxfam report was not arguing for less IMF lending, but rather for a less powerful "gatekeeper" role on the grounds that the IMF was allegedly preventing low-income countries from obtaining sufficient aid from donors. For a review of these and other similar criticisms, see Bird and Mosley (2005).

69

"while the Fund plays a relatively positive role in middle-income countries, it is debatable whether it is the appropriate institution for the small, structurally weak, low-income countries where the problems are of much longer-term nature and where democracy is also usually weakest."

Once one acknowledges that the boxes in which we tend to place countries analytically are arbitrary, debatable, and transitory (What is a "solvent emerging economy," and which countries fit?), the force of such arguments begins to fade. As an antidote, consider the more dynamic analysis of Michael Kremer, Alexei Onatski, and James Stock (2001), which provides an illustration and a tentative explanation for why countries cannot be treated as permanent members of a class.[7] Building on a model developed by Danny Quah (1993), they estimate long-run probabilities that poor or rich countries will become middle-income, or conversely. They find that a fall from richness is rare, but that countries do move between being poor or middle-income with greater frequency. Their suggested explanation for this stylized fact is that governments tend to experiment with various economic policy regimes until they find one that works. They continue to experiment until the cost of regime switching exceeds the expected growth and other benefits. Countries that reach the highest rungs of the distribution are unlikely to switch further and thus are likely to remain where they are. Less successful countries continue to experiment and thus might either rise or fall in the short run, but most should rise in the long run as better policy regimes are adopted.

A stark implication of this methodology is that the portion of middle-income countries is likely to rise quite sharply over the next few decades, assuming that poor countries are able to learn from the experience of their more successful forerunners. Since 1995, the IMF has removed eight countries from the list of those eligible for loans on concessional terms. Two or three decades from now, instead of the nearly 80 countries that are now classified as low-income, there could be as few as half that many. The numbers of both middle-income and high-income countries would rise, perhaps dramatically. Such an outcome is not inevitable, but the potential is there.

Looking back over the past two or three decades, it is not hard to find countries that have realized or at least begun to realize the potential to move up the ladder. Examples would include Botswana, Chile, China, Colombia, India, Korea, Turkey, and many once-poor fuel exporters such as Gabon, Libya, and Venezuela. Figure 4.3 illustrates the effect of this gradual progression on the IMF. For nearly the whole first decade of IMF operations (1947–55), the United States was the only creditor country. That monopoly ended when Canada qualified in 1956, and the next two decades saw a fairly steady rise as first Europe and Japan, then a few South American and other Asian countries,

---

[7] Thanks to Eduardo Borensztein for drawing attention to the implications of Kremer, Onatski, and Stock in this context.

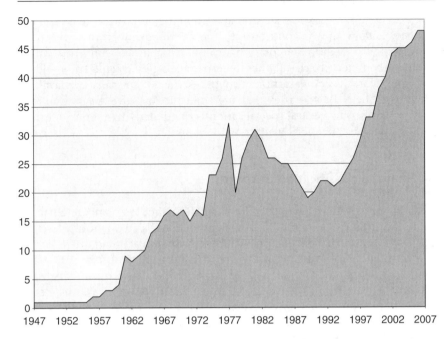

Figure 4.3 Number of IMF Creditors, 1947–2007

Note: Creditors are defined here as members with creditor position greater than 25 percent of quota. From 2000 defined as participants in the Fund's Financial Transactions Plan.

Source: See Figure 4.1

and finally the oil exporters of the Middle East joined the creditor ranks. The upheavals of the late 1970s and the 1980s brought a pause, but the globalization of the 1990s ushered in a new expansion of financial soundness and prosperity. At the end of 2007, the IMF had 52 creditor countries, including Chile and Colombia in South America, and Botswana and Libya in Africa.[8]

What underpins the IMF's role in this dynamic process is an understanding (a) that the purpose of the international financial system (of which the IMF is an integral part) is to help countries develop and move up the ladder and (b) that all countries need to pursue sound macroeconomic policies in order to succeed economically. Moreover, sustaining sound macroeconomic policies is neither easy nor free of cost. These points are examined further below, in Section III.

[8] Four of the 52 countries do not currently participate in the Fund's financial transactions plan, but they have creditor positions resulting from earlier purchases of their currencies by other member countries. For a current list of countries whose currencies are considered strong enough to use in IMF financial operations, see the IMF website, <http://www.imf.org>, under "financial transactions plan."

Even though the IMF does not and should not provide development finance, it does aim to contribute to the development process within its mandate, by providing temporary financing in support of countries' efforts to strengthen their policies. Rather than specializing *horizontally* by providing assistance to a select cross-section of countries, the IMF specializes *vertically* by offering to help all countries that are trying to improve macroeconomic policymaking. This vertical specialization is the underlying rationale for the IMF as a universal financial institution.

II. Financial classification of countries

As a basis for analyzing the contribution that IMF financial assistance might make for various groups of countries, the usual distinctions based on income level are not very helpful. What distinguishes countries with regular, intermittent, or rare demands for official assistance is the strength and stability of their national or fiscal finances, not the level of their per capita income. The correlation between the two is certainly positive, but it is far from perfect. Moreover, as Dorsey et al. (2008) have documented, private capital flows to low-income countries have increased sharply in the past decade, further blurring the line between that group and emerging market countries. An alternative taxonomy based on financial strength may be more informative.

In this scheme, the first group of countries includes those that have adequate domestic saving, supplemented by a steady, reliable access to private international capital markets, and usually with an ability to borrow in their own currencies with little or no premium for default or exchange risk. These *advanced financial economies* are very unlikely to face a need for IMF financing, although a marked deterioration in conditions could push them out of this box (as happened to Korea in 1997). This group currently would include most of the 30 members of the OECD and a scattering of other countries, but the membership at the margins is pretty unstable. South Africa, for example, has been more successful at borrowing abroad in its own currency than have OECD members Korea and Mexico. For different reasons, Sweden is far behind Australia in the portion of its public external debt denominated in its own currency (Hausmann, Panizza, and Stein, 2000). Saudi Arabia and some other major oil exporters presumably could borrow in their own currencies with little premium if they chose to do so, regardless of their level of industrialization or economic development.

The second category are the *emerging market economies*. These countries have a substantial ability to mobilize domestic savings and to supplement it with private international capital, both in debt instruments and in equity claims, but their access to international capital is not assured. These countries may face a significant credit risk premium and are unlikely to borrow in their own currency: the source of the "original sin" concept introduced to the finance literature by Eichengreen and Hausmann (1999). Access to international capital is thus both expensive and unreliable, which makes these countries good candidates as applicants for occasional and intermittent financial assistance from the IMF.

Membership of the emerging market group is inherently indefinite, especially around the margins. If it is defined broadly as comprising those countries that are neither advanced nor pre-emergent (as explained below), it probably includes close to 70 countries today.[9] At the top end, the ambiguity of the status of Korea and Mexico has been discussed above. Quite a few other countries, including those that have been admitted to EU membership since 2004, have begun to establish strong financial track records, and a number of those have been IMF creditors for at least the past few years. Many others clearly have emerging rather than advanced financial markets, but the bottom end is also fuzzy and unstable. In the 1970s, international banks were eagerly lending to Somalia, Sudan, and other low-income countries that today rely entirely on assistance from multilateral agencies and bilateral donors.[10] Since the early 1990s, Honduras, Nicaragua, and Papua New Guinea experienced economic deteriorations severe enough to qualify them for loans on concessional terms from the IMF.[11] On the positive side, many once-poor countries—Botswana, China, Dominican Republic, Egypt, and the Philippines, to name just a few— have graduated from reliance on official concessional assistance and are either in or close to the emerging market group. Others, though still having quite low per capita incomes, have also gained some access to foreign direct investment or other private capital inflows. In sub-Saharan Africa, that group has recently included the Gambia and Senegal, and others such as Uganda and Zambia have had intermittent success in this regard.

The third category includes the rest of the world: the countries that we might call *pre-emergent market economies*. These countries—which could be low- or middle-income and would include many of the countries that have so recently made the transition from centrally controlled to market economies—have little

---

[9] To define a narrow set of emerging market economies, Klingen, Weder, and Zettelmeyer (2004) use a list of 27 developing countries for which secondary markets existed for their sovereign debt for all or part of the period 1986–2001. IMF (2003), ch. 3, uses a similar definition but derives a somewhat more inclusive list (34 countries) based on more recent data. If countries with significant inflows of foreign direct investment are also included, the list expands significantly. For example, Basu and Srinivasan (2002) discuss seven sub-Saharan African countries that have inward FDI flows but not significant portfolio flows. Finally, for purposes of this analysis, it is appropriate to include those countries that have strong enough economies that they have borrowed from the Fund, if at all, only occasionally and intermittently.

[10] For these and other case studies, see Boughton (2001), chs. 14 and 16.

[11] Honduras and Papua New guinea were eligible for concessional loans in 1976–8 under the terms of the IMF Trust Fund, but none of the three was included in the initial list of eligible countries when the IMF resumed concessional lending in 1986. Honduras and Nicaragua were added in 1992, and Papua New Guinea was added in 2003.

or no access to private-sector international capital. They also generally have insufficient domestic saving to finance the capital investment and social services that are prerequisites for economic growth. Even if capital were available, many governments of pre-emergent economies cannot afford to take on unsubsidized debt, so they are almost entirely dependent on official development assistance and concessional borrowing from multilateral creditors. In terms of the number of countries, this third group is the most numerous (perhaps 80 or so), but—as noted above—countries do slide between this category and the emerging market group.

III. The modern role of the IMF

If the IMF is to be a universal institution, how can it best serve the needs of each of these three groups of countries? To answer this question, it is essential to keep in mind that the purpose of the institution—indeed, the purpose of the international financial system—is not just to help countries avoid mishaps, to help them run in place without stumbling. The purpose, at least for the latter two groups, is to help them grow. Over time, pre-emergent economies should emerge, and emerging markets should mature.

The main challenge facing most pre-emergent countries is development: economic, social, and institutional development. Among other challenges, these countries need better health systems, especially in the age of HIV–AIDS. According to the World Health Organization, the least-developed countries spend an average of US$13 per person per year on health, a sum that cannot possibly begin to reduce their enormous deficiencies in access to health care (see UNDP, 2003, ch. 5). Pre-emergent countries also need better education systems: more and better schools, more and better teachers, more pencils and books, better transportation systems for getting children to schools, more awareness of the value of educating girls as much as boys. At the same time, they need better access to clean water and sanitation facilities and better protection of the natural environment. Many of them need to diversify production so as to reduce dependence on one or two export commodities, but they need to diversify in ways that are consistent with their resource endowments and comparative advantages, and they need greater access to world markets. These are serious challenges that override and dominate the stabilization challenges on which the IMF famously focuses.

To meet these challenges, pre-emergent countries need more and better external support, predominantly in the form of reliable and effectively directed grants and highly concessional finance from donors. Because the IMF does not have and cannot provide that type of support on an ongoing basis, it is tempting to conclude that the institution is of little value for this group of countries. But pre-emergent countries also need to implement better policies, both for their own sake and to qualify for and attract development finance from donors. In that regard, in general terms, they need to improve their institutional structures, their systems of governance, their ability to raise tax revenues and control government spending, and—not least—their macroeconomic policies: fiscal policy, monetary policy, and exchange rate policies.

Several of these key targets for policy reform are within the IMF's mandate and field of expertise: macroeconomic policies, economic and financial governance, tax reform, and improved expenditure management. The IMF can help countries to make and adhere to policy commitments in these areas and to signal to donors that countries are making progress and are serious about reform. The financial role of the IMF is to commit enough money for a limited but sufficient time to enable a country to undertake reforms without endangering financial stability, and enough to ensure that the accompanying policy advice and conditionality will be taken seriously by both sides. Although this role might lead to a continuing indebtedness to the IMF over a period of several years in cases where an ongoing relationship is beneficial to the country, the amounts will normally be quite small in relation to the country's overall development needs. The temporary nature of the financing, its dependence on macroeconomic policy reforms, and its limited size are the key components that distinguish the IMF's role from that of official development banks.[12]

For emerging market economies, the overarching challenge is to develop an economic and financial strength comparable to that of the more advanced countries. In contrast to pre-emergent countries, where IMF financing is expected to be small but possibly of some persistence, here IMF financing is expected to be intermittent and quickly repaid, but possibly quite large. Korea provides a good illustration of a country that began as a pre-emergent borrower and was indebted continuously from 1974 to 1987, and then developed into a country that needed the IMF only as an emergency backup in 1997–2000.

Whereas the effectiveness of the Fund's role in pre-emergent economies depends on its ability to encourage and induce policy improvements and to catalyze support from other official creditors and donors, the effectiveness of lending to emerging market economies depends largely on the country's ability to restore stability quickly and on the ability of the process to restore market confidence and thus catalyze inflows from private capital markets.

For the advanced economies, there is a strong expectation—but no guarantee—that they will never have to borrow from the IMF. Nonetheless, every

---

[12] In practice, because Fund-supported programs in low-income countries usually include a broad array of structural as well as macroeconomic policy reforms, the signaling role of IMF support may be diluted as programs are suspended despite adequate progress on macroeconomic policies. Effectiveness requires that signals are clear and are not distorted by political pressures.

member country has the right to borrow under specified conditions to meet a balance of payments need. The IMF recognizes this right by maintaining a prudential balance of usable resources equal to 20 percent of the quotas of its creditor countries (as defined above; and see Treasurer's Department, 2001). Although most of these countries never will borrow, a few of them may. In any event, the existence of the IMF as a stand-by lender is an integral part of its contribution to global financial stability.

What links these various financial roles together is the policy advice that the IMF proffers regularly to all members, regardless of whether they are active borrowers, strong creditors, or in between. Because that advice always focuses primarily on the policy requirements for achieving and maintaining macro-economic and financial stability, its *elements* include some recurring and dominant themes. What varies more is the *context*. Consider the following examples relating to fiscal policy, which are drawn from recent staff reports on an advanced economy, an emerging market, and a pre-emergent country:[13]

- "The challenge [is] to sustain expenditure discipline, contain budgetary pressures, ... and anticipate costs of likely [tax] reform ... Continuing the pace of deficit reduction beyond the next two years will help place the long-run fiscal position on a sustainable basis." (Staff Report for the 2004 Article IV Consultation with the United States, p. 34.)

- "Staff commends the authorities' commitment to maintain expenditure restraint, keep public utility tariffs broadly aligned with operating costs, and refrain from any further tax reductions. Delivering on these commitments will be essential to maintain market confidence and meet the medium-term fiscal consolidation goals, as there is little scope for fiscal slippage." (2004 Staff Report on Uruguay, reviewing a stand-by arrangement, p. 21.)

- "There is ... a pressing need to strengthen budget execution and the quality of government spending, and achieve a more sustainable external debt position ... Although overall fiscal deficit targets have been met, persistent resort to supplementary appropriations has led to government spending outcomes that deviate from budget intentions, thus weakening the effectiveness of the budget as a development tool." (2004 Staff Report on Uganda, reviewing a PRGF arrangement, p. 20.)

While it is important for all countries to take such advice, the reasons differ. For pre-emergent markets such as Uganda's, macroeconomic stability has to be formulated in the context of—and in support of—a longer-run strategy aimed at achieving key development goals. Otherwise, conflicts will arise between development and stability (for example, cutting spending on health and

---

[13] These documents are available at <http://www.imf.org/external/country/index.htm>.

education services could help reduce a fiscal deficit, but at the expense of the country's development goals), and stability will be squeezed out as the lower priority. Hence, in the passages quoted above, while fiscal consolidation is a featured goal in all three cases,[14] the advice to Uganda focuses squarely on optimizing the budget "as a development tool." For the emerging-market country, Uruguay, the advice is aimed at maintaining market confidence. For the advanced economy of the United States, the advice is aimed at putting the budget on a course that can be sustained over the longer term and thus avoiding the need for a belated and disruptive policy reversal.

How realistic is this approach? Getting the words right is one achievement, and generating real economic progress is another. For a practical answer to this question, it is necessary first to acknowledge two obvious but not innocuous points. First, there is no ideal international financial system, simply because we do not live in an ideal world. The current system has flaws and weaknesses, as do all the alternatives that have been or might be proposed. Second, no agency can solve or even marginally alleviate all of the economic and financial problems in the world: development and stabilization, for all types of countries. Specialization is essential and inevitable.

Some multilateral agencies specialize *horizontally*, by country type, like the OECD (rich countries), the IBRD (middle-income), or IDA (low-income). While this horizontal specialization has the advantage of enabling a holistic approach to the agencies' policy advice, no institution can be expected to address the full range of problems that a country might face, especially for the least developed. Moreover, as this chapter has argued, allowance must be made for the tendency of countries to shift between categories. Alternatively, agencies can specialize *vertically*, by the type of problem, and stand ready to help any country that faces that type of problem. That is the logic behind the IMF.

Vertical specialization, however, has its own limitations. In particular, it requires a sophisticated understanding of the context in which policy advice and policy conditions are formulated. It also requires effective collaboration both with the affected countries and with other specialized agencies. The IMF cannot help pre-emergent countries unless it embeds its advice in a broader development strategy. That in turn requires working with the country to ensure that a solid strategy is in place, and it requires working with multilateral development banks and donor countries in support of that strategy.

The Monterrey Consensus (United Nations, 2002) now provides such a framework. All countries that have not already achieved all of their development objectives are urged to specify quantitative and time-bound goals (e.g.

---

[14] The choice of these examples does not imply that the IMF always advises countries to tighten fiscal policy. The Independent Evaluation Office (2003) concluded, on the basis of a detailed study, that the "evidence does not support the view that IMF-supported programs adopt a one-size-fits all approach to fiscal adjustment . . . [nor] the perception that programs always involve austerity by targeting reductions in . . . fiscal deficits or in public expenditure" (p. 4).

cut extreme poverty in half between 1990 and 2015), set out a realistic strategy and tactics for reaching those goals, and carry out the necessary institutional and policy reforms. Developed countries have a responsibility to ensure that the global economy is conducive to development and to provide the necessary financial and other support to developing countries. And international agencies have a responsibility to work together and with national governments to provide additional support, advice, and coordination (IMF and World Bank, 2004).

IV. Concluding thoughts

The aim of this chapter has been to set out an integrated framework for thinking about the constructive assistance that the IMF can provide to its member countries across the full spectrum of financial development. To be effective, that assistance must be not only well designed and well implemented, but also accepted as a legitimate contribution to the general welfare. When conflicts arise between the interests of creditor and debtor countries, a transparent and fair system for resolving those differences is essential. In particular, if a permanent group of creditors were to take effective control without an appropriate balance from the influence of the rest of the world community, the institution would be bound to lose credibility, to the detriment of both creditors and debtors. To minimize that danger, the system of governance of the institution should be adjusted periodically to reflect the evolution of the world economy.

The dynamic nature of the world economy, through which countries develop at different rates and shift—or at least know that they might shift—between providing and using the financial resources of the IMF, has in the past helped to ensure a measure of balance in the institution's governance. Maintaining and strengthening that balance is a key challenge in preserving the future value of the IMF as a universal financial institution. As more and more countries advance to the point where they stop viewing themselves as potential borrowers and as others borrow continuously for long periods and lose sight of the possibility of graduating from this dependence, the dangers of polarization of the membership and marginalization of the influence of borrowers become increasingly acute.

At the deepest level, the vision set out in this chapter requires good governance of the international financial system. As Pauly (1994) has reminded us, it requires "a deep sense that a global community exists" and "a vision of human solidarity" (p. 212). If an international agency imposes, or is perceived as imposing, the will of the powerful upon the weak, the benefits of universalism will be sadly diminished.

V. References

Basu, Anupam, and Krishna Srinivasan, 2002, "Foreign Direct Investment in Africa— Some Case Studies," IMF Working Paper WP/02/61 (March). Available at <http://www.imf.org/external/pubs/ft/wp/2002/wp0261.pdf>.

Bird, Graham, and Paul Mosley, 2005, "Should the IMF Discontinue Its Lending Role in Low-Income Countries?", in Gustav Ranis, James Vreeland, and Stephen Kosack (editors), *Globalization and the Nation State: The Impact of the IMF and the World Bank*, (Milton Park, UK: Routledge).

Boughton, James M., 2001. *Silent Revolution: The International Monetary Fund 1979–1989*, Washington: International Monetary Fund. Available at <http://www.imf.org/external/pubs/ft/history/2001/index.htm>.

——2005, "Does the World Need a Universal Financial Institution?", *World Economics*, Vol. 6, No. 2, pp. 27–46.

Dorsey, Thomas, Helaway Tadesse, Sukhwinder Singh, and Zuzana Brixiova, 2008, "The Landscape of Capital Flows to Low-Income Countries," IMF Working Paper WP/08/51 (February). Available at <http://www.imf.org/external/pubs/ft/wp/2008/wp0851.pdf>.

Eichengreen, Barry, and Ricardo Hausmann (1999), "Exchange Rates and Financial Fragility," paper presented at the Federal Reserve Bank of Kansas City Conference, *Issues in Monetary Policy*, 27–29 August, Jackson Hole, Wyoming.

Fischer, Stanley, 2001, "Farewell to the IMF Executive Board" (August 30). Available at <http://www.imf.org/external/np/speeches/2001/083001.htm>.

Hausmann, Ricardo, Ugo Panizza, and Ernesto Stein, 2000, "Why Do Countries Float the Way They Float?", Inter-American Development Bank, Research Department Working Paper No. 418 (May). Available at <http://www.iadb.org/res/publications/pubfiles/pubWP-418.pdf>.

Independent Evaluation Office, 2003, *Fiscal Adjustment in IMF-Supported Programs*, Washington: International Monetary Fund. Available at <http://www.imf.org/External/NP/ieo/2003/fis/index.htm>.

International Monetary Fund, 2003, *World Economic Outlook September 2003: Public Debt in Emerging Markets*, Washington: International Monetary Fund. Available at <http://www.imf.org/external/pubs/ft/weo/2003/02/index.htm>.

——2004, *Annual Report 2004*. Available at <http://www.imf.org/external/pubs/ft/ar/2004/eng/index.htm>.

——and World Bank, 2004, *Global Monitoring Report 2004: Policies and Actions for Achieving the Millennium Development Goals and Related Outcomes*, Washington: World Bank. Available at <http://siteresources.worldbank.org/GLOBALMONITORINGEXT/Resources/0821358596.pdf>.

Kapur, Devesh, and Moisés Naím, 2005, "The IMF and Democratic Governance," *Journal of Democracy*, Vol. 16, No. 1 (January).

Klingen, Christoph, Beatrice Weder, and Jeromin Zettelmeyer, 2004, "How Private Creditors Fared in Emerging Debt Markets, 1970–2000," IMF Working Paper WP/04/13, Washington: International Monetary Fund. Available at <http://www.imf.org/external/pubs/ft/wp/2004/wp0413.pdf>.

Kremer, Michael, Alexei Onatski, and James Stock, 2001, "Searching for Prosperity," NBER Working Paper 8250, Cambridge, Massachusetts: National Bureau of Economic Research. Available at <http://www.nber.org/papers/w8250>.

Meltzer, Allan H. (Chairman), 2000, *Report of the International Financial Institutions Advisory Commission (Meltzer Commission)*. Available at <http://www.house.gov/jec/imf/ifiac.htm> or <http://www.house.gov/jec/imf/meltzer.htm>.

Oxfam International, 2003, *The IMF and the Millennium Goals: Failing to Deliver for Low-Income Countries*, Oxfam Briefing Paper 54, September 2003. Available at <http://www.oxfam.org/eng/pdfs/pp030917_imf_mdgs.pdf>.

Pauly, Louis W., 1994, "Promoting a Global Economy: The Normative Role of the International Monetary Fund," in Richard Stubbs and Geoffrey R. D. Underhill (editors), *Political Economy and the Changing Global Order*, Toronto: McClelland & Stewart, Inc.

Quah, Danny, 1993, "Empirical Cross-Section Dynamics in Economic Growth," *European Economic Review*, Vol. 37, pp. 426–34.

Treasurer's Department, International Monetary Fund, 2001, *Financial Organization and Operations of the IMF*, Pamphlet No. 45, Sixth Edition. Available at <http://www.imf.org/external/pubs/ft/pam/pam45/contents.htm>.

United Nations, 2002, *Report of the International Conference on Financing for Development, Monterrey, Mexico, 18–22 March 2002*, A/Conf.198/11. Available at <http://www.un.org/esa/ffd/>, <http://daccess-ods.un.org/TMP/290299.7.html>.

United Nations Development Programme, 2003, *Human Development Report 2003*, New York and Oxford: Oxford University Press. Available at <http://hdr.undp.org/reports/global/2003/>.

World Bank, 2007, Annual Report. Table on country eligibility for borrowing is available at <http://web.worldbank.org/WBSITE/EXTERNAL/EXTABOUTUS/EXTANNREP/EXTANNREP2K7/0,,contentMDK:21508949~menuPK:4245297~pagePK:64168445~piPK:64168309~theSitePK:4077916,00.html>.

5

The Role of the IMF in Low-Income Countries: An Institutional Approach

Domenico Lombardi* (Oxford University and Brookings Institution)

I. Introduction

The International Monetary Fund is a multilateral institution comprising 185 members, including industrial, emerging, and low-income countries. Low-income members hold less than 10 percent of the institution's voting power and a roughly similar share of its quotas, which are based on the relative size of each member's economy.[1] Low-income members are a large group within the IMF, however; comprising 78 countries (see Table 5.A.1 in the Appendix), they make up more than 40 percent of the organization's membership. The purposes of the IMF, as set out in Article I of the Articles of Agreement, apply to the low-income members as much as to all the others. An IMF report (2004b) refers to the Fund's role in low-income countries as one of providing policy advice, financial programs, and assistance in capacity building in its areas of expertise and in accordance with its institutional mandate.

Yet views on the role that the IMF should play vis-à-vis this segment of its membership differ remarkably, and the topic has spurred considerable debate among academics, policymakers, and advocates from nongovernmental organizations. The debate has gained further momentum following the IMF's endorsement of the Millennium Development Goals (MDGs) and its refinement—still ongoing—of a "policy toolkit" in support of its low-income member countries. Sachs (2003) calls for a considerable step up in IMF involvement

* I acknowledge helpful comments received on an earlier draft from, but do not wish to implicate, Masood Ahmed, James Boughton, Valerio Crispolti, Peter Fallon, Pier Carlo Padoan, Mark Plant, Arrigo Sadun, Maria Fabiana Viola, Ngaire Woods, Joerg Zeuner, and the participants at a seminar delivered at Oxford University.

[1] At the time of writing of this chapter, the IMF Board of Governors is expected to approve a resolution that will increase the voting power of low-income and other developing countries by 2.7% of total votes (IMF 2008).

with its low-income members, while Rogoff (2004) argues for exactly the opposite. Birdsall and Williamson (2002) ask for an outright move of the Poverty Reduction and Growth Facility (PRGF), the Fund's concessional lending arm in support of low-income members, to the World Bank on the ground that the latter is better equipped to deal with this group of countries. Along similar lines, the well-known final report of the International Financial Institution Advisory Commission (2000), the "Meltzer Commission," concluded: "The International Monetary Fund should restrict its lending to the provision of short-term liquidity. The current practice of extending long-term loans for poverty reduction and other purposes should end." The Overseas Development Council report (2000) also underscored the need for the IMF to discontinue its role in the PRGF in favor of the World Bank, as did Bergsten (2005) in testimony before the US Senate. Most recently, the External Review Committee on Bank–Fund Collaboration recommended the IMF "to clarify its role in low-income countries," noting that its "financing activities in low-income countries is an area where it has moved beyond its core responsibilities" (2007, 10).

Given the prevalence of such criticism, it is important to ask what the rationale is—if any—for the Fund's involvement in low-income countries. Can economics help us better to understand this rationale? What does the Fund actually do for its low-income member countries, and how have its policies evolved in light of the commitments following, at least implicitly, from its endorsement of the MDGs? What challenges and tensions, finally, does the IMF currently face in pursuing these goals?

This chapter attempts to provide answers to these broad questions. Other issues, such as the role of the IMF in the context of the HIPC Initiative[2] or the cooperation with the World Bank, fall beyond the scope of this work. In particular, Section II lays out the underpinnings of the IMF's role in its low-income member countries. Section III offers a critical look at the Fund's lending policies and reviews ongoing developments, while Section IV considers some of the challenges the IMF faces in implementing its lending policies. Section V describes the Fund's surveillance activities in support of low-income members and reviews recent innovations. Section VI discusses related challenges and Section VII concludes.

II. Understanding the role of the IMF in low-income member countries

From a political economy perspective, the rationale for the IMF's engagement with low-income member countries is that it provides important information

---

[2] On this, please refer to Ch. 6, by Bird and Powell.

to investors and donors while offering a commitment technology to its membership. With regard to the former, given that information about the broad economic environment of an economy can be regarded as a public good—it benefits all potential and actual investors—a multilateral institution like the IMF is better equipped than individual investors to internalize the externalities that arise in this context.[3] While an individual investor may gather and retain information related to the profitability of a particular investment project and its related benefits, individual investors have inadequate incentive to undertake costly information-gathering activities to obtain data about the broader investment environment and the quality of policymaking in a given economy, and when they do gather such data, they are often disinclined to share it with others. A multilateral institution is in a better position to acquire such data efficiently and to share the informational public goods. In practice, a multilateral institution like the IMF engages in close dialogues with countries' governments to ascertain the state of their economies and the quality of their policies.

Although the informational role performed by a multilateral organization such as the IMF benefits all countries, low-income economies are well placed potentially to enjoy the greatest benefit from the information gathering. Some information-gathering activities are carried out by investors in economies with sizeable investment flows, but given the paucity of private international capital flowing into low-income countries' economies, these countries are unlikely to attract such investor-driven activities. Furthermore, as low-income countries are members of this multilateral organization, they may be more willing to cooperate and engage in a fruitful dialogue with this organization than with private investors, and their willingness to participate can, in turn, make the process of gathering accurate information easier. Donor countries that provide the bulk of official development flows are also members of this multilateral institution and are consequently able to enjoy the benefits of its informational activities in relation to low-income members. Rather than gather information bilaterally, it is more efficient for donor members to pool their resources and rely on a multilateral source.[4]

Rodrik (1995) notes that from the perspective of donor members, multilaterals also provide a useful commitment device to their member governments, as they enable donor members to commit resources for humanitarian and development ends. While donor members are theoretically able to pursue such lending bilaterally, experience shows that this ability is often overridden by political and strategic factors. A multilateral organization allows its donor

---

[3] Rodrik (1995) elaborates on this point.
[4] In an influential contribution, Burnside and Dollar (2000) have argued that aid is more effective when managed multilaterally rather than bilaterally.

members to commit themselves *ex ante* to concessional lending that they would be unlikely to commit to bilaterally *ex post*.[5]

The informational role played by a multilateral organization like the IMF is typically associated with lending activities that should be regarded as synergic to the multilateral's main function. As Rodrik (1995) points out, multilateral lending is meant to provide borrowing countries with an incentive to "open up their books" and engage more effectively with the institutions. For investors and donors, moreover, lending is typically assumed to boost the credibility of a multilateral's seal of approval, as a multilateral that lends money has a stronger incentive to monitor the quality of the policies being implemented in a member country than one that plays a strictly surveillance role.[6]

The multilateral nature of such lending allows institutions like the IMF to exercise conditionality, affecting the nature of policies implemented by the recipient country's government rather than simply monitoring their quality.[7] From the point of view of borrowing countries, conditionality may also provide a commitment technology to undertake decisions that, although desirable *ex ante*, would be difficult to carry out *ex post*.[8] While conditionality does not intrinsically require multilateral institutions—indeed, it has been in existence since long before the multilaterals were established after the Second World War—its multilateral nature helps to neutralize its intrusiveness in the national sovereignty of a borrowing country, making the intrusion more politically feasible and legitimate.[9]

An important feature typically attributed to multilateral conditionality is that it offers a way for further resources to be mobilized by providing other lenders with greater confidence that an appropriate reform program will be implemented and that, as a result, sound policies will return the economy to a path of sustainable growth. Although the empirical evidence on this so-called catalytic role of the multilaterals is mixed, recent contributions have emphasized its reality at least for low-income countries.[10] Rodrik (1995) finds that IMF lending, in contrast to lending by other multilaterals, appears to be

---

[5] In the case of IMF concessional lending, the IMF acts as a trustee of the resources committed by donor countries. IMF (2001a) elaborates on the Fund's financial structure and policies.

[6] On this, see Chs. 7 and 8, by Bevan and Lane respectively.

[7] The literature on IMF conditionality is quite extensive. See, among others, Goldstein (2000), IMF (2001b), IMF (2001c), IMF (2001d), and Boughton and Mourmouras (2004).

[8] Rodrik (1995) provides an example of this time inconsistency.

[9] Ferguson (1998), for instance, documents a case of sovereign lending from 1818 in which Prussia, bankrupted by the Napoleonic Wars, approached Nathan Rothschild for a loan.

[10] In this context, it may be helpful to clarify the difference between "catalytic effect" and "signaling." The latter "refer[s] to the conveying by the Fund of information that influences the financing decisions of outsiders, whether through some form of on/off mechanism or through the rendering of a multidimensional picture" (IMF 2004a). As a consequence, it encompasses, but is not limited to, the catalytic effect of Fund financing—the indirect signal sent by the Fund through the use of its own resources.

positively related to other capital flows. Bird and Rowlands (2002), relying on various research methodologies and on a wide sample and time period, come up with nuanced conclusions on the notion of catalysis that depend on the nature and the determinants of the capital flows that IMF lending is supposed to attract, and they offer evidence that the IMF's catalytic effect is likely to be stronger with respect to official bilateral aid flows. As aid donors are more likely to be concerned about a country's commitment to policy reforms that may boost the effectiveness of their aid flows than about the prospect of receiving a commercial rate of return from their disbursements, the relationship between IMF lending and other financial flows may substantially differ between low-income economies and emerging market economies. In other words, as the Independent Evaluation Office (IEO) report (2002) confirms, official donors are more likely than private creditors to rely on the IMF to provide a signal on the soundness of the macroeconomic policies of a member country.[11]

In a survey of donors (IMF 2005a), respondents confirmed that the IMF's signals constitute their main source of information about low-income economies and that they use them extensively when allocating aid flows, although not in a mechanistic way. Reliance on the IMF's signals appears to be more a matter of well-established policy than a formal requirement, but there are instances whereby the role of the IMF in catalyzing official assistance is formally codified. Paris Club debt treatment, for example, is generally conditioned on the existence of an IMF-supported arrangement, and the Enhanced HIPC and MDRI initiatives to relieve low-income economies from the burden of unsustainable debt likewise depend on a satisfactory performance under an IMF-supported arrangement.

In addition to lending, the IMF supports its members in developing the capacity to formulate and effectively implement policies, which is especially valuable for the low-income members, whose rule of law and institutional quality are often the weakest. Recent contributions to the literature on economic growth have underscored the importance of capacity building and the development of sound institutions as key ingredients for steady and sustainable growth,[12] strengthening the case for multilaterals to engage in and support capacity building in low-income countries as a central strategy in helping these countries exit the poverty trap.[13] While capacity building is not necessarily a distinctive feature of a multilateral organization, since it can be carried out on a

---

[11] For private creditors, the signal provided by the IMF appears as a possibly important element in a more articulated assessment of the economic status of a country. In this vein, recent research has found that Fund arrangements and publications of Fund documents have a favorable effect on interest rate spreads and stock prices. On this, see Kaminsky and Schmukler (1999), Glennerster and Shin (2003), and Mody and Saravia (2006).

[12] See, for instance, Rodrik (1998) and Rodrik, Subramanian, and Trebbi (2004).

[13] See Hakura and Nsouli (2003).

bilateral basis, a multilateral nonetheless has a remarkable institutional comparative advantage, as its role as information provider offers a distinct advantage in pooling and crafting the information for capacity-building activities in support of its members. The multilateral nature of institutions like the IMF clearly makes it easier for them to cooperate with member countries and to collect relevant information and experience. Their superior ability to interconnect with several members enables them significantly to share facts, events, and experiences of a relevant cross-section of their membership, to pool information, and to elaborate it accordingly. Multilaterals are a major repository of country data, facts, and experience, which, in turn, make it valuable for other members to access their knowledge.

In sum, the IMF fulfills its informational role through a range of activities that are typically bundled together, including lending, offering policy advice, and assisting with capacity building. IMF lending does not simply convey financial resources to a member country: it also provides these resources in the context of a macroeconomic framework agreed upon with the borrowing country. In the negotiations leading up to a financial arrangement, the IMF provides capacity building in the areas of its competence and offers advice on a wide range of policy issues, some of which do not formally fall under an agreed-upon program. Through its statutory surveillance activities—so-called Article IV surveillance—moreover, the Fund may draw the attention of a member's authorities to the desirability of entering into a lending arrangement with the Fund on the basis of the knowledge gathered about that member nation's economy.

Similarly, in discharging its surveillance role, the Fund may come to the conclusion that a member could benefit from the provision of technical assistance targeting at some specific areas. The knowledge gathered through the provision of such services in turn helps to reinforce the policy advice capabilities of the institution. In pursuit of a financial arrangement, the IMF may also offer technical assistance to a member in order to strengthen its capability to achieve a certain policy measure upon which the success of the arrangement depends. Conversely, gathering a better knowledge of the institutional strength and the political economy circumstances of a member through the provision of capacity building helps the IMF to sharpen its policy advice under both surveillance and lending activities. What is important to underscore is that these activities are bundled together, enabling the IMF to fulfill its informational role more effectively.

The rationale for the engagement of the IMF as a multilateral institution having been outlined, the next sections elaborate on the Fund's role in support of low-income members, leveraging on its expertise on macroeconomic policies and on how poor economies may benefit from it in terms of enhanced growth and poverty reduction.

III. Lending policies for low-income member countries

IMF concessional lending is provided through the Poverty Reduction and Growth Facility at a fixed interest rate of 0.5 percent, as compared to the charges levied on the use of the General Resources Account,[14] which, at current market interest rates, entail a degree of concessionality (or a grant element) of about one-third of the principal. The grace period for concessional loans is comparatively longer than that for standard IMF arrangements. A borrowing low-income member begins repaying a loan five and a half years after the disbursement of the first tranche, while the grace period for a standard credit tranche is two and a half years, which can be extended up to three and a quarter years. The maturity of a concessional arrangement is, at ten years, five years longer than that of a standard IMF arrangement.

In addition to PRGF-supported programs, lending on concessional terms is available for post-conflict members through Emergency Post-Conflict Assistance. Established in 1995, the facility provides assistance to members with urgent financing needs unable to develop a comprehensive economic program due to severe capacity limitations in the aftermath of a conflict. The facility—which often plays a valuable role as a bridge to a subsequent PRGF—has a subsidized interest rate of 0.5 percent for low-income members and a maturity between three and a quarter and five years, with access up to 50 percent of a member's quota.

In 2005, the IMF established the Exogenous Shocks Facility (ESF) to provide financial assistance to low-income countries hit by an exogenous shock. As such countries have a higher incidence of shocks than other developing countries, the facility is intended to provide assistance on concessional terms to support a program focusing on the adjustment to the underlying shock. For those economies that experience an exogenous shock while under a PRGF-supported program, the assistance is provided through an augmentation of the PRGF itself. The norm for annual access to the ESF is set at 25 percent of the member's quota, with a cumulative access limit of 50 percent of quota. So far no member has requested to benefit from this new facility.[15]

A. Recent trends

IMF concessional lending to low-income member countries dates back to the 1970s, as can be seen in Figure 5.1, which shows annual lending to the low-income membership. Concessional lending is thus not a new policy instrument, and over time it has been "blended" in varying proportions to GRA

---

[14] The rate of charge is determined as a function of the SDR rate, which, in turn, reflects yields on the international money market. As of March 31, 2008, the rate of charge amounted to 3.89% and the SDR rate to 2.7%.

[15] At the time of writing, the IMF has announced a review of the facility to make it more accessible.

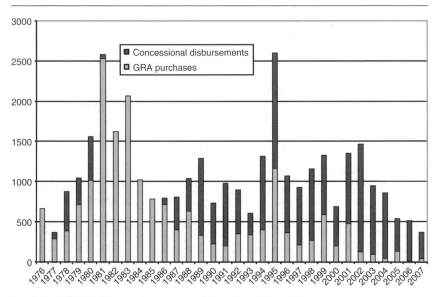

Figure 5.1 IMF Lending to Low-Income Members (SDR millions)

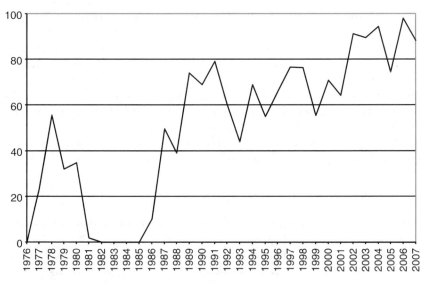

Figure 5.2 IMF Concessional Lending Compared to Total Lending to Low-Income Members (percent)

resources.[16] In the period between 1976 and 2007, lending to low-income members averaged SDR 1,092 million, with concessional lending contributing about SDR 514 million against a GRA lending average of 578 million. Figure 5.1 also shows that, apart from the spikes observed in connection with the early 1980s and mid-1990s, overall lending to low-income members has not increased systematically over time. What has increased is the proportion of concessional lending relative to GRA lending. Figure 5.2, which compares concessional to total lending to low-income member countries, makes this point clear, showing that the weight of concessional lending has steadily increased over time to reach 88 percent of all IMF lending in 2007.

How has lending to low-income member countries compared to the IMF's overall lending to its membership in the last 30 years? Figure 5.3 provides some answers. The bars in light gray show the absolute amounts lent by the IMF to the whole membership from its GRA Department, while those in black refer to the overall resources (concessional and nonconcessional) lent to low-income members only. Two aspects are noteworthy. First, the amount lent to low-income members from the concessional and nonconcessional arms has been relatively modest in comparison to the overall resources lent out. This has been particularly true in the last decade, when GRA lending spiked in response to the Mexican crisis (1995), the Asian crises (1997 and 1998), and,

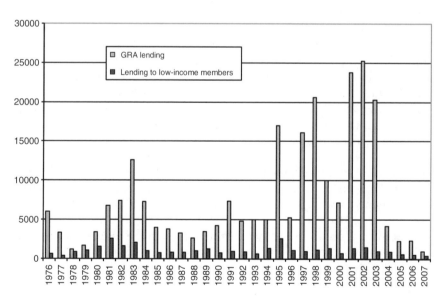

Figure 5.3 Total IMF Lending to Low-Income Members Compared to Total Lending to All Members (SDR millions)

[16] See Boughton in Ch. 3 for a historical account of IMF lending to low-income countries.

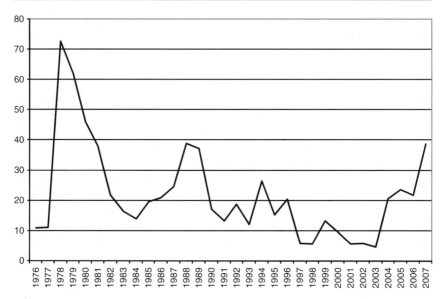

Figure 5.4 IMF Lending to Low-Income Countries as a Proportion of Overall GRA Lending (percent)

recently, the financial arrangements in support of Brazil, Argentina, and Turkey. Figure 5.4 displays lending to low-income countries as a percentage of overall GRA lending. Following the spike in the early 1980s, when several low-income economies began to cope with a growing and unsustainable debt, lending to low-income countries has steadily declined in proportion to overall GRA lending, reaching a plateau of about 4 percent in 2003, from which it has risen in the latest years on account of the drastic downsizing of the GRA portfolio. In fact, the proportion increased to 39 percent in 2007, reflecting the extraordinary decrease in GRA lending to SDR 959 million.

Table 5.1 illustrates the financial arrangements currently outstanding with the membership. Overall, the IMF is engaged with 32 members for a total of almost SDR 9 billion in committed resources. Twenty-four of these financial arrangements are with low-income members, corresponding to SDR 0.8 billion committed (or 10 percent of the total resources committed), while 8 billion (or 90 percent) has been lent to other members through the GRA Department. As Table 5.1 shows, those low-income countries that are currently engaged with the IMF receive financial assistance only on concessional terms.

B. Issues in program design

The Poverty Reduction and Growth Facility was established in 1999 at the end of a long debate, both internal and external to the IMF, about how to move

Table 5.1. IMF Lending Arrangements*

Member	Date of arrangement	Expiration	Amount	IMF credit outstanding
General Resources Account (GRA):				
Stand-By Arrangements				
Dominican Republic	31-Jan-05	30-Jan-08	437,800	346,522
Gabon	7-May-07	6-May-10	77,150	15,624
Iraq	19-Dec-07	18-Mar-09	475,360	0
Macedonia, former Yugoslav Republic of	31-Aug-05	30-Aug-08	51,675	0
Paraguay	31-May-06	31-Aug-08	30,000	0
Peru	26-Jan-07	28-Feb-09	172,368	0
Turkey	11-May-05	10-May-08	6,662,040	4,529,959
Total			**7,906,393**	**4,892,105**
General Resources Account (GRA):				
Extended Arrangements				
Albania	1-Feb-06	31-Jan-09	8,523	4,870
Total			**8,523**	**4,870**
Poverty Reduction and Growth Facility Trust				
Afghanistan, Islamic Republic of	26-Jun-06	25-Jun-09	81,000	35,800
Albania	1-Feb-06	31-Jan-09	8,523	52,131
Armenia, Republic of	25-May-05	24-May-08	23,000	99,923
Benin	5-Aug-05	4-Aug-08	6,190	2,640
Burkina Faso	23-Apr-07	22-Apr-10	6,020	23,720
Burundi	23-Jan-04	22-Jan-08	69,300	62,150
Cameroon	24-Oct-05	23-Oct-08	18,570	10,600
Central African Republic	22-Dec-06	21-Dec-09	36,200	31,244
Chad	16-Feb-05	15-Feb-08	25,200	35,264
Congo, Republic of	6-Dec-04	5-Jun-08	54,990	23,580
Gambia, The	21-Feb-07	20-Feb-10	14,000	4,000
Grenada	17-Apr-06	16-Apr-09	10,530	1,560
Guinea	21-Dec-07	20-Dec-10	48,195	40,930
Haiti	20-Nov-06	19-Nov-09	73,710	35,700
Kyrgyz Republic	15-Mar-05	31-May-08	8,880	94,814
Madagascar	21-Jul-06	20-Jul-09	54,990	27,060
Malawi	5-Aug-05	4-Aug-08	38,170	19,616
Mauritania	18-Dec-06	17-Dec-09	16,100	8,380
Moldova, Republic of	5-May-06	4-May-09	110,880	86,372
Nicaragua	5-Oct-07	4-Oct-10	71,500	53,680
Niger	31-Jan-05	31-May-08	26,320	25,380
Rwanda	12-Jun-06	11-Jun-09	8,010	5,133
Sao Tome & Principe	1-Aug-05	31-Jul-08	2,960	1,624
Sierra Leone	10-May-06	9-May-09	31,110	23,113
Total			**844,348**	**804,414**

* As of December 2007. Thousands of SDRs.
Source: IMF

forward from what was then called the Enhanced Structural Adjustment Facility (ESAF).[17] The essence of that debate was that for the PRGF to be an effective concessional lending instrument that supported the role of the IMF in low-income countries, its underlying program design had more closely to reflect the nature of low-income economies and their needs for pro-poor growth. Acknowledging the link between macroeconomic policies, growth, and poverty reduction policies, the PRGF program design is meant to provide a balanced framework for these elements to interact synergistically. While theoretical understanding of such a link is not yet fully developed, empirical studies suggest that the relationship may be indirect, relying on the impact that sound macroeconomic policies have on economic growth and the effect that the latter has on poverty reduction.[18] Dollar and Kraay (2002), for instance, find a one-to-one relationship between economic growth and income growth among the poorest segments of society in a large panel dataset. Using a sample of developing and transition economies, Epaulard (2003) finds that those countries that have been able to grow more are also the ones that have been more successful in tackling poverty. She does find, however, that the initial level of development and of income inequality affect the efficiency with which growth translates into poverty reduction. That is, the higher the inequality, the lower the absolute value of the elasticity of poverty with respect to growth; the higher the mean income, the higher the absolute value of such elasticity. All in all, this work suggests that growth is a necessary ingredient for reducing poverty and that pro-poor macroeconomic policies may affect the efficiency with which growth reduces poverty.

Other studies focusing on the link between indicators of macroeconomic performance on the one hand and measures of income inequality on the other have found some association between deflationary policies and improvement in the well-being of the poor. Romer and Romer (1998) have found that the income share of the poorest quintile of the population is inversely related to inflation. Bulir (2001) also investigates the relationship between inflation and income inequality and finds that the former affects the latter. His empirical analysis uncovers a nonlinear pattern whereby a reduction in inflation from very high rates significantly lowers income inequality, while a reduction from lower rates brings only negligible gains in terms of income equality. Epaulard (2003) investigates the link between inflation and poverty and finds that very high inflation is associated with a higher elasticity of the poverty rate to economic downturn but that at lower rates no significant relationship emerges between inflation and the elasticity of the poverty rate to growth or recession.

Along similar lines, a study by Moser and Ichida (2001) investigates the link between growth and non-income poverty as proxied by life expectancy

---

[17] See IMF (2000) and the External Evaluation of the ESAF (IMF 1998).
[18] See Cashin et al. (2003).

from birth, the infant mortality rate, and gross primary school enrollment in sub-Saharan Africa. They find that strong and sustainable economic growth leads to similarly strong and sustainable declines in non-income poverty. Importantly, they extend their analysis to explore to what extent the quality of growth affects such dynamics. Their results suggest that lower income inequality and greater provision of basic services lead to lower poverty levels for a given income level.

In the context of PRGF-supported programs, these findings have been operationalized in terms of higher outlays for education and health on the assumption that improvements in education and health, while being more easily measurable, have a beneficial impact on economic growth at the same time that they benefit the poor. Increased health and education expenditures are part of a broader framework that also envisages higher outlays for capital expenditures, including critical infrastructure, and focuses on economic governance to enhance economic growth.

The focus on pro-poor expenditure is no accident: social spending offers policymakers a policy device for the prompt provision of social services to the poorest segments of a society. Consistent with this working assumption, Lopez (2002) investigated the relationship between social spending and social outcomes as proxied by health and education indicators for countries in sub-Saharan Africa. His results confirm the working hypothesis that increased social spending is correlated to positive social outcomes as long as related budgetary allocations result in an increase in per capita social expenditures. There is, however, no evidence available so far that sheds light on the link between levels of social outlays and reduction of poverty, which is one of the objectives of PRGF-supported programs.

It is difficult to provide an accurate assessment of the pattern of social spending in PRGF-supported countries due to inconsistencies in data coverage that arise from the use of different definitions of social spending in different countries. Table 5.2 provides some insights by focusing on health and education expenditures, which obviously do not represent the universe of social spending but which nevertheless allow for a meaningful comparison across countries, as they enter government accounts on a more consistent basis. In the year prior to the establishment of a concessional arrangement, PRGF-supported countries exhibited a much lower level of social spending in comparison to their GDP (5.8 percent) than did non-PRGF-supported countries (7.8 percent). In the latest year for which such data are available, social spending had grown in PRGF countries while remaining, on average, flat in non-PRGF countries, reaching a ratio of 6.3 percent in proportion to GDP, an average rise of half a percentage point. As a result, the initial gap between PRGF and non-PRGF countries diminished in size from 2 percent of GDP to 1.5 percent.

The bottom part of Table 5.2 shows social spending as a proportion of total government expenditures. In this case, too, PRGF-supported countries

Table 5.2. Social Spending in PRGF and Non-PRGF Developing Countries (1)

	Sample size	Pre-PRGF year (2)	Latest year available (3)	Increase of the latest year from the pre-PRGF level
Social spending as a percent of GDP				
PRGF countries	41	5.8	6.3	0.5
Non-PRGF countries	46	7.8	7.8	0.0
Social spending as a percent of total government spending				
PRGF countries	41	22.3	24.1	1.8
Non-PRGF countries	46	24.4	25.2	0.8

(1) Data refer to the sum of public education and health spending and only cover developing countries with data available both for the pre-PRGF and for the latest year.
(2) For PRGF countries with programs in 1999–2007, the pre-PRGF year refers to the year preceding the first program; for non-PRGF countries, it refers to 2000, which is the mean pre-PRGF year for all program countries.
(3) Data for the latest year in the 2004–2006 period.

Sources: IMF and World Bank staff reports

underperformed non-PRGF countries in the year prior to the establishment of a concessional arrangement. The proportion of social spending in the PRGF-supported countries averaged 22.3 percent against 24.4 percent in non-PRGF countries. In the latest year for which data are available, however, PRGF-countries had increased their spending as a proportion of total government expenditures by 1.8 percent to 24.1 percent, while non-PRGF countries saw their expenditures rise by 0.8 to 25.2 percent. As a result, the initial gap between the two groups decreased from 2.1 percent to 1.1 percent. Along similar lines, a recent evaluation on the IMF's role in Africa (IEO 2007)[19] found that, on average, in the 29 sub-Saharan African PRGF-supported countries, public expenditures rose by about 2.5 percent over the period 1999 to 2005, compared to an increase of 1 percentage point over the previous six years.

As for the relationship between social spending and growth, Baldacci et al. (2008), using data from 120 developing countries, find that education and health spending positively affects the accumulation of education and health capital and, in turn, economic growth. The relevance of their study goes well beyond this evidence, however, as they employ a more general framework that takes into account the role of institutions and governance in mediating the nexus between social spending and its impact on growth. Their working assumption is that the effectiveness of social spending is positively influenced by a government's effectiveness. Their results clearly show that when governance is poor, health and education spending have virtually no impact on health and education indicators. They estimate, for instance, that all other things being equal, poor governance is associated with 1.6 percentage points less growth. Interestingly, they compare the effect of increases in education and health

---

[19] Salop, in Ch. 10, elaborates on the implications for the role of the IMF in low-income countries arising from this evaluation.

spending and show that for their subsample of low-income economies, the impact of poor governance on growth is generally larger than on the sample averages. In their sensitivity analysis of various regions, they show that sub-Saharan Africa would greatly benefit—more than other developing regions in the world—from increasing social expenditures. Furthermore, the multivariate framework enables the authors to investigate the effect of other macroeconomic variables on economic growth. In this vein, they find, for instance, that a reduction in the rate of inflation by 10 percentage points is associated with an average increase in economic growth of 0.5 percentage points. Similarly, a reduction of fiscal deficits by 1 percentage point of GDP is associated with a similar increase in growth, although this effect disappears in low-deficit environments. All in all, their study outlines the importance of reforms aimed at improving the efficiency of social spending.

In this connection, consider that an internal review of PRGF program design (IMF 2002a) noted that PRGF-supported programs focus on budget execution, placing emphasis on the efficiency and targeting of public spending to ensure that resources devoted to poverty reduction effectively reach their intended uses. Emphasis is also given to budget formulation by improving its usefulness as a relevant indicator of government fiscal policymaking. These findings are broadly supported by a recent IEO evaluation (IEO 2007).

On tax policy, PRGF program design aims to improve the equity and the administration of tax systems. Policy measures tend to include greater emphasis on "horizontal equity," that is, on making sure that taxpayers with equal incomes are treated on the same basis. Limiting tax exemptions and broadening the tax base are also goals under PRGF programs, while, on average, tax revenues are expected to increase by about 1 percent of GDP over the three-year period of a PRGF arrangement (IMF 2002a). The IEO (2007) has found that targets for revenue mobilization were generally more ambitious than in previous ESAF programs.

Another distinctive feature of the nature of PRGF arrangements as compared to other Fund financial arrangements is their emphasis on the distributional impact of major macroeconomic and structural reforms. According to an IMF study (2002a), about two-thirds of PRGF-supported programs include countervailing measures aimed at offsetting the impact of macroeconomic and structural policies on the poor. Such offsetting measures, however, have not often been backed by formal analytical studies undertaken through Poverty and Social Impact Analysis (PSIA), despite internal recommendations that they should. Even when PSIA has been made available from other agencies, such as the World Bank and DFID, it has not systematically fed into program design, according to the IEO (2007). Those analyses produced internally have been reported in PRGF documents, although the IEO could not find strong evidence that their results affected the design of PRGF programs.

C. Ownership and conditionality in PRGF program design

The most important feature of PRGF program design is that it is meant to reflect national ownership of underlying economic policies, which are formulated through an open and broad-based participatory process that results in a document produced by the country itself, the Poverty Reduction Strategy Paper (PRSP). Introduced in the year that the PRGF was established, the PRSP was meant to acknowledge the relevance of ownership in designing and effectively implementing growth-enhancing and poverty-reducing strategies. Building from a number of studies (for instance, Wood and Lockwood 1999) showing that reforms not owned by borrowing countries were poorly implemented and that conditionality alone was not enough to affect program performance, the PRGF made specific allowance for the need for borrowing member countries to be closely aligned to their PRSPs, which would also provide the basis for drawing the conditionality associated with an arrangement. In fact, conditionality and ownership do not necessarily involve a trade-off but can be regarded as complementary in the satisfactory implementation of an agreed-upon program of reforms. To the extent that conditions are based on a program owned by a country and are drawn up in close cooperation with the national authorities, they provide a compact for signaling to investors and donors the authorities' commitment to implementing their own policy agenda.

Conditionality may provide a transparent framework of engagement for both country authorities and the multilateral institution, both of which commit to a financial arrangement upon the fulfillment of certain conditions.[20] To the extent that conditionality reflects genuinely country-owned programs, it can enhance the ownership of reforms, providing reformist groups within the government and civil society with a commitment device to use as leverage against those lobbying for vested interests. In order to work in this way, however, conditionality must be limited to a set of actions deemed of critical importance for the success of the reforms and thus of the program itself (Boughton 2005).

The relationship between conditionality and ownership—if implemented to be mutually reinforcing—is likely to have a beneficial effect on catalysis. One of the reasons why the catalytic effect of IMF lending may be obscured in cross-country regression analysis is that other lenders base their decisions on a number of factors, including the quality of borrowing authorities' commitment to an agenda of policy reforms—that is, the degree of country ownership

---

[20] It is interesting to note that conditionality was not a feature of early IMF arrangements. To counteract the negative signal typically associated with a country borrowing from the IMF, the Executive Board began in 1952 to clarify the circumstances under which a member could borrow from the Fund. In particular, the notion of "upper credit tranche conditionality" was developed to signal that a member's policies were of sufficient strength effectively to address underlying balance of payments problems. See IMF (2004a).

of the program in question. Conditionality in itself is not informative of the willingness of a government to pursue a program of reform, nor can it be expected to provide an effective safeguard for IMF resources, as is commonly argued. Ownership, however, has the potential to make conditionality a more effective predictor.[21]

To be sure, there are a number of difficulties in making the notion of ownership operational in IMF policies. First, although ownership rests primarily with the government, broader inclusion of key stakeholders would be beneficial for building consensus around a program of reforms; given that personalities change over time, it would also boost the likelihood of a reform program's implementation. This underlines the importance of developing a genuine participatory approach such as the PRSP. Ownership is challenging because it is inherently dynamic, insofar as ownership of a given reform may originate within a restricted circle of high-ranking officials and then spill over to broader segments of a society. To make things more difficult, ownership is not normally observable before policies are actually implemented. And the notion of ownership does not necessarily imply the institutional capacity to implement an agreed-upon program of reforms (IMF 2001b; Boughton 2005).

These factors make the notion of ownership challenging to operationalize, especially for those institutions like the IMF that are external to the countries to which they are lending. Importantly, operationalizing ownership requires multinational lenders to have a deep knowledge of the political economy in which a given reform debate originates. The constraints posed by a given institutional setting and the key stakeholders able to affect the implementation of a reform program vary from country to country, and the IMF needs to build this awareness into its policies. It must ascertain, for instance, whether some constraints reflect a true institutional shortcoming or a lack of institutional capacity rather than a lack of commitment, and it must factor the results into its program design; in the latter case, for instance, technical assistance might help to overcome the problem. Again, this method requires substantial country-specific knowledge.

The IEO (2007) reports, however, that in some cases Fund missions listen too little and tend to impose their own views despite the rhetoric of "ownership." According to a survey carried out by the IEO, only about half the IMF staff interviewed admitted using the analytical work and experience of the authorities for PRGF analysis and design. When it comes to utilizing the PRSP as a basis for PRGF program design, only 40 percent of surveyed staff agreed that it provides the basis for the PRGF. However, twice as many noted that the PRGF provides the basis for the macroeconomic implementation of the PRSP.

---

[21] On the relationship between ownership and policy change, see Ivanova et al. (2003) and Killick, Gunatilaka, and Marr (1998).

Some further insights on the extent to which conditionality is associated with parsimony and ownership may be obtained from a recent evaluation of structural conditionality (IEO 2008).[22] In the arrangements made between 2001 and 2004, the review only found a marginal reduction in the average number of conditions—about 15 per program per year compared to about 16 in the arrangements from 1997 to 2000—whose streamlining was, instead, an objective of the new Conditionality Guidelines approved by the Board in 2002.[23] The review did find, however, a greater focus in the conditions increasingly clustered around "core areas," such as tax and public expenditure management policies and the financial sector, and away from non-core areas, such as privatization and civil service reforms.

Ownership is notoriously difficult to measure directly, and thus the review could only point to the extent to which one can observe indirect evidence that is consistent with authorities' increased ownership. For instance, the IEO (2008) reports that PRGF arrangements enjoyed greater compliance rates than nonconcessional GRA programs, although both types of programs exhibit relatively low compliance that becomes even lower in non-core sectors.[24] Yet the average compliance rate is not significantly correlated with the overall success of the individual program, and it exhibits substantial variation across sectors within individual programs. Successful programs have stronger analytical underpinnings in the areas affected by conditionality, and they exhibit well-specified medium-term roadmaps whose objectives are adequately articulated in terms of the sequencing and trade-offs linking the various conditions to the distortions that they aim to address.

Further insight on the relationship between conditionality and ownership can be inferred from whether conditionality is effective in bringing about follow-up reforms, which can be done by considering the degree to which compliance with a certain condition is followed by additional reforms in the same sector. All in all, the evaluation uncovers no significant correlation between compliance and continuity of reforms, casting doubt on the extent to which, on average, conditionality has worked as a tool to support overall economic reforms.

Finally, another conclusion of the IEO (2008) review, as well as of the IMF (2005b) internal review, is that conditionality on growth and supply-side measures has been severely cut back. There is a risk, in other words, that the program design underlying PRGF arrangements that have growth as one of their objectives has moved away from growth-related reforms. Even if this is in line with the Guidelines' emphasis on criticality, it has to be viewed in a

---

[22] This follows an internal review carried out in 2005. See IMF (2005b).

[23] These Guidelines followed up the Interim Guidance Note issued by the IMF's Managing Director in September 2001 aimed at streamlining conditionality.

[24] The average compliance rate for concessional arrangements is 61% in core sectors and 39% in non-core ones. In GRA-supported arrangements, the respective rates stand at 49% and 54%.

context in which the World Bank has not increased conditionality in those areas where the Fund has withdrawn.

IV. Challenging aspects of IMF lending policies

By strengthening its concessional programs to support growth and poverty reduction policies for its low-income members, the IMF has entered into an area different in several respects from its traditional stabilization programs. The latter aim to restore external viability in the short run by ensuring a rapid turnaround in the balance of payments, typically achieved by operating on the demand side, so that stability is accompanied, at least in the short term, by a reduction in growth. With PRGF arrangements, by contrast, program design has to accommodate the need of low-income economies to achieve objectives such as growth and poverty reduction rather than macroeconomic stability alone, and this new orientation requires a fundamental shift in the architecture of IMF-supported programs.

In practice, this creates an inherent tension with the typical IMF approach to program design, whose aim traditionally consists in helping countries to restore their external equilibrium following an adverse shock. Especially for those countries that have already attained macroeconomic stability and need fully to lift their growth potential to fight poverty, the challenge lies in determining the corresponding financing gap and a supportive macroeconomic framework. Operationally, it implies a greater focus on the supply side instead of—or in addition to—aggregate demand by concentrating on measures supportive of economic growth and private sector development, which are exactly those lacking according to the latest conditionality review (IMF 2005b).

From an empirical standpoint, it remains to be seen to what extent the PRGF has been able to achieve its challenging objectives. Given that it was introduced in 1999, reviews to date have been largely internal to the IMF and have typically focused on case studies or descriptive statistics, while a statistical analysis of the significance of the results achieved still has to be performed. According to a review carried out by the IMF (2003), the growth performance of those members that had a PRGF-supported program from 1998 to 2002 was better than that of non-PRGF low-income countries. Low-income economies as a group recorded a median growth rate of about 3.5 percent for the period 1998–2002, up from rates close to 3 percent in the 1980s. PRGF countries, by contrast, recorded a median growth rate of about 4.5 percent in the same period. These results are broadly based, and they also hold on per capita terms. In particular, per capita income growth, while averaging less than 0.5 percent in the 1980s, grew in excess of 1.5 percent in the period

1998–2002, with PRGF countries again recording a higher outcome. The favorable performance of PRGF-supported economies extends to other key macroeconomic variables. Inflation, for example, has steadily decelerated in PRGF countries, comparing favorably with other developing countries. Fiscal deficits, or reserve assets, have also shown favorable dynamics.

There is no comprehensive evidence yet available regarding the performance of PRGF-supported countries with respect to poverty reduction. As previously noted, this objective is instrumentally achieved primarily by targeting levels of pro-poor expenditures and by strengthening public expenditure mechanisms. While there seems to be agreement that increasing health and education expenditures may stimulate economic growth and improve distribution, there is no consensus on which policies are most effective in improving education and health (Cashin et al. 2001). Bevan and Adam (2001) argue that the link between health and education expenditures and poverty reduction that underlies PRGF program design is not empirically corroborated.

The IEO (2007) has found that PRGF program design typically focuses on the macroeconomic aspects of absorptive capacity by looking at "Dutch disease" and competitiveness risks, which, however, were found not be a concern for the countries in question. Program design paid almost no attention to sectors such as education, health, and infrastructure to gauge the extent of sectoral constraints on the overall aid absorptive capacity. More broadly, PRGF program design fell short of integrating the individual dimension of the analysis into an overall assessment that would take into account synergies and trade-offs, such as, for instance, the supply-side effects of infrastructures and how they feed into growth and macroeconomic stability.

Furthermore, the Fund does not appear to have set ambitious aid targets or to have identified additional aid opportunities in the context of PRGF-supported programs. While it has supported ambitious measures to mobilize domestic resources, the Fund has been less proactive in signaling incremental aid needs consistent with a country's own absorptive capacity and growth objectives, despite the recommendations of its own internal guidelines (IEO 2007).

More generally, it may be wondered to what extent program design in PRGF-supported programs has adopted a broader view of the right policy mix both conducive to sustainable growth and consistent with the objective of reducing poverty.[25] Given that the policy space does not partition neatly between poverty-reducing and "traditional" macroeconomic policies, poverty-reducing policies must be effectively integrated into the broader macroeconomic framework.[26] Consistent with such a goal, PRGF-supported policies would need to be underpinned by formal analytical studies undertaken through PSIA.

---

[25] See IMF (2005e).   [26] On this, see Bevan and Adam (2001).

V. IMF surveillance

Surveillance activities have a central importance to the role of the IMF as information provider.[27] This is especially relevant for low-income countries, where alternative information sources tend to be limited and local capacity often constrained.[28] The basis for surveillance is laid out in the Articles of Agreement—in particular, Article IV, which empowers the Fund to exercise surveillance over a member's economic policies and assess these policies in regard to their ability to contribute to economic growth and macroeconomic stability. Typically, this monitoring is conducted on an annual basis through "Article IV Consultations," whereby Fund staff meet authorities and representatives from economic and civil society in a member country. This policy dialogue then feeds into a staff report, which serves as a basis for an Executive Board appraisal of the member's policies.

A. Tailoring Fund signals to low-income members

Recently, discussions have focused on the most effective ways to convey information to outside creditors and donors beyond Article IV statutory consultations. In fact, while the latter imply an assessment of a member's economic policies, they do not entail an endorsement by the Fund. Furthermore, as they are statutory, Article IV consultations do not have a standard for entry, making it difficult for outside observers to appraise a country's performance against a clearly defined benchmark. Article IV consultations provide a multidimensional, textured assessment of a country's policies, moreover, while some donors and recipient countries would prefer a simple "on/off" signal.[29]

In terms of signaling, then, a financial arrangement tends to be regarded by donors and investors as a preferred alternative. A member has to *ask* for a Fund's arrangement, and only if the member's policies are of sufficient strength to be consistent with a clearly defined standard does it become eligible to enter into a financial arrangement with the Fund.[30] Financial arrangements also typically require more frequent assessment than the

---

[27] See Lombardi and Woods (2008) for a recent appraisal of IMF surveillance.

[28] The 2005 IMF survey confirms the widely held view that information produced by the Fund constitutes a main source of reference with regard to low-income economies (IMF 2005a, Annex I).

[29] Multidimensional signals entail a textured and articulated assessment about developments in a member country, typically covering the broader context in which authorities' commitments do or do not materialize. On the other hand, an "on/off" signal implies a binary assessment, as given, for instance, by a country passing or failing to pass a program review with the Fund.

[30] Such a standard is the so-called upper credit tranche conditionality, although for some select facilities (first credit tranche, emergency assistance for natural disasters, emergency post-conflict assistance) a different, lower standard applies.

standard annual Article IV consultations, thus conveying more timely information to interested parties. Importantly, financial assessments are defined on the basis of a country's performance against a quantitative macroeconomic framework and offer a multidimensional signal as well as an on/off signal based on whether a member completes the review as scheduled.

These considerations have arisen in a number of Board discussions on surveillance policy and led it to approve the Policy Support Instrument (PSI; see IMF 2005a).[31] The PSI is particularly suitable for those low-income members that do not need or want to enter into a financial arrangement with the Fund but are still expected to rely on assistance from donors on whom Fund signals could exert some catalytic effect. Its recent introduction aims (1) to offer macroeconomic technical assistance to low-income members; (2) not to unduly restrict applicants according to their balance-of-payments need, the PSI being an unfunded program; and (3) to send credible signals to the donor community by means of an agreed-upon macroeconomic framework consistent with the standard upper credit tranche.[32] For countries that do not wish to enter into a financial arrangement with the Fund, fearing that it might imply a weaker ownership, such a device may offer an alternative way to engage with the Fund and benefit from its signaling role. In fact, regardless of the degree of stabilization they have achieved, many low-income members are still expected to rely in the period ahead on donors' assistance, and such an instrument may provide the basis for a sound macroeconomic framework on which to leverage donors' support.

To understand the basic features of this signaling instrument better, it is helpful to draw a comparison to Staff-Monitored Programs (SMPs), which have also been used until recently as a signaling device by the membership, including low-income countries. SMPs were designed either to allow members to establish a track record toward obtaining a Fund arrangement or to signal the strength of members' policies by means of a quantitative macroeconomic framework. As their name indicates, SMPs are monitored by IMF staff, but they do not imply any endorsement by the Board, which is only kept abreast of developments in the context of Article IV consultations with members. This lack of Board endorsement, combined with the fact that the policies being monitored were generally not of a strength equivalent to those associated with an upper credit tranche arrangement, made clear that the flexibility associated with SMPs could result in signal ambiguity and in January 2003 led the Board to discontinue the use of this instrument for signaling purposes.

---

[31] At the time of writing, the IMF is conducting the first internal review since its introduction. On the PSI, see also Bevan in Ch. 7.

[32] According to the survey, of those low-income and donor members who responded as preferring on/off signals to multidimensional assessments, about half of them stated their preference (1) for a signal of a standard equivalent to that of an upper credit tranche arrangement and (2) for an explicit endorsement by the Board.

The new signaling instrument, the PSI, differs from an SMP in two important ways. It carries an explicit Board endorsement of the policies implemented by a member, obtained by means of regular reviews of developments in the country concerned and of its performance against a predefined macroeconomic framework. Furthermore, the PSI is specifically targeted to those members that have already established a track record toward a Fund arrangement. In fact, it implies a clear performance standard equivalent to that of an upper credit tranche arrangement, with specific quarterly or semi-annual targets for key variables.

In the context of signals provided by the Fund, donors have also identified the lack of information arising from delays in scheduled program reviews as a potential obstacle to the smooth delivery of their assistance. In this respect, the PSI entails a fixed schedule of reviews, thus enabling the Board to assess whether or not a member's policies meet the standard of upper credit tranche conditionality. Such an assessment is disseminated in a press release and supported by the publication of the relevant documentation. If the publication of such documents is delayed beyond a reasonable period, a press release is issued stating that the PSI has lapsed. The latter feature marks an important difference with respect to SMPs, where members benefited from the positive signal associated with the start of the program but then had limited incentives to follow up on their stated policies.

VI. Challenging aspects of IMF surveillance

The challenge for the IMF in providing effective advice to low-income members is effectively to tailor surveillance to the specifics of their economies, as it has done for its other members. Early IMF efforts to better understand key aspects of industrial and emerging middle-income member economies produced a stream of scholarship containing important policy contributions, including the monetary approach to the balance of payments and the Mundell–Fleming model (Boughton 2003). More recently, the IMF has sharpened its crisis prevention tools by giving greater emphasis to indicators of vulnerability, including models of early warning (Berg, Borenstein, and Pattillo 2005). A "balance-sheet approach" has been developed to assess underlying microeconomic sources of vulnerability. At the same time, the IMF—in cooperation with the World Bank—has set up a Financial Sector Assessment Program (FSAP) and taken the initiative on developing Reports on the Observance of Standards and Codes (ROSCs) to assess the soundness of members' financial sectors and their adherence to international standards of best practice (IMF 2005c; IMF 2005d). In the wake of the Argentine crisis, moreover, the Fund refined its analytical framework for assessing external and fiscal sustainability (IMF 2002b).[33]

[33] See Lane (2005) for a review of these recent developments.

A great need remains, however, to develop a better understanding of how low-income economies work, and the IMF could certainly contribute to this effort in its areas of expertise. In the context of assessing the medium-term viability of macroeconomic policies, the IMF developed a framework for analyzing debt sustainability in low-income economies (IMF 2006; IMF 2004c; IMF 2004d). The framework reflects some specific features of low-income economies, namely, that resources flowing to these countries are of an official nature and, as such, de-linked from market developments as reflected, for instance, in interest rate spreads.

The ability to signal incoming debt distress is of great importance to both lenders' and borrowers' ability to make good decisions. Creditors, in fact, tend to lend to those countries with a higher debt service in the hope of maintaining positive net transfers and avoiding abrupt adjustment of borrowing economies rather than lend to those recipients judged to have the soundest policies.[34] Conversely, when facing an increasingly unsustainable debt burden, borrowers have to allocate a rising share of their revenues and aid flows to service the debt, shifting away resources that could otherwise finance investments. Private investment is also affected, insofar as entrepreneurs hold back on investments when they are uncertain what share of their future revenues will go to tax authorities.

The new framework for debt sustainability that the IMF has developed in close cooperation with the World Bank is based on two pillars. In the first place, a wide set of debt burden indicators is assessed against country-specific thresholds based on the quality of a borrowing country's policies and institutions. Second, debt dynamics are assessed by projecting how the set of debt burden indicators will be affected by a baseline scenario and plausible shocks. The forward-looking nature of the analysis is meant to assist the multilaterals and their borrowing members in designing an appropriate borrowing strategy under which the terms of new financing will facilitate progress toward the MDGs and underpin the viability of macroeconomic and growth policies. For this goal to be feasible, however, lenders need to tailor the terms of their flows, including the mix between financing and grant volume, to the debt sustainability outlook of a recipient country. In this setting, the role of the IMF needs to be clearly spelled out, as the fact that it is both an information provider and a lender may create some embedded tensions.

Effective surveillance of low-income economies is, however, a matter of using the right analytical tools as much as of focusing on the right goals. In this respect, surveillance activities should be made to reflect the characteristics of low-income economies more systematically by taking into account the social impact of relevant macroeconomic policies, as well as the macroeconomic implications

---

[34] For the empirical evidence on defensive lending, see Birdsall, Claessens, and Diwan (2002) and Powell (2003).

of large resource transfers. Along similar lines, the IMF's endorsement of the MDGs should be reflected in its decision to operationalize them in surveillance activities. Sachs (2003) has argued that macroeconomic oversight should not be limited to the design of a macroeconomic framework consistent with current limited resources but should highlight the resource envelope required for low-income countries to achieve the MDGs. Leveraging its expertise, the IMF could provide low-income members with assistance in designing a macroeconomic framework compatible with the needed resource envelope in such a way as not to jeopardize macroeconomic stability.

In this setting, the greatest challenge for the IMF becomes to manage the relationship with donors appropriately. In assessing external financing re-quirements, the IMF sounds donors out before coming up with an aid figure that reflects what is likely to be available. This figure is then fed into medium-term macroeconomic and expenditures planning, as well as donor aid plans. There is a risk, however, that once this forecast becomes the IMF's own assess-ment, it carries significant weight with regard to donor ability and willingness to fulfill commitments. In other words, the very fact that the IMF says that a certain level of aid inflow is likely to materialize affects the likelihood that the aid will be offered. This highlights the opportunity for the Fund to assist country authorities in drawing more ambitious but still feasible aid scenarios, consistent with the economy's absorptive capacity.[35] The increasing trend toward budget support, moreover, amplifies donors' interest in engaging with the Fund. This is at odds, however, with donor reports that the IMF is not sufficiently proactive in engaging with them (IEO 2007).

VII. Concluding remarks

This study has highlighted the underpinnings of the IMF's role in dealing with its low-income members. The Fund engagement with such members is based not only on its nature as a universal financial institution but also on its role as an information provider and a commitment device, from which the low-income segment of its membership can most benefit. The IMF fulfills its role through a range of activities—including lending, offering policy advice, and providing assistance in capacity building—by which it conveys signals to investors and official donors, who thus become better aware of where to allocate their resources. From the point of view of low-income members, IMF assistance in setting up a stable macroeconomic framework can increase the efficiency with which domestic and donor resources are utilized, raising the social and private returns on investments.

---

[35] On this, see also Lombardi (2007).

Owing to the ability to provide a commitment device to its membership, the IMF can also make better use of its position by leveraging the volume and reducing the volatility of the resources flowing to low-income countries. This study has highlighted possible ways in which the IMF could take better advantage of its existing role, including implementing nonfinancial signaling arrangements as one way of improving dialogue with donors, as well as proactively assessing external financing requirements. Both reforms would take advantage of its capability to smooth coordination problems among its members. In the former case, official donors—who are also among the major shareholders of the institution—would need to acknowledge that the IMF does not necessarily need to back up its advice with its money in order for its advice to be credible. As donors sit on the IMF's Executive Board, they are ultimately responsible for monitoring the institution's policies. In the latter case, the Board would be given a more comprehensive assessment of member countries' macroeconomic outlook, and Executive Directors from donor countries would be in a better position to strengthen coordination in the delivery of ODA flows to which their respective capitals have committed.

VIII. References

Baldacci, Emanuele, Benedict Clements, Sanjeev Gupta, and Qiang Cui, 2008, "Social Spending, Human Capital, and Growth in Developing Countries," *World Development*, Vol. 36, No. 8, pp. 1317–41.

Berg, Andrew, Eduardo Borenstein, and Catherine Pattillo, 2005, "Assessing Early Warning Systems: How Have They Worked in Practice?" *IMF Staff Papers*, Vol. 52, No. 3, pp. 462–502 (Washington, DC: International Monetary Fund).

Bergsten, Fred, 2005, "Reform of the International Monetary Fund," Testimony before the Subcommittee on International Trade and Finance, Committee on Banking, Housing, and Urban Affairs (Washington, DC: US Senate).

Bevan, David, and Christopher Adam, 2001, "Poverty Reduction Strategies and the Macroeconomic Policy Framework," Paper prepared for the Department for International Development (London).

Bird, Graham, and Dane Rowlands, 2002, "Do IMF Programmes have a Catalytic Effect on Other International Capital Flows?" *Oxford Development Studies*, Vol. 30, No. 3, pp. 229–49.

Birdsall, Nancy, Stijn Claessens, and Ishac Diwan, 2002, "Will HIPC Matter? The Debt Game and Donor Behaviour in Africa," CEPR Discussion Paper 3297 (London: Centre for Economic and Policy Research).

—— and John Williamson, 2002, *Delivering on Debt Relief: From IMF Gold to a New Aid Architecture* (Washington, DC: Center for Global Development and the Institute for International Economics).

Boughton, James, 2005, "Who's in Charge? Ownership and Conditionality in IMF-Supported Programs," in Gustav Ranis, James Raymond Vreeland, and Stephen Kosack (editors), *Globalization and the Nation State: The Impact of the IMF and the World Bank* (Milton Park, UK: Routledge).

—— 2003, "On the Origins of the Fleming–Mundell Model," *IMF Staff Papers*, International Monetary Fund, Vol. 50, No. 1, pp. 1–9.

—— and Alex Mourmouras, 2004, "Whose Programme Is It? Policy Ownership with Conditional Lending," in David Vines and Christopher L. Gilbert (editors), *The IMF and Its Critics: Reform of Global Financial Architecture* (Cambridge, UK: Cambridge University Press).

Bulir, Ales, 2001, "Income Inequality: Does Inflation Matter?" *IMF Staff Papers*, Vol. 48, No. 1, pp. 139–59 (Washington, DC: International Monetary Fund).

Burnside, Craig, and David Dollar, 2000, "Aid, Policies, and Growth," *American Economic Review*, Vol. 90, No. 4, pp. 847–68.

Cashin, Paul, Paolo Mauro, Catherine Pattillo, and Ratna Sahay, 2003, "Macroeconomic Policies and Poverty Reduction: Stylized Facts and Overview of Research," in Christopher Edmonds (editor), *Reducing Poverty in Asia: Emerging Issues in Growth, Targeting, and Measurement* (Cheltenham, UK: Edward Elgar).

Dollar, David, and Aart Kraay, 2002, "Growth Is Good for the Poor," *Journal of Economic Growth*, Vol. 7, pp. 195–225.

Epaulard, Anne, 2003, "Macroeconomic Performance and Poverty Reduction," IMF Working Paper 03/72 (Washington, DC: International Monetary Fund).

External Review Committee on Bank–Fund Collaboration, 2007, *Report of the External Review Committee on Bank–Fund Collaboration* (Washington, DC: International Monetary Fund and World Bank).

Ferguson, Niall, 1998, *The House of Rothschild: Money's Prophets, 1798–1849* (New York: Viking Press).

Glennerster, Rachel, and Yongsek Shin, 2003, "Is Transparency Good for You, and Can the IMF Help?" IMF Working Paper 03/132 (Washington, DC: International Monetary Fund).

Goldstein, Morris, 2000, "IMF Structural Conditionality: How Much Is Too Much?" (Washington, DC: Institute for International Economics).

Hakura, Dalia, and Saleh Nsouli, 2003, "The Millennium Development Goals, the Emerging Framework for Capacity Building, and the Role of the IMF," IMF Working Paper 03/119 (Washington, DC: International Monetary Fund).

Independent Evaluation Office, 2008, "Evaluation of Structural Conditionality in IMF-Supported Programs" (Washington, DC: International Monetary Fund).

—— 2007, "The IMF and Aid to Sub-Saharan Africa" (Washington, DC: International Monetary Fund).

—— 2002, "Evaluation of Prolonged Use of IMF Resources" (Washington, DC: International Monetary Fund).

International Financial Institution Advisory Commission, 2000, *Final Report* (Washington, DC: US Congress).

IMF, 2008, "Reform of Quota and Voice in the International Monetary Fund—Report of the Executive Board to the Board of Governors" (Washington, DC: International Monetary Fund).

—— 2006, "Review of Low-Income Country Debt Sustainability Framework and Implications of the MDRI" (Washington, DC: International Monetary Fund).

IMF, 2005a, "Policy Support and Signaling in Low-Income Countries" (Washington, DC: International Monetary Fund).

——2005b, "Review of the 2002 Conditionality Guidelines" (Washington, DC: International Monetary Fund).

——2005c, "Financial Sector Assessment Program—Review, Lessons, and Issues Going Forward" (Washington, DC: International Monetary Fund).

——2005d, "The Standards and Codes Initiative—Is It Effective? And How Can It Be Improved?" (Washington, DC: International Monetary Fund).

——2005e, "Review of PRGF Program Design—Overview" (Washington, DC: International Monetary Fund).

——2004a, "Signaling by the Fund—A Historical Review" (Washington, DC: International Monetary Fund).

——2004b, "The Role of the Fund in Low-Income Countries" (Washington, DC: International Monetary Fund).

——2004c, "Debt Sustainability in Low-Income Countries—Proposal for an Operational Framework and Policy Implications" (Washington, DC: International Monetary Fund).

——2004d, "Debt Sustainability in Low-Income Countries: Further Considerations on an Operational Framework and Policy Implications" (Washington, DC: International Monetary Fund).

——2003, "Role of the Fund in Low-Income Member Countries Over the Medium Term—Issues Paper for Discussion" (Washington, DC: International Monetary Fund).

——2002a, "Is the PRGF Living Up to Expectations? An Assessment of Program Design," IMF Occasional Paper 216 (Washington, DC: International Monetary Fund).

——2002b, "Assessing Sustainability" (Washington, DC: International Monetary Fund).

——2001a, "Financial Organization and Operations of the IMF," Pamphlet Series, No. 45 (Washington, DC: International Monetary Fund).

——2001b, "Strengthening Country Ownership of Fund-Supported Programs" (Washington, DC: International Monetary Fund).

——2001c, "Conditionality in Fund-Supported Programs: External Consultations" (Washington, DC: International Monetary Fund).

——2001d, "Structural Conditionality in Fund-Supported Programs" (Washington, DC: International Monetary Fund).

——2000, "Key Features of IMF PRGF-Supported Programs" (Washington, DC: International Monetary Fund).

——1998, "External Evaluation of the ESAF: Report by a Group of Independent Experts" (Washington, DC: International Monetary Fund).

Ivanova, Anna, Wolfgang Mayer, Alexandros Mourmouras, and George Anayiotos, 2003, "What Determines the Implementation of IMF-Supported Programs?" IMF Working Paper 03/8 (Washington, DC: International Monetary Fund).

Kaminsky, Graciela, and Sergio Schmukler, 1999, "What Triggers Market Jitters? A Chronicle of the Asian Crisis," *Journal of International Money and Finance*, Vol. 18, pp. 537–60.

Killick, Tony, Ramani Gunatilaka, and Ana Marr, 1998, *Aid and the Political Economy of Policy Change* (London: Routledge).

Lane, Timothy, 2005, "Tensions in the Role of the IMF and Directions for Reform," *World Economics*, Vol. 6, No. 2, pp. 47–66.

Lombardi, Domenico, and Ngaire Woods, 2008, "The Politics of Influence: An Analysis of IMF Surveillance," *Review of International Political Economy*, Vol. 15, No. 5, pp. 709–37.

—— 2007, "The Role of the IMF in Low-Income Countries: Recent Issues," *World Economics*, Vol. 8, No. 4, pp. 191–5.

Lopez, Paulo Silva, 2002, "A Comparative Analysis of Government Social Spending Indicators and Their Correlation with Social Outcomes in Sub-Saharan Africa," IMF Working Paper 02/176 (Washington, DC: International Monetary Fund).

Mody, Ashoka, and Diego Saravia, 2006, "Catalysing Private Capital Flows: Do IMF-Programmes Work as Commitment Devices?" *Economic Journal*, Vol. 116, July, pp. 843–67.

Moser, Gary, and Toshihiro Ichida, 2001, "Economic Growth and Poverty Reduction in Sub-Saharan Africa," IMF Working Paper 01/112 (Washington, DC: International Monetary Fund).

Overseas Development Council, 2000, *The Future Role of the IMF in Development* (Washington, DC).

Powell, Robert, 2003, "Debt Relief, Additionality, and Aid Allocation in Low-Income Countries," IMF Working Paper 03/175 (Washington, DC: International Monetary Fund).

Rodrik, Dani, Arvind Subramanian, and Francesco Trebbi, 2004, "Institutions Rule: The Primacy of Institutions Over Geography and Integration in Economic Development," *Journal of Economic Growth*, Vol. 9, No. 2, pp. 131–65.

—— 1998, "TFPG Controversies, Institutions, and Economic Performance in East Asia," in Yujiro Hayami and Masao Aoki (editors), *The Institutional Foundation of Economic Development in East Asia* (London: Macmillan).

—— 1995, "Why Is There Multilateral Lending?" NBER Working Paper 5160 (Cambridge, MA: National Bureau of Economic Research).

Rogoff, Kenneth, 2004, "The Sisters at 60," *The Economist*, July 24, pp. 65–7.

Romer, Christina, and David Romer, 1998, "Monetary Policy and the Well-Being of the Poor," NBER Working Paper 6793 (Cambridge, MA: National Bureau of Economic Research).

Sachs, Jeffrey, 2003, Remarks delivered at the informal seminar for IMF Executive Directors "The Millennium Development Goals," unpublished (Washington, DC: International Monetary Fund).

Wood, Angela, and Matthew Lockwood, 1999, *The "Perestroika of Aid?": New Perspectives on Conditionality* (London: The Bretton Woods Project).

APPENDIX

Table 5.A.1. IMF Low-Income Members*

Afghanistan	Liberia
Albania	Madagascar
Angola	Malawi
Armenia	Maldives
Azerbaijan	Mali
Bangladesh	Mauritania
Benin	Moldova
Bhutan	Mongolia
Bolivia	Mozambique
Burkina Faso	Myanmar
Burundi	Nepal
Cambodia	Nicaragua
Cameroon	Niger
Cape Verde	Nigeria
Central African Rep.	Pakistan
Chad	Papua New Guinea
Comoros	Rwanda
Congo, Democratic Rep.	Samoa
Congo, Rep.	São Tomé and Principe
Côte d'Ivoire	Senegal
Djibouti	Sierra Leone
Dominica	Solomon Islands
Eritrea	Somalia
Ethiopia	Sri Lanka
Gambia	St. Lucia
Georgia	St. Vincent
Ghana	Sudan
Grenada	Tajikistan
Guinea	Tanzania
Guinea-Bissau	Timor-Leste
Guyana	Togo
Haiti	Tonga
Honduras	Uganda
India	Uzbekistan
Kenya	Vanuatu
Kiribati	Vietnam
Kyrgyz Rep.	Yemen, Rep.
Lao, P.D.R.	Zambia
Lesotho	Zimbabwe

* As of October 2007.
Source: IMF

Part III

IMF Policies and Financing in Low-Income Countries

6

Financier or Facilitator? The Changing Role of the IMF in Low-Income Countries

Graham Bird (University of Surrey) and Dane Rowlands
(Carleton University)

I. Introduction

The International Monetary Fund's involvement in low-income countries (LICs) has attracted a great deal of attention over recent years. The key issue relates to what role the Fund should be playing and how it should be playing it. Should it merely give advice about short-run stabilization policy designed to reduce inflation and correct currency misalignment, or should its advice spread out to incorporate a wide range of longer-term structural adjustment issues? Should it be lending to LICs and, if so, should its lending be limited to the short run? Would it be preferable for the Fund to desist from lending to LICs altogether and focus instead on encouraging others to provide external finance in support of both short-run adjustment and longer-run development?

The Fund's approach to, and institutional framework for, dealing with poor countries has changed over the years. Prior to the early 1960s, developing countries were not seen as warranting special treatment and conventional stand-by arrangements were deemed to be the appropriate modality for lending to them. In 1963, and with the introduction of the Compensatory Financing Facility (CFF), it was institutionally recognized that export instability could be a source of particular difficulty for poor countries, and the CFF was designed to provide financial compensation for export shortfalls that were beyond their control. Initially the CFF had low conditionality, although this was changed in the early 1980s. In 1974, the Extended Fund Facility (EFF) was introduced ostensibly to provide longer-term finance in support of more fundamental economic reform, and the 1970s also witnessed the introduction of a Trust Fund to subsidize loans to poor countries drawing under the Oil Facility which was itself designed to help countries affected by the sharp rise in oil prices in 1973–4. By the mid-1980s the concept of structural adjustment was in its ascendancy and the Fund introduced its own Structural Adjustment Facility (SAF) and then the Enhanced Structural Adjustment Facility (ESAF). These combined the longer-term perspective of the EFF with the idea of subsidization.

Having been modified and renamed at the end of the 1990s, the Poverty Reduction and Growth Facility (PRGF) has remained the principal mechanism through which the IMF assists its poor country members. However, concerns have been expressed within parts of the Fund about the prolonged use of IMF resources by poor countries and, against a background of often not wishing to tie up its resources, the Fund has gradually shifted attention toward offering policy support (under the auspices of a new Policy Support Instrument) rather than financial assistance, arguing that it is the endorsement of policies that poor countries are seeking from the Fund as a way of encouraging others— particularly aid donors—to lend. At the same time, an Exogenous Shocks Facility has been added to the Fund's portfolio of lending windows to allow it to provide financial help in cases where shocks in countries eligible for PRGF loans result in a shortfall of foreign exchange that endangers the pursuit of economic reform.

In any event, while the range of facilities and instruments through which the IMF attempts to assist poor countries has evolved and continues to evolve, the presence of poor countries among the Fund's clients has remained continuous.

Some observers have claimed that, as a consequence, the Fund has unwisely intruded into the territory formerly occupied more exclusively by the World Bank and aid donors. Accusations of mission creep have been made where the "creep" applies both to the range of countries in which the Fund is involved and to the breadth and depth of the conditionality embodied in the programs that it supports. As a consequence, the observers often go on to argue that the Fund has sought to become, or has allowed itself to become, a development agency rather than the balance of payments agency that it was originally intended to be. This, they suggest, is unfortunate since the Fund's institutional comparative advantage lies in dealing with short-run balance of payments disequilibria rather than long-run development.[1]

The debate about the role of the IMF in LICs has been given sharper focus since 2000 because of the international community's commitment to meet the Millennium Development Goals (MDGs). In this context, it is natural to consider the part that the IMF can play. Furthermore, the Fund is itself going through a period of institutional introspection as it considers its medium-term strategy. An important element in this exercise is to define more clearly the best way for it to assist its poorer member countries.

---

[1] A clear statement of this point of view may be found in the Meltzer Report (IFIAC, 2000).

Once one gets beyond broad and sweeping generalization about the IMF's purpose, the issues are far from simple and clear cut. Indeed, they are complex and overlapping. Low-income countries face a wide array of economic, political, and social problems to which there are no quick, easy, or universal solutions. From the perspective of economics, LICs need an appropriate blend of short-run stabilization policy, longer-term economic reform, and external finance. Reliance on any one of these components on its own will be inadequate; not least because they are interconnected. Thus, the enhanced availability of external finance allows countries to pursue longer-term policies that may not have an immediately beneficial impact on their balance of payments. Without such external finance, the emphasis will need to be placed on short-run stabilization and adjustment. This shift in emphasis in turn has implications for short-run consumption and investment, and longer-term economic growth and development, and therefore also has important political and social ramifications.

The complexities spill over to the detailed debate about the Fund's role in LICs since, at present, the IMF fulfills functions in all the aforementioned areas. Its traditional rationale relates to short-run stabilization and the provision of short- to medium-term balance of payments finance. Since the mid-1980s, however, and as noted above, it has become involved in longer-term structural adjustment and lending. It is in the context of structural adjustment that the distinction between balance of payments policy and development policy has become particularly blurred and it is this increased blurring that has galvanized accusations of mission creep. It has also made it more difficult to be precise about the division of labor between the Fund and the World Bank. For while it is easy to say that the Fund is a balance of payments agency and the World Bank is a development one, the question remains at what point a longer-term balance of payments policy becomes a development strategy.

It is not just a matter of identifying the optimum blend of short-run stabilization, long-run economic reform, and external financing—a challenge that is hard enough to meet—but also of determining the best institutional arrangements for bringing it about. What contribution should the IMF be making in order to secure the optimum blend?

Answering this question requires analysis of areas where the Fund is at its most and least effective. However, to argue that the IMF is not very effective in a particular role is not necessarily to argue that a different agency is, or would be, more effective. Moreover, a debate about the role of the IMF in LICs requires an assessment of not only contemporary comparative advantage but also dynamic comparative advantage. For example, in one set of economic and political circumstances, it may be that it is more effective to organize financial flows to LICs via the Fund. In a different set, it may become more effective to organize financial flows in other ways, such as through conventional bilateral foreign aid. The role of the Fund in LICs may therefore need to change over time to reflect changing circumstances.

No single chapter can hope to do justice to the myriad of themes that are raised in the above discussion. Here, therefore, we concentrate much more narrowly on two of them.[2] First, the chapter explores the underlying logic of the IMF's involvement in LICs. Why is it that such a large number of IMF programs are with LICs? Second, it analyzes the adjustment and lending roles that the Fund can play in those LICs that turn to it for assistance. However, our treatment of adjustment will be fairly cursory and our attention will focus on external financing, not only in its own terms but also in terms of its repercussions for adjustment. The Fund can make a direct contribution to adjustment via conditionality, but it can also influence adjustment indirectly via its effect on the availability of external financing. In particular, the chapter investigates the relationship between the IMF and bilateral foreign aid.

Has the Fund been a substitute for or a complement to bilateral aid? If there is complementarity, does this work through the impact of the IMF on economic policy via conditionality or through the effect of IMF lending on liquidity? Or are IMF programs and bilateral assistance "joint products"? How might the relationship change as a consequence of any "scaling up" of foreign aid? Does this mean that the Fund needs to place more emphasis on its role in facilitating the effective use of external finance from other sources, and less on its role as a financier of low-income countries?

II. IMF arrangements in low-income countries

Between the collapse of the Bretton Woods system and the 1982 debt crisis, a division of labor seemed to be taking shape that involved private capital markets lending to emerging and middle-income countries and the IMF (and other official sources) lending to the poor countries that were unable to attract private capital. For the most part, the Fund's clientele were poorer developing countries, though debt problems did begin to drive some middle-income countries to the IMF. It was this latter trend that was dramatically exaggerated after 1982. The Fund has continued to lend to low-income countries. But it has also lent to those emerging economies that encounter economic and financial crises of one form or another, and to countries in transition from command-based to market-based systems. From our point of view, however, the central point is the enduring nature of IMF lending to LICs.

Table 6.1 provides summary confirmation of this observation. Access to the Fund's concessionary PRGF is conditional on a country's low-income status.

---

[2] A fuller review of the issues and the literature pertaining to the IMF's relationship with low-income countries may be found in Bird (2005), a source upon which, in places, we draw quite heavily.

Table 6.1. IMF Arrangements in Effect as of April 30, 1997–2008

Financial year	Number of arrangements				Amount committed under arrangements as of April 30 (in millions of SDRs)			
	Stand-by	EFF	PRGF	Total	Stand-by	EFF	PRGF	Total
1997	14	11	35	60	3,764	10,184	4,048	17,996
1998	14	13	33	60	28,323	12,336	4,410	45,069
1999	9	12	35	56	32,747	11,401	4,186	48,334
2000	16	11	31	58	45,606	9,798	3,516	58,920
2001	17	8	37	62	34,906	8,697	3,298	46,901
2002	13	4	35	52	44,095	7,643	4,201	55,939
2003	15	3	36	54	42,807	4,432	4,450	51,689
2004	11	2	36	49	53,944	794	4,356	59,094
2005	10	2	31	43	11,992	794	2,878	15,664
2006	10	1	27	38	9.534	9	1,770	11,313
2007	6	1	29	36	7,864	9	1,664	9,536
2008	7	2	25	34	7,507	351	1090	8,949

Sources: IMF Annual Report, 2007, and IMF Financial Statements, 2008

Although, in principle, LICs can also draw on the Fund under nonconcessionary stand-bys and extended arrangements, few do so. For example, in the early 1980s only the better-off or oil-rich sub-Saharan countries such as Gabon and Nigeria had stand-by arrangements. For each year in the period from 1997 to 2008 PRGF arrangements accounted for more than half of total IMF arrangements. Out of an aggregated total of 602 arrangements over the entire period, 390 of them were made under the PRGF, representing 65 percent of the total. In this sense, IMF arrangements are dominated by those with LICs. But, of course, LICs receive relatively small loans; after all they are generally small countries. This means that IMF lending is dominated by loans to middle-income and emerging economies, and this in turn means that the Fund's ongoing involvement in LICs is sometimes somewhat overlooked.

The above empirical observations lead on to a fairly natural question. Why do LICs dominate the portfolio of IMF arrangements? Is it that the Fund has actively sought to develop its portfolio of lending in this way or is it more simply a reflection of basic economic circumstances?

III. What motivates IMF programs in low-income countries?

The question just posed may be approached at different levels of sophistication. There is a relatively large literature that examines the determinants of IMF arrangements covering both economic and political variables.[3] One approach would be to examine whether LICs seem to experience those factors

---

[3] This literature is summarized in Bird and Rowlands (2001a and 2007).

that exert a significant influence to an extent greater than that of other country groupings. An exercise similar to this has been conducted by Bird et al. (2004) and IEO (2002) in seeking statistically to identify factors that distinguish prolonged users of IMF resources from temporary users. Much of the growth in the prolonged use of IMF resources has been accounted for by LICs, and the characteristics of prolonged users have been found to match quite closely those conventionally associated with relatively poor countries. However, to pursue this approach in detail would constitute a full chapter in its own right. Here therefore we adopt a looser and more generic approach, but one that meets our immediate requirements.

The purpose of the IMF, as articulated in its Articles of Agreement, is to help countries deal with balance of payments problems that have become unsustainable. The heavy incidence of arrangements with LICs would, on this basis, suggest that many low-income countries encounter unsustainable balance of payments deficits, and do so to a greater degree than other country groupings.

Data drawn from *International Financial Statistics* do indeed imply that, relative to other country groupings, LICs tend to experience fairly persistent current account deficits. But is this misleading? A detailed analysis of the behavior of current account imbalances over the period 1970–2001 has recently been undertaken by Edwards (2004). Unfortunately from our point of view he conducts his analysis on a regional basis rather than on the basis of income per capita. His Asia region therefore includes middle-income emerging economies as well as low-income developing countries. It is his African region that includes the greatest concentration of poor countries. His results show that, as a percentage of GDP, African countries have tended to have the highest mean current account deficit over 1970 to 2001. However, only 7 of the 49 African countries are *persistent* "high deficit" countries. This implies that poor countries encounter relatively severe current account balance of payments difficulties but that deficits are usually reversed quite rapidly either, one supposes, as a consequence of beneficial shocks neutralizing negative ones, or as a result of induced policy responses that are designed to offset the effects of negative external shocks or more persistent adverse trade effects on the balance of payments.

Indeed, without access to external finance, countries are, in principle, forced to eradicate deficits. For this reason, data on current account deficits are not a good measure of payments problems. A sufficiently strict demand deflationary policy may reduce the level of imports to such a degree that a trade deficit is eliminated or a surplus created. But this is not necessarily a signal of a healthy balance of payments since, at the same time, economic growth may have been curtailed. The balance of payments deficit is in effect being suppressed, and macroeconomic disequilibrium is being reflected by low economic growth rather than by a current account deficit.

Faced with temporary negative shocks, countries may, in principle, deplete international reserves which are, after all, held as an inventory against trade instability and other external shocks. But low-income countries often tend to hold low reserves, despite their vulnerability-induced need, because of the high opportunity cost of holding them. Holding reserves may therefore be a relatively inefficient way of meeting the liquidity needs of low-income countries. It may be preferable to have access to credit as and when it is needed.

Unfortunately, low-income countries generally have poor access to private capital markets, making this source of finance untenable as a substitute for reserve holdings. For example over the period 2000–2002, and according to World Bank data, private capital flows to LICs were $18,365 million, whereas equivalent flows to middle-income countries amounted to $489,638 million. Consequently LICs need to turn to official sources of finance such as bilateral aid or the IMF to enable them to sustain their trade deficits. In practice, of course, it may not be a matter of either/or, since lending from bilateral aid donors and from the IMF may be connected—something that we explore in more detail later in this chapter. The reality, as reflected by Table 6.1, is that, as a consequence of their balance of payments problems, LICs have frequently been pushed toward the IMF. But, in spite of the Fund's infusion of liquidity, they have also often experienced a reasonably rapid, but usually temporary, reversal in their balance of payments. If this is a fair representation of the facts, does it imply that the Fund is playing a beneficial role in allowing LICs to adopt optimal balance of payments strategies or is it failing in this role?

IV. Balance of payments strategy in low-income countries: in pursuit of the optimum blend of adjustment and external financing

Previous sections show that, as a group, low-income countries have encountered relatively frequent current account balance of payments deficits and that they have often made use of IMF resources. Recent theory relating to the current account views deficits as the consequence of intertemporal consumption smoothing. Following on from conventional national accounting identities, deficits are presented as reflecting deficient saving relative to investment. Other things being constant, an increase in saving is then anticipated to lead to a broadly equivalent "improvement" in the current account. The absence of solid empirical evidence supporting this proposition has resulted in additional theoretical and empirical investigation designed to see whether the basic intertemporal model may be salvaged.

However, even proponents of this approach accept that it is of relatively limited relevance for emerging economies and perhaps even less relevant for low-income countries.[4] There are the ubiquitous problems of satisfactorily

---

[4] The presentation of the current account in an intertemporal framework is often credited to Sachs (1981). It formed an underlying theme in the standard text by Obstfeld and Rogoff (1996). More recent contributions that extend the basic analysis in a portfolio context include

explaining saving and investment, but there is also greater uncertainty about the future, consequent upon the vulnerability to shocks, and the more binding nature of financing constraints that are encountered in low-income countries. As a result, current account deficits, normalized for country size, will become unsustainable and problematic in poor countries before they would in advanced ones.

Prior to the vogue for the intertemporal consumption-smoothing model, the current account balance of payments was traditionally analyzed using absorption, monetary, and structural approaches. Indeed, the saving–investment approach is derived from the absorption model. To a large degree these approaches may be integrated within a Mundell–Fleming (IS–LM–BP) framework. Current account deficits (or, indeed, overall balance of payments deficits) can then be represented as the consequence of excessive domestic consumption, fiscal deficits, and monetary expansion, as well as structural factors relating to the nature of domestic production and exports, the pattern of trade, and domestic productivity and efficiency.

Each of these explanations probably has a part to play in explaining current account deficits in low-income countries. Certainly monetized fiscal deficits are not uncommon in poor countries. But a key feature of countries in an early stage of development is their low level of economic diversification. If primary products exhibit a relatively low income elasticity of demand, and if poor countries have a high degree of export concentration on them, they will experience a secular weakening in their current accounts. With a low price elasticity of demand, export success in terms of volume may fail to translate into success in terms of export revenue. Superimposed on an adverse movement in the terms of trade, there may also be significant export instability that makes balance of payments management yet more challenging.[5] The difficulty may be as much associated with export excesses, which lead to lapses in terms of the conduct of macroeconomic policy, as with export shortfalls.

How can low-income countries respond to the current account balance of payments deficits they encounter? As noted earlier, one possibility is that the response comes from elsewhere inasmuch as aid inflows to some extent cover trade deficits, making them more sustainable. More generally, governments, in effect, have to make a choice about the extent to which they attempt to correct trade imbalances or finance them. Beyond this, they then have to choose the most appropriate means of adjustment and method of financing.

Kraay and Ventura (2000, 2002), and Ventura (2003). In similar vein see Edwards (2002). However, models that emphasize changes in portfolios as a reaction to changing perceptions of risk, as well as adjustment costs in investment, are probably not as relevant in the context of low-income countries, where capital inflows that mirror current account deficits take the form of aid.

[5] As noted earlier, studies of the prolonged use of IMF resources have identified these structural characteristics as being significant determinants.

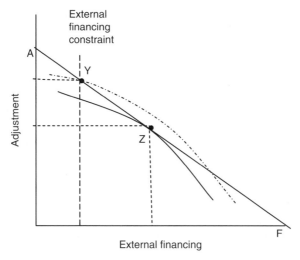

Figure 6.1 The Choice of Balance of Payment Strategy

In principle, the choice between adjustment and financing depends first on whether the deficit is temporary or permanent, second on the relative costs of adjustment and financing, and third on the social time preference rate. A financing-intensive strategy seems most appropriate where deficits are temporary, where the cost of financing is low relative to that of adjustment, and where there is a high social discount rate. The choice is illustrated in Figure 6.1 which shows consumption choices over two periods. The intercept A on the vertical axis illustrates full first-period (short-term) adjustment which is assumed to involve a contemporary consumption sacrifice. Intercept F on the horizontal axis involves short-term (first-period) financing. This enables the current sacrifice to be avoided but involves incurring a larger future (second-period) sacrifice when loans have to be repaid with interest. Governments then have to choose the optimum point on the AF trade-off. This depends on their preferences as between contemporary and future consumption—the idea of smoothing is relevant here. The optimum combination of adjustment and financing will occur where the marginal rate of substitution between current and future consumption sacrifices equals the marginal rate of transformation between them (point Z in Figure 6.1). This optimum will be affected by the slope of AF, which reflects the relative costs of adjustment and financing, and the slope of the community (governmental) indifference curves in Figure 6.1, reflecting the country's preferences.

Given this simple conceptual framework, a number of assumptions about low-income countries may be made. Assumption 1 is that short-term (i.e. rapid) adjustment involves a relatively high cost. This could be the consequence of a relatively low degree of economic flexibility and low demand and supply elasticities. It could also be related to relatively low marginal propensities to import and the strategic developmental importance of imports. Assumption 2 is that there will be a high discount rate such that current consumption is strongly preferred to future consumption.

This preference, combined with a diminishing marginal productivity of capital, may explain why domestic saving falls short of investment in low-income countries and therefore why current account deficits appear in the first place. Taken together, this implies that low-income countries will prefer a balance of payments strategy that involves relatively large current financing and more gradual adjustment, rather than rapid adjustment and little financing. However, their choice will be constrained. With little access to private capital markets, and relatively low holdings of international reserves, and assuming only relatively modest inflows of aid, governments may be forced to select what they perceive as a sub-optimal strategy, such as point Y in Figure 6.1.

Of course, there are problems in defining an "optimal" balance of payments strategy. Can this be done technically on the basis of economic considerations alone, or does it need to incorporate political economy factors? A technically superior strategy may, in effect, turn out to be redundant if it involves political costs that prove unacceptable. Furthermore, a strategy perceived as superior by one government in isolation may be globally inferior when externalities are taken into account. For example, a beggar-my-neighbor strategy may be deemed globally undesirable. There is a growing literature on the political economy of policy reform and this can be applied to balance of payments policy as much as to other areas of policy. With regard to Figure 6.1, while point Z represents the government's preferred policy mix, the government may be self-serving. Point Z will not necessarily represent the best policy mix from either the broader national or international perspective.

The general observation that in choosing a balance of payments strategy poor countries may be more constrained and have less flexibility than other countries may be conceptually illustrated by using a figure originally designed by Cooper (1968). The vertices of Figure 6.2 show three alternative ways of responding to a current account balance of payments deficit: external financing, adjustment based on the exchange rate, and adjustment based on managing domestic aggregate demand. However, there may be economic and/or political constraints on the extent to which each of these may be used, shown by lines F, E, and D. These delineate an area of flexibility in terms of the design of balance of payments policy for advanced, emerging, and low-income countries. For advanced economies there is a relatively large area of flexibility and these countries can exploit it in a way that enables them to avoid borrowing from the IMF. For emerging economies this may also be true for much of the time. However, in the midst of a crisis, the financing constraint becomes more binding and the area of policy discretion is sharply reduced such that they may need to turn to the IMF for financial assistance (as shown in Figure 6.2b).

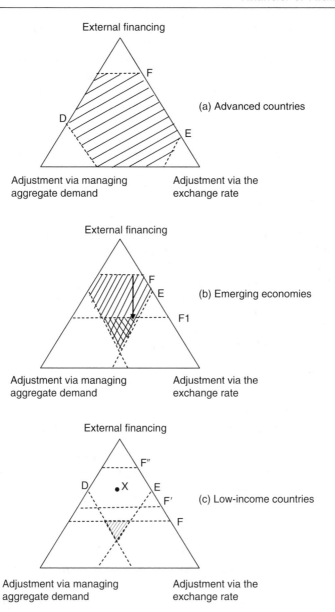

Figure 6.2 Balance of Payments Policy Options

For low-income countries shown in Figure 6.2c, let us assume that there is a persistently binding financing constraint, and that there may be economic and/or political factors that more sharply militate against demand compression or exchange rate devaluation. The area of balance of payments policy flexibility is therefore much smaller and these countries are more likely to seek assistance regularly from the IMF. Structural adjustment is not directly shown by the figure but, given its relatively long-term nature, will be constrained by a lack of external finance. Additional financing to some extent allows structural adjustment to substitute for adjustment based on managing aggregate domestic demand.

But what if IMF lending is itself limited so that the external financing constraint is still acutely binding. In Figure 6.1, while IMF lending will shift the external financing constraint line to the right, the optimum blend of financing and adjustment may still be precluded. In Figure 6.2, while the financing constraint will be shifted upwards the additional finance provided by the Fund may be insufficient to allow the country to adopt a balance of payments strategy incorporating the optimum combination of short-run stabilization, long-run adjustment, and external financing as reflected, for example, by point X.

V. Assessing the IMF's role in pursuing the optimum blend

The conceptual framework presented in the previous section allows us to articulate a two-dimensional role for the IMF in LICs. One dimension is to seek to relax any external financing constraint that prevents LICs from adopting the optimum blend of adjustment and financing. The constraint may be relaxed either by means of the IMF lending itself or by means of its encouraging others to lend. In the absence of adequate external finance, countries will be forced to adopt a sub-optimal path of adjustment. Since adjustment will need to have a rapid effect on the balance of payments, it will more often that not have to focus on compressing aggregate demand. Such compression often implies that either investment or the capital component of government expenditure will need to fall, with the latter possibly having a further negative effect on the former. There will then be negative effects on economic growth. Alternatively, consumption and the current component of government expenditure will need to fall, with this having a negative impact on contemporary living standards. There may then be serious political opposition, with the result that programs become more difficult to implement.

The second dimension of the Fund's role is to ensure that, where the external financing constraint has been relaxed, LICs are encouraged to take the opportunity provided by this to implement the optimum blend of adjustment and financing, rather than to substitute out of adjustment altogether. The IMF needs to help avoid the danger illustrated in Figure 6.2c. Here, either as a result of enhanced IMF lending or as a result of other additional capital flows, F shifts significantly toward the relevant vertex, to F″. As shown in the figure, this, in principle, allows the country concerned to reduce short-run stabilization by relaxing demand management policies and by allowing increased exchange rate misalignment. Conceptually, point X in Figure 6.2c represents a hypothetical optimum blend of demand management policies, exchange rate policy, and longer-run economic reform, supported by the requisite external financing. The Fund's role should be to assist countries in reaching point X and staying there. This will not be possible if there is inadequate external financing. But adequate external financing does not, on its own, guarantee that point X will be reached. Visual inspection shows that point X is just one outcome; many other outcomes are feasible in the space bounded by D, E, and F″.

It is within this conceptual framework that many of the issues that have conventionally been raised in debates about the Fund's role in LICs may be placed. These relate to the adequacy of IMF lending, the ability of the IMF to induce bilateral aid donors to provide official finance, the design and effectiveness of IMF conditionality, the implementation of IMF programs, and the prolonged use of IMF resources. In essence, all of these are associated with the basic question of whether the IMF helps LICs to reach point X.

In the remainder of this chapter we focus on the first two topics in the above list. In particular we examine in more detail the relationship between IMF involvement in LICs and bilateral aid flows. We say little about IMF conditionality, implementation, and prolonged use, although we have covered these topics elsewhere (see, for example, Bird, 2005). We do, however, say something about the implications of external financing for these issues. We also explore how the relationship between the IMF and foreign aid may change in the light of any prolonged "scaling up" of aid.

VI. Relaxing the external financing constraint: the IMF and foreign aid

In the mid-1990s flows of foreign aid in real terms diminished and there was talk of aid fatigue. External financing for LICs was becoming a more binding constraint. In this context, the Fund's role in LICs related, in considerable part, to whether it was able to substitute its own lending for conventional bilateral aid flows and whether it could galvanize aid donors to increase their lending. The latter issue was part of a broader discussion of the catalytic effect of IMF lending on other capital flows, which, however, tended to focus on the relationship between IMF involvement and private capital flows (see, for example, Bird and Rowlands, 2002). Given their generally poor access to private markets, this relationship was less relevant for LICs.

The underlying logic of the relationship between the IMF and foreign aid is complex and contains a number of elements. We pose these as questions since it is difficult to provide clear a priori answers. Will richer countries that ultimately provide the resources to LICs regard multilateral assistance orchestrated through the IMF as a complement to or a substitute for bilateral aid? Will they tend to modify multilateral aid in the same or the opposite direction? And is this relationship symmetrical? Will bilateral aid donors and multinational agencies have different objective functions; might bilateral aid, for example, be more heavily influenced by the political and commercial interests of individual donors?[6] Will IMF programs "crowd out" foreign aid as they encourage countries to eliminate fiscal deficits, the financing of which may constitute a motive for giving aid? For this reason some critics have suggested that IMF programs will lead to a "tapering out" of aid precisely in those countries demonstrating a good track record of implementing IMF programs (see, for example, Collier and Gunning, 1999). What will bilateral donors be looking for from IMF programs? Will they be hoping that IMF lending helps overcome short-term liquidity problems or are they more concerned about the conditionality component as a way of ensuring that recipients pursue sound economic policies? Are aid donors seeking to delegate the role of monitoring economic policy and performance to the IMF? If so, does a country's record on implementing IMF programs affect its future access to foreign aid?

Elsewhere we have tried to supply an empirical answer to some of these questions (Bird and Rowlands, 2006). Examining 48 low-income countries over the period 1974–2000, we investigated the determinants of Official Development Assistance (ODA). Our principal objective was to explore the impact of IMF programs on aid flows while conditioning for other influences. As we anticipated, we found that stand-by and extended agreements did not significantly affect ODA. However, concessionary programs under the PRGF and its predecessors were positively and significantly linked to ODA. The association appeared to be stronger where there was stricter conditionality, as reflected by ESAF programs as compared with SAF programs.

Our results also suggested that the Fund's liquidity role was relatively unimportant inasmuch as there was no significant link between ODA and the size of IMF purchases relative to GDP. However, even the conditionality role remained open to some question since having a record of incomplete programs did not appear to exert a significant impact on contemporary ODA. Donors did not seem to be dissuaded from providing aid as a consequence of poor past implementation. Perhaps donors are content to delegate the design and monitoring of conditionality to the IMF, with the Fund's endorsement of a program providing sufficient justification for them to give financial support. Certainly

---

[6] For an analysis of the determinants of bilateral aid, see Alesina and Dollar (2000).

126

the strong statistical association we discovered did not seem to result from a catalytic effect induced via liquidity and signaling. Instead, it more likely reflects a convergence of interests between the IMF and aid donors.

For this chapter we adopted a slightly different approach from the one reported in Bird and Rowlands (2006). To test the connection between the IMF's activities and bilateral foreign aid we estimate a model of per capita official development assistance (ODA). The explanatory variables, derived from the extant literature, include per capita income, population, economic growth performance, the importance of imports to the economy, real international interest rates, reserve adequacy, the debt-service ratio, the debt-to-GDP ratio, the level of civil rights repression, and the presence of a newly signed IMF agreement. All data are taken from the World Bank World Development Indicators except the civil rights variable, which is taken from Freedom House, and the IMF variable which is constructed from IMF Annual Reports.

There are two innovations relative to Bird and Rowlands (2006). First, the dependent variable is *per capita* ODA inflows into a country as opposed to ODA itself (although the results are in fact qualitatively similar when different versions of the ODA variable are used). Second, we formally correct for the possibility that the presence of an IMF program is not independent of the factors that affect development assistance decisions, introducing a selection bias. To correct for selection, we use a treatment effects model with explanatory variables derived from the literature on the pattern of IMF program allocations.

We ran the model for the period 1976–2000 on an unbalanced panel dataset of 570 observations covering 48 low-income countries (as classified by the World Bank). The results are presented in Table 6.2. Four important observations emerge from our analysis. First, the model does a reasonably good job of identifying important determinants of per capita ODA inflows into low-income countries, although models of individual donor behavior may yield superior results in terms of differentiating the motivations of individual donors. For example, within the set of low-income countries there appears to be a statistically weak bias against the poorer countries in the sample, and those with larger populations. Countries with high debts and heavier dependence on imports also seem to attract more ODA per capita, while countries with fewer civil freedoms receive less aid per capita.

The second observation relates directly to the link between IMF programs and ODA. The positive and statistically significant coefficient on the signing of IMF programs suggests that a new IMF agreement is associated with an increase in ODA of nearly US$ 36 per person. This is a reasonably substantial amount, and reinforces earlier studies linking the activity of the IMF to bilateral donor assistance. Third, although not reported here, additional estimations indicate that the positive association between ODA and Fund programs is present primarily in the post-1990 period following the end of the Cold War.

Table 6.2. Treatment Effects Model for *per capita* ODA Flows

Variable	Coefficient estimate	Normal statistic
GNI per capita	0.0130†	1.66
Population (millions)	−0.309 ***	−2.67
Population squared (million^2)	0.0003 **	2.41
GDP growth (lagged)	0.0655	0.4
Imports/GDP (lagged)	45.7***	3.38
Real LIBOR	0.107	0.29
Reserves/Imports (lagged)	22.7	1.49
Debt-service ratio	22.4†	1.82
Debt/GDP (lagged)	13.5***	4.72
Civil rights repression	−7.91***	−3.8
IMF program	35.7***	5.26
Constant	31.7*	2.12
	Selection equation	
GNI per capita (lagged)	−0.000399***	−2.62
GDP growth (lagged)	−0.00549	−0.6
Reserve adequacy (lagged)	−1.16***	−2.74
Change in reserves (lagged)	0.00104	1.24
Current account balance (lagged)	0.381	0.55
Change in current account (lagged)	−0.0000000269***	−3.15
Real exchange rate depreciation (lagged)	0.0000166	0.12
Debt-service ratio (lagged)	0.423	1.34
Debt/GDP (lagged)	0.0540	0.58
Imminent rescheduling indicator (lagged)	0.0154	0.16
Past IMF agreements	0.523***	3.92
Fixed exchange rate indicator (lagged)	0.207†	1.77
Constant	−0.299	−1.38
Number of observations	570	
ρ	−0.821***	
Probability $\rho = 0$	0.00	

Robust normal test statistics appear in parentheses. The symbols ***, **, *, and † indicate statistical significance at the 2%, 5%, 10%, and 20% levels for two-tailed tests. The parameter ρ is the covariance between the estimating and selection equation. If ρ = 0, then the selectivity correction is not statistically important.

Bilateral and multilateral donor activity seems to have become increasingly coordinated. Finally, the hypothesis that ODA per capita and IMF programs are determined independently ($\rho = 0$) is clearly rejected, suggesting that selection bias is important. There is strong evidence to support the hypothesis that ODA and IMF programs are positively correlated and at least partially determined by joint processes.

Formally correcting for selection bias does not change substantially many of our earlier conclusions about the relationship between IMF programs and ODA. Other research (Powell, 2003) has discovered a statistically highly significant relationship between IMF programs that were on track and ODA.

In terms of the questions posed at the beginning of this section, our empirical investigation suggests the following answers. IMF programs and foreign aid are complementary. Any differences between the motivations for IMF lending and bilateral aid seem to have narrowed since 1990. IMF lending does not seem to crowd out foreign aid and there is nothing to suggest that tapering out is an important problem. Aid donors are not looking to the IMF to provide substantial amounts of liquidity but, by the same token, do not reduce their aid flows to compensate for the provision of liquidity by the Fund. The results are consistent with, though not definitive evidence of, the proposition that aid donors instead appear to look to the IMF to monitor economic policy and performance in aid recipients. There is a reasonable presumption that, over the period from the mid-1970s through to the end of the 1990s, bilateral aid flows to LICs would have been lower without the IMF than they were with it.

VII. Is the role of the IMF in low-income countries changing?

How have things changed since 2000? The *big* change was that up until the mid-2000s aid fatigue was replaced by aid regeneration, as illustrated by Figure 6.3. Moreover, there has been an increasing, though incomplete, consensus based on empirical research that aid is effective, and most effective when accompanied by sound economic policies.[7] Finally, the "quality" of bilateral aid has improved as the degree of tying has been sharply reduced. Donor interest motives for bilateral aid have been joined by recipient need motives, and the politics of aid have changed to include concern about corruption and governance in recipients rather than purely the military and strategic concerns of donors.

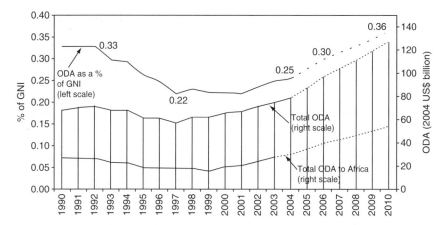

Figure 6.3 DAC Members' Net ODA 1990–2004 and DAC Secretariat Simulations made in 2005 of Net ODA in the period 2006 to 2010.

Source: OECD, Development Assistance Committee Statistics, 2005

[7] For a survey of the literature see Hudson (2004).

In terms of our earlier conceptual framework the external financing constraint was being relaxed and this reduced the need for direct IMF lending to LICs. If IMF loans are perceived as a residual, attempting to fill the gap between the need for external finance and the supply of it from aid donors, the size of this residual was narrowing (we return to this in a moment).

An implication of an increase in external financing, as shown earlier in Figure 6.2c, is that a larger number of balance of payments strategies become feasible; less emphasis needs to be placed on short-run adjustment. The optimum strategy will now appear within the feasible set, whereas previously it was outside it because of the external financing constraint. In these circumstances the role of the Fund changes. Prior to the increase in foreign aid, its role was to seek to relax, as far as possible, the financing constraint by direct lending and by galvanizing foreign aid. Beyond this, it was to minimize the difference between the actual balance of payments strategy adopted and the (infeasible) optimum strategy. With any scaling up of foreign aid, the Fund's role becomes that of helping LICs to select and implement the optimum balance of payments strategy from the (expanded) set of options.

Prior to the scaling up of aid in the first half of the 2000s, proposals to introduce a sharper division of labor between the IMF and aid donors based on comparative advantage were limited by the apparent unwillingness of donors to increase aid and by the donor interest motivations that lay behind it. The changes in foreign aid reported above provided more scope for a sharper distinction. While donors can supply aid, it would be inefficient for them individually to provide conditionality. The transactions costs would be excessive and there would be problems of coordinating conditionality across donors. Conditionality may be perceived as a public good that is much more efficiently provided by the IMF. In principle, the combination of expanded external finance from aid donors and conditionality from the IMF could jointly ensure adequate and effective foreign aid.

If this all looks easy, it isn't. The broad conceptual picture presented above masks difficult and fundamental problems relating to the role of the IMF in LICs. Here we mention but do not explore them. However, the cursory treatment they receive should not be interpreted as reflecting their relative importance. As we just said, they are fundamental. First, what is the optimum blend of external financing, short-run and long-run adjustment? This incorporates issues relating to inflation and exchange rate misalignment, fiscal policy, monetary policy, and exchange rate management. It incorporates issues relating to long-run economic reform and economic liberalization. And it also incorporates issues relating to the potential problems associated with aid inflows in terms of Dutch disease, absorptive capacity, macroeconomic management, and debt sustainability. Second, what is the appropriate role for the IMF relative to that of the World Bank in identifying and sponsoring this optimum blend? Relevant in this context is the finding reported by the authors elsewhere that, however elusive it is in general, the IMF may be better able to exert a catalytic effect on other capital flows than is the World Bank (Bird and Rowlands, 2000, 2001b, and Bird, Mori and Rowlands, 2000). Third, is conditionality an appropriate modality for encouraging LICs to implement the optimum blend of economic policy? These questions themselves raise a myriad of further questions relating to the design of IMF conditionality, its implementation, and the prolonged use of IMF resources by LICs. And this is without getting into the details of the instruments through which the Fund deals with LICs, in particular the PRGF, and the significance of debt relief as part of the overall picture. It also bypasses issues of governance both in the LICs and in the IMF. We do not pursue the above issues simply because they require much more detailed discussion than we can afford to give them in this chapter. However, we conclude this section with an observation. If aid donors begin to place heavier emphasis on IMF conditionality, this will increase the bargaining power of the Fund with LIC governments, but it will also increase the imperative that IMF conditionality is well designed and supports an appropriate balance of payments strategy. Unlike the projections shown in Figure 6.3, real aid flows after 2006 actually tended to fall and this once more raises the question of whether the Fund needs to be a financier as well as a facilitator.

VIII. Should the Fund retain an independent financing role in low-income countries?

Ultimately foreign aid involves a transfer of real resources from richer to poorer countries, and it will largely be up to the richer countries as to how they wish to engineer this transfer. Do they opt for conventional bilateral ODA? Do they increase contributions to multilateral agencies? Or do they select newer and less conventional conduits for aid such as increased allocations of SDRs, or international taxation of one form or another? Again, these questions raise a host of interesting issues. In the first half of the 2000s it seemed that the donor countries had chosen ODA and debt relief as their preferred routes. They remained reluctant to increase the lending capacity of the IMF or to establish new mechanisms for transferring resources to poor countries.

By the end of the 2000s these preferences seemed to be changing again as aid flows were diminishing and there was renewed interest in the direct lending role of the IMF. Apart from this, the future of direct lending by the IMF to LICs depends on a number of things. It depends on whether the credibility of IMF conditionality is influenced by the willingness of the Fund to tie up its own resources. It depends on whether the Fund will do a better job of monitoring programs if its own resources are involved. And it depends on whether the Fund can mobilize its own resources more rapidly than it can mobilize bilateral aid. If the answer to all of the above is positive, then a case may be made for the Fund to continue to have an independent lending role in LICs. The logic of this may be illustrated by a more specific example. Take a case where an IMF program has been agreed upon but is then blown off course by an unexpected and temporary negative trade shock. Its temporary nature will favor a financing rather than an adjustment response. But it may take too long to organize bilateral aid donors to provide additional assistance. Here is a role that the Fund should be well positioned to play. Should the trade shock turn out to be more permanent, in association with an enduring change in the terms of trade, longer-run adjustment in the form of export diversification may be required and aid donors could support this. Thus, while the scaling up of aid in the first half of the 2000s shifted the division of labor between the IMF and aid donors in favor of the latter providing more of the external financing needed by LICs, there may also be a division of labor within this financing role, with the Fund providing rapid-response finance designed to protect agreed policy strategies from unforeseen short-term contingencies. With the intro- duction of the Exogenous Shocks Facility, this appears to be the broad direc- tion in which the Fund is moving. But changes in the amount of bilateral aid may create a need to reassess things as the Fund attempts to help LICs design and implement the most appropriate balance of payments strategies.

IX. Concluding remarks

For many years a common theme emerging from discussions with staff at the IMF was that poor countries needed more foreign aid rather than more lending from the Fund. The argument was that the IMF was not well suited to deal with the long-term balance of payments problems that low-income countries en- counter. At a time when additional foreign aid was not forthcoming, the Fund responded by introducing facilities designed to provide longer-term finance supporting structural adjustment. But if external financing is inadequate, a binding constraint is placed on how quickly balance of payments adjustment needs to be achieved. In turn, short-run adjustment is likely to mean com- pressing aggregate domestic demand and this, in turn, is associated with many of the problems that have been observed in the Fund's dealings with LICs. The issues involved are, of course, much more complex than this, but even so, the broad conceptual caricature remains.

This chapter has explored how a lack of balance of payments sustainability has led to LICs' making relatively heavy use of IMF resources. It also discusses how an optimal balance of payments strategy may have been ruled out by the binding nature of the external financing constraint that LICs have encoun- tered. It goes on to analyze in some detail the historical relationship between IMF involvement and bilateral aid in LICs.

In the first half of the 2000s there was a marked upward trend in foreign aid. This seemed to suggest that the Fund's role as a financier in low-income countries could diminish and that it could focus more on providing an input to the design of adjustment and via this facilitate the provision of aid. However, since the mid-2000s flows of foreign aid to LICs have failed to achieve the degree of "scaling up" that was envisaged in 2005 and this implies that the Fund's role as a financier may remain important for some years to come.

X. References

Alesina, Alberto, and David Dollar, 2000, "Who Gives Aid to Whom and Why?" *Journal of Economic Growth*, 5, 1, 33–63.

Bird, Graham, 2005, "The IMF and Poor Countries: Towards a More Fulfilling Relationship," in Jan Joost Teunissen and Age Akkerman, eds., *Helping the Poor? The IMF and Low Income Countries*, The Hague, Forum for Debt and Development.

——Mumtaz Hussain and Joseph Joyce, 2004, "Many Happy Returns? Recidivism and the IMF", *Journal of International Money and Finance*, 23, 231–71.

——Antonella Mori, and Dane Rowlands, 2000, "Do the Multilaterals Catalyze Other Capital Flows? A Case Study Analysis," *Third World Quarterly*, 21, 3, 483–503.

——and Dane Rowlands, 2000, "The Catalyzing Role of Policy-Based Lending by the IMF and the World Bank: Fact or Fiction?" *Journal of International Development*, 12, 951–73.

—— ——2001a, "IMF Lending: How Is It Affected by Economic, Political, and Institutional Factors?" *Journal of Policy Reform*, 4, 3, 243–70.

—— ——2001b, "World Bank Lending and Other Financial Flows: Is There a Connection?" *Journal of Development Studies*, 37, 5, 83–103.

—— ——2002, "Do IMF Programmes Have a Catalytic Effect on Other Capital Flows?" *Oxford Development Studies*, 30, 229–49.

—— ——2006, "The Demand for IMF Assistance: What Factors Influence the Decision to Turn to the Fund?" in Gustav Ranis, James Raymond Vreeland and Stephen Kosack, eds., *Globalization and the Nation State: The Impact of the IMF and World Bank*, 231–62, London, Routledge.

—— ——2007, "The IMF and the Mobilization of Foreign Aid," *Journal of Development Studies*, 43, 5, 856–70.

Collier, Paul, and J.W. Gunning, 1999, "The IMF's Role in Structural Adjustment," *Economic Journal*, 109, F634–F651.

Cooper, Richard, 1968, *The Economics of Interdependence*, New York, McGraw-Hill.

Edwards, Sebastian, 2002, "Does the Current Account Matter?", in S. Edwards and J.A. Frankel, eds., *Preventing Currency Crises in Emerging Markets*, University of Chicago Press.

——2004, "Current Account Imbalances: History, Trends and Adjustment Mechanisms," *IMF Staff Papers*, 51 Special Issue, 1–49.

Hudson, John, 2004, "Introduction: Aid and Development," *Economic Journal*, F185–F190.

Independent Evaluation Office (IEO), 2002, *Evaluation of the Prolonged Use of IMF Resources*, Washington, DC, IMF.

Independent Evaluation Office (IEO), 2003, *Fiscal Adjustment in IMF-Supported Programs*, Washington, DC, IMF.

International Financial Institution Advisory Commission (IFIAC), 2000, *Report of the International Financial Institution Advisory Commission*, Washington, DC: US Government Printing Office.

Kraay, A. and J. Ventura, 2000, "Current Accounts in Debtor and Creditor Countries," *Quarterly Journal of Economics*, 115, 4, 1137–66.

—— ——2002, "Current Accounts in the Long and Short Run," *2002 NBER Macroeconomics Annual*.

Obstfeld, Maurice, and Kenneth Rogoff, 1996, *Foundations of International Macroeconomics*, MIT Press.

Powell, Robert, 2003, "Debt Relief, Additionality, and Aid Allocation in Low Income Countries," IMF Working Paper 03/175, Washington, DC, International Monetary Fund.

Sachs, Jeffrey, Richard N. Cooper, and Stanley Fischer, 1981, "The Current Account and Macroeconomic Adjustment in the 1970s," *Brookings Papers on Economic Activity*, 12, 1, 201–82.

Ventura, Jaume, 2003, "Toward a Theory of Current Accounts," *The World Economy*, 26, 4, 483–512.

7

The IMF's Approach to Macroeconomic Policy in Low-Income Countries

David Bevan (Oxford University)

I. Introduction

This chapter focuses on four related concerns. In Section II, the possibility is explored of how the IMF can remain fully engaged with low-income countries without (usually) having a loan program in place. Section III looks at how the commitment to a more flexible macroeconomic approach might be better implemented within the general framework of the Poverty Reduction and Growth Facility (PRGF). Section IV examines the Fund's approach to the debt sustainability issue, in the context of concessionality. Section V briefly considers the nature of the technical assistance offered by the IMF and how well tailored this is to the circumstances of low-income countries, and Section VI concludes.

While all these concerns are of long standing, there have been substantial developments in recent years. (An earlier discussion, pre-dating these, is Bevan, 2005.) Among these developments, seven are particularly significant. They are:

- The adoption of a joint Bank–Fund framework for debt sustainability assessments (DSF) in April 2005.
- The publication of the Fund's Medium Term Strategy (MTS) in September 2005.
- The introduction of the Policy Support Instrument (PSI) in October 2005.
- The introduction of the Exogenous Shocks Facility (ESF) in November 2005.
- The introduction of the Multilateral Debt Relief Initiative (MDRI) in January 2006.
- Various reports of the Fund's Independent Evaluation Office, especially "The IMF and Aid to Sub-Saharan Africa" (IEO SSA) in March 2007.

- An extensive set of Fund studies on the management of scaled-up aid, exemplified by the working paper "Fiscal Management of Scaled-Up Aid" issued in September 2007.

These developments have materially altered the landscape in respect of the first concern, by introducing an instrument that involves close engagement without having a loan attached. As well as rehearsing the arguments in favor of such a change, Section II examines the new instruments (PSI and ESF), the extent to which they achieve the underlying objective, and how they have been viewed by Fund critics.

The second concern, over flexibility, remains live if somewhat confused. Section III draws a distinction between the common complaint, that the IMF generally takes too restrictive a stance, and the subtler criticism, that it is insufficiently supportive of the exploration of policy alternatives. It takes a view on how much support there is for each claim, drawing on IEO SSA as well as relevant Fund research. The suite of Fund papers examining scaling up does represent a shift in the Fund's position, and a clearer articulation of what that position is.

The MDRI and DSF have major implications for the third concern, over debt sustainability. While they both constitute improvements, Section IV argues that they do not adequately address the real issues.

The MTS included a discussion of how Fund technical assistance might be better focused, by giving area departments the central role in setting priorities. While this is a welcome development, it does not get to the heart of the major concerns in this area, which involve the difficulties many low-income countries face in systematically assessing their macroeconomic policy options. Section V offers a brief discussion of this issue.

Before we proceed with this agenda, one point should be clarified. In some quarters, the IMF is portrayed as a very homogeneous, unreflective, and inflexible entity, so that radical, externally imposed surgery is required if substantial improvements in its performance are to be achieved. However, this is more caricature than characterization. It is true that the Fund has a mixed record in low-income countries, as elsewhere, and has sometimes adopted unhelpfully rigid and repressive positions. On other occasions, it has shown itself to be both flexible and innovative. In the present context, it has in recent years been extremely active in discussing—often internally—what alternative principles and instruments might be appropriate for its dealings with low-income countries. In other words, substantial elements within the Fund have been very constructively engaged in the general debate about its future role in this context. The present chapter is in part a commentary on these Fund positions, and references are limited to a handful of Fund documents.

II. The pros and cons of IMF loans to low-income countries

The traditional loan activity of the Fund was nonconcessional, and for short-term balance of payments support. It first moved into concessional finance during the mid-1970s following the first oil shock. For the last twenty years, the bulk of its financial support to low-income countries has been concessional, most recently overwhelmingly so. However, the degree of concessionality has not been high compared, for example, with the World Bank's International Development Association (IDA) loans to the same group of countries. This is not because the Fund charges a markedly higher interest rate—it charges only 0.5% pa on its most concessional loans, under the PRGF; it is because the loan has to be repaid much more quickly—to be fully repaid within ten years, as opposed to the IDA's forty years. According to the convention for calculating the degree of concessionality, PRGF loans currently only have a "grant element" of about 27% (IMF 2004b, footnote 8). If these resources were offered by some "third party" donor, and were therefore detached from the rest of the IMF package, it is not obvious that a low-income country would wish to accept them.

Given the dependence on recycling money within the Fund's concessional apparatus, simply extending the repayment period would mean that the supply of fresh loans would be sharply reduced. Achieving high concessionality of IMF loans to low-income countries, at current volumes, would require radical alterations to IMF procedures, and also substantially enhanced funding from bilateral donors. However, it is far from clear that the IMF is an appropriate vehicle for concessional funds. The core strength to which it aspires, after all, is as an arbiter of fiscal and monetary prudence, and of good macroeconomic management more generally, and this sits uncomfortably with the provision of soft money.

The conundrum arising from this discussion can be summarized as follows. Low-income countries are in need of highly concessional finance, or better yet, outright grants. The Fund currently provides, via the PRGF, what might be described as "semi-concessional" finance. Alterations to its procedures and its own financing that would permit it to move to highly concessional loans or grants could in principle be organized, but it is far from clear what purpose would be served by diverting part of a given total flow of concessional finance through the Fund, as opposed to its being delivered via multilateral development agencies such as the World Bank, or directly by the bilaterals themselves.

In its ruminations about the rationale for its loans to low-income countries, the Fund used two rather different taxonomies of potential justifications. One of these highlights differences in the potential recipients in terms of their recent history. The other does so in terms of their financing needs. Each taxonomy and its accompanying rationale is discussed briefly—there are inevitably some overlaps between the two—and then some inferences are drawn.

A. Rationale within a historical taxonomy

This taxonomy is intended by the Fund (IMF 2003) to represent a stylized continuum along which low-income countries may move. Four intervals along the continuum are distinguished. The first is characterized by extremely weak government institutions, both political and economic. Members of this group include, but are not confined to, *post-conflict countries*, for which there is a dedicated facility, Emergency Post-Conflict Assistance (EPCA), a sort of less-demanding precursor of the PRGF. In the second group are countries that have weak but growing institutional capacity and have begun to get to grips with macroeconomic stabilization, and are dubbed *early stabilizers*. They have developed a Poverty Reduction Strategy Paper (PRSP) as a framework for policy and for coordinating relations with the international community, but this is incomplete and fragile. They are regarded as being appropriate candidates for a PRGF, subject to safeguards. In the third group are countries that have more developed institutions in place, and where macroeconomic stability has been established for some time; these are the *mature stabilizers*. The PRSP process is now fairly well established, but there is still a role for major Fund involvement and hence further access to a PRGF. Finally, the fourth group consists of countries where governance and macroeconomic management have evolved still further, even though they remain low-income. These are dubbed *pre-emerging market economies*; they are deemed no longer to need a program relationship along the lines of the PRGF, so the Fund reverts to a surveillance function.

This taxonomic continuum is highly stylized, and it is far from clear that countries will progress along it, rather than getting trapped at particular points, or even cycling within a range. Nonetheless, it seems a useful way of characterizing the range of circumstance encountered in low-income countries. It is particularly important to note that history matters in this context: similar fiscal and monetary strategies may have very different consequences in countries with different past performance in policymaking and governance. Hence current policy options may be heavily circumscribed by the past. The conclusion is that this type of taxonomy may be helpful in encouraging the Fund to treat systematically different types of country in systematically different types of way. Incidentally, it does not serve to say that each country should be simply treated "on its merits" without using any grouping device at all. While each country does indeed need to be studied in its own right, this must be done from within some organizing framework. The reason is that systematic analytic thinking is required about different sorts of economy, and how best to manage and develop them, and this requires construction of archetypes—such as an "early stabilizer" for example. Indeed, much of analytic macroeconomic thinking has been devoted to just two archetypes, an "industrialized country" (a thinly disguised USA), and a "middle-income country" (usually a compound of several Latin American economies). There has been very little systematic thought given to the particular properties of low-income countries, even though they have sufficiently different characteristics that extrapolating from the other two groups is likely to be highly inappropriate.

The real problem with the taxonomy is that it is tied, not just to the type of attention required from the Fund, but to particular loan instruments. There seems no case for arguing that a "pre-emerging market economy" that remains low-income will not still need, and be able to use, a substantial flow of concessional finance. Indeed it may well be able to absorb a higher flow than an "early stabilizer". In terms of need and absorptive capability, there seems no argument for forcing it to graduate from concessional finance, and indeed it is not being argued that *other* sources of such finance should be withdrawn, only the Fund's.

So why should economies that have poor institutions and are poorly governed, or that are at a relatively early stage in escaping from that state, be eligible for concessional finance within a Fund program, when countries further down the road are not? Two arguments have been advanced in support of this position. The first is that the Fund is better able to press for improved policies within a program than it is via simple surveillance arrangements, and it needs this extra leverage in the earlier parts of the spectrum, but not in the later ones. In fact there is little evidence to support this contention. There has been much analysis of the so-called "prolonged use" of Fund resources (IMF 2002), which has increasingly involved low-income countries that are institutionally weak, and have several programs in sequence, often without a break between them. Prolonged use is indeed implied by this rationale if countries need a substantial period to work their way down the spectrum to become a "pre-emerging market economy". But the evidence is that this type of prolonged program involvement has not led to significant changes in performance.

The second argument relates to signaling. Resources provided by the Fund are often small relative to those provided by other multilaterals and by the bilaterals, but they are highly leveraged, since availability of these other resources may be contingent on the Fund's providing a "seal of approval" for the recipient country's policies. (It should be noted that the Fund itself is decidedly uncomfortable with the gatekeeping role which has been wished on it.) The argument is that for this signaling function to be credible, the Fund must "put its money where its mouth is" and put its own funds at risk. This is particularly important for recipient governments whose own credibility is weak, but is unnecessary for those with convincing track records; hence the asymmetric treatment of countries along the spectrum. This seems a peculiar argument. The usual case for asserting that a signal must be costly for it to be believed is that the signaler is supposed to have an incentive to mislead the other party. But that is not the case here. Indeed, it is more likely to be the converse. The Fund is more likely to provide a genuinely disinterested judgment on a country's circumstances, prospects, and policies if it is *not* financially committed. When it has funds at risk, the largest threat to timely repayment is withdrawal of support by these other agencies, and an adverse judgment by the Fund would be a critical trigger for such withdrawal. Hence there is a conflict of interest. In other circumstances, we would think it bizarre that, for example, an auditor should be required to have a financial interest in companies it audited. Even apart from the conflict of interest issue, there is another reason for having misgivings about the Fund's program involvement in these cases. It is natural to claim that adopting the recommended package will lead to material improvements in performance, such as acceleration in the growth rate. Since these improvements have usually not materialized, this has imparted an upward bias to forecasts for low-income countries within Fund programs, with a number of unhelpful consequences.

B. Rationale in terms of financing needs

This taxonomy (IMF 2004b) also has four categories. It distinguishes between countries with "continuing balance of payments needs", those with "limited balance of payments needs", those requiring emergency post-conflict assistance, and those suffering exogenous shocks. In the past, somewhat ironically, low-income countries in the latter two categories have been eligible for Fund resources only on nonconcessional terms. The Fund acknowledges that these cases would be best handled by grants from other donors, and that in future, if Fund resources are required, they should be concessional, and, in the post-conflict context, more extended than hitherto. (The former issue has been partly addressed by the adoption of an Exogenous Shocks Facility, see below.)

Here we focus on the first two categories, which reflect the Fund's dilemma in providing (via sequences of three-year programs) what is essentially long-term assistance under the guise of balance of payments correction. What is a continuing balance of payments problem? Any low-income country that could usefully absorb substantially more resources than it currently produces would run a large current account deficit if it could. If it is in receipt of net aid inflows, remittances, or capital inflows, it will be able to do so. If it is not in receipt of these, and excluding the unlikely case where it has substantial foreign assets, it will not be able to do so. We might characterize a country in the second situation as being poor and starved of resources, but it would be odd to characterize it as having a continuing balance of payments problem. The Fund acknowledges the difficulty, saying that "protracted [balance of payments] problems may not necessarily be associated with large current account deficits . . . [A] small current account deficit could be associated with severe constraints imposed by limited availability of external financing or foreign reserves rather than an absence of balance of payments needs" (IMF

2004b, Box 3). But this seems to be semantic hair-splitting. The only low-income countries *without* a continuing balance of payments problem on this argument would be those with such good access to concessional finance that absorptive capacity had become the binding constraint. Fund lending under this heading is tantamount to development assistance, not to balance of payments support.

As regards the category of countries with limited balance of payments need, the justification for Fund finance—under its own articles—is weaker still. In consequence, Fund staff have argued for a bewildering variety of program relationships with little or no finance attached; these include "low-access" PRGFs, "precautionary" PRGFs, an "Enhanced Monitoring Policy", and "post-program monitoring". In the present context, the details of these various schemes are not important; what they all share is two very plausible perceptions. The first is that countries in this category may still benefit from an enhanced dialogue with the Fund that goes beyond ordinary surveillance. The second is that there is no good "hook" on which to hang the provision of substantial Fund finance, or indeed any need for it. Where they differ is in the judgment over whether enhanced surveillance will only be credible if part of some sort of lending program, or whether this is unnecessary.

C. The Policy Support Instrument

After these extended discussions, the Fund undertook a survey of PRGF-eligible countries and of donors as to how its "instruments and practices might be adapted to support sound policies in low-income members, in particular those that do not need, or want, to use Fund resources" (IMF 2005b, p. 3). Much of the survey was concerned with the signaling issue, and whether there was a need for a new, nonborrowing instrument, with a quantified medium-term macroeconomic framework, specific quarterly targets, and semi-annual reviews. Nearly 80 percent of the PRGF-eligible countries agreed there was such a need, and only one-third of donors felt that the Fund's on/off signal would cease to be credible if it did not put its own money on the line. The PSI was created in response. It is intended for the category of PRGF-eligible countries that have been categorized as mature stabilizers. It has a duration of one to three years, which could be extended to four, and there would presumably be a possibility of renewal. There is a distinction between assessment criteria, which need to be waived if missed to allow completion of a review, and indicative targets; there is a requirement that the program be fully financed; and so on. In other words, the PSI is remarkably similar to a PRGF with the exception that is does not involve Fund financing.

It should be noted that, along the spectrum of Fund involvement, there has recently been another vehicle for providing enhanced Fund support of policies, and close engagement with countries, that does not involve Fund *endorsement* of these policies. This has been labeled "intensive surveillance" and involves closer monitoring and greater frequency than the usual (typically annual) Article IV consultations. Thus if countries simply wished for a more intensive dialogue than that provided by these consultations, there would be no need for the new instrument; the requirement is already covered. It follows that the requirement for the PSI is really about endorsement and the signaling that it offers; countries are prepared to accept conditionality, not because it carries relatively expensive IMF financing, but because it encourages enhanced grants and concessional loans. Since its introduction in October 2005, five countries have signed up for it (Nigeria, Uganda, Cape Verde, Tanzania, and Senegal).

One advantage of a PRGF is that it offers the possibility of rapid enhancement of financing if a program country suffers an adverse external shock. To provide a PRGF-eligible country that opted for a PSI a similar avenue, the Exogenous Shocks Facility was introduced immediately after the PSI. This was lodged within the PRGF Trust. In contrast to the long-standing Compensatory Financing Facility (CFF), which has not been utilized in recent years, the ESF would be available on (PRGF) concessional terms, over 1–2 years, and could be triggered rapidly for a country with an on-track PSI (IMF 2006). Qualifying shocks would include terms-of-trade shocks, natural disasters, export demand shocks, and conflict or crisis in neighboring countries, where these are expected to have temporary adverse balance of payments effects. These effects would be assessed "judgmentally". The important category of aid shocks is excluded on the some-what contentious ground that it would be difficult to separate endogenous from exogenous aid shocks. The ESF seems a sensible adjunct to the PSI, but it has not yet been used, and may share the fate of its more expensive cousin, the CFF.

A number of commentators are very critical of the PSIs that have been agreed to date, on the ground that they contain much the same level and type of conditionality as PRGFs, without supplying any finance. But that is surely to miss the point. If the purpose of the conditionality is to induce adherence to appropriate policies, and/or to demonstrate that this adherence has been achieved, there does not seem any good reason for the definition of the set of appropriate policies to differ between PRGFs and PSIs. If the conditions are *inappropriate*, for example a blanket insistence on privatization, then that is equally unacceptable in both. A more apposite distinction between the two cases might be that the balance in the debate that determines what is appro-priate should have shifted, with the view of the country authorities becoming more decisive.

There are two other issues involving the progression in Fund involvement following a PSI phase. The first is whether this should involve either a phase of intensive surveillance, followed by a reversion to standard Article IV surveillance, or a direct shift to the latter. In any event, it would be for a country's authorities to decide which was preferred. The second is whether the Fund should move more systematically into the role of a ratings agency; its evaluations would move from being predominantly on/off to being more nuanced, and multidimensional. If so, these ratings could, for example, be incorporated in the World Bank's Country Policy and Institutional Assessment (CPIA), of which more below. There are at least three perspectives on this: the first is that the Fund should minimize its role as a ratings agency, and stick to its role in validating—or not—the overall thrust of policy; the second is that it should go somewhat further, supplementing this on/off judgment with a more nuanced commentary on different aspects of policy and its implementation; the third is that it should buy into a more mechanical if judgmental assessment, along the lines of the CPIA. There seems to be some merit in moving from the first to the second step, but the third may be very problematic, though some authors feel these difficulties are exaggerated (see, for example, Radelet, 2006).

Finally, there is the question of what should happen if the Fund was forced by major funders, notably the USA, to withdraw from development finance altogether, and restrict its loans to explicit short-term balance of payments support. This would make the PRGF system difficult to maintain, and there would be a question as to whether the PSI could be adapted for currently PRGF-eligible countries which are not mature stabilizers. This would seem to be manageable, though probably undesirable; the element of cumulative progression/graduation that is now possible would be lost, and the disciplinary force of the present system would be corrupted.

D. Conclusions

It seems clear that the Fund should continue to be very actively engaged across the range of low-income countries, in those cases where this is acceptable to the countries themselves. This engagement should include support in policy formulation as well as some form of enhanced macroeconomic monitoring and surveillance as an input to other donors' decisions. It is clear that these relationships need not be embodied in loan programs. The Fund has expressed a number of anxieties about its role as gatekeeper; most of these are caused by, or exacerbated by, the fact that continuation or suspension of a Fund program is regarded as a sort of on- or off-switch. It should be much easier for the Fund to provide nuanced and qualified approval or disapproval of a country's policies now that it does not necessarily have the previous type of lending program involvement. A progression, initially coupled with formal conditionality, performance criteria and the like, but no longer with a loan arrangement, progressing through a process of intensive surveillance and culminating in the

Fund's usual annual "Article IV" consultations, should permit a much more flexible approach.

It is true that this argument depends on donors learning to accept that the Fund's signaling should actually be more, not less, informative and accurate in the absence of a Fund lending program. If, to the contrary, they do not, and the net aid flow falls in consequence, this change might involve a deterioration from the status quo. A related risk is that the Fund as an institution may find it difficult to maintain the same commitment of staff resources and intensity of scrutiny if its own resources are not at risk. In either case, retention of something like the current arrangements might then be a second best. In any event, it will be necessary to keep the functioning of the PSI under close review. As experience is gained, the balance of advantage in pursuing this approach more generally can then be better gauged, and the force of the various caveats better assessed.

III. Towards a more flexible macroeconomic approach

If we leave aside the financing aspects of the PRGF for a moment, what does its general design imply about the way in which the Fund is attempting to interact in the Poverty Reduction Strategy process? The "key features" of the PRGF (IMF 2000) are organized under seven headings or categories. These are:

A. Broad participation and greater ownership
B. Embedding the PRGF in the overall strategy for growth and poverty reduction
C. Budgets that are more pro-poor and pro-growth
D. Ensuring appropriate flexibility in fiscal targets
E. More selective structural conditionality
F. Emphasis on measures to improve public resource management/accountability
G. Social impact analysis of major macroeconomic adjustments and structural reforms

This is an ambitious prospectus, and while it seems clear that the Fund has put serious effort into the attempt to deliver it, the results so far have been mixed. This is not surprising, since these categories are very different qualitatively. The Fund itself notes that its "contribution needs to become more narrowly focused on the institution's core areas of expertise (see sections E and F), but at the same time more consistent with the broad approach to poverty reduction (sections B, C, and G) and with enhanced country ownership (sections A and D)" (IMF 2000). Thus the key features are symmetric neither in respect of the expertise that the Fund brings to bear, nor in the extent to which the Fund could undertake to deliver on them even if it had the expertise to do so. In this respect, they represent a sort of portrait of what the Fund would like a PRGF to look like, but implementing this vision depends not only on the Fund's own staff, but on a variety of other actors.

More generally, not enough attention has been given to how real in-country improvements in institutions and process can be assisted and assessed, on a country by country basis, and there has been too much emphasis on procedures and paperwork. Unsurprisingly, macroeconomic policy design has proved to be a peculiarly difficult area in which to foster broad participation, and the Fund's attempts to do so have been spasmodic at best. As with much else in the PRSP concept, there are delicate issues here, especially those of intrusion in the domestic political process. In the remainder of this section, the focus is on the fourth category, of fiscal flexibility.

A. Ensuring appropriate flexibility in fiscal targets

The Fund has interpreted this almost entirely in terms of how to accommodate possible variations in external financing or other external shocks. For example, it asks how expenditure might be varied if greater aid receipts became available than those originally projected. The other legitimate concern of fiscal policy, in respect of domestic financing, has been much less addressed. Fund staff appear to have behaved rather passively under this head; if a government comes forward with alternative fiscal scenarios, they will engage in dialogue. If not, then the Fund does not set out to explore alternatives with government. Even if a government takes it on itself to explore its fiscal options, Fund staff often effectively restrict the agenda to the foreign financing dimension. Given the difficulty of these matters, and given the limited technical capacity of several recipient governments, this seems unsatisfactory. Of course it is right that the government, and not the Fund, should exercise political choice over its fiscal options within the space of prudent policies. However, in defining the limits of this space, a government may well need sympathetic and competent assistance, which the Fund is—or could become—well placed to supply. To date, it has either taken a rather passive view, or, all too often, continued to press for further fiscal tightening when the need for that has passed.

These issues are far from trivial. To offer a specific example, consider a government which has successfully disinflated the economy, has received Heavily Indebted Poor Country (HIPC) relief, and has secured a substantial net concessional inflow, but still has excessive domestic debt. It has a choice between a more or less rapid retirement of its domestic debt, at the cost of a more or less severe reduction in its social spending. How should it strike this balance? While this is ultimately a political decision, it still needs to be an informed one, and the likely consequences of different courses of action are not self-evident. (How rapidly may domestic interest rates be expected to fall? How rapidly may domestic private credit and investment be expected to respond?) Similarly, what are the likely absorptive capacity constraints in the event of substantial increases in offers of concessional aid, and how best might they be neutralized?

It appears that the Fund has not given much thought to how it should assist countries to explore the issue of flexibility. This seems to be a major lacuna in present arrangements. It is almost certainly not sufficient simply to suggest that country teams should take the point on board. It would more likely require the Fund to give active and coordinated consideration to how best to approach the matter. This would have to include detailed consideration of the potential conflict between confidentiality and transparency, and also of how to introduce a mechanism for monitoring the Fund's own inputs and their consequences. In the latter case, a far more systematic rolling review of Fund country forecasts is required inter alia. The in-country vehicle with which this process could most appropriately engage is the Medium Term Expenditure Framework (MTEF). This is now up and running in many low-income countries, and being introduced in most of the others. Since the focus is also on growth, a longer-term perspective, however speculative, is also required. A handful of countries have begun to develop such perspectives, in Long Term Expenditure Frameworks (LTEFs), often in the context of planning to meet the Millennium Development Goals.

B. Inflexibility as excessive conservatism

Critics of the Fund's alleged inflexibility usually have a different complaint: they believe that it insists on overly conservative macroeconomic programs, blocking the use of available aid. It is important to understand the mechanisms through which this might happen.

These might take the form of preventing the government from *spending* the aid, which would require a widening of the fiscal deficit (excluding aid). Alternatively, they could involve preventing the country from *absorbing* the additional resources, which would require a widening of the current account deficit (excluding aid). Or they could involve a mixture of the two. Spending depends on fiscal policy, while absorption depends on monetary and exchange rate policy. If the government receives aid-in-kind, or uses the aid to finance additional imports, spending and absorption are both equal to each other and to the aid inflow. However, at least in part, the government is likely to sell aid dollars to the central bank, and use the local counterpart currency to finance spending on domestically produced goods. The level of absorption then depends on how much of this additional foreign exchange the central bank sells, with consequences for the exchange rate and the domestic interest rate.

The obvious response to increased aid is both to spend and to absorb it, but there may be circumstances that call for a different approach. If a country's foreign exchange reserves are severely depleted, hampering the management of the economy, it will be important to rebuild them, so that the aid should be saved as dollars, and neither spent nor absorbed. Similarly, it may be appropriate for a government with an excessive fiscal deficit, or a high level of domestic debt, to choose to absorb but not spend additional aid. The aid is used as a substitute for domestic financing, and to increase the credit available to the private sector. Conversely, the combination of spending and not absorbing is unlikely to be justified: the aid is being used to build foreign exchange reserves, so is not available to finance increased spending. Hence the spending increase requires increased domestic financing and, if this is prudent, the increased spending could take place without any increase in aid.

IMF programs routinely involve restrictions on fiscal and monetary magnitudes. The question is whether these have been set in a way that prevents the absorption and/or spending of aid. It is helpful to distinguish between two cases, one involving within-year aid volatility, the other more sustained shifts in aid levels. The IMF has for many years handled within-year volatility by a system of adjustors, which specify how excesses and shortfalls against forecast aid are to be handled. These adjustors have often been asymmetric, requiring that any excess be saved and any shortfall at least partly met by spending reductions. The pattern of adjustors has varied in apparently random fashion between countries and between programs for the same country. They have typically not been accompanied by any systematic rationale, and have on average a depressing effect on both spending and absorption.

The more interesting case in the context of possible scaling up is whether IMF programs have similar effects in the more sustained case. This was one of the main concerns addressed in the IEO's report on the IMF and aid to sub-Saharan Africa. The central finding was that

PRGF-supported macroeconomic policies have generally accommodated the use of incremental aid in countries whose recent policies have led to high stocks of reserves and low inflation; in other countries additional aid was programmed to be saved to increase reserves or to retire domestic debt. Reserves in the two–three months-of-imports range were found to be the threshold for determining whether the increased aid should be used to expand the current account deficit or to increase reserves. The estimated inflation threshold for determining whether the country got to spend or save additional aid lies within the 5–7 percent range. (IEO: IMF 2007a, p. 2)

While both the quantitative methodology and the interpretation have been disputed, not least by Fund staff, these broad results suggest that it would be difficult to make the accusation stick that the Fund routinely blocks the use of aid. Indeed the reserves threshold seems to be incautiously low.

While the tentative verdict is that the Fund is probably not guilty of the blocking charge, there is clear evidence that the textbook response of full absorb-and-spend is surprisingly rare. One IMF study (IMF 2005d) analyzed the experience of five African countries, described as "relatively well-governed", that had experienced a recent surge in aid inflows. The PRGF-supported programs in these countries appear to have been compatible with an absorb-and-spend response, but this took place in none of them. In two—Ethiopia and Ghana—both absorption and spending were very low. Both had precarious initial reserve levels, and, in Ghana's case, had suffered from very high aid volatility. Hence the response had some justification. In the other three—Mozambique, Tanzania, and Uganda—spending exceeded absorption, creating a surge in domestic liquidity; this led variously to high inflation or a sharp rise in interest rates. In effect, the fiscal authorities set out to spend the aid, but the monetary authorities declined to permit equivalent absorption, because of fears about international competitiveness and an unwillingness to see the exchange rate appreciate.

In brief, there does appear to be a real issue over whether increased aid gets used, but the behavior of the Fund is not at the root of it. The undesirable outcome of spending without absorption seems to reflect a failure of coordination between the fiscal and monetary authorities. "Independent" central banks were generally felt to be desirable because they would be more conservative than the fiscal authorities and act as a brake on any excesses of the latter. This made some sense in an era when the fiscal authorities did indeed have a tradition of profligacy. In more recent times, their behavior has been much more prudent, and it may be undesirable for their use of aid inflows to be inhibited. One possibility would be to alter the objectives of the central banks. Their independence lies in the operational freedom they have to pursue these objectives, not in choosing their own objectives. The existing objectives lie in targeting no more than moderate inflation and interest rates while smoothing exchange rate movements. In principle it would be possible to add some medium-term absorption target in respect of aid inflows, either directly, or indirectly, by limiting the duration of any period in which reserves were accumulated above some upper bound.

While the IMF may not be the source of the problem, it could play a more constructive role in the search for ways of mitigating it. It has certainly been devoting increased attention to the issue of how increased aid should be managed, and produced no fewer than five papers on the subject in June 2007 alone, which lay out the issues. These papers stress the importance of establishing a medium-term framework, with better coordination of fiscal, monetary, and exchange rate policies, and of associated institutional improvements. They also state as a guiding principle for program design that "the Fund aims to bring all low-income members to the point where all aid can be fully and effectively spent and absorbed" (IMF 2007b, paragraph 27). The same document noted that "real appreciation has often been a concern, but rarely a problem" (IMF 2007b, p. 3). Collectively, the papers document a desirable shift in stance by the Fund, as well as a much clearer statement than hitherto of what that stance actually is.

IV. Debt sustainability

There has been an outpouring of work on this issue, from all types of participant in the development process, including the Fund itself. The overwhelming bulk of this work has focused on external debt. Some of it has been devoted to characterizing unsustainable debt in terms of "debt distress", where countries are forced to run up significant arrears, seek rescheduling, or access non-concessional Fund lending. (Notice that this categorization excludes countries with excessive debt service burdens which avoid these three symptoms at the cost of savage cuts in domestic expenditures.) The probability of distress, so defined, is found to be a function of the level of the debt burden, the quality of policies and institutions, and shocks that affect GDP growth. The inference is then drawn that the financing mix made available to low-income countries should reflect these factors.

The Fund, jointly with the World Bank (IMF and IDA 2004a, 2004b) proposed a new framework for the analysis of debt sustainability, based on "two broad pillars". The first is to estimate indicative country-specific external debt-burden thresholds that depend on the quality of a country's policies and institutions. The second is to provide an analysis and interpretation of actual and projected debt-burden indicators under a baseline scenario and in the face of plausible shocks. This broad approach was subsequently adopted, though with rather more conservative thresholds than originally proposed (IMF and IDA 2005, 2006). Part of this increased conservatism reflected a natural caution on the part of the Boards of the two institutions to reduce the chances of an early return to debt distress. Part of it reflected a concern that, following the substantial additional debt relief under the Multilateral Debt Relief Initiative (MDRI), low-income countries might be vulnerable to new and not very concessional sources of finance—the so-called free rider problem. This danger was perceived to be the more acute since the reduced debt service obligations under the MDRI were sometimes partly offset by reduced flows of new concessional finance.

Even so, implementing this framework will almost certainly imply an increase in the concessionality of the financing made available to low-income countries, including an increase in the volume of grants. If donors and creditors fail to make these adjustments, the implication will be that recipient countries might have to refuse some aid, even when concessional, if it were not sufficiently concessional to permit them to stay within the calculated sustainability thresholds.

The relation between these country-specific thresholds and those used in the ongoing HIPC Initiative is somewhat awkward, since the latter are uniform across countries. The International Financial Institutions (IFIs) have argued that this is unproblematic, since the HIPC arrangements address existing debt overhangs by providing debt relief, while the new framework is intended to provide forward-looking guidance. However, this seems disingenuous; had a country-specific view been evolved in time, it would have been bizarre not to tailor debt relief to it. Since it was not, the effect of HIPC completion will be to locate graduating countries in very different positions relative to their country-specific thresholds. For most countries, these thresholds will be somewhat higher than those under HIPC, sparing the Bretton Woods Institutions the embarrassment of immediately requesting a further round of debt forgiveness for countries that have already benefited from the HIPC process. Despite these assorted caveats, some attempt to move to a more country-specific basis is a definite advance, reducing the very arbitrary nature of the existing arrangements. Another improvement is the acknowledgment that domestic debt must also be taken into account, though the new framework is far less concrete on how this integration is to be accomplished.

While these developments definitely mark an advance, they still fall some way short of being fully satisfactory. Any forward-looking exercise is probabilistic and subject to being overtaken by events. However good the prior analysis and empirical work may be, attempting to determine a sustainable threshold involves an exercise of judgment. A conservative judgment risks unduly constraining the country's expenditure program, or else requiring a degree of concessionality that cannot be delivered. Being less conservative raises the probability that debt distress will in fact occur. More specifically, whether a judgment is in fact conservative or not depends crucially on the accuracy of forward projections, most notably of growth rates, and both the Fund and the Bank have in the past tended to be very overoptimistic about these for low-income countries. The emphasis on perceived policy "quality" may also prove very problematic in practice. This judgment is to be based on the World Bank's Country Policy and Institutional Assessment (CPIA), a blend of evidence-based and subjective components the details of which have until quite recently been jealously kept secret by the Bank, and whose merits have been hotly disputed. Finally, the proposals do not address the conflict of interest problem, where the Bank and Fund are acting as arbiters of a country's debt sustainability at the same time as being involved in lending to it. This problem has been reduced, but not eliminated, by the MDRI.

However, there is a more fundamental problem here; it is that debt sustainability is a very slippery concept, and may not be the appropriate one, especially for low-income countries. To place this proposition in context, consider briefly the idea of optimal debt, in the case where this is nonconcessional, and where neither repudiation nor forgiveness is an issue. Then in principle there will be some path for debt which will be optimal given international interest rates and domestic investment opportunities. It would not be worth incurring more debt than this, because the additional investment that could be financed would not have a sufficiently high return to finance the additional cost. Even so, it *would* be possible to incur more debt and still service it; it would be sustainable even if above the optimal level. If borrowing were raised sufficiently further (assuming willing and presumably short-sighted creditors), it would eventually become unsustainable, in the sense that a default would become inevitable. Between the two will be a range of debt levels which are sustainable though undesirable. A key difference needs to be noted between the concepts of optimality and sustainability, and the level of debt that can be carried under each. Optimality relates mostly to the relation between the domestic rate of return and the international interest rate; sustainability to the relation between the growth rate (of GDP, or possibly of exports) and this interest rate.

Now consider the consequences of starting with a given level of debt in these circumstances. A larger debt imposes larger debt service obligations, and reduces the productive expenditure the government can make in future, given its expected future tax revenues. What level of external debt would a government choose to inherit on acceding to power, if it had the choice? The answer, clearly, is none at all, or better still, an indefinitely large volume of foreign assets (negative debt).

How does this relate to the current and prospective circumstances of a low-income country which has been highly indebted, has received debt forgiveness under HIPC, and is eligible for concessional finance? Concessional finance has three characteristics which distinguish it from nonconcessional finance, apart from the obvious one of being cheaper. First, access to it is rationed in the present. Second, access to it will be withdrawn at some point in the future. Hence it will not be possible to roll it over indefinitely. Third, the actual degree of concessionality is unclear, since there could be future debt forgiveness in certain circumstances. Furthermore, these characteristics are not independent. For example, a rapidly growing country would tend to lose access and be unlikely to obtain forgiveness in future compared to a country that remains in a low-income trap. All this makes the concessional case quite different from the conventional one. In a sense, concessional debt is a little like a common form of student loan—also made on concessional terms, definitely repayable if the recipient does well, with some form of forgiveness if the recipient does not. In each case, the financing instrument takes the form of debt in good times, and equity in bad times. The difference between the two is that the terms of forgiveness are clearly spelled out *ex ante* under student loan schemes, but are only determined probabilistically and *ex post* in the development context.

This cannot be an efficient mechanism, either in terms of signaling, or in terms of incentives.

There seem to be four propositions for low-income countries arising from this discussion. The first is that there is no clear way of assessing sustainable limits for external debt. What now seems easily sustainable might prove not to be so if *future* access to concessional finance were quickly withdrawn. What now seems unsustainable might prove unproblematic if there were further debt forgiveness in future. Second, there may be a complete divorce between a country's capacity to absorb aid and its capacity to accept more concessional indebtedness according to any arbitrary rule concerning sustainability, such as the HIPC criteria, or even the more refined criteria now being implemented under the DSF.

Third, if the real purpose of aid is to assist development, then the criterion should be to allocate available aid resources between countries according to their need and capacity to use and absorb these resources. It does not seem helpful to interpose an additional constraint reflecting some alleged limit on debt sustainability as a subsidiary rationing mechanism. Of course, it would be possible in principle continually to vary the grant element in loans so that a level of resource transfer determined by donor willingness and the capacity of the recipient country could be kept consistent with a net present value of debt that obeyed some HIPC-type rule, or country-specific variant of this. But this would be onerous to compute and virtually impossible to implement, as well as seeming to serve no useful purpose.

Hence and fourth, if this argument is accepted, there is little merit in persevering with concessional loans to low-income countries, as opposed to moving comprehensively to a grant mechanism for delivering aid. There are, of course, counter-arguments.

One of the arguments for retaining concessional loans is that they provide a disciplinary mechanism that would be absent under a pure grant regime. However, this is contestable. With concessional finance of the IDA type, for example, the "discipline" is deferred for so long that a different government is likely to be in power before it (weakly) binds. Indeed it is very likely to be perverse, with governments being called to account for the actions of their predecessors, but not for their own. No serious incentive mechanism design would have these properties. A related argument is that, despite this mismatch in time, at least loans—whoever incurred them—act to discipline current government because of the need to cover the associated debt service. But this is a two-edged sword, since the donor community shrinks from enforcing a default on itself. Hence large gross donor flows may provide an illusory degree of discipline. In many respects it is the net flow which constitutes the real discipline, and that would remain under a straight grants system. In consequence, a performance-based grants system could, if desired, provide a more flexible disciplinary device than a system based on loans.

Another argument often made in favor of persevering with loans is that it would require some re-engineering of the International Financial Institutions to permit them to operate on a grant basis instead of a loan basis. However, while this may be an important difficulty as a matter of practical operations, it is hard to accept that it could not be circumvented if the will was there.

V. Technical assistance

The Fund's commitment to providing technical assistance (TA) is substantial, amounting to more than 10 percent of its activity, with more than 40 percent of this directed to low-income countries. It intends the effort both to strengthen countries' capacity to formulate and implement appropriate macroeconomic, financial, and structural policies, and to assist more directly in the design of associated reforms. It acknowledges that providing TA to low-income countries is especially difficult, usually involving "a daunting reform agenda, limited absorptive capacity, weak institutions, only a thin layer of skilled officials and low retention rates for those who are qualified, and lack of equipment, among other constraints" (IMF 2004a, p. 13).

It has been criticized, not least by its own Independent Evaluation Office (IEO: IMF 2005a), for the weak link between TA priorities and Poverty Reduction Strategy Papers, a major shortcoming given that the PRSPs were supposed to become the main vehicle for guiding IMF priorities in low-income countries. This reflects the general lack of a medium-term (multi-year) perspective, as well as a systematic failure of inter-donor coordination in TA activities.

The Fund, reasonably enough, wishes to focus its TA within its areas of core expertise, which are taken to be macroeconomic policy formulation and management; tax policy and revenue administration; expenditure management; monetary policy; the exchange rate system; financial sector sustainability; and macroeconomic, external, fiscal, and financial statistics. These areas, in combination, are taken also to cover the design of poverty-reducing and growth programs, and of debt sustainability analyses. What is rather odd is that this array of capabilities is not deemed to include expertise in analyzing a recipient government's "resource envelope". The IEO, for example, worries that the Fund may have over-promised what it can deliver, "given prevailing resource constraints and its comparative advantage. One example concerns the determination of a medium-term external resources envelope that strikes the right balance between needs, sustainability, and realism... Clearly, these are vital components of the overall strategy, but it is not clear that the IMF is well suited to deliver them" (IMF 2004c, p. 6). It is obviously true that responsibility for this determination rests squarely with the domestic authorities, but that is true for the whole of policy. It seems peculiar that the Fund should feel well placed to advise on macroeconomic policy generally, but not on this very central component of it.

The Fund's Medium Term Strategy (IMF 2005d) proposes to improve the focus and relevance of the technical assistance program by giving the area departments a central role; it also proposes increased use of internal and external evaluation. These steps reflect the Fund's response to the IEO report (IMF 2005c). Going beyond the Fund's own concerns about prioritization, delivery, and monitoring of TA, there are three more general concerns about its activities in this area. Unsurprisingly, they are closely related to each other.

First, there is the problem alluded to previously, that much macro-analytic economic thinking is informed by the study of archetypical economies very far removed from the characteristics of low-income countries. There is tremendous scope for fresh thinking here. To be fair to the Fund, it has recently been active in this area, with a lot of in-house research on low-income countries (see for example Gupta et al. 2004); it has also set out to foster research among academics and others by convening conferences. However, there remains scope for a more systematic attack on the problem of how best to model low-income countries, so that a richer analytic perspective and more focused policy prescriptions can be developed.

Second, there is a need to fill the lacuna previously discussed, as regards the Fund actively helping the governments of low-income countries to explore the "policy space" within which prudent judgment may be exercised. It is for governments to make choices within this space, but many of them require much more structured assistance in defining the prudential limits. In the past, the Fund was able to form a view relatively easily. Many of its low-income clients were outside any reasonable definition of the prudential policy space and more stringency was incontrovertibly required. Now, however, a substantial number of these countries have achieved a real measure of stabilization, and real, though often subtle, policy choices must be made. The Fund will have to work harder to respond to the challenge of assisting governments in these new circumstances. Given capacity constraints within the countries, simply reacting passively should not be the Fund's default position.

Third, much of the Fund's more detailed technical assistance and advice needs to be revisited in the light of empirical findings, and, hopefully, a richer analytic perspective. To give one example, the Fund has consistently advocated the replacement of (highly distortionary) trade taxes by value added taxes which are levied, in principle, uniformly on both imported and domestically produced goods. This advocacy rests on two propositions, first that it is possible to make such a substitution in a revenue-neutral way, and second, that it will result in lower efficiency losses. Both these propositions rest on a modeling framework which presupposes well-functioning markets with good information flows. Neither of these are likely to hold in low-income countries, so the advocacy is based on questionable premises. In fact there has recently been both theoretical work which challenges the efficiency assumption, and empirical work which challenges the revenue neutrality assumption. This does not necessarily mean the advice has been wrong, but it does imply that much more care is needed in formulating it. Similar issues arise in other areas of the Fund's expertise, for example in respect of trade policy.

VI. Conclusion

The name of the IMF's main vehicle for involvement with low-income countries signals an underlying tension. It is not possible to refer to poverty reduction and growth without taking a long view. Indeed, even with sustained high growth, it will take twenty-five years before most of these countries have graduated from low-income to lower-middle income status. Given its expertise, and their capacity weaknesses, it is entirely appropriate for the Fund to sign up for the long haul with these countries. However, the long haul sits uncomfortably with the Fund's lending activities, which are supposed to focus on balance of payments support. Describing a need for development lending as a need for continuing balance of payments support seems a little strained.

Rather than sit astride this uncomfortable fence, it would be better for the Fund to move one way or the other. Either it could move into properly concessional long-term development lending, if that were desired to underpin its roles as adviser, disciplinarian, and gatekeeper. This lending would no longer be described as providing balance of payments support, but be explicitly to support macroeconomic policy management, and would require major revision of the Fund's articles. Alternatively, the Fund could move out of the (revolving) long-term loan business altogether. Of these three options, on balance the last seems preferable. One of the ironies of the debate over the IMF's role in the development arena is that some positions are supported by commentators of extremely different political views. In particular, the view that it should exit this component of its loan portfolio is shared both by those who would like to see a massive expansion in the total net aid flow, and by those who would like to see it taper off; it is also shared both by those who would like to see a retreat by the IMF into a narrow focus on short-term balance of payments issues, and by those who wish to see its current substantial commitment to long–term development questions maintained or even expanded. The concern of those in the last group must be that exit from the long-term loan activity could be used as a lever to press for other forms of reduction in the Fund's role.

Assuming that this can be avoided, there is a strong case for a strengthening in the underpinning of the Fund's technical assistance functions, to develop a more focused low-income analytic perspective, to build its own capacity to assist countries to explore their macroeconomic options, and more systematically to evaluate its technical advice in the light of the outcomes it has induced.

There is also an issue as to the balance between the two objectives specified in the PRGF, and their relation to the Fund's traditional mandate in respect of stability. The desirability of poverty reduction is beyond argument, and it is appropriate for the distributional implications of macroeconomic policies to be examined closely, so that, if necessary, adjustments can be considered, or some form of offset. However, this is not an area that plays to the Fund's strengths, and signing up to it has had costs. Arguably, the Fund has allowed itself to be deflected from the difficult but necessary task of extending its horizon, and examining how macroeconomic policy can best be designed to combine the maintenance of stability with the acceleration of growth. During a recent history where donor concerns have privileged social sector spending over infrastructure, the Fund has too readily acquiesced in a process determining the composition of public expenditure that may have serious adverse consequences for future growth in many low-income countries.

VII. References

Bevan, D., 2005, "The IMF and Low-Income Countries", *World Economics,* April–June, pp. 67–85.

Gupta, S., B. Clements, and G. Inchauste (eds.), 2004, *Helping Countries Develop: The Role of Fiscal Policy*, IMF.

—— et al., 2007, "Fiscal Management of Scaled-Up Aid", IMF WP/07/222.

IMF, 2000, "Key Features of IMF PRGF-Supported Programs", August.

—— 2002, "Evaluation of the Prolonged Use of IMF Resources", Independent Evaluation Office.

—— 2003, "Role of the Fund in Low-Income Member Countries over the Medium Term: Issues Paper for Discussion", Policy Development and Review Department, July 21.

—— 2004a, "Review of Technical Assistance", Office of Technical Assistance Management, February 17.

—— 2004b, "The Fund's Support of Low-Income Member Countries: Considerations on Instruments and Financing", Finance and Policy Development and Review Departments, February 24.

—— 2004c, "Evaluation of the IMF's Role in Poverty Reduction Strategy Papers and the Poverty Reduction and Growth Facility", Independent Evaluation Office.

—— 2005a, "Evaluation of the Technical Assistance Provided by the International Monetary Fund", Independent Evaluation Office, January 31.

—— 2005b, "Policy Support and Signalling in Low-Income Countries", June 10.

—— 2005c, "Conclusions of the Task Force on IMF Technical Assistance", July 12.

—— 2005d, "The Macroeconomics of Managing Increased Aid Inflows: Experiences of Low-Income Countries and Policy Implications", August 8.

——2005e, "The Managing Director's Report on the Fund's Medium-Term Strategy", September 15.

——2006, "Guidance Note on the Exogenous Shocks Facility", January 27.

——2007a, "The IMF and Aid to Sub-Saharan Africa", Independent Evaluation Office, March.

——2007b, "Aid Inflows: The Role of the Fund and Operational Issues for Program Design", June 14.

——and IDA 2004a, "Debt Sustainability in Low-Income Countries: Proposal for an Operational Framework and Policy Implications", February 3.

————2004b, "Debt Sustainability in Low-Income Countries: Further Considerations on an Operational Framework and Policy Implications", September 10.

————2005, "Operational Framework for Debt Sustainability Assessments in Low-Income Countries: Further Considerations", March 28.

————2006, "Applying the Debt Sustainability Framework in Low-Income Countries Post Debt Relief", November 6.

Radelet, S., 2006, "The Role of the IMF in Well-Performing Low-Income Countries", in E. Truman, ed., *Reforming the IMF for the 21st Century*, Institute for International Economics, Washington, DC.

8

Signaling, Aid, and IMF Financial Arrangements for Low-Income Countries

Timothy Lane* (Bank of Canada)

I. Introduction

It is widely recognized that the IMF's primary responsibility in low-income countries (LICs) is to provide a macroeconomic framework aimed at "promoting stability and high-quality growth". This entails advising the countries on the design of their macroeconomic policies, monitoring the policies being implemented, and signaling to donors and other international financial institutions that the policies are on track toward their objectives. While the IMF continues to provide financial arrangements for many LICs—which, indeed, now constitute the vast majority of its borrowers—the primary reason for such involvement is, to an increasing extent, to provide a context for aid and other financing, while its role in directly satisfying these countries' financing needs has increasingly become secondary. The "no-money programs" provided under the Policy Support Instrument (PSI) introduced in 2005 are a limiting case of this trend.

This shift in the IMF's role reflects several important, and related, developments in LICs that underscore the longer-term nature of these countries' needs for financing. One important factor has been the improvement in the macroeconomic performance of many low-income countries: whereas in the past, many of these countries were plagued by short-run balance of payments problems, accompanied by high inflation and other macroeconomic instability,[1] which called for short-term financing, increasing numbers of countries have

* This chapter reflects helpful comments from James Boughton and Domenico Lombardi. The author is responsible for any remaining shortcomings. At the time when the chapter was written, he was a staff member of the IMF. Views expressed are those of the author and do not necessarily represent the view or policies of either the IMF or the Bank of Canada.

[1] See for instance Bredenkamp and Schadler, 1999.

overcome these problems and graduated into the category of "mature stabilizers" (IMF, 2003). At the same time, the experience of fostering economic development during the past several decades calls for humility in tackling the enormous challenges remaining in overcoming poverty through sustainable growth.[2] Whereas in the 1980s and early 1990s the IMF repeatedly provided financing to LICs through the Enhanced Structural Adjustment Facility on the assumption that significant headway would be made during a three-year program period (Bredenkamp and Schadler, 1999), it is now increasingly accepted that progress will require persistent effort over a much longer period—not only through action to remove structural distortions but on a broader front including institutional reform and human capital development which may take a generation to yield results. The focus of international development efforts on achievement of the Millennium Development Goals (MDGs) has brought an increased focus on longer-term objectives together with the expectation of substantial scaling up of aid. A related development is the problem of debt sustainability: the build-up of unsustainable debt in LICs in the 1980s and 1990s, and the succession of debt relief packages provided in response, has led to much greater emphasis on the need for a large share of grants in the financing mix. For these reasons, the IMF's financing—with a maturity of at most 7 years—has become an increasingly minor part of the overall financing picture.[3] It is agreed that, apart from providing financing to cope with exogenous shocks (e.g. related to bad weather, natural disasters, and sharp movements in the terms of trade), the IMF's role in financing low-income countries should be limited.[4]

These changing conditions have led to a substantial reduction in the IMF's financing to low-income countries. In the 24 new PRGF arrangements approved during 2005–6, access was an average of 12 percent of quota, about one-third of the average during the previous 15 years. Moreover, gross disbursements under the Fund's PRGF facility in 2005–6 were about half of the Fund's average 1990–2000 lending to low-income countries; and repayments exceeded disbursements. The PSI further accentuates this shift, with the possibility of a program-like relationship in the absence of any IMF financing. Thus, when the recent Report of the External Review Committee on Bank–Fund Collaboration (the "Malan Report") stated that the IMF should not engage in development lending, it was validating a trend that was already well established (IMF and World Bank, 2007). This trend requires fresh

---

[2] See for instance Easterly, 2002.

[3] The relatively short maturity of the IMF's PRGF financing also implies that it is less concessional than other LIC financing flows, despite its low interest rate of 0.5 percent per annum.

[4] After this chapter was written, there has been an expansion of IMF financing for LICs that are dealing with the effects of the global financial crisis and recession. It remains to be seen how large and sustained that increased financing will be, and the implications for the IMF's signaling role in a low-income country context.

thinking on the institution's role in a context where most financing is being provided by other bilateral and multilateral lenders.[5]

In this context, the IMF's financial arrangements have continued to be used as a framework for other financing. A program establishes a set of macroeconomic projections and associated policies, together with periodic reviews and explicit markers for monitoring performance over time—performance criteria, prior actions, structural benchmarks, and indicative targets.[6] The initial approval of a policy program by the IMF, and thereafter the assessment of whether performance under the program is on- or off-track—usually linked to whether a country retains its access to IMF financing—remain an important signal for other donors and lenders, often called the "seal of approval". Under the PSI, this signal is detached from any actual financing provided by the IMF, but it remains linked to the design and monitoring of a program.

A recent survey confirmed that such signals from the IMF were used by virtually all major donors, albeit not always in a mechanical way, with their importance varying depending on type of institution and type of assistance (IMF, 2005a). Such a seal of approval is particularly important in the context of debt relief, with an on-track IMF program used as an explicit condition for Paris Club restructurings and for debt reduction under the Heavily Indebted Poor Countries (HIPC) Initiative and later Multilateral Debt Relief Initiative (MDRI).[7] The Fund's signaling is more important for budgetary support than for project aid.

A related issue is the role of an IMF-supported program in the volume of aid envisaged under the program, which, if it exceeds aid commitments, may be associated with a "financing gap". The nature and the role of a financing gap is widely misunderstood, with the perception that the IMF determines the amount of aid that may be delivered to an individual country. This aspect of Fund-supported programs thus warrants further discussion.

This chapter explores these two uses of IMF-supported programs: the seal of approval and the financing gap. The remainder of the chapter is structured as follows. Section II discusses the seal of approval, presenting a simple model for thinking about the seal of approval, and uses it to motivate a discussion of the limitations of this approach. Section III discusses the logic of the financing gap

---

[5] This has been stressed most recently by the Independent Evaluation Office in *An Evaluation of the IMF and Aid to Sub-Saharan Africa* (2007).

[6] Performance criteria are formal conditions that must be either observed or waived by the IMF's Executive Board if the country is to retain access to successive installments of IMF financing. Program reviews entail a broader forward-looking assessment of whether the program is on track to achieve its objectives, as well as to confirm or revise performance criteria for the period ahead (which have usually previously been established as indicative targets); structural benchmarks (and in some cases indicative targets—which also often indicate the performance criteria currently envisaged—are used to lay out the contours of such reviews. Prior actions are steps the authorities agree to take before the Fund's management will recommend approval of a financial arrangement or completion of a review.

[7] In addition to completion of successive program reviews, Fund staff often give donors and other lenders assessment letters indicating the current status of an IMF-supported program.

in an IMF-supported program and its limitations as a measure of a country's financing needs. Section IV concludes the paper.

II. The IMF "seal of approval": rationale and implications

A. Basic questions

In considering the IMF's signaling role vis-à-vis donors and other creditors, three basic questions first need to be considered.[8] First, what information is being provided by such a signal, and why is it needed? Second, why should it be the IMF that provides the information—that is, why do donors not collect the information themselves? Third, why should the signal typically be linked to access to IMF financing?[9]

With regard to the first question, an on-track IMF-supported program is widely viewed as an indication that sound macroeconomic policies are being pursued by the country; such an indication is likely to be relevant to donors in deciding how to allocate scarce aid to where it can be used most effectively. Donors and multilateral lending institutions have stressed the need for aid delivery to be accompanied by appropriate policies and institutions in the target countries (OECD, 2005). Broadly, this view is based on evidence suggesting that "aid is effective where good policies are in place" (Burnside and Dollar, 2000)—despite considerable disagreements on the robustness of this evidence (e.g. Easterly et al., 2004), as well as on the specifics of what constitutes "good policies". There is widespread agreement that policies conducive to macroeconomic stability—including stable growth, moderate inflation, and the absence of acute external imbalances—are a key element of policy needed for aid to be used effectively. The need to ensure that aid is disbursed in the context of sound policies and institutions—particularly with regard to the fiscal framework—becomes increasingly important with the continuing shift in the composition of aid from project aid toward general budgetary support.

With regard to the IMF's role in monitoring aid-receiving countries' policies, it is plausible to suppose that there may be benefits both to specialization and to coordination. The IMF, as an institution focusing on macroeconomic policy issues in a wide range of countries, may arguably have a comparative advantage in this area. The basis for this comparative advantage is not necessarily a higher level of technical expertise than in other institutions, or the use of more sophisticated models; rather, it is a large body of practical experience and institutional memory in monitoring policies, including in a context where

---

[8] Cottarelli and Giannini (2002) examine the related issue of signaling as the basis for the catalytic effect on capital markets. Marchesi and Thomas (1999) develop a theoretical model of conditionality as a screening device in that context.

[9] An excellent historical survey of signaling by the Fund is presented in IMF (2004a).

data limitations require both a strong capacity to scrutinize available information and a considerable element of informed judgment. Coordination may be efficient, as it reduces duplication of monitoring effort and helps avoid a situation in which LICs are subject to a plethora of different (and potentially conflicting) monitoring standards. At the same time, though, coordination can be a two-edged sword, potentially adding to aid variability to the extent that aid provided by a variety of agencies is turned on and off in response to the same signal (Collier, 1999; Bird and Rowlands, 2004).

But why has the signal of policies typically been linked to IMF program financing? At times, the concept of burden-sharing vis-à-vis other donors and creditors is invoked; but this should surely not be of critical importance, given that the major members of the IMF are, by and large, the same as those of other international institutions and the donor community. Another possible consideration is that the IMF may be able to obtain greater leverage over policies when its own funds are in play. In general, though, the IMF's leverage—or put otherwise, the recipient country's incentive to implement program conditionality—should depend on the total amount of financing that hinges on implementation, not only on the portion provided by the IMF.

Arguably a more important reason for IMF's financial involvement with low-income countries is the importance of "money on the table" as a way of binding the IMF itself into a monitoring relationship. For instance, the Malan Report noted that "a program was one way of ensuring the Fund's engagement in these countries" (IMF and World Bank, 2007, p. 44). The Fund is likely to devote greater resources to a program country, and its assessment of macroeconomic policies is likely to be undertaken—and taken—more seriously, if they are linked to financing. This rationale is based on the perception that the IMF's fiduciary responsibility to provide its financing on the basis of "adequate safeguards" for its resources (and those of the PRGF Trust Fund) is a stronger basis for its policy assessments than its mandate for broader-based joint assessments of countries' Poverty Reduction Strategy Papers (PRSPs) or its responsibility to provide "firm surveillance" of economic policies.[10] At the same time, because a financial arrangement strengthens the IMF's own incentives to monitor program implementation strictly, it also gives the IMF greater leverage over the policies implemented under the program.

B. A simple model

The foregoing arguments can be presented in a simple model of delegated monitoring under asymmetric information. This model involves three players: the national authorities, the donors, and the Fund. It is assumed that the

---

[10] Such perceptions are in part behind recent steps to strengthen the Fund's surveillance in the context of the Medium-Term Strategy (IMF, 2005c). These steps include clarifying the legal basis for surveillance (the 1977 decision) and establishing a formal "remit-accountability-independence" framework for evaluating surveillance.

authorities and the donors have a broadly shared objective—such as poverty reduction and sustained growth—which depends on costly actions to be undertaken by both: the authorities implement policies that can make aid more effective, while the donors provide aid (which could be either grants or concessional financing). This assumption is of course a simplification: for instance, in practice donors may base their decisions in part on ideological biases or narrow national interests, and the authorities may also be motivated by a variety of political considerations.

The outcome q depends both on policy actions by the authorities, x (such as policies to ensure macroeconomic stability), and on financing, f, provided by donors:

$$q = q(x, f) \tag{1}$$

where $q_x, q_f > 0$; $q_{xx}, q_{ff} < 0$; $q_{xf} < 0$

Suppose that the policy actions entail a cost c to the authorities—capturing the economic, political, and social costs of implementing these actions. Then the cost faced by the authorities is

$$c = c(x, a) \tag{2}$$

where $c_x > 0$; $c_{xx} > 0$; $c_{xf} < 0$

The authorities seek to maximize

$$u = q - c \tag{3}$$

The donors' objectives, in turn, depend on the outcome q as well as on the cost of the financing they provide, f.

$$v = q - f \tag{4}$$

In the case where all information is common knowledge to both parties, agreement can be reached on a combination of financing and policies that will maximize the outcome subject to the costs. This yields a cooperative solution characterized by the following conditions:

$$q_x = \theta c_x \tag{5a}$$
$$q_f = (1 - \theta) \tag{5b}$$

Here, θ is a parameter that may be interpreted as the relative bargaining power of the country and the donors. The conditions imply that the combination of aid and policy action delivered reflects the marginal costs and benefits of each. In this case, there is no need for a third party such as the Fund to be involved.

The cooperative equilibrium characterized by equations (5a) and (5b) requires, however, that the authorities be able to commit themselves to undertaking the policy action x and that the donors can also commit themselves to providing aid, f. If no such commitment is possible, the result is a Nash equilibrium characterized by

$$q_x = c_x \tag{6a}$$
$$q_f = 1 \tag{6b}$$

This implies less aid and less macroeconomic policy effort than in the cooperative solution, since the authorities cannot internalize their ability to catalyze more aid through stronger policies and the donors cannot internalize their ability to induce stronger policies through higher aid.

It may be possible to come closer to the cooperative solution by finding a third party—the Fund—that can monitor the authorities' policy actions and plans. Suppose that the Fund faces a fixed cost of monitoring m which is lower than the cost of monitoring faced by donors. One can visualize this cost as comprising not only the resource costs of staff involved in program monitoring, but also the political "cost" of making a candid assessment of policies that the authorities may not like. Let us also assume that the authorities, but not the donors, can observe whether the Fund is monitoring their policies.

The Fund is also a lender. It provides financing s in lieu of part of the donors' financing (i.e. the total financing provided, and thus the outcome for growth, is unaffected). In the event that this financing is repaid, it carries a rate of return r; the opportunity cost of the financing is b. The fraction of this financing that is repaid, p, depends on the policy action taken by the authorities. Then the Fund lends only if

$$(1+r)p(x) \geq b \tag{7}$$

In the event that the Fund does not monitor the policy action, the authorities will choose their policy action independently in line with the Nash solution x_N as given by (6a). In the event that the Fund monitors, it can observe the actual value of x. Thus it monitors only if the increased amount repaid multiplied by the financing provided by the Fund is sufficient at least to compensate for the fixed cost of monitoring:

$$s(1+r)[p(x) - p(x_N)] \geq m \tag{8}$$

In this setup, the Fund can, in effect, be delegated to monitor a cooperative agreement between the donor and the country. The donors agree to make their aid conditional on the Fund's decision to provide short-term financing, which in turn depends on the policies monitored by the Fund. The financing provided by the Fund needs to be sufficient to give it an incentive to carry out the monitoring, that is, satisfying equation (8).

However, the full cooperative outcome (minus the Fund's monitoring costs) can only be achieved if the macroeconomic policies that influence aid effectiveness are agreed by the country and the donors. If it is the Fund rather than the donors that reach agreement on policies, the outcome depends on how the Fund's responsibilities are specified. Here are a couple of possibilities. If the Fund is given only the responsibility of "lending on adequate safeguards", it may specify a repayment prospect p_s and lend only provided that policies are sufficiently strong to achieve that target repayment:

$$x_s \text{ such that } p(x_s) = p_s \tag{9}$$

This may yield policies that are either stronger or weaker than those that would be agreed between the authorities and donors in the cooperative solution (5).

Alternatively, the Fund may internalize the outcome for the country, q, as part of its own objectives, and bargain over the effort involved in achieving it. This case can be represented as maximizing an objective function depending both on the overall outcome for the country, q, and on the potential financial cost to the Fund:

$$w = q + s[(1 + r)p(x) - b] \tag{10}$$

If the Fund negotiates a policy program with the authorities, the result may be characterized as a solution along the contract curve, given by

$$q_x = (1 - \phi)c_x - \phi s(1 + r)p_x \tag{11}$$

where ϕ is a parameter representing the relative bargaining power of the Fund and the authorities.

This model provides a simple framework for thinking about the Fund's role in providing a signal of macroeconomic policies in aid-receiving countries. First of all, it formalizes the idea that having its own resources at stake "keeps the IMF honest" in its role of monitoring policies and providing a candid assessment of these policies to donors. It suggests that the amount of IMF financing provided needs to be of some minimum size to overcome the costs (which should be interpreted as including political costs) of providing such an assessment. At the same time, it suggests that there may be a tension between policy monitoring geared to the IMF's traditional role of safeguarding its resources (as given by equation (9)) and creating an environment conducive to aid effectiveness (as given by (5a)). This tension is a simplified representation of the tension between the application of IMF conditionality to measures that are critical to the macro-economic objectives of the program over the program period,[11] and the longer-term macroeconomic policies and institutions that may be important to the effectiveness of aid in promoting growth over the longer term.

C. Implications and limitations

First of all, it is important to consider the implications of this model—with the idea that IMF financing is used to "keep the IMF honest"—for the shift to low-access and "no-money programs" (as in the PSI). As the volume of IMF financing diminishes—with low-access and no-money programs—the condition that the IMF's financing be sufficient to provide incentives for the IMF to monitor is less likely to be satisfied. The stated IMF policy is that diminished financing is not intended to be accompanied by any weakening of conditionality; the PSI, in particular, is to carry "upper-credit-tranche conditionality", mimicking the mo-dalities of program monitoring used in normal financial arrangements. However, the logic of the signaling model suggests that reduced financing is likely to be associated with reduced incentives for the Fund to monitor—as reflected a reduction in both the resources devoted to low-income countries and the candor with which program implementation is assessed. To counter this risk, it is important to clarify the Fund's responsibilities (as noted in the Malan Report) and to move ahead with other steps to strengthen the IMF's accountability for its monitoring of countries' economic policies as envisaged in the Medium-Term Strategy (IMF, 2005c) and the 2007 Surveillance Decision.

Another implication of this discussion is that the tension between objectives could be alleviated if the IMF has the ultimate objective such as poverty reduction and sustainable growth as part of its objective function—even while focusing only on monitoring policies conducive to macroeconomic stability—in which case financing by the IMF should be limited to what is needed to give it the incentive to monitor policies effectively. However, it also suggests that, when financing is reduced or eliminated, the monitoring should not necessarily emulate the monitoring mechanism designed to safeguard the IMF's resources: rather, the absence of financing provides an opportunity to improve program design and monitoring in a way that is better tailored to the desire to increase the effectiveness of aid. Recent initiatives to increase the quota share and voice of developing countries at the expense of advanced creditor countries may contribute to such a shift.

At the same time, it is important to recognize the limitations of the model just presented. First, it assumes that implementation of an IMF-supported program

---

[11] This test of "macro-criticality" is prescribed under the IMF's 2002 Conditionality Guide-lines (IMF, 2002).

ensures sound macroeconomic conditions that bring about effective use of aid and long-term sustainability. The large literature on the macroeconomic experience with IMF-supported programs provides mixed results on this premise. There is some evidence that IMF-supported programs in low-income countries have been associated with higher growth, but not with debt sustainability (e.g. IMF, 2004b; Ghosh et al., 2005). At the same time, there are dissenting views in the literature, presenting findings that IMF-supported programs have adverse impacts on growth (e.g. Przeworski and Vreeland, 2000; Barro and Lee, 2005). This questions the premise that policies monitored under IMF-supported programs are highly conducive to translating aid into long-term growth.

Another issue is that, given that donor governments themselves have a major role in the governance of the IMF, they may exert pressure to provide a favorable assessment to justify aid decisions already taken, destroying the value of the signal while perpetuating IMF financing.[12] This issue was stressed in a study by the Independent Evaluation Office, which identified the seal of approval role as a major reason for prolonged use of IMF resources (Independent Evaluation Office, 2002). To the extent that this assessment is valid, it suggests that the IMF's assessments acted more to provide political cover for donors' aid allocation decisions than to provide a signal to guide those decisions. There is also the possibility that bureaucratic politics within the IMF may influence its assessments.

Another key question is the extent to which performance under an IMF-supported program is indicative of future performance—an issue that could not be addressed in the atemporal model presented above. Here, a key element is debt sustainability, which could be viewed as one of the main rationales for IMF involvement in LICs: macroeconomic policies underpinning debt sustainability are important to ensure that concessional financing does not leave the country with an unsustainable debt burden. Evidence suggests, however, that IMF-supported programs in low-income countries have not, on average, achieved fiscal or external sustainability (IMF, 2004b). With regard to fiscal sustainability, an underlying issue is the quality of fiscal adjustment: while evidence suggests that fiscal adjustment is more likely to be sustainable if it is implemented through cuts in current expenditure, in practice it is more likely to be implemented through postponement of investment or through revenue increases (Tanzi and Davoodi, 2000). IMF-supported programs are often designed with the objective of improving the quality of fiscal policy to ensure that fiscal adjustment can be sustained: this is one of the purposes of including structural reforms as an important component of program design, although evidence of whether these reforms do underpin greater sustainability is mixed (Bulíř and Moon, 2005).

As a related issue, program conditionality often in itself is intended in part as a signal of future policies. This idea is found, in particular, in the case of prior

---

[12] Of course, member countries may also press for an unfavorable assessment for other political reasons, which may also weaken the value of the signal.

actions—that is, steps that the authorities have to undertake as a condition for program approval or for completing a program review. In many cases, prior actions are explicitly discussed as a signal of the authorities' commitment to implement the remaining elements of the program (Ramakrishnan and Thomas, 2006). This use of prior actions is, in principle, discouraged under the 2002 Conditionality Guidelines; however, those guidelines are aimed at streamlining conditionality and putting greater emphasis on program owner-ship rather than micro-management—and these are steps that tend to go in the direction of augmenting the importance of identifying suitable signals of future performance. The use of program conditions as a signal requires a balancing of the authorities' costs and benefits of "going through the mo-tions" of implementing certain policies to gain access to IMF financing—provided not only directly by the IMF, but also by donors, as implied by the standard economic theory of signaling (Spence, 1974). In principle, it becomes harder to use conditionality as a signal within a program when a larger volume of financing is tied to program approval—including aid and especially debt relief (as under the HIPC and MDRI initiatives).

In conclusion, while the model suggests that the IMF can play a role in signaling sound macroeconomic policies for the benefit of donors, it also suggests that there may be a tension to the extent that the requirements for aid effectiveness and for repaying short-term financing to the Fund do not coincide. The steps that have been taken include creating an institutional mandate to support sustainable growth and poverty reduction, while detach-ing that support from substantial financing.[13] This suggests that the Fund's assessments should continue to put greater stress on long-term issues, includ-ing debt sustainability, institution building, and the overall policy framework, based on a candid overall assessment and realistically paced progress toward improvements—with correspondingly less preoccupation with the attainment of quarterly targets for macroeconomic aggregates. Fresh ideas are also needed, however, to devise a framework for addressing these issues.

III. The financing gap

An IMF-supported program is predicated on a particular level of financing, both in the current period and in the future. If that level of financing has not already been committed by donors and from other sources, a "financing gap" occurs. The IMF is often (incorrectly) viewed as dictating each country's aid

[13] These results depend on the assumption that both the donors are motivated primarily by longer-term objectives such as poverty reduction and sustained growth in the recipient country. Otherwise, putting the IMF's money at risk may limit donors' ability to pursue ideological or geopolitical motives at the expense of the recipient country's growth—and the shift to no-money programs may weaken that safeguard.

allocation based on its financing needs—with IMF staff presenting donors with a "financing gap" that needs to be filled. Thus, it is important to consider the nature of a financing gap and under what circumstances it can occur.

As a starting point, consider the following basic identity: the volume of financing F_t—which, in low-income countries, typically consists mainly of aid and concessional financing—is equal to the difference between income Y_t and absorption A_t, plus any accumulation of reserves ΔR_t:

$$F_t = \Delta R_t + A_t - Y_t \tag{12}$$

As the simplest and most general level, one may assume that both income and absorption are functions of the policy content of the program, which can be represented by a vector x_t. They also depend on a vector of endogenous variables y_t which (depending on the monetary and exchange rate regime) may include variables such as exchange rates, interest rates, and domestic prices. They also depend on exogenous variables z_t, which, for instance, include economic conditions in trading partners, the terms of trade, and various supply factors.

$$A_t = A(x_t, y_t, z_t) \tag{13a}$$
$$Y_t = Y(x_t, y_t, z_t) \tag{13b}$$

On the basis of these general relationships, a program specifies a set of envisaged macroeconomic and structural policies, $x_t, x_{t+1}, \ldots$ that satisfy identity (12), substituting from (13) given the projected financing $F_t, F_{t+1}, \ldots$. This simply formalizes the principle that a program must be "fully financed". Given this constraint, a program generally tries to satisfy other objectives, including for economic growth.

Within this very simple framework, it is clear that *ex post* there can be no financing gap, since equation (12) holds by definition. If the financing envisaged under the program is not forthcoming, some other variable must adjust. Here, there are three obvious possibilities. One is that the policies x_t, may be different from those envisaged—e.g. government spending may need to be lower, or monetary policies tighter, than planned. A second is that some of the endogenous variables y_t would be different from those envisaged—e.g. the real exchange rate may be more depreciated. Either of these first two possibilities implies that the current account, and thus absorption and/or national income, adjusts. A third possibility is that the country runs down international reserves R_t below the level envisaged. Any of these possibilities imply that the program can no longer be implemented as planned: its macroeconomic framework and related policy assumptions are no longer attainable.

Given the unpredictability of aid, it is very likely that, *ex post*, aid will turn out to be higher or lower than envisaged. But, a central principle of conditionality is that a program is only recommended for approval if it is likely to be implemented (IMF, 2002)—otherwise it makes no sense to monitor the authorities' program implementation. Thus, programs are generally meant to be predicated on realistic estimates of the aid that is likely to be forthcoming. Staff predict aid based on a variety of sources, including donor commitments and other more informal sources of information, and design the program on the assumption that this aid will be spent and absorbed (IMF, 2007b). There is thus a circularity in the notion that the Fund dictates aid through its financing assumptions: the program itself is predicated on a best guess of that financing, so if donors took that as a guide to the financing they were to provide, this would only be guiding them to behave in line with the IMF staff's expectations, including by delivering on their commitments.

So what would be the meaning of setting forth a program in which there is expected to be a financing gap? In the notation above, that would imply a policy program in which

$$F_t^* = \Delta R_t + A(\mathbf{x}_t, \mathbf{y}_t, \mathbf{z}_t) - Y(\mathbf{x}_t, \mathbf{y}_t, \mathbf{z}_t) \tag{14}$$

giving rise to a gap, $F_t^* - F_t$. But since a program with a gap cannot actually be implemented, the financing gap may essentially serve as a rhetorical device to elicit more aid; alternatively, it could serve to persuade the country to undertake more adjustment, taking aid as given. To the extent that such a gap is used successfully to persuade donors to deliver F_t^*, the gap disappears and the program becomes feasible; otherwise, the program would need to be revised to bring it into line with realistic financing assumptions. In practice, neither the financing nor the associated policies is exogenous; determining the volume of financing and associated policies may involve an iterative process, with communication between the authorities, donors, and Fund staff.

Given this logic, programs rarely assume unfilled financing gaps. In practice, they may do so to a limited degree, for instance to draw attention to the need to cover the recurrent costs of investment projects that are already under way (IMF, 2007b). Such gaps are more often posited for future years, for which quantitative macroeconomic performance criteria have not yet been set. But these gaps are generally constrained by perceptions of donors' willingness ultimately to fill them.

An alternative approach to devising financing gaps would be to base them on broader targets. One could, for instance, take as a starting point a target long-run growth rate for the economy, perhaps that associated with the Millennium Development Goals. On the basis of that growth rate, one could devise the associated capital requirements using the incremental capital output ratio (ICOR). Alternatively, one could use the basic Harrod–Domar growth model to determine the warranted rate of growth together with the associated investment requirements and financing needs; such an approach is, however, based on outmoded economic theory which does not stand up to econometric scrutiny (Easterly, 1999). More modern growth literature suggests that growth stems not mainly from capital accumulation, but from productivity gains associated with human capital development and learning by doing; devising the financing needs associated with the latter analysis is a problem for which there is no well-defined solution. But, in addition to these methodological conceptual difficulties, a key point is that specifying a country's financing needs is a counterfactual exercise based on the premise that donors will in fact supply the needs identified; it is thus conceptually distinct from devising a program as a basis for monitoring a country's macroeconomic performance.

Finally, the logic of financing gaps suggests that the IMF should determine the level of aid that a country needs. This approach is fundamentally at odds with the idea that aid is generally beneficial—if only by supporting consumption in the face of widespread poverty—and that one can always devise a suitable macroeconomic program to make effective use of it. In this context, the key question is how aid should be allocated across countries—since some countries are better able than others to use an extra dollar of aid to propel growth. But to address that question would call for an explicitly cross-country analysis of aid allocation, rather than the specification of financing needs and gaps for individual countries.[14]

IV. Conclusions

This chapter has discussed two traditional aspects of the use of IMF-supported programs as a framework for aid: the use of an on-track IMF financial arrangement as a trigger for aid; and the use of the "financing gap" from an IMF-supported program as an indication of a country's financing needs.

The chapter examines the logic of using a Fund-supported program to monitor policies to ensure that they are sufficiently sound to ensure that aid can be used effectively. It uses a simple model of delegated monitoring to illustrate the idea that a financial arrangement can be used as an incentive mechanism for the Fund. In this framework, the amount of financing provided is dictated, not by the country's financing needs, but by the need to give the IMF a sufficient stake in the country's macroeconomic policies to create an incentive for it to provide a thorough and candid assessment of policies. A critical assumption of the model is that monitoring is costly—where the costs can be construed not only narrowly as the resource costs of gathering and scrutinizing data, analyzing developments in economic variables, and so on, but also as the political costs of making candid policy judgments that may not be to the authorities' liking.

While this analysis makes sense of the signaling role of IMF financial arrangements, it also points to its limitations. First, the IMF's financing must be of a

---

[14] A much more important input into the provision of financing to low-income countries is the debt sustainability assessments undertaken jointly by the IMF and World Bank.

certain minimum size to ensure the credibility of its policy assessments; there is a tension between this requirement and countries' diminished needs for the kind of financing the IMF provides—as reflected in the dwindling importance of IMF lending to low-income countries. Second, to the extent that the probability that the Fund is repaid depends on policies differently from the effectiveness of aid—e.g. to the extent that the latter depend on longer-term dimensions of policy—compliance with IMF conditionality is an imperfect measure of policy soundness. Third, to the extent that donors may put pressure on the IMF to approve program financing, the incentive mechanism breaks down. Fourth, to the extent that program conditions may be important, not in themselves but as signals of future policies, this within-program signaling mechanism may break down: as more aid becomes contingent on IMF program approval, the authorities' incentive to "go through the motions" becomes stronger.

All of these considerations thus point in the direction of a different approach, where the Fund has an explicit mandate to pursue the objectives of sustained growth and poverty alleviation. The IMF's mandate would need to be confined to providing a candid assessment of whether macroeconomic policies are consistent with achieving these objectives; no financing would be required. This would require the development of a broader approach to policy assessment than the current one, which focuses largely on observance of performance criteria for macroeconomic aggregates. For this approach to be fully effective, stronger mechanisms for accountability and independence would need to be established—as envisaged for the Fund's surveillance under the 2007 Surveillance Decision.

The chapter also discusses the limitations of the "financing gap" in an IMF-supported program as a guide to foreign aid. It notes, in particular, that a financing gap implies a lack of internal consistency in a macroeconomic program. As generally applied, this concept involves an element of circularity: programs are designed to be fully financed, and thus to generate financing needs that correspond to realistic expectations of the aid that is likely to be forthcoming. In the event that the financing gap were unfilled or over-filled, that would merely mean that the policies, or other macroeconomic assumptions, would need to be altered. A financing gap thus entails a counterfactual exercise, used as a rhetorical device to elicit more aid. This kind of argumentation is giving way to a fuller analysis and dialogue with donors and member countries on the implications of aid, with a view to increasing its effectiveness in supporting poverty reduction in low-income countries.

V. References

Barro, Robert, and Jong-Hua Lee, 2005, "IMF Programs: Who is Chosen and What are the Effects?" *Journal of Monetary Economics*, Vol. 52, No. 7 (October), pp. 1245–69.

Bird, Graham, and Dane Rowlands, 2004, "Financing Balance of Payments Adjustment: Options in the Light of the Elusive Catalytic Effect of IMF-Supported Programs", *Comparative Economic Studies*, Vol. 46, No. 3, pp. 468–86.

Bredenkamp, Hugh, and Susan Schadler (editors), 1999, *Economic Adjustment and Reform in Low-Income Countries* (Washington: International Monetary Fund).

Bulíř, Aleš, and Javier Hamann, 2003, "Aid Volatility: An Empirical Assessment", *IMF Staff Papers*, Vol. 50, No. 1, pp. 64–89.

—— and Timothy Lane, 2004, "Aid and Fiscal Management", in *Helping Countries Develop: The Role of Fiscal Policy*, edited by Sanjeev Gupta, Benedict Clements, and Gabriela Inchauste (Washington: International Monetary Fund).

—— and Soojin Moon, 2005, "Long-Term Fiscal Development and IMF Conditionality: Is There A Link?", in *IMF-Supported Programs : Recent Staff Research*, edited by Ashoka Mody and Alessandro Rebucci (Washington: International Monetary Fund), pp. 245–59.

Burnside, Craig, and David Dollar, 2000, "Aid, Policies, and Growth", *American Economic Review*, Vol. 90 (September), pp. 847–68.

Collier, Paul, 1999, "Aid 'Dependency': A Critique", *Journal of African Economics*, Vol. 8, No. 4 (December), pp. 528–45.

Cottarelli, Carlo, and Curzio Giannini, 2002, "Bedfellows, Hostages, or Perfect Strangers? Global Capital Markets and the Catalytic Effects of IMF Crisis Lending", IMF Working Paper WP/02/193.

Easterly, William, 1999, "The Ghost of Financing Gap: Testing the Growth Model of the International Financial Institutions", *Journal of Development Economics*, Vol. 60, No. 2 (December), pp. 423–38.

—— 2002, *The Elusive Quest for Growth* (Cambridge, Massachusetts: MIT Press).

—— David Roodman, and Ross Levine, 2004, "Aid, Policies, and Growth: Comment", *American Economic Review*, Vol. 94, No. 3 (June), pp. 774–80.

Ghosh, Atish, Timothy Lane, Alun Thomas, and Juan Zalduendo, 2005, "Program Objectives and Program Success," in *IMF-Supported Programs : Recent Staff Research*, edited by Ashoka Mody and Alessandro Rebucci (Washington: International Monetary Fund), pp. 3–16.

IMF, 2002, "Guidelines on Conditionality" (September), available at <http://www.imf.org>.

—— 2003, "The Role of Fund in Low-Income Member Countries Over the Medium Term" (July), available at <http://www.imf.org>.

—— 2004a, "Signaling by the Fund: A Historical Review", available at <http://www.imf.org>.

—— 2004b, "Fund-Supported Programs: Objectives and Outcomes", available at <http://www.imf.org>.

—— 2005a, "Policy Support and Signaling in Low-Income Countries" (June), available at <http://www.imf.org>.

—— 2005b, "Review of PRGF Program Design: Overview" (August), available at <http://www.imf.org>.

—— 2005c, "The Managing Director's Report on the Fund's Medium-Term Strategy" (September), available at <http://www.imf.org>.

—— 2007a, "The Role of the Fund in the PRS Process and Its Collaboration with Donors", available at <http://www.imf.org>.

IMF, 2007b, "Aid Inflows: The Role of the Fund and Operational Issues for Program Design", available at <http://www.imf.org>.

—— 2007c, "Fiscal Policy Response to Scaled-Up Aid" (June), available at <http://www.imf.org>.

—— and World Bank, 2007, "Report of the External Review Committee on Bank–Fund Collaboration" (February), available at <http://www.imf.org>.

Independent Evaluation Office, 2002, *Evaluation of Prolonged Use of IMF Resources* (Washington: International Monetary Fund).

—— 2007, *An Evaluation of the IMF and Aid to Sub-Saharan Africa* (Washington: International Monetary Fund).

Lane, Timothy, 2005, "Tensions in the Role of the IMF and Directions for Reform", *World Economics*, Vol. 6, No. 2 (April–June).

Marchesi, Silvia, and Jonathan Thomas, 1999, "IMF Conditionality as a Screening Device", *Economic Journal*, Vol. 109 (March), pp. C111–29.

OECD, 2005, "Paris Declaration on Aid Effectiveness", March (Paris: OECD), available at <http://www.oecd.org>.

Przeworski, Adam, and James Raymond Vreeland, 2000, "The Effect of IMF Programs on Economic Growth", *Journal of Development Economics*, Vol. 62, No. 2 (August), pp. 385–421.

Ramakrishnan, Uma, and Alun Thomas, 2006, "The Incidence and Effectiveness of Prior Actions in IMF-Supported Programs", IMF Working Paper WP/06/213.

Spence, Michael, 1974, *Market Signaling: Informational Transfer in Hiring and Related Screening Processes* (Cambridge, Massachusetts: Harvard University Press).

Tanzi, Vito, and Hamid Davoodi, 2000, "Corruption, Growth, and Public Finance", IMF Working Paper WP/00/182.

9

Debt Relief in Low-Income Countries: Background, Evolution, and Effects

Graham Bird (University of Surrey) and Robert Powell (IMF)

I. Introduction

The landmark event of the 1980s was the so-called "Third World" debt crisis. In the minds of some observers this threatened the stability of the international monetary system. It certainly spawned a large amount of economic research, led to a sequence of policy initiatives, and, again in the minds of some, recreated a systemic role for the International Monetary Fund to play; a role that had been lost with the demise of the Bretton Woods system. However, media attention focused almost exclusively on the external debt problems of emerging economies in Latin America. With the securitization of Latin American debt under the auspices of the Brady Plan toward the end of the 1980s, media interest in developing country debt abated.

Largely overlooked or ignored by media discussion at the time were the debt difficulties of low-income countries. The characters involved in this dimension of the Third World debt drama were different. The debtors were poor and much less economically and politically significant. The creditors were mainly official rather than private. Thus the default stand-offs between large and powerful middle-income countries on the one hand, and influential and strategically important private international banks on the other, that were a feature of the Latin American debt crisis, were absent in the case of low-income countries.

It is only as the international community began to show more concern with the issue of global poverty that, in turn, greater attention became paid to poor country debt. Mounting public interest was associated with a growing awareness of the "debt burden" carried by many poor countries. The strengthening desire to do something to assist LICs culminated in the United Nations' commitment, in 2000, to achieve the Millennium Development Goals; substantial debt reduction has been viewed as a key element in this endeavor.

This chapter traces the evolution of poor countries' external debt problems and the various policy initiatives that have been pursued in an attempt to alleviate and eventually eradicate them. Early parts of the chapter examine why, in principle, debt problems arise and provide an assessment of which factors have been of particular importance in the case of low-income countries. They discuss in general the range of policies that can be directed toward dealing with debt difficulties and in particular evaluate the economics of debt relief. Later parts of the chapter describe and explain how measures designed to deal with the LICs' debt problems have evolved in the period from the mid-1980s through to the mid-2000s. They also analyze the effects of these measures, and in particular the question of additionality: did debt relief operations result in increased resource flows to LICs? A final part of the chapter briefly considers the future evolution of LIC debt and the extent to which the debt problems of LICs have been adequately addressed. It also explores the role of the IMF in this context.

II. What are "debt problems"? And why do they arise?

What constitutes a debt problem? Although easy to ask, this question is, in practice, very difficult to answer. One way of attempting to sidestep it is to claim that countries have debt problems when their debt has reached an unsustainable level. But this merely begs the further question of the level at which debt becomes unsustainable. Debt sustainability comprises elements of both the ability and the willingness of countries to meet their outstanding debt obligations. A country's ability to meet them will depend on the extent to which it can generate the necessary domestic savings, as well as the extent to which savings can be transferred into foreign exchange. With strong economic growth, saving may be expected to rise. Moreover, with economic growth, a given stock of debt will become smaller in relation to GDP. It is for this reason that debt may become more sustainable even though it has grown in absolute terms. Similarly, the path of a country's debt service ratio (the ratio of debt service payments to export revenue) depends importantly on the pattern of export growth. The rapid growth of exports may enable a country better to sustain a higher level of debt service payments.

Much of the analysis of debt sustainability resorts to projections of economic growth and export growth. But apart from the large measure of uncertainty surrounding such projections which seriously undermines their reliability, with sensitivity analysis often illustrating the wide range of potential outcomes, further difficulties remain. Quickly summarized these include the following. First, there is no a priori way of establishing what levels of key debt ratios demarcate the boundary between debt that is sustainable and that which is not. One is forced to resort to empirical regularities from which there may be significant deviations (Underwood, 1990). Second, although projections may suggest a trend, trade shocks—or other types of shocks—create instabilities about the trend. Negative shocks have been shown to be a significant determinant of debt difficulties (Kraay and Nehru, 2006). Third, a country's ability to manage any particular level of debt depends on new capital inflows, since new inflows allow existing obligations to be met. As a consequence, even with no change in, or improving, debt ratios or debt service ratios, debt may become less sustainable if new inflows diminish. By the same token, an increase in new inflows may make a given amount of debt more sustainable in the short run. Finally, the sustainability of debt depends importantly on the quality of the economic policies pursued by the indebted countries, as well as on institutional and governance factors that may themselves affect the quality of economic policy and, as a consequence, economic and export growth. Good policies and good governance will make any given amount of debt, as shown by conventional indicators, more sustainable, and vice versa.

Beyond the already complex issue of ability, there is the further issue of willingness to pay. At what point will an indebted country become unwilling to make the sacrifice necessary to remain current with its debt-servicing obligations? Ultimately this comes down to an evaluation of the benefits and costs of default; an evaluation that will be made simultaneously by debtors and creditors. After all, creditors will be anxious to avoid a situation where indebted countries opt to default, and they will therefore monitor circumstances to assess the probability of its happening. From a debtor's perspective the benefit from nonpayment is clearly the resources that are not paid. The costs incurred depend on the reaction of creditors, about which debtors (and indeed perhaps creditors as well) will be uncertain. Not unrelated to this, costs will also depend on the value that an indebted country places on its reputation as a well-behaved debtor.

When the uncertainties associated with a country's willingness to pay are combined with the difficulties in estimating its ability to pay, it becomes yet clearer why defining debt problems and measuring debt sustainability are very far from trivial tasks. Indeed, in many respects, they fundamentally underpin the evolution of policies pursued by creditors in dealing with LIC debt.

It may reasonably be supposed that policies to deal with debt are more likely to succeed when they target the causes of the problem. But this gives rise to another difficulty, since the causes of debt problems may be diverse. In principle, there are a number of factors that may be involved. Briefly, debt problems are likely to arise where the marginal productivity of capital borrowed is less than the rate of interest on the loans, where a low domestic saving rate does not rise, and where there is only limited export growth, such that the net foreign exchange position of the indebted country fails to improve. Beyond this, the willingness of an indebted country to meet its outstanding debt obligations will be influenced by the sign and size of net transfers. Where these become negative, debt problems are more likely to follow.

Within the framework presented above, a number of other factors may be identified as influencing the occurrence of debt problems. These relate, inter alia, to the microeconomic management of external financing, the size of the debt that is taken on and the terms on which it is contracted, the conduct of macroeconomic stabilization and adjustment policy, the quality of governance and the level of corruption, trends in the terms of trade, the incidence of negative trade shocks, adverse movements in exchange rates, and the willingness of creditors to provide new loans. As this list implies, debt problems are likely to be caused in part by internal factors, such as economic mismanagement, and in part by external factors such as adverse movements in the terms of trade. They are unlikely to have just one cause.

III. How can debt problems be handled?

In principle, there are a number of responses to a situation where external debt has become unsustainable. It is relatively straightforward to list them. They include default by the indebted country; economic adjustment or productivity enhancing reform in the indebted country to free up or generate additional foreign exchange to pay creditors; economic expansion elsewhere in the world to allow indebted countries to increase export revenue; new financing to provide the resources necessary to meet outstanding obligations; debt rescheduling to provide indebted countries with more time to pay; and debt relief designed to reduce the net present value of the stock of debt.

Listing the options is, of course, the easy part. There are problems with each of them. To a significant degree, policy evolves whereby, having adopted one approach, problems with it lead on to the adoption of another approach, only then to discover the problems with that one.

Default has the downside of being uncoordinated. Its effects will therefore be uncertain. Where serious macroeconomic imbalances exist, early adjustment in debtors may focus on compressing aggregate demand since the short-term options for the expansion of aggregate supply may be limited. In turn this can have a negative effect either on growth, where investment and the capital component of government expenditure fall, or on contemporary living standards, where it is consumption and the current component of government expenditure that decline. Moreover, there may be adverse spillover effects. Adjustment through economic expansion in the rest of the world encounters political economy constraints, since creditor countries will only want to pursue policies that they see as being in their own best interests, and, in any case, unorchestrated expansion may lead to global economic instability and to rising world interest rates. New financing or debt restructuring may alleviate short-run liquidity problems but may either increase or leave unaffected the stock of debt. There is the danger that the time bought by rescheduling may be ill used by debtors, allowing inappropriate economic policies to be retained, with these leading to larger problems in the future.

Debt relief that aims to reduce the stock of debt to sustainable levels may appear to be a way of circumventing many of the above problems. It can be coordinated or controlled by creditors. It reduces the need for extremely contractionary economic policies in debtors and protects long-run growth. It does not require creditor countries to change their own domestic economic policies. It reduces the stock of debt and, if this creates debt sustainability, it removes the need for, and the transactions costs of, quasi-perpetual rescheduling. It may also have a relatively high political payoff for creditor countries at a relatively low economic cost (Krugman, 1990). We return to many of these issues and to a discussion of the problems associated with debt relief a little later in the chapter. But before doing so, and against the background established so far, we move on to explore the causes of debt problems in low-income countries and to examine the way in which the policies of creditors have evolved in an attempt to deal with them.

IV. The build-up of debt in low-income countries during the 1980s and 1990s: underlying causes

A reasonable premise might be that a number of the factors identified above are likely to have contributed to the increasing debt problems encountered by many LICs during the 1980s and 1990s. LICs are frequently characterized by weak economic management, deteriorating terms of trade, and vulnerability to external shocks. These problems formed the basis for the introduction of the Heavily Indebted Poor Countries (HIPC) initiative, co-sponsored by the IMF and World Bank, that was launched in 1996. Is the evidence consistent with this premise?

Brooks et al. (1998) examine empirically, over the twenty years prior to 1996, the main factors behind the increasing debt problem in a representative sample of ten poor countries whose debt burdens where judged to be excessive (Bolivia, Cameroon, DR Congo, Côte D'Ivoire, Ghana, Nicaragua, Niger, Uganda, and Zambia). In all cases the external debt-to-exports ratio was at relatively modest levels in the late 1970s, generally 200 percent or lower. Bolivia's ratio was 260 percent, and in four countries (Cameroon, Ghana, Niger, and Uganda) it was lower than 100 percent. However, by the mid-1990s, the debt-to-exports ratios had increased by at least three or four times in most cases. In Nicaragua, for example, the ratio increased from 200 percent in the late 1970s to 2,500 percent in the early 1990s, while in Uganda, the ratio increased to 1,100 percent. In four other cases (Côte D'Ivoire, DR Congo, Niger, and Zambia), the ratio exceeded 500 percent by the 1990s. Only in Cameroon, Ghana, and Kenya did the debt-to-exports ratio increase at a more modest pace (reaching 300–400 percent). In Bolivia, the ratio reached a peak of almost 900 percent in 1987.

In Nicaragua and Uganda, the two cases with the largest increases in the debt-to-exports ratio between the periods 1976–80 and 1991–5, the ratios rose as a result of a large increase in the nominal debt stock (some 600 percent in US dollar terms) combined with a significant fall in exports over the same period (14–18 percent in US dollar terms). The external borrowing did not appear to have been used to enhance effective export capacity. Indeed, the need for borrowing and rescheduling to support adjustment efforts arose in part because of weak export performance. In contrast, the relative success of Kenya in limiting the increase in its debt burden reflected success in achieving high export growth in parallel with substantial borrowing. In the DR Congo and Zambia, smaller increases in debt stock were less manageable because of inferior export growth. In Bolivia, a debt accumulation of 450 percent was unmatched in the long run by any growth in exports.

In another study Kraay and Nehru (2006) empirically examine the determinants of debt distress in low-income countries over the period 1970–2001. Using probit regressions, they find that a "substantial fraction" of the cross-country and time-series variation in the incidence of debt distress can be explained by three factors: the debt burden, the quality of policies and institutions, and shocks. Further discussion of the debt build-up in LICs may be found in Claessens et al. (1996), Cohen (1996), and Easterly (2002).

The general conclusion emerging from the literature on the build-up of LIC debt is that the causes were varied and interrelated. In most cases, no single factor was responsible. Rather it was a combination of factors that led to the increase in the LIC debt burden. These included (i) exogenous factors, such as adverse terms-of-trade shocks and, to a lesser extent, adverse weather conditions; (ii) the lack of sustained adjustment policies, particularly when facing exogenous shocks, which gave rise to substantial financing needs and failed to strengthen the capacity to service debt; this included slow progress in most cases with structural reforms that would have helped promote the sustainable growth of output and exports; (iii) the lending and refinancing policies of creditors, particularly the lending on commercial terms with short repayment periods by many creditors in the 1970s and early 1980s combined with the nonconcessionary rescheduling terms for most of the 1980s; (iv) the failure of debtor countries to follow clear debt management strategies, driven in part by excessive optimism by creditors and debtors about the prospects for increasing export earnings and thereby for building debt-servicing capacity; (v) the lack of sufficiently careful management of the currency composition of debt; and (vi) political factors, including war and civil strife.

V. The response of creditors to low-income country debt: from rescheduling to relief

Faced with growing debt difficulties in many LICs, official creditors have responded with a sequence of incremental policy initiatives (Evans, 1999; Daseking and Powell, 2002; and Sachs, 2002). The early strategy involved the comprehensive rescheduling of payments falling due combined with new lending packages linked to structural adjustment programs supported by the IMF, in order to try to ensure that the opportunity to adjust was not wasted. By the late 1980s, however, the assumption of ultimate recoverability of much of the debt started to be seriously questioned by many creditors. The accounts of the official export credit agencies (ECAs) came under much closer scrutiny as the impact of earlier lending policies began to be reflected in their net cash flow positions (Stephens, 1999).

As a consequence many aid agencies started to forgive their aid-related debts in the late 1970s and 1980s. Thereafter, various initiatives were launched to deal with official bilateral claims on low-income countries. These led to agreements reached at G7 summits in Toronto (1988), London (1991), Naples (1994), Lyons (1996), and Cologne (1999). The agreements gradually shifted the focus of Paris Club rescheduling techniques from simple cash flow (or program financing) support to more complex mechanisms aimed at slowing the growth of, or reducing the stock of, debt. By 1996, debt relief from multilateral creditors was also placed on the agenda as part of the IMF and the World Bank's comprehensive approach incorporated in the Heavily Indebted Poor Countries (HIPC) initiative (IMF, 2008). In 1999, the HIPC initiative was enhanced to provide deeper and faster relief to qualifying LICs, and to strengthen the link between the provision of debt relief and poverty reduction efforts. By this time, debt relief had become intricately linked to aid allocation and poverty alleviation. The agreement on the Millennium Development Goals and subsequently the Monterrey Consensus, which linked policy reforms in recipient countries to stronger financial support from donors, focused the minds of the international community on various methods of providing additional resources to support countries' efforts to boost growth and reduce poverty. By 2005, the major multilateral and bilateral creditors had agreed to provide 100 percent debt forgiveness to those LICs reaching the "completion point" under the enhanced HIPC initiative, and established the Multilateral Debt Relief Initiative (MDRI).

As implied above, the motivations for the changes in policy are, at one level, reasonably easy to explain. The shortcomings of one approach led to the adoption of another. Initially, nonconcessional rescheduling organized by the Paris Club was motivated by the hope that loans would eventually be fully repaid. Most export credit agencies (ECAs) continued to keep loans to LICs on their books at full face value. The switch toward debt relief that aimed at reducing the stock of debt was largely in recognition of the fact that actual repayments were less than contractual ones. The emphasis was on trying to bring contractual obligations more into line with what was actually happening. It was only with later initiatives that the motivation became that of lowering actual debt service being paid with a view to freeing up additional budgetary resources.

At another level, however, the evolution of debt relief initiatives is a complex story. Not all creditors had similar economic and political relationships with LICs, and policy therefore had to find compromises between them. Individual creditors remained mindful of the budgetary implications of debt operations, in both the near and the long term. And there was also the fact that, even within creditor countries, there were often disagreements between ECAs and aid agencies. The latter often did not want to see an increased fraction of a given aid budget being used to underwrite old ECA credits. The evolution of policy at the international level therefore reflected the outcome of the interplay between these various influences. However, rather than explaining this in detail here, we instead focus on the rationale and effects of debt relief initiatives since the introduction of the Toronto terms in 1988. Upon what economic basis did enhanced debt relief operations seem appropriate and what has been their track record?

VI. Debt relief: the underlying issues applied to low-income countries

There are a number of well-established issues associated with debt relief. Posed as questions they include the following: will debt relief merely reward countries that have taken on excessive debt and have mismanaged their economies; will it absorb scarce resources and redistribute assistance away from more needy countries that may have pursued better economic policies; will it create additional resources and will the additionality be limited only to indebted countries; will it enable indebted countries to reduce debt indicators to sustainable levels and avoid the need for further rescheduling, thereby avoiding future transaction costs? We return to these questions in the next section.

However, the principal theoretical issue associated with debt relief relates to debt overhang. The basic notion here is that indebted countries need to have a certain level of investment in order to generate the economic growth that will eventually make a given level of external debt manageable. But, at the same time, there will be limits on the extent to which they are prepared to sacrifice contemporary consumption. Beyond a point, debt obligations may become so high that the consumption threshold becomes a binding constraint and indebted countries will reduce investment in order to support consumption. The excess debt acts as a tax on investment and long-term adjustment. This, in turn, reduces the future capacity of the country to repay debt.

In the context of the theory of debt overhang, debt relief which is aimed at eliminating the overhang or, in other words, that part of debt that is unsustainable, benefits both debtors and creditors. Debtors can enjoy faster rates of economic growth and can avoid the ramifications of unilateral default. Creditors can similarly avoid the costs on them of default and can increase the probability of receiving further repayment of the debt that is not forgiven.

Debt overhang may be reinterpreted and illustrated by the so-called debt relief Laffer curve, shown in Figure 9.1. The analogy with the conventional Laffer curve is that, by reducing the stock of debt over the range CL, the present value of expected future debt repayments may be increased by strengthening the incentive to pursue investment and economic reform.

A remaining issue, however, is whether the theory of debt overhang is as relevant to LICs as it was to the indebted middle-income countries for whom it was originally developed. There are certainly differences. For middle-income countries external debt was largely private. By 1987, net transfers were turning negative, with the probability of unilateral default rising as a consequence. Debt relief also held out the prospect of increasing the secondary market value of the remaining stock of debt. For LICs, their debt was largely official, net transfers remained positive, and the secondary market was fairly irrelevant. In circumstances where higher levels of debt are compensated by increased inflows of aid, the concept of debt sustainability has reduced meaning, since any level of debt can be made sustainable by adjusting aid inflows. In this context, conventional debt indicators, in themselves, say little about sustainability. Deteriorating indicators could indeed be associated with increased debt sustainability if aid inflows increase more than proportionately. There will be no incentive for indebted countries to default if this carries a high risk of their

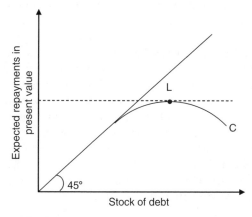

Figure 9.1 Debt Relief Laffer Curve

losing a more than equivalent amount of resources through an induced reduction in aid.

But from a creditor's point of view what is the logic of providing indebted
countries with aid merely in order for them to use it to meet outstanding debt
obligations? It may prevent default, but it may eventually seem neater from an
accounting point of view and more efficient in terms of transactions costs, to
reduce the amount of debt to a sustainable level, and allow aid to be used for
other purposes. This was the conclusion that official creditors seemed to have
reached toward the end of the 1980s. The debate then related instead to the
level at which debt became sustainable, and the extent to which creditor
countries wished to provide low-income countries with additional resources.

VII. The effects of debt relief on low-income countries

A number of studies have attempted to estimate the effects of recent debt relief
initiatives for LICs (Birdsall et al., 2001; Bird and Milne, 2003; Powell, 2003;
Powell and Bird, 2006; Ranis and Stewart, 2001; World Bank, 2003, 2006).
Three issues are important in an assessment of these initiatives. The first is
whether they have resulted in additional resource flows to LICs. The second
is whether they have been associated with an improvement in economic
policy. And the third is whether they have achieved the objective of creating
debt sustainability.

A. Additionality

Has debt relief to LICs been additional? This apparently simple question is, in
fact, not so simple, since additionality may be interpreted and measured in
various ways. One way examines whether debt relief is additional for the countries receiving it, inasmuch as there is no decline in the foreign aid they receive.
A second way is to examine the impact of debt relief on actual net resource
transfers. The recipients of debt relief may not have been meeting their contractual obligations beforehand and relief may therefore be largely "cosmetic."
Of course, it is possible that although actual debt payments decline, implying
additionality in this sense, aid is simultaneously reduced with the result that net
resource transfers decline. A third way of measuring additionality is to examine
the effect of debt relief on all poor countries, and not just those receiving debt
relief. While it may be additional for recipients it may be "subtractual" for other
low-income countries. Financial assistance may be redirected away from LICs
that are not eligible for debt relief according to the criteria of the schemes (or
more generally nonparticipants) and toward participants. A source of confusion
in discussions of debt relief is that while it may be additional according to one of

the above interpretations, it may simultaneously not be according to either one or both of the others.

Elsewhere we have undertaken a reasonably detailed regression analysis of additionality in the case of 45 sub-Saharan economies over the period 1988–2002, a period that covers both pre HIPC and post E-HIPC years (Powell and Bird, 2006). To do this we estimate a model of aid allocation and include into this debt and debt relief variables. Our work, upon which we report more fully below, builds on earlier contributions. Splitting their sample of sub-Saharan African (SSA) countries into high and low debt countries, Birdsall, Claessen and Diwan (2001) find that for the high debt group, debt reduction does not lead to an increase in net transfers. This result is consistent with the claim that debt reduction diminishes the motivation for donors to provide aid. Making a distinction between HIPCs and non-HIPCs among 50 LICs, Marchesi and Missale (2004) find that higher debt stocks are associated with higher net transfers in the case of HIPCs but with lower transfers in the case of non-HIPCs. This supports the suggestion by Bird and Milne (2003) that the theory of debt overhang is less relevant in the case of some LICs where aid has been increased to help them meet their debt obligations. Ruiz-Arranz, Cordella and Ricci (2005) confirm that, over the period 1970–2002, the relationship between net transfers and the level of debt was negative only for non-HIPCs. Looking at a more recent period, however, the World Bank (2006) concludes that HIPC debt relief has been significantly additional to other net resource transfers both in the aggregate and individually for 21 out of 28 countries. Their report notes that net transfers to HIPC countries doubled from $8.8 billion in 1999 to $17.5 billion in 2004, while transfers to other LICs grew by only a third. In an earlier study, Ranis and Stewart (2001) had claimed that the HIPC scheme had an adverse effect on the distribution of financial assistance to poor countries by diverting attention toward debt and away from the overall pattern of net resource transfers, and that this had worked to the disadvantage of LICs not eligible for HIPC relief.

Our own research, alluded to above, discovers a nuanced and time-variant picture of additionality. For the period 1988–94 (pre Naples terms and HIPC) we find that there was a relatively strong negative relationship between the debt burden of SSA countries and overall net transfers. We find debt relief to have had a positive and significant effect on resource flows. In the subsequent period (1995–2002), heavily indebted SSA countries no longer seemed to receive systematically lower resource transfers from aid donors. Meanwhile relief continued to have a significant and positive effect on resource transfers.

Apparently, immediately following the negotiation of the Toronto and, subsequently, London terms, African countries with high debt burdens received reduced cash transfers per capita, when allowance is made for other factors influencing aid flows. This is consistent with the argument that aid donors regarded high debt countries as insolvent and un-creditworthy and as being

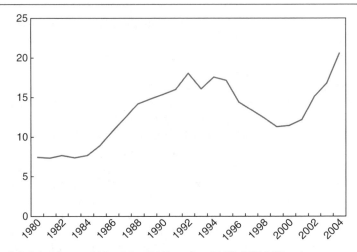

Figure 9.2 Sub-Saharan Africa: Net Aid Transfers (NAT) (US$ billions)

Sources: Organization for Economic Cooperation and Development/The Development Assistance Committee; data are adjusted using the methodology of Roodman (2006).

unable to accommodate additional, albeit concessional, loans. This may in part explain why incremental forms of debt relief were introduced, culminating in the enhanced HIPC initiative, in order to reduce the burden of debt. Perhaps, at this time, creditors saw debt overhang, with its negative incentive effects, as a problem and as a barrier to economic reform. Rather than opting to give additional conventional aid in order to compensate for higher levels of debt, attention focused instead on reducing debt and moving over to the provision of grants rather than loans. The period from 1994 to 1999 saw falling aggregate transfers to sub-Saharan Africa (Figure 9. 2).

Donors then started to pay closer attention to the conduct of economic policy in determining the further allocation of aid. Indeed latterly, aid, in combination with sound economic policy, good governance, and debt relief, has become more broadly perceived as a mechanism for meeting the needs of recipients. Thus in the period following the implementation of the Naples terms in 1994 and the introduction of the HIPC initiative in 1996, there was also an increase in grants to highly indebted SSA countries, and indebtedness no longer seemed to be a significant impediment to resource transfers. Having created an environment in which debt overhang had been mitigated, donors now placed a greater emphasis on policy performance. However, while we find that debt relief under the HIPC initiative has therefore, on average, been additional for those countries involved, we also discover that for much of the period studied up until 2000, aggregate net aid transfers to SSA as a group (including non-HIPC countries) fell in both real and nominal terms. This could imply that the additionality to countries receiving debt relief was at the cost of those not receiving it, although the absence of a counterfactual warns against claiming that debt relief had this causal effect.

B. Economic policy

While the impact of debt relief may, in principle, be judged in terms of its effect on the conduct of economic policy in those countries receiving it, this is, in principle, very difficult to assess. The principal problem is that of knowing what economic policy would have been in the absence of debt relief. Debt relief operations may affect economic policy in two ways. First, there is the involvement of the IMF and the conditionality associated with IMF programs. Second, there are the incentive effects associated with reducing or removing debt overhang which are assumed to encourage economic adjustment and reform. The incentive effects associated with debt overhang will be less pronounced in countries that are experiencing a positive net transfer of international capital. If indebted LICs are also receiving foreign aid which is, in turn, linked to the quality of domestic economic policy, debt relief itself may, at best, have a marginal and indiscernible effect. The quality of economic policy will be largely determined by factors other than the amount of debt relief delivered.

In its most recent evaluation of the HIPC initiative, the World Bank (2006) observes that countries that have passed the "completion point" started out with higher scores on key policy ratings as compared with other LICs and tend to continue to score higher, while countries not yet at the completion point have on average the lowest ratings of all LICs. Those not yet even at the decision point are likely to have still lower ratings. However, this observation does not tell us anything about the effects of debt relief. Rather, it suggests that countries with relatively good policies can reach the completion point, while countries with poor policies not only encounter debt problems but also find it very difficult to emerge from them.

C. Debt sustainability

The rationale of debt relief schemes has been to adjust the stock of debt in participating LICs in such a way that debt becomes sustainable. The acid test of the schemes is therefore whether they have achieved this objective. Again, however, there are hurdles in the way of applying this test, since, as we discussed earlier in the chapter, there are significant measurement problems in analyzing debt sustainability. This having been said, the HIPC initiative defined three eligibility criteria and the effects of the initiative may therefore be evaluated in terms of whether participants have been able to improve their debt situations in terms of them.

The World Bank's recent evaluation is not sanguine (World Bank, 2006). While debt stock and debt ratios were reduced, the Bank observes that "in 11 of 13 post-completion point countries for which data are available the key indicator of external debt sustainability has deteriorated since completion point. In eight of these countries, the ratios have come to once again exceed HIPC thresholds" (World Bank, 2006, p. xi). While the implementation of the MDRI significantly reduced the debt stocks of most completion point countries to well below the HIPC sustainability thresholds, the bottom line is that although the debt relief initiatives may make things better for participating countries than they would otherwise have been, they are not themselves able to contain the rate of accumulation of new debt in future and assure sustainability.

VIII. The future of debt policy: the role of the IMF

The experience with debt relief operations in LICs confirms that they should be seen as only part of a package of reforms. The benefits of debt relief will be offset if other parts of the package deteriorate. Debt relief does not rule out the need for foreign aid in LICs, but experience with debt problems does strengthen the argument for grants as opposed to loans, and does counsel against the uncontrolled accumulation of new debt. Similarly debt sustainability depends on the pursuit of appropriate economic policies. In part, these will involve stabilization measures to keep inflation low and to avoid currency misalignment, but they also include long-term policies aimed at export diversification, good governance, and increased economic efficiency. Even with increasing diversification, negative external shocks will make debt less sustainable and may lead to debt problems in some countries. Not only do shocks have an adverse effect on export earnings but they also tend to affect negatively rates of economic growth and other key macroeconomic variables and thereby make a given stock of debt less manageable.

These general observations imply a continuing role for the IMF in alleviating the debt problems of LICs. For a number of LICs there remains the unfinished agenda of the HIPC initiative and MDRI. The Fund can also help LICs that have received comprehensive debt relief to design and implement sustainable debt management strategies, and to conduct regular debt sustainability analysis, so as to help avoid a renewed build-up of debt to unsustainable levels in future. The Fund can exert an impact on economic policy via conditionality either in conjunction with new lending under the PRGF, or through the recently introduced Policy Support Instrument (PSI) which focuses on the strengthening of economic policy rather than on the provision of new lending. Via these mechanisms the Fund can also exert a beneficial effect on aid flows and the effectiveness of aid. It can also seek to insulate programs of economic adjustment from the effects of negative external shocks. The recently introduced Exogenous Shocks Facility is designed to help do this. Finally, the Fund can be an advocate for multilateral trade reform that seeks to provide a global environment in which LICs can earn foreign exchange via exports. The problem is less in delineating the broad direction that the IMF should be taking than in ensuring that it designs policies that deliver the required effects.

IX. Concluding remarks

Debt relief to low-income countries is "work in progress." Debt relief operations have conferred significant benefits on countries reaching the HIPC completion point and benefiting from the MDRI. Some other countries, however, have not yet been able to emerge from their debt problems. Reducing debt does not guarantee that remaining debt will always be sustainable, and reforms covering the design of economic policy, export diversification and growth, as well as the terms of new aid flows continue to be important for maintaining sustainability into the future. Moreover, although the evidence suggests that early concerns that debt relief would be financed by existing aid budgets and that recipients would lose with the one hand what they were being given with the other have proved largely misplaced, there is evidence to suggest that there has been some overall redirection of financial assistance toward heavily indebted countries. It does not necessarily follow that the resulting distribution of assistance to low-income countries is optimal. Indeed counter-arguments can be made to suggest just the opposite.

The IMF remains a key player in debt relief operations, and, in many ways, occupies a unique position since its role and activities span many of the components of a holistic approach to dealing with the economic problems that LICs face, of which unsustainable levels of external debt may be one. The Fund is often an LIC creditor, but it can also exert an influence over the design of economic policy in LICs, on aid flows, and on contingency financing. Recent reforms adopted by the Fund are a positive step but only time will tell how effective they are.

X. References

Bird, Graham, and Alistair Milne, 2003, "Debt Relief for Low Income Countries: Is It Effective and Efficient?" *World Economy*, Vol. 26, No. 1, pp. 43–59.

Birdsall, Nancy, Stijn Claessens, and Isaac Diwan, 2001, "Will HIPC Matter? The Debt Game and Donor Behavior," Carnegie Endowment for International Peace Economic Reform Project Paper 3, Washington.

Brooks, Ray, Mariano Cortes, Francesca Fornasari, Benoit Ketchekman, Ydahlia Metzgen, Robert Powell, Saqib Rizavi, Doris Ross, and Kevin Ross, 1998, "External Debt Histories of Ten Low-Income Developing Countries: Lessons from Their Experience," IMF Working Paper 98/72 (Washington: International Monetary Fund).

Claessens, Stijin, Enrica Detragiache, Ravi Kanbur, and Peter Wickham, 1996, "Analytical Aspects of the Debt Problems of Heavily Indebted Countries," in *External Finance for Low-Income Countries*, eds. Zubair Iqbal and Ravi Kanbur, pp. 21–48 (Washington: International Monetary Fund).

Cohen, Daniel, 1996, "The Sustainability of African Debt," World Bank Policy Research Department Working Paper No. 1691.

Daseking, Christina, and Robert Powell, 2002, "From Toronto Terms to Enhanced HIPC Initiative: A Brief History of Debt Relief for Low-Income Countries," *International Economic Policy Review*, Vol. 2, pp. 39–58.

Easterly, William, 2001, "Think Again: Debt Relief," *Foreign Policy*, 127, pp. 20–6.

——2002, "How Did Highly Indebted Countries Become Highly Indebted? Reviewing Two Decades of Debt Relief," *World Development*, Vol. 30, No. 10, pp. 1677–96.

Evans, Huw, 1999, "Debt Relief for the Poorest Countries: Why Did It Take So Long?" *Development Policy Review*, Vol. 17, No. 3, pp. 267–79.

IMF, 2008, "Debt Relief Under the Heavily Indebted Poor Country (HIPC) Initiative," IMF Factsheet, March, Washington.

Kraay, Aart, and Vikram Nehru, 2006, "When Is External Debt Sustainable?" *The World Bank Economic Review*, Vol. 20, pp. 341–65 (Washington: World Bank).

Krugman, P., 1990, "Debt Relief is Cheap," *Foreign Policy*, 80, pp. 141–52.

Marchesi, Silvia, and Alessandro Missale, 2004, "What Motivates Lending and Aid to HIPCs?" Working Paper Series, Centro Studi Luca d'Agliano, No. 189 (Milan, Italy).

Powell, Robert, 2003, "Debt Relief, Additionality, and Aid Allocation in Low Income Countries," IMF Working Paper 03/175 (Washington: International Monetary Fund).

——and G. Bird, 2006, "Aid and Debt Relief in Africa: Have They Been Substitutes or Complements?" processed (Washington: International Monetary Fund).

Ranis, G., and F. Stewart, 2001, "The Debt-Relief Initiative for Poor Countries: Good News for the Poor?" *World Economics*, Vol. 2, No. 3, pp. 111–24.

Roodman, David, 2006, "An Index of Donor Performance," Center for Global Development Working Paper 67 (revised November 2006).

Ruiz-Arranz, Marta, Tito Cordella, and Luca Antonio Ricci, 2005, "Debt Overhang or Debt Irrelevance? Revisiting the Debt Growth Link," IMF Working Paper 05/223 (Washington: International Monetary Fund).

Sachs, Jeffrey, 2002, "Resolving the Debt Crisis of Low Income Countries," *Brooking Papers on Economic Activity*, Vol. 33, Issue 2002-1, pp. 257–86.

Stephens, Malcolm, 1999, *The Changing Role of Export Credit Agencies* (Washington: International Monetary Fund).

Underwood, John, 1990, "The Sustainability of International Debt," manuscript, World Bank.

World Bank, 2003, *The Heavily Indebted Poor Countries (HIPC) Debt Initiative: An OED Review* (Washington: World Bank).

World Bank, 2006, *Debt Relief for the Poorest: An Evaluation Update of the HIPC Initiative*, Independent Evaluation Group (Washington: World Bank).

10

The Role and Performance of the IMF in Aid to Low-Income Countries: Lessons from Evaluation

Joanne Salop* (Joanne Salop Consulting)

I. Introduction

A recent evaluation by the Independent Evaluation Office of the IMF examined the role of the IMF in aid to sub-Saharan African countries.[1] Its analysis and findings provided an inside look at how the IMF actually implemented an important initiative—the transformation of the Enhanced Structural Adjustment Facility (ESAF) into the Poverty Reduction and Growth Facility (PRGF). Much of the evaluation is relevant to the subjects of this book. Hence the inclusion of this chapter, which gives an overview of the evaluation's findings and conclusions.

The evaluation covered 1999–2005. This was a time of improving macroeconomic performance in much of sub-Saharan Africa (SSA), with increasing growth and decreasing inflation. It was a time when aid to SSA recovered from earlier declines, debt relief gained momentum, and donors began to move to multi-donor budget support. It was a time when the Poverty Reduction Strategy (PRS) process and the HIPC Initiative were mainstreamed within the IMF and the

* The author would like to thank IEO management and staff for their comments on an earlier draft of this chapter, especially T. Bernes, J. Hicklin, M. Berndt, and S. Standley—without implicating them in any way. All views on the interpretation of the evaluation's analysis, findings, and conclusions as set out in this chapter—and all errors—are the sole responsibility of the author, who was the IEO project leader for the evaluation. The evaluation team included M. Berndt, M. Kaufman, S. Kayizzi-Mugerwa, S. Standley, and T. de Vaan.

[1] See Independent Evaluation Office (2007). The evaluation was initiated in late 2005, and the report was submitted to IMF Executive Directors at the end of January 2007. Executive Directors discussed the report along with the IMF management and staff responses—as well as a further comment by the IEO—on March 5, 2007. The package was subsequently published verbatim, with translations of the report available in French and Portuguese. See <http://www.ieo-imf.org/eval/complete/eval_03122007.html>.

World Bank. It was a time—in late 1999—when the IMF replaced the ESAF with the PRGF as its primary lending instrument for low-income countries. Much heralded at its introduction, the PRGF was advertised as a new way of working, building on the openness of the PRS process, and involving more direct measures for accelerating poverty reduction and growth and for identifying the associated financing requirements.

As the above changes unfolded during the period, variations on long-standing criticisms of the IMF's work in SSA emerged, with three providing a point of departure for the evaluation's analysis of the underlying facts and policies. The first was that IMF-supported programs blocked the use of available aid to SSA through overly conservative macroeconomic programs. The second was that such programs lacked ambition in projecting, analyzing, and identifying opportunities for the use of aid inflows to SSA countries, which may in turn have tempered donors' actual provision of aid. The third was that IMF-supported programs did little to address poverty reduction and income distributional issues despite institutional rhetoric to the contrary.

In considering the validity (or not) of this critique, the evaluation analyzed the facts of IMF programs in relation to IMF policies and pronouncements. In gathering the facts, the evaluation utilized internal IMF data and documents to which the IEO had privileged access because of its institutional mandate and responsibilities. In assembling the relevant policy framework, it started with IMF Board-approved policies and management's translations of Board decisions into operational guidance to staff. IMF communications, through management and senior staff speeches, press releases, articles, and correspondence with newspapers, were also considered as important channels for articulating IMF positions and informing external audiences about what the IMF had undertaken to do. At various stages, the evaluation team sought the views and inputs of stakeholders—both formally and informally—inside and outside the Fund.

In the event, the evaluation found major differences in perceptions about both what the institution had committed to do on aid and poverty reduction—even among IMF Executive Directors and senior staff—and what it actually did in PRGF programs. Internally, the differences were due to several factors, starting with a lack of consensus about the IMF's policies and role in low-income countries among members of the Board. In addition, turnover in IMF senior management and staff deprived the institution of the leadership on the aid and poverty reduction agenda that had underpinned the PRGF's introduction. This loss of leadership was also important for working-level staff, some of whom—like some Board members—questioned whether and how the Fund should be engaged with low-income countries.

Externally, official IMF communications blurred rather than clarified the institution's commitments and accountabilities on aid and poverty reduction—given concerns about the aforementioned criticisms. Meanwhile, IMF partnerships with the World Bank in support of the PRS process, global monitoring of policies and actions for achieving the Millennium Development Goals (MDGs), and related initiatives provided convenient vehicles for the IMF to showcase its commitment to poverty reduction and the other MDGs. However, these initiatives were more aspirational than operational for the Fund, saying little about its institutional commitments or actions at the country level. The result was mixed messages about the appropriate benchmarks for assessing IMF operational performance.

Against this background of ambiguity and confusion, the evaluation focused narrowly on programs supported by the PRGF—in an attempt to sharply distinguish IMF policies, accountabilities, and operational performance from those of other partners, including the Bank. It concentrated on aid—the principal source of external financing for most SSA countries—and in particular on how PRGFs interfaced with country recipients and donors in shaping the provision and use of aid in the pursuit of poverty reduction and other development goals. The PRGF lens yielded a significant body of documentary evidence for cross-country examination and evaluation, covering 29 SSA countries during the 1999–2005 evaluation period.[2]

The evaluation relied on data from several sources. The first was an unpublished IMF internal database for PRGF programs.[3] These data were used in the evaluation's empirical analyses of the SSA countries in the evaluation sample and the non-SSA countries in the evaluation control group. The second was internal documentary and staff-interview evidence for desk reviews of about half the sample countries. These desk reviews permitted the team to investigate in more depth some of the findings emerging from the evaluation's more aggregative empirical work. The third involved country case studies—of PRGF programs in Burkina Faso, Ghana, Mozambique, Rwanda, Tanzania, and Zambia—involving extensive in-country interviews and meetings with the authorities, donors and other partners, and civil society representatives. Finally, the evaluation team surveyed the authorities, donors, civil society, and the staff of the African Development Bank, the United Nations Development Programme, the World Bank, and the IMF.

The remainder of this chapter distills key points from the evaluation. Sections II–IV summarize the evaluation evidence with respect to the three

---

[2] The evaluation's focus on 1999–2005 was selected to coincide with the PRGF period, while avoiding operations that were still in progress, in line with the IEO's mandate not to interfere with ongoing operations. This prohibition is also important for the IEO's independence and perceptions thereof, which could be compromised if the IEO took positions on ongoing operations and then subsequently evaluated those same operations on their completion.

[3] The database—Monitoring of Fund Arrangements (MONA)—includes program targets (and selected projected and actual variables) associated with the use of Fund resources. It includes data on 600 ESAFs/PRGFs, between 1993 and 2005, which were used for the evaluation's empirical analysis. See Annex B of Independent Evaluation Office (2007) for further details. See also Berndt (2007).

criticisms set out above. Section V reports on the evaluation's analysis of communications. Section VI presents conclusions and a brief postscript, taking into account follow-up within the IMF through the end of 2007, when this chapter was prepared.

II. Accommodation of aid in PRGF program design

In assembling the evidence, the evaluation focused on the implications of the design of PRGF-supported programs—and the associated macroeconomic targets—for the accommodation of aid. This focus provided a basis for assessing external criticisms that the IMF "blocked" the full use of available donor funding. In investigating this allegation, the evaluation looked across countries at how anticipated changes in aid mapped into bottom-line changes in *programmed* levels of the current account (as a measure of the change in programmed levels of net imports) and fiscal deficits (as a measure of the change in programmed levels of net fiscal spending). It also looked at how programs dealt with uncertainties in the aid forecast, especially through the design of "automatic adjusters" for reacting to unanticipated shortfalls or windfalls in aid inflows within the program period.

As detailed below, the evaluation found that macroeconomic stability issues were paramount in the design of PRGF programs, including with respect to the implications for the aggregate use of aid. PRGFs did not take into account sectoral issues, related to the composition of aid or their implications for growth, poverty reduction, or program design. PRGF-supported macroeconomic programs generally accommodated the use of incremental aid, or not, depending on a country's external position (as measured by its initial stock of international reserves), and its internal position (as proxied by the inflation rate). In line with this finding, the evidence also showed that as SSA macroeconomic performance improved over the period, the accommodation of aid in SSA PRGFs increased and the stance of PRGF automatic adjusters eased.

The evaluation found that these staff practices were broadly consistent with Board-approved policy on the accommodation of aid, management guidance, and staff inclinations—though often at odds with the preferences of the IMF's civil society and other critics. However, neither the practices nor the policies were openly communicated to donor partners and civil society stakeholders—even in cases when civil society specifically asked staff about them. The evaluation concluded that these findings helped to explain why some outside observers perceived the Fund as "blocking" the use of aid: PRGFs in countries with reserve levels below and/or inflation rates above the respective thresholds were likely to program the saving of at least part of additional aid.

A. Current account adjustment

The evaluation's empirical analysis found reserves in the 2–3 months-of-imports range to be the observed threshold for determining whether/how much incremental aid could be "absorbed"—that is, whether increased aid was programmed to be used to expand the current account deficit or to increase reserves.[4] For countries with reserve stocks above the threshold, incremental aid was reflected in higher programmed levels of net imports—and the associated macroeconomic variables that would generate such outcomes—while for countries with reserve stocks below the threshold, incremental aid did not translate into such increases.

The evaluation found that on average, SSA PRGFs called for less current account adjustment than had SSA ESAFs. As late as the second half of the 1990s, most ESAFs called for significant current account adjustment in the initial program year, but PRGFs did not call for such adjustment. The evidence points to two main factors for the difference between the two periods—increased expectations regarding aid inflows for the initial program year and higher initial reserve stocks—both of which translated into higher import levels. Abstracting from these two factors, the evaluation found no evidence of an independent shift over time in program design with respect to the programmed absorption of increased aid.

B. Fiscal adjustment

Inflation was identified as a major driver of cross-country differences in programmed spending of incremental aid, in part proxying the role played by domestic debt and related considerations. According to the evaluation's empirical analysis, countries with inflation rates below a threshold in the 5–7 percent range generally could spend the bulk of anticipated aid increases in the form of increased fiscal deficits; whereas, countries with inflation rates above this threshold generally could spend significantly less of such increases. Similar to the findings on current account adjustment, secular improvements in domestic macroeconomic performance drove reduced fiscal adjustment in PRGFs, and in turn greater accommodation of aid—with no evidence of an independent shift in program design.

These findings were broadly corroborated by the evaluation's desk reviews and case studies and also by the evaluation's interview and survey evidence. Consistent with Fund policy on single-digit inflation and the spending and absorption of aid, program documents frequently cited the control of inflation as a factor in explaining program design, especially the setting of monetary and fiscal targets.[5] Desk reviews showed that domestic debt

---

[4] See IMF (2005a). See also Berg et al. (2007).   [5] See IMF (2005b).

considerations loomed large in PRGFs, with many programs—such as those in Ghana and Mozambique among the evaluation case studies—limiting domestic financing of the government amid concerns about inflation, debt sustainability, and private-sector crowding out. Interviews with staff—and the results of the evaluation survey—confirmed that concerns about inflation and debt were key drivers of macroeconomic program design.

C. Automatic adjusters

The evaluation also examined PRGF programs to see how they dealt with "aid surprises," both positive and negative. Almost all SSA PRGFs include automatic "adjusters" to deal with unanticipated aid windfalls or shortfalls. Such adjusters set out the pre-programmed modification of targets affecting the degree of current account and/or fiscal adjustment; they typically cover six-month periods, with longer-term implications for program design taken up at the next review.[6] Within this short-term horizon, adjusters were generally calibrated toward macroeconomic prudence, with full savings of aid windfalls and only partial financing of shortfalls. The evidence indicated that as country performance improved over the years, and with that improvement the reduced rates of current account and fiscal adjustment noted above, the calibration of the automatic adjusters also eased. In the evaluation's case study countries, for example, such easing afforded more spending of windfalls in Burkina Faso, Ghana, Mozambique, and Tanzania and more financing of shortfalls in Mozambique, Rwanda, and Tanzania.

The evaluation found adjusters to be a major source of controversy among civil society critics of the IMF—in part because of poor communications between Fund staff and civil society representatives. The Fund failed to communicate both the limited time frame to which the adjusters applied and their evolution over time in line with country performance, while civil society representatives read PRGFs' legalistic language on adjusters as clear evidence of aid blocking. For example, Mozambique's program adjusters—which called for the saving of aid inflows above programmed levels—were interpreted by civil society critics as a way for the Fund to directly *block* the use of aid, while Fund staff saw them as a way to manage the short-term macroeconomic implications of volatile aid flows. Subsequently, the formulation of the adjusters was changed to allow for full spending of aid windfalls, linked to priority poverty-reducing expenditures—but the civil society representatives had not been informed about the changes, despite efforts on their part to find out from Fund staff.

---

[6] See IMF Policy Development and Review Department (2006a).

III. Forecasting, analysis, and mobilization of aid

The evaluation examined PRGFs' analysis of, and impact on, aid flows. This examination provided a basis for considering critics' concerns that IMF actions (or lack thereof) adversely influenced the level of aid. Consistent with the civil society critique, the evaluation found that PRGFs neither set ambitious aid targets nor identified additional aid opportunities where absorptive capacity exceeded projected aid inflows. It found that PRGF aid forecasts were unbiased for the immediate program period, but overly conservative for programs' outer-years, although the latter showed signs of adapting to changing aid trends. IMF staff did little to analyze additional policy and aid scenarios or to share the findings of any such analysis with the authorities and donors. Nor were they proactive in mobilizing aid resources, a topic where the IMF Board remained divided and IMF policy—and operational guidance to staff—was unclear. On the other side, the evaluation found strong evidence that PRGFs catalyzed aid through their macroeconomic assessment and support for country efforts to improve the underlying macroeconomic environment and fiscal governance.

A. Forecasting aid flows

PRGF aid forecasts have long concerned IMF critics, who saw them as unnecessarily conservative with a chilling effect on public spending and donor aid plans.[7] The evaluation found that PRGF aid forecasts were generally accurate (or slightly optimistic) for the program period one year ahead,[8] but under-predicted aid in the *outer*-years. The under-prediction, in turn, seems to have reflected recognition lags about the changing aid patterns in PRGF aid forecasts. During the ESAF era, aid to SSA countries (and to other low-income countries) had typically tapered down over the medium term. But in the PRGF era, rather than tapering down, aid outcomes in SSA PRGF countries increasingly stayed flat. This opened up gaps between actual levels of aid and what the respective PRGFs had projected several years before. The evaluation did find some evidence suggesting that PRGF projections have begun to catch up with the changing trends in aid tapering, with the evaluation's case studies of five major aid recipients—Burkina Faso, Ghana, Mozambique, Rwanda, and Tanzania—showing a shift in 2005–6 with respect to reduced tapering of projected aid compared with previously, and even increases in some cases, reflecting improved country macroeconomic conditions and aid prospects.

---

[7] See, for example, Oxfam International (2003).
[8] This finding was not new to the evaluation, but the evaluation's analysis did reaffirm it. See OECD Development Assistance Committee (2005).

The evaluation found little in PRGF Board documents about the derivation of the aid forecast and its underlying assumptions. PRGF documents alluded to the degree of donor support, noting the importance of good country performance in sustaining donor flows and aid predictability, the need for improvements in donor coordination, and—during the early part of the PRGF period—the desirability of reducing aid dependence. But in-depth discussion of how the forecast was actually made—along with key assumptions—was rare. This lack of transparency meant that readers could not understand (or challenge) the basis for key program assumptions. Nor could they use Fund documents to track donor actions against promises—although there have been good-practice exceptions, where quarterly aid projections and actuals were included in PRGF documents, as for example in the Tanzania program.

B. Analyzing aid absorptive capacity

Looking behind PRGF Board documents into the supporting documentation in the staff files, the evaluation also examined the staff's analysis of aid absorptive capacity. In line with the earlier discussion on the accommodation of aid, it found explicit attention to macroeconomic issues. In some cases, the documents also considered "Dutch Disease" and competitiveness risks, which were generally found not to be a concern for the forecast levels of aid inflows, and accordingly did not affect the proposed accommodation of aid suggested by the country's reserve stock and inflation rate. But there was no analysis of aid absorptive capacity constraints or availabilities in education, health, or infrastructure, notwithstanding the obvious cross-sectoral implications for competitiveness, the supply response, and growth, for example, of developments in infrastructure.

But even for macroeconomic issues, there was no systematic analysis of absorptive capacity for potentially *higher* levels of aid than the aid forecast underpinning the program—or "alternative scenarios." PRGF analysis was grounded in a single aid forecast, considered by staff to be the most likely scenario. This single-scenario approach was consistent with IMF policy, but lacking in clarity, in part reflecting differences of views among Fund Executive Directors and in part reflecting the conflation of staff work on PRGFs on the one hand and on Poverty Reduction Strategy Papers (PRSPs) and Article IV consultations on the other. For example, during the 2004 and 2005 Board discussions of PRSP implementation, Executive Directors had considered how "alternative scenarios" could help to bridge gaps between realism and ambition in national Poverty Reduction Strategies and provide a possible basis for the scaling up of aid at the country level.[9] They "concurred that Fund staff should help those countries that sought assistance in preparing such

[9] See IMF (2004a) and IMF (2005c).

scenarios." However, there was no consensus in the Board for including such alternative scenarios in PRGF program requests and reviews—a distinction that was not always clear to Fund observers.

C. Mobilizing aid

The evaluation looked at the Fund's approach to the mobilization of aid, especially the question of its possible role in seeking expanded levels of donor assistance. Of course, given that Fund staff did not do the underlying analysis of aid absorptive capacity, as discussed above, they were not in a position to carry out informed discussions about possibly higher levels. Nor, according to the survey results, did the authorities see much attention to it—either in the Fund's dialogue with donors or in its dialogue with them on PRGF design. Donors were even more negative on the question of the importance that Fund teams attached to different aid (and policy) scenarios. And they gave low marks for Fund staff proactivity in engaging with them on aid issues both one-on-one and in formal and informal meetings. Where donors gave much higher marks was on the Fund's macroeconomic assessment, which most reported as playing a catalytic role in their own aid decisions about aid commitments and disbursements.[10]

In interpreting these findings, the evaluation noted their broad consistency with IMF policy, which supports the PRGF's catalytic role in fundraising but which is far more cautious on a staff "mobilization" role. Whether the latter is authorized or not depends on the underlying function—with *advice on aid* an acceptable role but *advocacy for aid*, not. The evaluation also highlighted the unresolved differences in views among Executive Directors on this topic, with many calling for a narrow scope in which the Fund can analyze, advise, and catalyze aid "based on sound assessments of financing gaps and macroeconomic implications of aid flows . . . [and others preferring] . . . a broader role of the Fund, including in promoting and coordinating aid inflows for MDG purposes."[11]

IV. PRGF key features

The evaluation also explored other dimensions of PRGF programs, in particular how actual practice compared with institutional undertakings about the "key features" meant to distinguish the PRGF from the ESAF.[12] As detailed below, the evaluation found the Fund's best performance on its work with governments on fiscal governance and domestic revenue mobilization, two

---

[10] See IMF (2005d).   [11] See IMF (2004b).
[12] See IMF (2000). See also IMF Policy Development and Review Department (2000).

areas very close to the institution's core mandate. The worst was on normative financing for pro-poor and pro-growth programs, where the original thinking had been that the PRGF would highlight financing gaps. But—in line with the above discussion of alternative scenarios and the mobilization of aid—this did not happen. In between were the surprising finding that PRGFs helped to safeguard government spending for pro-poor programs more than for pro-growth programs and the Fund's mixed performance on poverty and social impact analysis (PSIA).

Taken as a whole, the IMF implemented the "key-features" agenda when the required action either was in line with its core macro mandate (as in fiscal governance) or did not challenge the boundaries of that mandate and was consistent with other Fund initiatives, such as HIPC (as in protecting pro-poor spending out of a programmed level of overall spending). It did not implement those features that involved an analysis of alternative financing scenarios or the consideration of the supply-side nexus between aid and growth, and in turn the implications for macroeconomic program design. Nor did it pro-actively manage the interface with the World Bank on the growth agenda, aid scenarios, or the analysis of poverty and social impacts.

A. Pro-poor and pro-growth budgets

When the PRGF was first introduced, the expectation was that it would help countries to develop budgets that were more "pro-poor and pro-growth."[13] In the event, the evaluation found that the Fund did a better job of supporting spending for pro-poor programs, in health and education, than it did on pro-growth programs, for example in infrastructure. The evaluation concluded that Fund staff monitored compliance with HIPC commitments, which generally directed debt service savings to health and education and related programs and through that monitoring helped to protect pro-poor spending. Pro-growth spending programs, such as in infrastructure, fared less well in PRGFs, largely because they were less protected by countries' HIPC-related undertakings.

More generally, the evaluation found that the Fund did little to take into account spending composition issues—especially between the social sectors and infrastructure—despite the relevance of that composition for the economy's supply-side response, growth, and in turn the design of the macroeconomic program on the one hand and poverty reduction on the other.[14] Here, the evaluation argued *not* that the Fund should duplicate or displace the work of the World Bank on the composition of public expenditures and aid,[15] but rather that it should be a more active and engaged partner with the Bank—and user and

---

[13] See IMF (2000).   [14] See Bevan (2005), and Foster and Killick (2006).
[15] See World Bank (2005). See also Estache (2006).

requestor of timely analysis—in these and other areas of material relevance to its own work, in line with the agreed division of labor between the two institutions.

B. External financing needs for pro-poor and pro-growth budgets

While staff did encourage countries to adhere to their HIPC commitments on pro-poor spending, the evaluation found they did little to signal the incremental aid needs for financing larger pro-poor and/or pro-growth spending, as indicated in the key-features agenda and the PRGF Handbook.[16] As discussed earlier in this chapter—and reflecting the policy cautions discussed there with respect to the IMF Board—Fund staff were *not* proactive in analyzing alternative aid scenarios or normative aid requirements for meeting national growth and development objectives. Nor did they discuss donors' additional aid opportunities where country absorptive capacity exceeded projected aid flows.

Similar reservations apply a fortiori to the consideration of possibly higher aid commitments for pro-poor and pro-growth programs in education, health, and infrastructure. But there was another complication as well—related to collaboration between the IMF and the World Bank. As between the two, the Bank is the lead agency in these sectoral areas, but the evaluation found that Bank–Fund collaboration did not work well therein.[17] This said, Fund and Bank staff undertook several exercises that covered a range of objectives and levels of complexity in the design of alternative scenarios. But these exercises were de-linked from their respective PRGF programs, which remain decidedly most-likely-scenario processes.

C. Poverty and social impact analysis

From the launch of the PRGF, social impact analysis was to inform the consideration of distributional impacts of program design and the identification of countervailing measures to offset adverse impacts.[18] Fund staff were generally not expected to do the PSIA analysis themselves, but rather to integrate the analysis of partners, especially of World Bank staff, into program design. Subsequent Board discussions repeatedly emphasized the importance of such analysis for PRGF program design and called for systematic treatment of impacts and countervailing measures in PRGF documents.[19] They also highlighted the fact that the World Bank was the lead agency on PSIA, given its role as the lead agency on poverty reduction.[20]

---

[16] See IMF Policy Development and Review Department (2006a) and (2006b).

[17] The evaluation found these collaboration problems to be due to the undermanagement by both the Fund and the Bank of the practical modalities associated with the requesting and delivering of analytic work across institutional lines. This issue also received considerable attention in the context of World Bank and IMF staff follow-up to the February 2007 *Report of the External Review Committee on Bank–Fund Collaboration*. See IMF and World Bank (2007).

[18] See Inchauste (2002), Robb (2003), and Kpodar (2006).

[19] See IMF (2003) and (2004b).   [20] See IMF (2004a).

The evaluation found that PSIAs carried out by the World Bank and other agencies did not systematically inform PRGF program design, although there were exceptions. During interviews, IMF staff said that most PSIAs prepared by other agencies generally lacked the necessary timeliness, relevance, and/or quality to underpin PRGF design. It was for this reason that the Fund's PSIA unit, set up primarily to help staff integrate PSIAs done by others into PRGF-supported programs, had become a producer of PSIAs. The findings of PSIAs carried out by IMF staff are now typically reported in PRGF documents, although there is less evidence of material influence on PRGF program design. World Bank staff indicated that to undertake PSIAs in support of PRGFs, their work programs would need to include specific requests with the supporting resources. The evaluation concluded that the Fund needed to be more pro-active in managing the PSIA interface with the Bank, while at the same time avoiding the duplication of Bank capacities and programs.

D. Fiscal governance

In contrast to the other PRGF key features, the evaluation found that the Fund did well in helping countries to mobilize domestic revenues and to strengthen fiscal transparency and accountability. Both have been substantial areas of PRGF focus, with extensive discussions of budgetary control and transparency issues in program documents and structural conditionality framed in a variety of ways—from prior actions and performance criteria to indicative targets and benchmarks—frequently supported by technical assistance. The evaluation concluded that this increasing emphasis reflected the confluence of (i) traditional concerns about macroeconomic stability and the underlying processes and systems for ensuring budget execution and reporting; (ii) shareholder concerns about governance and the need to ensure the proper disposition of debt service savings from the HIPC Initiative, and the Multilateral Debt Reduction Initiative more recently; (iii) donor interest in improving country fiduciary systems as a quid pro quo for their own shift to budget support instruments; and (iv) effective Bank–Fund collaboration, with country teams supported by technical specialists in both institutions focused on their respective areas of comparative advantage—collaboration arrangements that contrasted sharply with those on other issues.

V. External communications

The evaluation also looked into Fund communications, drawing on evidence from surveys, face-to-face interviews, and reviews of Fund institutional communications, issues of particular relevance to the themes of this book. It found that staff communicated most often and most effectively—although not without complaints—with the country authorities. Staff communicated to a much lesser degree with donors, while in-country communications with civil society representatives were extremely limited. At headquarters, institutional communications portrayed the IMF as more proactive on the MDGs, alternative scenarios, and the mobilization of aid than Board policies and staff operational practices indicated.

A. Staff communications

The evaluation team met with and surveyed representatives of ministries of finance and central banks, and also with sectoral colleagues in ministries of health, education, and infrastructure and related agencies, albeit to a lesser extent. Contributing to an earlier cited evaluation conclusion, many ministry of finance officials complained about what they saw as the Fund's overemphasis on pro-poor spending and neglect of pro-growth spending on infrastructure. Contrary to the expectations of the evaluation team, representatives from education and health ministries did not complain about Fund-related pressures on their spending plans, and some praised the discipline they said it helped instill in their finance colleagues. But as noted earlier, those ministries were major beneficiaries of funding from HIPC savings, which may have favorably inclined them toward the IMF. Representatives from infrastructure ministries generally made two points: (i) the need to broaden the criteria for priority expenditures to include basic infrastructure projects, a plea that was sometimes specifically supported by their colleagues in the health ministries, based on a recognition that investments in water and roads are necessary to meet the health MDGs; and (ii) their desire to loosen Fund-imposed constraints on borrowing abroad to finance high-return investments in infrastructure.

Donor representatives gave Fund staff high marks for their macroeconomic assessment and the PRGF's catalytic role in triggering their own disbursements, but much lower marks for staff proactivity in engaging with donors. On a closely related point, they focused (both in interviews and in survey responses) on the growing importance of general budget support by donors—and reliance on the Fund's macroeconomic analysis—and the implications for the donor–IMF relationship. Two pressure points were identified with respect to demands on resident representatives' and mission chiefs' time. First, the increase in budget support and budget support donors in a number of countries has raised donor interest in an ongoing dialogue with the IMF on macroeconomic issues in the context of working groups and task forces on medium-term expenditure frameworks, inter alia. Second, there are critical moments in the budget/donor calendar when information about the IMF macroeconomic assessment is essential. These two pressure points placed a premium on the availability of Fund staff to engage with local donor groups, especially at critical stages of the budget-support timeline, which sometimes strained relationships between donors and IMF staff.

IMF engagement with country-based members of civil society was found to be limited and ineffective. The very clear message from civil society survey responses—and from the evaluations team's face-to-face meetings with civil society groups during the country visits—was that Fund staff are generally unknown and unavailable to civil society in SSA. Yet this remains a blindspot for IMF staff. About 80 percent of Fund staff respondents reported progress in their engagement with civil society over the past five years, compared with only 20 percent of civil society respondents. For the future, majorities of all respondent groups—including the authorities and Fund staff—agreed that greater outreach efforts would be important. The evaluation team's face-to-face interviews with civil society representatives reinforced the finding of limited interaction with IMF staff. They pointed to even more limited agreement on assumptions about how Fund-supported policies impact the use of aid and poverty reduction and the MDGs.

B. Institutional communications

The evaluation found that institutional communications overstated the IMF's commitment to aid mobilization, advocacy for aid, and alternative scenarios for achieving the MDGs. For example, the IMF website (and other channels) reported that the Fund contributed to country efforts to achieve the MDGs, inter alia, through its "role in mobilizing donor support."[21] It further stated that the IMF helps poor countries achieve the growth levels needed to reduce poverty through inter alia "advocating for increased aid" from developed countries and that it encourages countries to develop and analyze alternative frameworks for achieving the MDGs. Similarly, in responding to Jeffrey Sachs, Thomas C. Dawson, then Director of the Fund's external relations department stated: "that same sense of urgency [that characterized IMF follow-up to the G8 call for IFI debt relief] is present when IMF teams work with countries and development partners . . . to consider their strategies for meeting the MDGs."[22]

These and other communications suggest proactive operational involvement with countries in the pursuit of the MDGs, both through strategy development and advocacy for funding. Yet they are at variance with the evaluation's findings about IMF policies and practices. As noted earlier, the Fund Board has not agreed on the inclusion in PRGFs of alternative scenarios for meeting the MDGs or other goals or on an operational role for the Fund on aid advocacy. Nor did Fund

---

[21] See <http://www.imf.org/exetrnal/np/exr/facts/mdg.htm>.
[22] See Dawson (2006).

mission chiefs and resident representatives surveyed for the evaluation see much connection between their operational work and the MDGs.

VI. Conclusions and postscript

Different stakeholders have interpreted the evaluation's evidence and findings differently. At one end of the spectrum, IMF operational staff interpreted the evidence as confirming that they had indeed implemented Board-approved policies—on the accommodation, forecasting, and mobilization of aid and related issues; they also emphasized SSA's improving macroeconomic results, which they attributed to their advice, at least in part. At the opposite end of the spectrum, civil society representatives interpreted the same evidence as validating long-standing concerns about aid blocking, conservative forecasting, and insufficient attention to poverty reduction.

Both views have some validity. Staff did *block* the use of aid in some cases, albeit in line with Board-approved policy, which called for spending and absorption of aid to the extent consistent with macroeconomic stability, although they were not open about their practices. Staff were *conservative* in forecasting aid, albeit also in line with policy that called for PRGFs to be grounded in single most-likely aid scenarios. But at the same time staff did help *protect* spending on health and education, in line with HIPC undertakings, although they did not consider the linkages between the composition of aid and spending and the macroeconomic forecast, outturn, and program, as civil society would have liked. In other words: Fund operational staff generally acted in line with Fund policies; it was the policies that civil society was in effect criticizing. However, the Fund made it difficult for civil society and other external observers to know exactly what the institution's policies were—compounded by the virtual absence of in-country communications about what particular Fund-supported programs were doing and by institutional miscommunications from headquarters that overstated the Fund's commitment to aid mobilization, advocacy for aid, and alternative scenarios for achieving the MDGs.

But this is not the entire story. The underlying debate was more complicated than a case of a divided but generally conservative Executive Board versus the institution's more liberal civil society critics. There was also the pivotal—and evolving—position of Fund management and senior staff. They had initially espoused some of the civil society agenda, embodied in the PRGF's key features. But during implementation, they stepped back from parts of the key features, including on the all-important normative financing requirements for pro-poor and pro-growth spending, the key feature of most relevance to the civil society aid critique. This stepping back reflected turnover in the Fund's senior team, depriving the agenda of the leadership needed to forge a consensus in the face of (i) deep divisions within the Board, and among staff, on the role of the Fund in low-income countries and (ii) a complicated relationship with the World Bank in areas of mutual concern. Instead, Fund management adopted a more passive stance on these issues, leaving important policy issues unresolved and/or ambiguous and the institution's external communications unchecked, setting the stage for the confusion on Fund policies and practices that the evaluation found and undermining the institution's credibility and reputation on the low-income country agenda.

Against this background, the evaluation made three "stop-loss" recommendations for rebuilding institutional integrity and improving the coherence of the institution's policies and actions relating to aid to, and poverty reduction in, SSA. First, it called on the Board to clarify relevant policies one way or the other and for management to provide clear guidance to staff on the implementation of those once-clarified policies and to ensure candid communications about Fund policies and practices. This recommendation also included a specific point on the proactive management of the relationship with the World Bank in areas of mutual concern, such as on growth, aid, and the analysis of poverty and social impacts. Second it called on management to ensure effective and transparent implementation monitoring to strengthen accountabilities and external perceptions thereof. Third, it called on management to clarify expectations concerning staff interactions with donors and civil society and then to follow through on them.

During subsequent Board discussions, the IMF Executive Board and management broadly supported the evaluation's recommendations. Executive Directors clarified and reaffirmed existing policies on forecasting aid and the use of alternative aid scenarios, the spending and absorption of aid, and the formulation of "adjusters" in PRGFs. Executive Directors also underscored the importance of complementing greater policy clarity with measures to ensure that IMF communications are consistent with IMF policies and practices, and of strengthening staff interactions with local donor groups and civil society. Nevertheless, questions remain about management's plans for monitoring and evaluating the implementation of the recommendations, including the clarified policy on PRGFs. The next Board review of the PRGF is scheduled for 2010. To maximize impact on staff behavior and institutional accountability, an explicit monitoring framework will be needed long before then, setting out benchmarks to be used in measuring and assessing IMF performance.

A postscript is warranted on three recent developments, building on the evaluation's lessons learned.

- First and foremost is the arrival of the new Managing Director, who signaled early on a particular interest in the Fund's engagement with low-income countries. This may mark an opportunity for moving beyond the clarification of policies and the monitoring of implementation, to the provision of leadership on the relevant policy frontier. But as learned in the evaluation, balancing the tensions between the views of management and the support of the Board and staff will clearly require a close watch to ensure institutional coherence and integrity throughout the process, and to avoid a new round of disconnects between institutional communications on the one hand and institutional policies and practices on the other.

• Second, responding to concerns from shareholders about the decline in Fund income, Fund management launched a major exercise to cut costs, designed to complement ongoing efforts to enhance the revenue side of the Fund's finances. This exercise places a premium on the Fund's focusing narrowly on its areas of responsibility, working in partnership with other agencies, especially the World Bank, and saving resources by avoiding duplication. In light of the lessons learned from the evaluation, it also places a premium on open communications about what the Fund is accountable for in the context of such partnerships—and the specific benchmarks by which *its* performance will be measured.

• Third, in October 2007, Fund and Bank management issued the Joint Management Action Plan (JMAP) following up on the report of the External Review Committee on Bank–Fund Collaboration. The JMAP set out protocols for improving staff coordination and collaboration between the two institutions, including with respect to Bank staff's supplying sectoral analysis to Fund staff as inputs into PRGFs' analysis of aid, the supply response, and growth. These protocols have the potential for decreasing operating costs while increasing analytic depth in both institutions. But the realization of this potential will require proactive management from *both* sides of 19th Street, utilizing formal systems for requesting and tracking inputs from the other institution, including clear accountabilities, in line with the lessons learned from the evaluation.

VII. References

Berg, Andrew, Shekhar Aiyar, Mumtaz Hussain, Shaun K. Roache, Tokhir N. Mirzoev, and Amber Mahone, 2007, "The Macroeconomics of Scaling Up Aid: Lessons from Recent Experience," IMF Occasional Paper 253 (Washington, DC: International Monetary Fund).

Berndt, Markus, 2007, "The Macroeconomic Treatment of Aid Increases in IMF-Supported Programs," IEO Working Paper, BP/07/2 (Washington, DC: International Monetary Fund).

Bevan, David, 2005, "An Analytical Overview of Aid Absorption: Recognizing and Avoiding Macroeconomic Hazards," Paper presented at Maputo Seminar on Foreign Aid and Macroeconomic Management (Oxford: Oxford University Department of Economics).

Dawson, Thomas C., 2006, "IMF Focus Is to Help Nations Grow Even When Aid Promises Fall Short," Letter to the Editor, January 3 (London: Financial Times).

Estache, Antonio, 2006, "Infrastructure: A Survey of Recent and Upcoming Issues," Paper presented at the World Bank ABCDE Conference in Tokyo (Washington, DC: World Bank).

External Review Committee on Bank–Fund Collaboration, 2007, *Report of the External Review Committee on Bank–Fund Collaboration* (Washington, DC: International Monetary Fund and World Bank).

Foster, Mick and Tony Killick, 2006, "What Would Doubling Aid Do for Macroeconomic Management in Africa?" (London: Overseas Development Institute).

IMF, 2000, "Key Features of IMF PRGF-Supported Programs" (Washington, DC: International Monetary Fund).

—— 2003, "Concluding Remarks by the Acting Chair: Aligning the Poverty and Growth Facility and the Poverty Reduction Strategy Paper (PRSP) Approach" (Washington, DC: International Monetary Fund).

—— 2004a, "The Acting Chair's Summing Up: Poverty Reduction Strategies—Progress in Implementation" (Washington, DC: International Monetary Fund).

—— 2004b, "The Acting Chair's Summing Up: The Role of the Fund in Low-Income Member Countries" (Washington, DC: International Monetary Fund).

—— 2005a, "The Macroeconomics of Managing Increased Aid Flows: Experiences of Low-Income Countries and Policy Implications" (Washington, DC: International Monetary Fund).

—— 2005b, "The Acting Chair's Summing Up: Review of PRGF Program Design" (Washington, DC: International Monetary Fund).

—— 2005c, "The Acting Chair's Summing Up: Poverty Reduction Strategies—2005 Review of the Poverty Reduction Strategy Approach—Balancing Accountabilities and Scaling Up Results" (Washington, DC: International Monetary Fund).

—— 2005d, "Implementation of the Policy Support Instrument" (Washington, DC: International Monetary Fund).

—— and World Bank, 2007, "Enhancing Collaboration: Joint Management Action Plan (Follow-up to the Report of the External Review Committee on World Bank–IMF Collaboration)" (Washington, DC: International Monetary Fund and World Bank).

IMF Policy Development and Review Department, 2000, "Key Features of PRGF Arrangements: Checklist," Memorandum from Jack Boorman to Heads of IMF Area Departments (Washington, DC: International Monetary Fund).

—— 2006a, "A Handbook for the Staff on PRGF Arrangements" (Washington, DC: International Monetary Fund).

—— 2006b, "Staff Report Checklist: POD Review Work" (Washington, DC: International Monetary Fund).

Inchauste, Gabriela, 2002, "Poverty and Social Impact Analysis in PRGF-Supported Programs," IMF Policy Discussion Paper No. 02/11 (Washington, DC: International Monetary Fund).

Independent Evaluation Office, 2007, "The IMF and Aid to Sub-Saharan Africa" (Washington, DC: International Monetary Fund).

Kpodar, Kangni, 2006, "Distributional Effects of Oil Price Changes on Household Expenditures: Evidence from Mali," IMF Working Paper 06/91 (Washington, DC: International Monetary Fund).

Organization for Economic Cooperation and Development, Development Assistance Committee, 2005, "Baselines and Suggested Targets for the 12 Indicators of Progress: Paris Declaration on Aid Effectiveness" (Paris: Organization for Economic Cooperation and Development).

Oxfam International, 2003, "The IMF and the Millennium Development Goals: Failing to Deliver for Low Income Countries," Oxfam Briefing Paper, No. 54 (London: Oxfam International).

Robb, Caroline, 2003, "Poverty and Social Impact Analysis—Linking Macroeconomic Policies to Poverty Outcomes: Summary of Early Experience," IMF Working Paper 03/43 (Washington, DC: International Monetary Fund).

World Bank, 2005, "Infrastructure and the World Bank: A Progress Report," Paper presented to the Joint Ministerial Committee of the Boards of Governors of the Bank and the Fund on the Transfer of Real Resources to Developing Countries (Washington, DC: International Monetary Fund and World Bank).

11

Participation in IMF Programs and Income Inequality

Patrick Conway* (University of North Carolina)

I. Introduction

Income within economies became more unequal in the majority of develop-ing and transition economies between 1988 and 1998.[1] Figure 11.1 illustrates this, with a negative percent change indicating a fall in the mean income of the lowest quintile relative to the population mean: 62 of the 89 countries exhibited a reduction. Concurrently, participation of developing countries in IMF programs grew both in the number of countries participating and in the frequency of the programs in each country.[2] Is there a causal link from the one to the other?

The determinants of income inequality within countries have been exten-sively studied.

- Kuznets (1955, 1966) began the discussion with the "inverted-U hypothesis"—the notion that income will become more unequal as countries achieve larger incomes per capita up to a watershed level of income per capita, and then will become more equal with further development. The evidence for this hypoth-esis has typically been cross-country in nature: ranking the countries j in ascending order by income per capita, the inequality measure for small income per capita will worsen as income per capita increases until a turning point, and then will grow larger on average for countries with still higher per capita income.

* Thanks to Jim Boughton for encouraging this line of research, and to Branko Milanovic for making the data used in this chapter available.

[1] Figure 11.1 is based on data collected by Branko Milanovic from household surveys in 108 developing and transition countries. Milanovic (2004) and Milanovic (2005) report details of these data. These data are available at <http://econ.worldbank.org/projects/inequality>.

[2] This tendency in IMF participation is documented in Conway (2007).

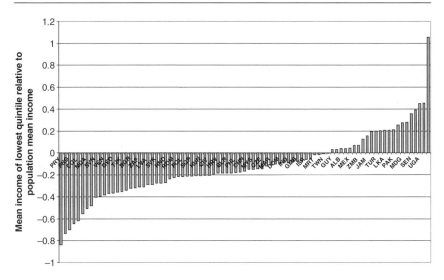

Figure 11.1 Percent Change in Inequality Ratio, 1988–98

- Li et al. (1998) finds in an unbalanced panel of Gini coefficients of middle- and low-income countries that the cross-country differences in income inequality represent about 92 percent in the variation of the Gini while within-country differences were responsible for only 1.4 percent.[3] They identified political liberty and developed financial markets as two potential contributors to income equality, and found in estimation that more-developed financial markets were significantly associated with increased income equality.

- Deininger and Squire (1998) use panel data to demonstrate that the Kuznets curve does not hold intertemporally for a given country. There is evidence in the cross-sectional data of such a relationship. Those in the lowest quintiles of the income distribution see significant increases in relative income from growth-promoting policies.

- Ravallion (2001) discovers an independent effect of openness on income inequality: greater openness is associated with increased inequality among the least developed countries. Dollar and Kraay (2002), by contrast, conclude that openness has similar effects at the top and the bottom of the income distribution, with mean incomes in all deciles rising. Milanovic (2005) summarizes the results of these and other studies of the interaction of openness and inequality by noting that results support both interpretations. His own analysis supports the conclusion that openness, *ceteris paribus*, leads to increased income inequality.

---

[3] The remainder was due to definitional differences in Gini computation across countries.

The contribution of participation in IMF programs to income inequality will be quite complex. The stylized fact that income inequality is relatively unchanging over time suggests that IMF programs may not have measurably large effects on income inequality. The finding that participation in IMF programs will retard economic growth at first but stimulate it in the longer run, first noted by Khan and Knight (1981) and corroborated by Conway (1994), suggests that the program's positive contributions to income equality may only be observed in the longer term. By contrast, the conditionality associated with IMF programs can constrain state welfare spending (for example, income support payments and subsidies) and thus lower the relative income and expenditure of those in the lowest deciles of the population.[4]

Garuda (2000) studied the impact of IMF programs on income distribution (Gini coefficients and the share of total income held by the poorest quintile) through a cross-country estimation strategy. He used the propensity-score method to ensure a matching of participating and nonparticipating countries, and found that for those countries predicted *ex ante* to be most likely to participate in an IMF program the impact of participation is to increase income inequality. Interestingly, however, this negative effect of the IMF program is reversed when countries less likely *ex ante* to participate in IMF programs are considered. Garuda interprets the likelihood of participation to be related to the degree of existing external and internal imbalance: the greater the likelihood, the worse the imbalance. Those countries participating in IMF programs because of severe imbalances are the ones whose income inequality worsens, while those participating with relatively mild imbalances are the ones whose income inequality is reduced.

In this chapter, I present an empirical analysis of the determinants of income distribution in 108 developing countries over the period 1988 to 1998. The data are the developing-country subset of those used by Milanovic (2005), augmented by information on the cumulative prior participation of the country in IMF programs over the preceding 10 years.[5] Just as in Li et al. (1998), I conclude that the majority of variation in income inequality is cross-country in nature: this component of income inequality will depend primarily upon the development characteristics of the countries, and not on participation in IMF programs. I also find, however, that cumulative past participation in IMF programs has a positive effect on the share of income held by the lowest quintile of the population in those countries for which observations are available at different times. This effect is robust to the inclusion of other developmental indicators.

[4] Rudra (2002) notes that while welfare spending in the OECD countries rose (from 12% to 16%) in the period 1972–95, welfare spending in less-developed countries fell (from 3.2% to 2.5%) from 1972 to 1995.
[5] For the transition economies, the cumulative prior participation variable is defined for the preceding five years to ensure coverage.

II. Definitions, methodology, and data

In this chapter I will examine the mean income of the lowest quintile of the population relative to the population mean as the measure of income inequality: as the ratio rises, inequality is reduced.[6]

The mean income of quintile i in country j in time t (m_{ijt}) can be defined by the mean income of country j at time t (m_{jt}) and an inequality ratio (I_{ijt}).

$$m_{ijt} = m_{jt} \, I_{ijt} \qquad (1)$$
$$\text{or} \quad (m_{ijt}/m_{jt}) = I_{ijt}$$

By construction, I_{ijt} is nondecreasing with decile: $I_{kjt} \geq I_{ijt}$ for $k \geq i$. Assumption of a Pareto distribution of incomes provides greater structure to the specification. With minimum country-j income of X_{jt} and Pareto inequality parameter $k_j > 1$, the mean incomes for quintile i and the inequality ratio I_{ijt} can be rewritten:

$$m_{ijt} = (k_j/(k_j - 1))X_{jt} * 5 * [(1 - \alpha_{i-1})^{(k_j-1)/k_j} - (1 - \alpha_i)^{(k_j-1)/k_j}]$$
$$m_{jt} = (k_j/(k_j - 1))X_{jt}$$
$$I_{ijt} = I_{ij} = 5 * [(1 - \alpha_{i-1})^{(k_j-1)/k_j} - (1 - \alpha_i)^{(k_j-1)/k_j}] \qquad (2)$$

where α_i represents the upper bound of quintile i: for the lowest quintile, $\alpha_1 = 0.20$, $\alpha_0 = 0$, and the expression becomes

$$I_{1jt} = I_{1j} = 5 * [1 - (0.80)^{(k_j-1)/k_j}] \qquad (3)$$

In this specification the inequality ratio for the lowest quintile is independent of time but does depend upon the inequality parameter k_j. As k_j rises, the value of I_{1j} converges to unity (and the distribution of income becomes more equal). More generally, k_j will be a function of time as well. My goal in the following sections is to identify those significant determinants of k_{jt}, and then consider whether IMF participation contributes significantly in addition to those.

The data used in this chapter have been assembled by Branko Milanovic of the World Bank from household surveys at the national level and used in Milanovic (2005). Once developed countries are excluded, there are 108 developing and transition countries for which at least one income-distributional observation is available. Milanovic reports the ratios of mean income by decile to mean income for the country as a whole for the years 1988, 1993, and 1998 when available. Of the 108 countries, there are 19 with observations in only one of the years, 28 with

---

[6] The data include measures of all quintiles, not just the lowest, and so the analysis of the chapter could be extended in the future to describe the evolution of the entire income distribution.

observations in two of the years, and 61 with observations in all three years. In addition to these, Milanovic reports information on other potential explanatory variables: in this chapter I will use mean per capita income (y_{mjt}) in purchasing-power-parity (PPP) terms, the index of democratic institutions (D_{jt}), the openness ratio (O_{jt}), the ratio of M_2 to nominal GDP as an indicator of financial deepening (M_{jt}), the ratio of government expenditure to GDP (G_{jt}), and the real interest rate (R_{jt}). For each of these last five variables, I create the "period-t" value by averaging the observations for the previous five years (in other words, the values from t-5 to t-1). I calculate a measure of cumulative prior participation in IMF programs (P_{jt}) from the quarterly series used in Conway (2007), including participation in Stand-by, EFF, Structural Adjustment, Enhanced Structural Adjustment, and Poverty Reduction and Growth Facilities. The period-t measure for this variable is the percentage of the time t-10 to t-1 (in years) that the country was participating in IMF programs.[7]

III. Cross-sectional income inequality in developing and transition countries

The Kuznets U remains a cross-sectional feature of the data on income inequality in developing countries, although when the transition economies are added the relationship becomes less pronounced. Figure 11.2 illustrates the

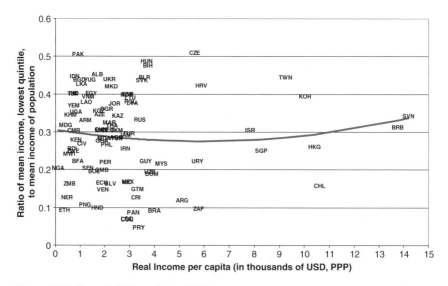

Figure 11.2 Kuznets U Hypothesis, 1998

[7] For transition economies, I calculate cumulative participation over the previous five years.

ratio I_{1j1998} of the mean per capita income for the lowest 20 percent of the population to the mean per capita income for the entire population for each country j in 1998. The Kuznets U pictured is the predicted value calculated by regressing this ratio on the mean and mean squared of per capita income (in PPP terms) in each country.

Each country's location on the figure is indicated by its three-letter acronym. While a slight U shape is evident, the coefficients of the underlying regression are insignificantly different from zero. Table 11.A.1 reports the regression results in the first two columns (see the appendix).

The transition economies tend to lessen the significance of this cross-sectional relationship: they tend to have intermediate real income per capita and relatively high mean income ratios. When the transition economies are excluded in 1998 there are 67 countries remaining; for those, the Kuznets U is significantly evident in the data. The third and fourth columns in Table 11.A.1 report the results of that regression, while Figure 11.3 illustrates the derived Kuznets curve.

While the Kuznets U hypothesis is the most famous of explanations for the evolution of income inequality, the introduction noted a number of other potential explanations: openness, financial deepening, democratic institutions, and the impact of participation in IMF programs. While these have valid theoretical roots, they are in practice quite different to distinguish among. There are two major difficulties in testing these hypotheses in econometric work. The first difficulty is the high correlation among advances in

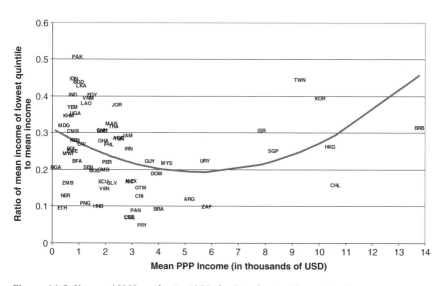

Figure 11.3 Kuznets' U Hypothesis, 1998, for Developing Countries Alone

these various dimensions. Table 11.A.2 illustrates the significant correlations (in bold numbers) among measures for the alternative explanations considered by Milanovic (2005). Four of the six, in particular, are significantly correlated with the measure of mean income used in estimating the Kuznets U. The second difficulty is the less-than-complete coverage for some of the empirical measures. There are 258 country–year observations of income share of the lowest quintile in the dataset, and complete coverage is only possible with y_{mjt} and P_{jt}. The openness indicator is only available for 86 percent of the sample, and the financial-deepening indicator is only available for 60 percent of the sample. Real interest rates and government expenditures indicators are available for less than half, and when both are included only one-third of the sample can be used.

This is unfortunate, for the censoring involved with data availability is not innocuous. Table 11.A.3 reports the means of the y_{mjt}, P_{jt}, and I_{1jt} variables by availability of explanatory variable. Those missing in each case will have participated less on average in IMF programs than those for which we have data. Those missing in each case also tend to have more equal income distributions than those for which data are available. The countries with $Demo_{jt}$ missing have larger mean income than those for which data are available.

There will thus be a trade-off to keep in mind when adding these explanatory variables with incomplete coverage—more complete hypothesis testing, but for a censored sample.

It is unfortunately beyond the scope of this chapter to decipher the common causes of the movements in the explanatory variables.[8] I will assume that the other explanatory variables have a potentially nonlinear component determined by their level of development, and that the real income per capita is a valid instrument for the level of development. I use cross-country regressions in this sample to identify the component of the variables due to shifts in level of development, and consider the residual from that regression to be the non-development-component of the explanatory variable.[9] For example, if the estimated equation is specified as:

$$O_{jt} = a + b * y_{mjt} + c * (y_{mjt})^2 + \varepsilon_{Ojt} \tag{4}$$

ε_{Ojt} is then the openness indicator used in the regressions. Similar indicators are derived for cumulative prior participation in IMF programs (ε_{Pjt}), democratic institutions (ε_{Djt}), and financial deepening (ε_{Mjt}).

Table 11.A.4 reports the results of Kuznets regressions building upon Table 11.A.1 with the addition of explanatory indicators as regressors. The first pair

[8] Rodrik et al. (2004) provides a nice econometric decomposition of the contributions of integration and institutional development to economic growth and concludes that "institutions rule".
[9] Those regressions are reported in the Appendix, Table 11.A.1.

of regressions in Table 11.A.4 is identical to those of Table 11.A.1: the left-hand side reports the results for all developing and transition countries, while the right-hand side reports the results for developing countries alone. When the indicator of cumulative prior IMF participation is added, the sign in both sets of regressions is negative—increased prior IMF participation leads on average to increased inequality. This effect is significant for the complete sample, but insignificant for the developing countries alone.

When both IMF participation and country openness indicators are added, ε_{Ojt} has an insignificant coefficient in both sets of regressions—and 14 percent of the observations (all from transition countries) are excluded. This has an important effect on the Kuznets U coefficients, with the significant inverted-U shape of the preceding regressions replaced with the expected (though insignificant) U shape. The impact of IMF participation remains significant in the full sample, although smaller in magnitude than in the preceding regression.

When the indicator for democratic institutions is added, the full sample shrinks further to only 80 percent of the original size. The ε_{Djt} increases income inequality in both samples by a comparable and significant amount. IMF participation and openness are both insignificant in this sample. When financial deepening is added, the sample shrinks still further—to 56 percent of the original size. ε_{Mjt} enters with positive sign and significant coefficient: the greater the financial depth of a developing or transition country, the greater the equality of income. The coefficient on ε_{Djt} becomes insignificant, while for the developing-country sample the openness indicator comes in with negative and significant coefficient.

Correlation coefficients among the adjusted variables are reported in Table 11.A.5, and these indicate the source of shifting significance and coefficient magnitude as regressors are added.[10] Even after the joint dependence on the level of development has been removed, these explanatory variables remain highly correlated. Participation in IMF programs is significantly and positively correlated with the degree of democratic institutions, and significantly and negatively correlated with the degree of financial deepening. The more democratic countries also tend to be significantly shallower financially than the less-democratic countries in the sample.

While we may not be able to state a priori the causal relationships between institutional depth, financial depth and openness, we can postulate that participation in IMF programs does not make a significant contribution to the pattern of income inequality across developing countries at any point in time, and does not in transition plus developing countries once other factors (financial depth, democratic institutions) are introduced. In fact, if we expect

---

[10] When the correlation matrix is created for 1998 alone, the pattern and magnitude of correlation coefficients is quite similar. This indicates that the pattern observed here is due to cross-country variation rather than time-series variation.

participation in an IMF program to have an effect on income distribution, we anticipate that its effect will be observed over time. I turn to that possibility in the next section.

IV. Measuring the intertemporal impact of participation in IMF programs on income inequality

The derivation of the inequality ratio in equation (3) suggests that deviations in this ratio will be largely due to cross-country differences in k_j. That derivation of the inequality ratio has no intertemporal component at all—a country j will remain with constant I_{1jt} in every t. In reality, the inequality coefficients are not constant. Figure 11.4 illustrates the empirical frequency of the percentage change in I_{1jt} from the value five years earlier.[11] While near-zero change is the modal outcome overall, there are substantial numbers of observations with large percentage changes in this ratio. In this section I investigate whether these changes can be attributed to participation in IMF programs on average.

The dependent variable in this section is $\lambda_{20jt} = \Delta I_{20jt}/I_{20jt-1}$: the change in inequality ratio in country j from period t-1 (five years earlier) to period t. Considering percentage changes should remove the development-level effects, and will also eliminate one observation per country considered. Table 11.A.6 reports the results of Kuznets-like regressions on λ_{20jt}.

The initial panel in Table 11.A.6 reports the result of a regression of the percentage change in the inequality ratio on the lagged mean and lagged mean squared of per capita real income.[12] The Kuznets U is evident in the percentage change as well; that is, the percentage change in the mean income of the lowest quintile relative to overall mean income is initially declining as countries become more developed and then rises for the most-developed countries in the sample. This pattern is evident in all specifications reported in Table 11.A.6. The Wald statistics indicate the joint significance of the two coefficients on per capita real income at the 95 percent level of confidence.

When cumulative participation in IMF programs is added to the regression, the coefficient is both positive and significant on ε_{Pjt} in most specifications.[13]

---

[11] The graph points measure the number of observations falling in the range from 10 percentage points below to the point listed on the graph. For example, the observations at 0 represent all observations with values between −10 and 0.

[12] For example: if the dependent variable is λ_{20k98}, then it measures the percentage change from 1993 to 1998 in mean income of the lowest quintile in country k divided by the mean income for country k. The right-hand side variables are the real per capita income in 1993 in country k and that variable squared.

[13] Inclusion of ε_{Pjt} in this regression means that I am using the cumulative participation in IMF programs from 1988 to 1997 adjusted to exclude development-level effects to explain the percentage change from 1993 to 1998 in the inequality ratio. Inclusion of ε_{Pjt-1} implies that the cumulative participation in IMF programs from 1983 to 1992 would explain the percentage change from 1993 to 1998 in the inequality ratio.

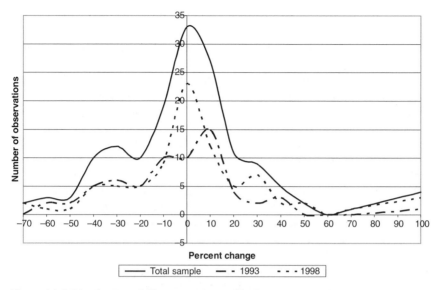

Figure 11.4 Distribution of Changes in Inequality Ratio over Five Years

The greater the prior participation in IMF programs, the more positive the change in the inequality ratio. The cumulative participation variable lagged one period (i.e. five years) takes the opposite sign but is insignificantly different from zero. As the other potential explanatory variables are added to the regression the coefficient on ε_{Pjt} changes very little in magnitude, while the other explanatory variables always make an insignificant contribution to the regressions. The Wald statistics for these latter cases test the joint significance of the coefficients on the additional variables (ε_{Ojt}, ε_{Mjt}, ε_{Djt}) and reject significance in all cases. While the coefficient on ε_{Pjt} is itself insignificant in the final panel, this is due to the shrinking sample size leading to increased standard errors rather than a reduction in the estimated coefficient.

As a test of the robustness of these results, I included $\Delta y_{mjt}/y_{mjt-1}$, $\Delta \varepsilon_{Pjt}/\varepsilon_{Pjt-1}$, $\Delta \varepsilon_{Mjt}/\varepsilon_{Mjt-1}$, $\Delta \varepsilon_{Djt}/\varepsilon_{Djt-1}$, and $\Delta \varepsilon_{Ojt}/\varepsilon_{Ojt-1}$ as additional regressors in the appropriate regressions, creating an error-correction specification. These contemporaneous percentage-change regressors were always insignificant and never changed the significance of the Kuznets U coefficients or the IMF participation effect.

V. Conclusions and extensions

We can restate the initial hypothesis as follows: once other factors determining income inequality are controlled for, is there an independent and significant effect of participation in IMF programs on income inequality? On the basis of the evidence provided here, I conclude that it will be difficult to attribute any of the cross-country differences in income inequality to participation in IMF programs. However, there is a significant and pro-equality effect of participation in IMF programs evident in the intertemporal dimension of the data.

The problem in identifying the cross-country effects begins with the difficulty in assigning causality among the potentially important variables, but does not end there. Cross-country regressions like these are based upon the implicit assumption that the process generating income inequality from the independent variables is identical across countries. There are also, as Milanovic (2004) documents, significant differences across countries in administration of household surveys and in calculation of income quantiles. In the end, these results should be taken as suggestive; the rejection of the hypothesis that participation in IMF programs is responsible for cross-country differences in income inequality seems warranted, but will require more detailed work to be made definitive.

The significant impact of IMF programs on the time path of income inequality is evident in these data, but it is important to recognize that for each country there are at most two observations of differenced data. This is not a feature that allows confidence in describing the time path of adjustments in income inequality due to participation in IMF programs, Rather, I establish that on average the participation in IMF programs is significantly associated with an adjustment toward greater income equality.

This does not invalidate the complaint that IMF programs tend to reduce government expenditure on goods aimed at the poor: those complaints may well be true, since government expenditures of this type will in many cases not enter the calculations of inequality based upon household surveys. This concern will be a useful direction for further research.

This research design is predicated on the absence of sub-groups of countries with strongly different experiences; if they exist, these sub-groups should be addressed explicitly. I have begun this in the current chapter by redoing the analysis with transition economies excluded. Such an exclusion is natural, since the most important income-distributional event during the data period was the end of the Soviet Union and the relatively more unequal income distributions that followed. Given that the successor states of the Soviet Union had both (a) strongly worsened income equality after independence and (b) no prior participation in IMF programs, the positive effect of participation on income equality could well be an artifact of that event. Redoing the analysis for only the developing countries demonstrates that this was not a defining factor in the results reported here, but more attention to such sub-groups will be useful in future research.

Garuda (2000) serves as the benchmark for work relating IMF programs to income inequality, but owing to the difference in research design the results here are not directly comparable. I can suggest one qualification to Garuda's conclusions, and one direction in which this chapter should be extended. First, the qualification: Garuda's result that those more in need of IMF programs are more likely to lose from them is probably an artifact of the cross-country dimension of income inequality. Here, the propensity to participate will be strongly correlated with developmental indicators, and the sorting going on in that paper could simply be the sorting picked up by my developmental regressors. Second, the extension: the participation variable P_{jt} in this chapter could be enhanced by considering the prior likelihood of participation. Once the analysis is confined to the intertemporal dimension—one that Garuda (2000) did not consider—the possibility remains that Garuda's conclusions will be reaffirmed here.

VI. References

Conway, P. 1994: "IMF Lending Programs: Participation and Impact", *Journal of Development Economics* 45, pp. 365–91.

—— 2007: "The Revolving Door: Duration and Recidivism in Participation in IMF Programs", *Review of Economics and Statistics* 89/2, May, pp. 205–20.

Deininger, K. and L. Squire, 1998: "New Ways of Looking at Old Issues: Inequality and Growth", *Journal of Development Economics* 57, pp. 259–87.

Dollar, D. and A. Kraay, 2002: "Growth is Good for the Poor", *Journal of Economic Growth* 7/3, pp. 195–225.

Garuda, G. 2000: "The Distributional Effect of IMF Programs: A Cross-Country Analysis", *World Development* 28/6, pp. 1031–51.

Khan, M. and M. Knight, 1981: "Stabilization Programs in Developing Countries: A Formal Framework", IMF Staff Papers 28, pp. 1–53.

Kuznets, S. 1955: "Economic Growth and Income Inequality", *American Economic Review* 45, pp. 1–28.

—— 1966: *Modern Economic Growth.* New Haven, CT: Yale University Press.

Li, H., L. Squire, and H. Zou, 1998: "Explaining International and Intertemporal Variations in Income Inequality", *Economic Journal* 108, pp. 26–43.

Milanovic, B. 2004: *Worlds Apart: Global and International Inequality 1950–2000.* Princeton, NJ: Princeton University Press.

Milanovic, B. 2005: "Can We Discern the Effect of Globalization on Income Distribution? Evidence from Household Surveys", *World Bank Economic Review* 19/1, pp. 21–44.

Ravallion, M. 2001: "Growth, Inequality and Poverty: Looking Beyond Averages", *World Development* 29/11, pp. 1803–15.

Rodrik, D., A. Subramanian and F. Trebbi, 2004: "Institutions Rule: The Primacy of Institutions over Geography and Integration in Economic Development", *Journal of Economic Growth* 9/2, June.

Rudra, N. 2002: "Globalization and the Decline of the Welfare State in Less Developed Countries", *International Organization* 56/2.

APPENDIX

Table 11.A.1. Regression Results, Kuznets U Hypothesis

	All developing and transition economies		Excluding transition economies	
	Coefficient	Std. error	Coefficient	Std. error
Full sample:				
Intercept	0.277 *	0.018	0.304 *	0.016
y_{m98}	0.020 *	0.009	−0.027 *	0.009
$(y_{m98})^2$	−0.0014 *	0.0007	0.0025 *	0.001
R^2	0.02		0.05	
F value	2.52		5.19 *	
Critical F(2,N-2)	3.02		3.03	
N	258		186	
1998:				
Intercept	0.304 *	0.028	0.317 *	0.027
y_{m98}	−0.010	0.014	−0.043 *	0.015
$(y_{m98})^2$	0.0009	0.001	0.004 *	0.001
R^2	0.01		0.13	
F value	0.45		4.80 *	
Critical F(2,N-2)	3.11		3.14	
N	93		66	
1993:				
Intercept	0.292 *	0.025	0.295 *	0.025
y_{m93}	−0.002	0.013	−0.021	0.013
$(y_{m93})^2$	0.0004	0.001	0.002	0.001
R^2	0.004		0.02	
F value	0.17		0.55	
Critical F(2,N-2)	3.11		3.14	
N	93		70	
1988:				
Intercept	0.209 *	0.043	0.293 *	0.036
y_{m88}	0.091 *	0.023	−0.011	0.022
$(y_{m88})^2$	−0.007 *	0.002	0.002	0.002
R^2	0.18		0.02	
F value	7.83 *		0.51	
Critical F(2,N-2)	3.13		3.18	
N	72		47	

* indicates significance at 95 percent level of confidence.

Table 11.A.2. Pearson Correlations among Independent Variables

	y_{mjt}	$Open_{jt}$	M_{2jt}/Y_{jt}	DFI_{jt}/Y_{jt}	$Demo_{jt}$	Gov_{jt}/Y_{jt}	$Rintr_{jt}$
y_{mjt}							
$Open_{jt}$	**0.40**						
	(223)						
M_{2jt}/Y_{jt}	**0.41**	**0.49**					
	(153)	(152)					
DFI_{jt}/Y_{jt}	**0.14**	**0.56**	−0.01				
	(215)	(209)	(147)				
$Demo_{jt}$	**0.33**	0.03	−0.10	**0.13**			
	(233)	(206)	(147)	(201)			
Gov_{jt}/Y_{jt}	0.17	**0.23**	**0.22**	0.11	0.06		
	(111)	(110)	(109)	(108)	(109)		
$Rintr_{jt}$	0.10	−0.06	0.05	0.03	0.06	−0.00	
	(122)	(122)	(122)	(120)	(117)	(85)	
CP_{jt}	**−0.29**	**−0.20**	**−0.39**	−0.03	0.12	−0.14	0.10
	(258)	(223)	(153)	(215)	(233)	(111)	(122)

Numbers in parentheses are the number of observations used in calculating correlation.
Statistics in bold are significantly different from zero at 95 percent level of confidence.

Table 11.A.3. Means of Variables of Interest for Missing and Non-missing Observations

	Number missing	I_{20jt}		CP_{jt}		y_{mjt}	
		Missing	Not missing	Missing	Not missing	Missing	Not missing
$Open_{jt}$	35	0.48	0.29	0.02	0.36	2.86	2.75
$Demo_{jt}$	25	0.36	0.31	0.06	0.34	4.38	2.59
Gov_{jt}/Y_{jt}	147	0.34	0.29	0.25	0.39	2.56	3.04
$Rintr_{jt}$	136	0.35	0.27	0.20	0.43	2.56	3.00
M_{2jt}/Y_{jt}	105	0.35	0.29	0.18	0.39	2.50	2.95

Source: author's calculation.

Table 11.A.4. Independent Impact of Explanatory Variables

	All developing and transition economies		Excluding transition economies	
	Coefficient	Std. error	Coefficient	Std. error
Full sample:				
Intercept	0.277 *	0.018	0.302 *	0.017
y_{mt}	0.020 *	0.009	−0.027 *	0.009
$(y_{mt})^2$	−0.0015 *	0.0008	0.0025 *	0.001
R^2	0.02		0.05	
F value	2.52		5.19 *	
Critical F(2,N-2)	3.02		3.03	
N	258		183	

(continued)

Table 11.A.4. (Continued)

	All developing and transition economies		Excluding transition economies	
	Coefficient	Std. error	Coefficient	Std. error
Adding IMF participation:				
Intercept	0.277 *	0.018	0.302 *	0.027
y_{mt}	0.020 *	0.009	−0.027 *	0.015
$(y_{mt})^2$	−0.0014 *	0.0007	0.0025*	0.001
ε_{Pjt}	−0.114 *	0.028	−0.019	0.026
R^2	0.08		0.06	
F value	7.45		3.61 *	
Critical F(2,N-2)	3.02		3.03	
N	258		183	
Adding IMF participation and openness:				
Intercept	0.299 *	0.017	0.302 *	0.016
y_{mt}	−0.006	0.009	−0.027 *	0.009
$(y_{mt})^2$	0.0007	0.0007	0.0025 *	0.001
ε_{Pjt}	−0.055 *	0.027	−0.022	0.027
ε_{Ojt}	−0.026	0.016	−0.020	0.015
R^2	0.03		0.07	
F value	1.87		3.18 *	
Critical F(2,N-2)	3.02		3.03	
N	223		183	
Adding IMF participation, openness and democratic institutions:				
Intercept	0.298 *	0.017	0.307 *	0.017
y_{mt}	−0.005	0.009	−0.032 *	0.009
$(y_{mt})^2$	−0.0005	0.001	0.003 *	0.002
ε_{Pjt}	−0.045	0.028	−0.015	0.027
ε_{Ojt}	−0.024	0.017	−0.021	0.016
ε_{Djt}	−0.007 *	0.002	−0.007 *	0.002
R^2	0.06		0.12	
F value	2.70 *		4.62 *	
Critical F(2,N-2)				
N	206		171	
Adding IMF participation, openness, democratic institutions and financial deepening:				
Intercept	0.303 *	0.023	0.327 *	0.019
y_{mt}	−0.008	0.012	−0.049 *	0.010
$(y_{mt})^2$	0.001	0.001	0.004 *	0.001
ε_{Pjt}	−0.026	0.036	0.035	0.031
ε_{Ojt}	−0.048	0.030	−0.099 *	0.026
ε_{Djt}	−0.005	0.003	−0.003	0.002
ε_{Mjt}	0.072 *	0.035	0.121 *	0.033
R^2	0.09		0.28	
F value	2.35		7.16 *	
Critical F(2,N-2)				
N	146		119	

Source: author's calculations; GMM estimation.

Table 11.A.5. Pearson Correlations among Adjusted Variables

	ε_{Pjt}	ε_{Ojt}	ε_{Djt}	ε_{Mjt}
ε_{Pjt}	**1.00**			
	(258)			
ε_{Ojt}	−0.07	**1.00**		
	(223)	(223)		
ε_{Djt}	**0.24**	−0.11	**1.00**	
	(233)	(206)	(233)	
ε_{Mjt}	**−0.28**	0.38	**−0.23**	**1.00**
	(153)	(152)	(147)	(153)

Numbers in parentheses are the number of observations used in calculating correlation.
Statistics in bold are significantly different from zero at 95 percent level of confidence.

Table 11.A.6. Intertemporal Impact of Explanatory Variables on λ_{20jt}

	All developing and transition economies		Excluding transition economies	
	Coefficient	Std. error	Coefficient	Std. error
Full sample:				
Intercept	0.090	0.049	0.056	0.057
y_{mt-1}	−0.084 *	0.022	−0.057	0.033
$(y_{mt-1})^2$	0.007 *	0.002	0.005	0.003
R^2	0.07		0.03	
Wald	18.8 *		10.41 *	
N	150		102	
	Adding IMF participation:			
Intercept	0.043	0.050	0.016	0.058
y_{mt-1}	−0.076 *	0.022	−0.051 *	0.023
$(y_{mt-1})^2$	0.007 *	0.002	0.005 *	0.002
ε_{Pjt}	0.298 *	0.102	0.270 *	0.135
ε_{Pjt-1}	−0.118	0.101	−0.128	0.123
R^2	0.12		0.07	
Wald	9.24 *		4.01	
N	150		102	
	Adding IMF participation and openness:			
Intercept	0.008	0.055	0.015	0.058
y_{mt-1}	−0.049 *	0.024	−0.051 *	0.024
$(y_{mt-1})^2$	0.005 *	0.002	0.005 *	0.002
ε_{Pjt}	0.260 *	0.114	0.271 *	0.134
ε_{Pjt-1}	−0.113	0.106	−0.129	0.124
ε_{Ojt}	0.100	0.108	0.007	0.137
ε_{Ojt-1}	−0.107	0.101	−0.007	0.128
R^2	0.07		0.07	
Wald	1.20		0.00	
N	117		102	

(continued)

Table 11.A.6. (Continued)

	All developing and transition economies		Excluding transition economies	
	Coefficient	Std. error	Coefficient	Std. error
	Adding IMF participation and democratic institutions:			
Intercept	0.035	0.055	0.019	0.060
y_{mt-1}	−0.068 *	0.028	−0.049	0.027
$(y_{mt-1})^2$	0.006 *	0.003	0.005 *	0.002
ε_{Pjt}	0.317 *	0.105	0.278 *	0.134
ε_{Pjt-1}	−0.133	0.109	−0.094	0.128
ε_{Djt}	−0.005	0.012	−0.016	0.016
ε_{Djt-1}	0.006	0.010	0.006	0.014
R^2	0.12		0.09	
Wald	0.34		1.69	
N	139		98	
	Adding IMF participation and financial deepening:			
Intercept	0.024	0.061	0.013	0.062
y_{mt-1}	−0.061 *	0.026	−0.051	0.026
$(y_{mt-1})^2$	0.006 *	0.002	0.005 *	0.002
ε_{Pjt}	0.248	0.134	0.263	0.145
ε_{Pjt-1}	−0.142	0.126	−0.165	0.149
ε_{Mjt}	0.028	0.064	0.016	0.069
ε_{Mjt-1}	0.015	0.064	0.056	0.062
R^2	0.10		0.10	
Wald	0.30		0.91	
N	90		80	

Source: author's calculations; GMM estimation.

Part IV

The Role of Low-Income Member Countries in the Governance of the IMF

12

Governance Matters: The IMF and Sub-Saharan Africa

Ngaire Woods (Oxford University)

I. Introduction

The IMF has found it extremely difficult to facilitate successful economic growth, development, and policy reform in Africa. This is puzzling from the outside because on the face of it the IMF looks very powerful vis-à-vis African countries. It has considerable resources, knowledge, and expertise compared with its inter-locutor agencies on the ground. Borrowers in Africa are among the least likely to have access to alternative sources of finance. And the institution has worked with African countries for a long time. But after more than two decades of engage-ment, the IMF's main borrowers in sub-Saharan Africa do not seem to have been well served by the institution. A recent evaluation of IMF aid to sub-Saharan Africa found "ambiguity and confusion about IMF policy and practice on aid and poverty reduction" on the continent and "a disconnect between the IMF's external communications on aid and poverty reduction, and its practice in low-income countries" (Independent Evaluation Office of the IMF 2007).[1]

This chapter argues that the IMF's failures in Africa cannot be divorced from the governance of the institution. The above-cited report highlights the failure of the Board and Management of the organization to ensure "clarity on what they should do on the mobilization of aid, alternative scenarios, and the application of poverty and social impact analysis" (Independent Evaluation Office of the IMF 2007, p. 3). These conclusions and their implications are further underscored by a yet more recent evaluation of the IMF's governance (Independent Evaluation Office of the IMF 2008).

At the Board level, low-income countries have insufficient voting power to give them appropriate incentives to engage meaningfully in deliberations

[1] See also Ch. 10, by Joanne Salop.

and decisions. The Executive Board of the IMF is dominated by the wealthiest economies who command more than 40 percent of votes of the organization. By contrast, sub-Saharan African countries, who account for a quarter of the membership of the IMF, have just over 4 percent of the vote. Belgium (population 10 million) has more votes than Nigeria, Ethiopia, Zambia, Tanzania, Mozambique, and South Africa combined (total population around 300 million).

Although the IMF's Board typically does not resort to voting, voting power and quotas strongly underpin calculations as to when a decision has been reached (typically described as "consensus"). In recent years Board members report that the collegial and consensual nature of decision making has eroded sharply making voting power yet more important. This renders the voice of developing countries on the Board yet weaker. As one former Executive Director from South Africa has put it, the miniscule voting power of African and other developing countries renders it almost impossible for them to put items on the agenda (Rustomjee 2005). Simply to muster enough voice to be heard is a gargantuan task.

The international community has recently committed itself to enhance the voice and capacity of developing countries in the institution. The modest reform package includes a tripling of basic votes (which are allocated to all countries regardless of their economic size) to increase the voice of low-income countries and a mechanism to maintain the share of basic votes in total votes in future, and an additional Alternate Executive Director for the two chairs representing large African constituencies (IMF 2008). These may well be helpful steps but properly to assess them requires considering what the real problems with the IMF's engagement with the continent have been, and whether governance reform of any description could make a difference to the IMF's work in sub-Saharan Africa.

II. Why does governance matter?

There are three reasons to expect that governance might affect the IMF's impact in sub-Saharan Africa. The first reason concerns the *responsiveness* of the organization. The argument here is that the capacity of the institution to generate pertinent and relevant programs and instruments for its low-income members could be enhanced if low-income members have an incentive to voice their concerns and priorities within and to the organization *and* if others have an incentive to listen. The presumption would be that a failure to listen in the past has led to insufficient responsiveness which has hindered the quality of efforts on the part of the IMF. To assess this argument, we need to examine the quality of those efforts and to explore under what conditions the IMF has "listened" (or not), to whom, and why.

A second reason why better representation or voice by African countries might alter the IMF's performance has more directly to do with *effectiveness*. Here the argument is that for the IMF's work to have positive effects in sub-Saharan African countries would require the institution to establish early and deep engagement with governments and sufficient "buy-in" from them and their societies to make the organization's work and advice effective. The governance structure of the organization offers one way to build some degree of "buy-in"—indeed the origins of the current governance structure in which the US is heavily represented and empowered was precisely in order to ensure the US would participate and engage deeply. As the institution has become more heavily involved in Africa, a change in the structure of representation adequately to reflect this has not occurred. By examining the recent history, we can assess why this might make a difference.

A third way in which governance affects the IMF's impact is because it affects the organization's *accountability*. The Board of the IMF sets the priorities of the organization and oversees their implementation, their impact, and their evolution. In theory at least, the Board monitors the performance and work of the senior management of the organization. The managing director and senior staff, in turn, hold to account all other staff working for the organization. Needless to say, all players across the organization have an incentive to meet the desiderata of those members of the Board who can most powerfully affect their careers and direction of work. If there is little scope for sub-Saharan African countries to play a role in this, the risk is that the priorities and needs of the continent will constantly be under-served by a system which skews accountability toward meeting the preferences of other more powerful groups. By examining the recent history we can assess this argument and examine whether alternative arrangements might produce different effects.

This chapter will examine the evidence of the past two decades of IMF engagement in Africa to ascertain how responsiveness, effectiveness, and accountability have worked, and what, therefore, might be changed by a change in the governance structure of the institution.

III. Setting priorities: the IMF's approach to Africa

In the early 1980s the IMF plunged into a widespread debate about what kind of economic reform would work in Africa.[2] Up until the late 1970s most developing countries had favored a statist approach to development, using economic planning, import-substitution-industrialization, price controls, credit rationing, state-owned enterprises, and government control of agricultural marketing (Van de Walle 2001; Lofchie 1994; Killick 1990a; Waterbury

---

[2] This section draws on ch. 6 of Woods 2006.

1999). In Africa the approach was reiterated in the Lagos Plan of Action set out by the Organization for African Unity in 1980. The concern of African leaders advancing the plan was to shift the continent away from its dependence on the export of basic raw materials, which "had made African economies highly susceptible to external developments" (Economic Commission for Africa 1980, preamble). To this end, the plan focused on increasing Africa's self-reliance, promoting industrialization, and building up regional and sub-regional cooperation and integration.

In the IMF in the early 1980s, the African or Lagos view of Africa's needs was rejected. The Lagos approach to development faced two severe challenges. First, it required resources and by the early 1980s most African countries were in economic crisis. Hit by the increase in oil prices in 1973–4 as well as a slump in commodity prices, many had increased their borrowing in the 1970s so that by 1980 they faced a world economic downturn with a huge debt burden on their backs. There was a huge gap between the resources required for a renewed push toward industrialization and what was available. External donors were unlikely to come forward, in part because industrialized countries faced problems of inflation and a downturn in their own economies. Also skepticism had grown among governments in several industrialized countries about the statist approach to development. This was the second challenge faced by the Lagos approach.

The IMF Board was dominated by members whose ideological climate had changed dramatically in the early 1980s. In the United States, the United Kingdom, and Germany, President Reagan, Prime Minister Thatcher, and Chancellor Kohl espoused a new antistate, antigovernment, free-market rhetoric. Their hostility to government spending, industrial policy, and the welfare state soon spread into their view of aid. Suddenly the focus was on the failures of development policy in the 1970s (Bauer 1984; Tucker 1977). In the worst cases in Africa the state-owned, state-driven economic model had created and sustained a kleptocratic state. Across the continent as a whole, economic development seemed at the time to have failed. In the twenty years from 1960 to 1980 the average annual rate of growth for Africa was about 4.8 percent, dropping to 2.9 percent for the least developed countries (Economic Commission for Africa 1980). At the time these figures were treated as disastrous, although by the late 1990s they looked like a golden age of development on the continent. For example, over the period 1990–2001 Africa suffered a 0.2 percent average annual decline in gross national income (World Bank 2003, ch. 1).

Against the background of scarce aid resources and skepticism about state-centered development, the IMF defined conditionality for Africa in the 1980s within two important assumptions. First, the IMF treated the primary cause of the 1980s crisis in sub-Saharan African countries as internal rather than external to each country. Eschewing African leaders' concerns about external shocks and constraints and how these might be mitigated (a central theme of the Lagos Plan), the institution focused its attention on actions indebted governments needed to take. The IMF chose to reject the state-centered industrialization model, which had prevailed until the end of the 1970s, and to focus on reducing the state in the hope that this would enhance the role of the private sector.

The IMF's approach began first and foremost with a requirement that governments undertake stabilization policies to reduce the budget deficit and stem inflation. This was evident in the conditions attached to loans during the 1970s. The Fund's largest loan at the time was to Zambia, which took out its first stand-by arrangement with the IMF in 1973 when its border with Rhodesia was closed by that country's white-controlled minority government of Ian Smith, who was trying to suppress the majority struggle for control in that country. Among many other effects, the border closure severely disrupted Zambia's commercial transportation system, decimating the country's trade (Boughton 2001, p. 787).

In 1976 and 1978 Zambia took out two further IMF loans, this time as its economy, heavily dependent on copper exports, was rocked by shifts in the world copper price. In each program the Fund required the Zambian government to take measures to reduce inflation and trim the deficit. In these terms Zambia succeeded and indeed this spurred further IMF offers of assistance (IMF External Evaluation 1998, p. 95; Callaghy 1990, p. 290; Boughton 2001, p. 291). However, a 50 percent reduction in the deficit between 1976 and 1979 was essentially achieved by cutting recurrent and capital expenditure, and this policy soon caused a political backlash that wiped out the gains of reform (Callaghy 1990, p. 290).

Even as Zambia met its core program conditions, its debts mounted alarmingly, and by the early 1980s Zambia could no longer repay the IMF in a timely fashion (Boughton 2001, p. 787). For the IMF this spelled out the need for deeper measures of "structural adjustment," while critics argue that the case of Zambia in the 1970s underlined the extenuating impact of external factors— political, strategic, and economic (Economic Commission for Africa 1982).

The alternative to the tough stabilization approach taken by the IMF— which African members probably would have pushed, had they had more voice in the organization—was a more explicitly gradualist approach to reform as advocated by many development economists at the time. The Economic Commission for Africa produced an African Alternative Framework as a conceptual starting point, although this did not include specific program designs (Economic Commission for Africa 1989). A more specific alternative was drawn up by an independent team of advisers to Uganda, sponsored by the Canadian International Development Research Centre, who advocated a program of economic stabilization and reform while retaining several key elements of the existing system of centralized planning and control (Uganda

Economic Study Team 1987). Likewise, a three-person group drew up an alternative plan for Tanzania (McDonald and Sahle 2002). At the core of gradualist alternatives was an attention to attenuating the vulnerability of African economies to world markets, exogenous economic shocks, and their reliance on exporting primary commodities—in the case of Uganda 90 percent of its export earnings came from global coffee markets (Loxley 1986).

The issue that the G7-dominated IMF marginalized was commodities.[3] Commodity exports lay at the core of the problem for many low-income developing economies. Their reliance on exporting commodities laid a vicious economic trap for three reasons. First, access to markets for commodities was (and still is) tightly controlled by industrialized countries who, instead of opening their markets, operate tight discretionary policies. Second, the price and demand for many primary commodities was in a long-term decline, which meant that even if the volatility in world prices for commodities were alleviated, an alternative long-term strategy was still required. Finally, the possibilities for poor countries to pursue a longer-term strategy of moving away from raw commodities into semi-processed and processed goods were blocked by industrialized countries who applied higher and higher barriers to these goods, effectively kicking away the development ladder from any countries trying to move up it: a 1988 United Nations Conference on Trade and Development (UNCTAD) study showed industrialized countries were applying twice the level of nontariff barriers to manufactured goods from developing countries compared to what they were applying on manufactured trade with each other (UNCTAD 1989; Chakravarthi 1989).

A more African approach to the continent's crisis in the 1980s would have recognized that all small, low-income economies were being buffeted by factors beyond their control, including shifts in terms of trade, in capital flows, and in world interest rates. Calling on small, low-income economies to adjust their own economies was like exhorting passengers in a lifeboat to paddle faster when their raft is in the middle of the Atlantic Ocean in a hurricane. No matter how impressive the efforts of the passengers, it is unlikely that their paddling will bring them to safety. Without a coherent approach to international conditions, it was clear to some economists that the "adjustment" programs being foisted on one country at a time would not work. The fallacy in the IMF's approach was, as Tony Killick expressed in 1990, that adjustment "has come to be viewed primarily as something to be undertaken by deficit countries, with no equivalent pressure for action on surplus countries" (Killick 1990b).

The IMF was not sufficiently responsive to its African members, even as it began so extensively to work with them. Instead, the institution remained

---

[3] The 1963 Compensatory Financing Facility provided the possibility of only very limited and short-term alleviation and shareholders failed to expand it in the 1980s.

beholden to major shareholders in the institution who had extended loans to African countries throughout the 1960s and 1970s for a variety of geostrategic, postcolonial, economic, and domestic political reasons. In the 1980s, finding that their aid-dependent partners could not repay even the most concessional loans, the creditor countries directed the IMF to expand its engagement, thrusting the institution into a more active role in Africa, without altering its governance.

By the end of the 1980s the IMF was playing a key role coordinating the region's relations with creditors, setting down the conditions debtors needed to meet in order to continue borrowing not just from itself but from all donors. Sub-Saharan African countries had become massively indebted throughout the decade. The total debt of countries on the continent doubled between 1979 and 1985 and doubled again by the early 1990s. The value of their external debt as a share of gross national product (GNP) rose from around 25 percent in 1980 to more than 80 percent in 1994. As the IMF coordinated reschedulings in the 1980s, the debt burden of African countries increased sharply. As debt-service payments were postponed, outstanding debt was increased as debt-servicing obligations were added to the capital sum.

The IMF's injection of resources was seriously limited. In March 1986 the Structural Adjustment Facility (SAF) was created in the IMF with $3.2 billion to provide loans to the poorest countries (essentially the same as those eligible for assistance from the Bank's International Development Association) with balance of payments difficulties. However, after strong US opposition to new or easy money, the facility was meagerly funded from repayments on previous loans to the IMF's Trust Fund (Boughton 2001, p. 646). Likewise, strong UK opposition tightly limited the Enhanced Structural Adjustment Facility (ESAF) in 1987 with the US administration arguing that it needed to concentrate on securing appropriations for the International Development Association (IDA) from Congress and refusing to countenance selling some of the IMF's gold stock in order to finance the new facility (and US approval was a *sine qua non* since such a sale required 85 percent of total voting power on the Board of the Fund).

The Enhanced Structural Adjustment Facility magnified the bargaining power of the IMF vis-à-vis Africa. It combined much-needed loans with particularly far-ranging and high-level conditionality covering medium-term policy changes and short-term monetary and fiscal management. It was a prerequisite for loans from all other bilateral donors and other international funding programs. Fund conditions were thus "at the top of the hierarchy of donor conditionality" not because of the amount of resources that the Fund transferred but because the Fund was the lead coordinator (IMF External Evaluation 1998, p. 26).

Loans from the IMF in the 1980s reflected new stringent constraints on creditor countries: a squeeze on resources as their industrialized country members responded to general economic downturn; and a new ideological imprimatur imposed very rapidly and forcefully in each institution when the Reagan administration took office (Boughton 2001; Kapur et al. 1997). These constraints meant that it was easier for the IMF to call on borrowers to tighten their belts than it was to extract more resources from industrialized country members, or indeed even their cooperation in macroeconomic coordination. In short, the priorities and policies of the organization, as it implemented far-reaching initiatives in Africa, were being set without sufficient input from the countries most affected.

IV. Implementing policies without responsiveness

A core part of the IMF's stated mission in sub-Saharan Africa throughout the 1980s was to bring about economic reform. Effectively to do this, the organization needed close relations with governments, and policy prescriptions which responded appropriately to rapidly changing political and economic circumstances. The case of Senegal, a leading recipient of aid per capita in Africa from 1980 to 1987, illustrates the way politics, economics, and conditionality were intertwined. It highlights the extent to which the IMF's governance structure enabled the organization to be unresponsive to the rapidly shifting needs and constraints of African borrowers.

In the late 1970s, economic crisis and a collapse in revenue from peanut exports on which Senegal depended brought reformer Abdou Diouf to power, first as prime minister and then as president (Mbodji 1991). In a first flurry of reform, Prime Minister Diouf took a loan from the IMF's Extended Fund Facility. The loan required the government to cut its current account deficit by more than half, almost double net public savings by 1985, increase overall investment from 16 percent in 1981 to 18 percent in 1985, and achieve a 4 percent annual growth rate of GDP (World Bank 1989c; Ka and Van de Walle 1994, p. 309).

The IMF loan soon ran into difficulty. Bad weather affected exports and necessitated greater food imports, public debt was higher than originally admitted, and fiscal revenues actually declined from 1981 to 1984 (Ka and Van de Walle 1994, p. 311). The IMF loan was discontinued in January 1981 and replaced by a one-year stand-by arrangement. For a government facing a sharp drop in the export price of peanuts and in the run-up to an election, it was increasingly difficult to sustain unpopular, contractionary reforms (Landell-Mills and Ngo 1991, p. 48; Mbodji 1991, pp. 124–5). For some analysts this demonstrated that Diouf's political base was too narrow and technocratic with insufficient grounding in political parties, the political process, and electoral politics of Senegal—a constraint that soon began to change (Ka and Van de Walle 1994).

Immediately after the 1983 elections in Senegal, Diouf began to consolidate his political power. He eliminated the post of prime minister and limited the power of the National Assembly, strongly reinforcing his position as president. He also began to usher a new breed of technocrats into positions of authority across all ministries, enhancing and streamlining the capacity of the government to negotiate with external aid and lending agencies and to undertake new economic policies. Principal among the new breed of officials was Mamoudou Toure, a former IMF official who was to lead Senegal's structural adjustment effort from 1985.

By mid-1984 Senegal enjoyed a new IMF loan (and three newly approved World Bank loans) (IMF–Senegal 2004; World Bank 2004). The government embarked on a program of economic reform. Government expenditure was slashed, credit was controlled, and fiscal and current account deficits were both cut. As Senegal struggled with an exchange rate fixed within the African Financial Community (CFA) franc zone and fluctuating against the dollar, it relied heavily in the period 1980–7 on foreign aid flows, which grew by about 18 percent per year, totaling about one-fifth of Senegal's GDP.

By 1987 the president's reform agenda faced powerful opposition. Austerity and cuts in government spending soon led to student boycotts, school closures, strikes, and union opposition to the government. In the aftermath of the 1988 election a state of emergency was called by the government as opponents of the government went on a rampage, and even once order had been restored, public demonstrations against reform continued. In the spring of 1989 riots took on an ethnic dimension as tensions with neighboring Mauritania spilt over into the streets of Dakar, forcing Mauritanian shopkeepers out.

The IMF succeeded in supporting the government to undertake stabilization, but longer-term reforms seemed to be slipping rapidly out of reach. The key technocrats in charge of structural adjustment—Mamoudou Toure and Cheikh Hamidou Kane—both left government in March 1988. Meanwhile, key structural adjustment policies were reversed in the face of the need to shore up political support and the government's lack of revenue. For example, the government had removed trade protective tariffs as a core part of a relatively successful new industrial policy (Boone 1991). By 1988, the policy was reversed because the government needed the revenues that tariffs produced and a small number of large, powerful businesses lobbied against it (Ka and Van de Walle 1994). While outside commentators accuse the IMF (and other donors) of having imposed conditions that were too detailed and copious to be implemented and too seldom enforced (Ka and Van de Walle 1994, p. 329), Senegalese critics of structural adjustment in that country argue that it imposed unsustainable and unacceptable costs in health, sanitation, education, and literacy (Ndiaye 2003).

In retrospect, a survey of the assumptions underpinning the IMF's plan makes clear why it failed. During the 1980s, the IMF (and World Bank) justified the program in Senegal as one which, after the initial stabilization and a first phase of adjustment, would achieve an annual growth rate of around 3.8 percent. This prediction was based on some extraordinary premises. For example, it was assumed that liberalization in agriculture and industry would produce an immediate "supply response." In other words, farmers could and would rapidly increase production in response to greater market freedom. Similarly, industry would expand as privatization and liberalization attracted new credit and permitted new export sectors to flourish. Unsurprisingly (given all other cases of stabilization and structural adjustment) new policies would take much longer to produce change, and in Senegal there were technical and environmental factors along with wide fluctuations in world market prices of exports and low international peanut prices that prevented an expansion of food production and exports (Landell-Mills and Ngo 1991, p. 52). In respect of industry, the establishment of new private-sector activity and increased investment would require at the very least a more developed banking system. More generally, in the words of one scholar examining the evidence in the textile industry, "Senegal's Structural Adjustment programs offered no economically viable or politically acceptable means of restructuring the existing textile industry" (Boone 1991, p. 146).

The problem with the Fund's approach to Senegal was that while it fitted well with the priorities of the IMF's most powerful members (to reduce their commitments to Africa in the face of their own straitened economic circumstances), it did little to balance the external and internal possibilities and constraints facing Senegal. One such constraint was the country's inability to devalue its currency. As a member of the West African Monetary Union, Senegal was locked into the CFA franc zone arrangements. In essence this left the government with only two real instruments of adjustment: cutting government expenditure, and controlling exports and imports. The overvalued CFA franc made the latter extremely difficult.

Why did the IMF accept and support Senegal's currency arrangement? In economic terms a permanently fixed and externally guaranteed exchange rate coupled with a supranational central bank should promote low inflation and encourage savings, investment, and growth. These benefits have been reviewed by several IMF and World Bank economists (Bhatia 1985; Devarajan and de Melo 1987; Elbadawi and Majd 1992). Certainly low inflation was achieved within the franc zone and some scholars go further and positively correlate the currency arrangement with growth (Devarajan and de Melo 1987; Guillaumont et al. 1988). However, these studies also show that members did not benefit equally. Indeed, smaller countries such as Senegal did much worse than the larger members (Medhora 2000). Furthermore, the most obvious benefit of the currency arrangement—exchange rate stability—may well have been illusory for Senegal since the real effective exchange rate was more unstable than the nominal effective exchange rate (de Macedo 1986). In economic terms there was (and still is) genuine debate and disagreement as to the merits and demerits of Senegal's currency arrangement through the 1980s.

For the IMF there was a further political reason underpinning support for Senegal's currency arrangement. As it is one of France's former colonies and largest aid recipients, decisions about Senegal are led by France's preferences, with other powerful shareholders in the international institutions loath to intervene in respect of what they recognize as a special sphere of influence. Senegal's currency arrangements in the 1980s were part of France's CFA franc zone encompassing the West African Monetary Union and a currency union among the central African states across which France guaranteed the convertibility of the common currency—the CFA franc (Medhora 1992). France vigorously opposed CFA franc devaluation and fought any Fund recommendations in this respect. The French position was not robustly challenged and altered by the Board.

The IMF's governance structure did not ensure that the institution "heard" and adapted to the escalating problems faced by African governments during the 1980s, nor did it provide adequate oversight of IMF policies in the region. The fact was that conditionality and structural adjustment were not working: one worldwide survey of 305 IMF programs from 1979 to 1993 found implementation failure in 53 percent of cases, where failure was defined as a country not implementing 20 percent or more of the program's conditions (Killick 1996). A number of evaluations undertaken by the IMF also provide evidence. Combing through the studies, which use a variety of methodologies, it is difficult to find any evidence that countries that entered into programs of structural adjustment with the IMF did any better than countries that did not.[4] It was not until the late 1990s that the IMF Board finally commissioned an independent evaluation of its work in Africa (IMF External Evaluation 1998).

V. To whom should the institution be accountable?

The IMF's work in Africa over the past two decades has been characterized by extreme slowness in responding to challenges on the ground, by ineffectiveness in achieving stated goals, and by a lack of accountability for poor advice, poor outcomes, or inappropriate priorities. Each of these problems has a direct link to the governance of the organization. If affected countries were more engaged in informing the organization—through its staff, its senior management, and its Board—if they had greater confidence in working with the organization, and if they were able to hold it more closely to account, then it could be argued that the IMF could have done its job better. So how could the governance structure be improved?

---

[4] See the excellent summary of the IMF's own analysis from 1988 onwards in Boughton 2001 and the ESAF review (IMF External Evaluation 1998).

A. Better representation through increased basic votes

Basic votes were originally distributed in equal numbers to all members of the institution. They were a symbol of state equality in institutions which other-wise allocated votes proportional to economic weight. Currently basic votes represent just 2.1 percent of total votes in the IMF. At the founding of the institution, they represented just over 10 percent of votes. The result has been to erode equality among members in a subtle way. If basic votes were to be brought back to their original level, the effect on African constituencies in the IMF would be fairly small. It would raise their voting power by just under 2 percentage points.

This would not alter the power balance within the institution. However, more subtle effects might be achieved. First, an increase in basic votes would permit African countries to change constituencies and to form smaller ones in which each could participate more fully and better hold their representative to account (more on this below). Second, at the margins, a modest increase in voting power could enhance the incentive on powerful members to consult African members. That said, there is a more effective way to do this.

B. Creating an incentive to consult African members through double-majority voting

An alternative to increasing basic votes in the IMF, or a way significantly to leverage an increase in basic votes is to introduce a double-majority voting system which protects the right of small countries within the organization. Proposals in this vein have been prepared by advisers to the German government as well as by scholars working on the governance of multilateral development banks.

Already in the IMF a double majority is required to alter the Articles of Agreement as well as to expel a member or deny a member state benefits. This means not just that there must be 85 percent of voting power agreeing with an amendment, but a 60 percent majority of members. Other inter-national organizations also use double-majority voting (e.g. the EU Council of Ministers, the Global Environment Facility in the World Bank). The effect of a double-majority voting rule applied to a wider range of decisions would be to ensure that the Board's consensus reflected not only a majority of voting power but also the support of a majority (or set percentage) of members of the organization—achieving a similar effect to basic votes (as above).

Applying a double-majority voting rule to a wider range of decisions would require amending the articles (which itself requires the double majority out-lined above). But this would not be extraordinary. Many such changes have been undertaken in the past—in particular so as to expand the range of decisions for which a special majority is required (i.e. a simple majority of 85% of voting power as opposed to a double majority).

The impact? As argued above in respect of basic votes, at present the G7 members of the IMF command just over 40 percent of voting power and need only find one further Executive Director's vote in order to pass a decision. In other words, ten or so members of the institution can pass a measure. A double-majority voting rule would mean that decisions would have to command not only 50 percent of voting power, but also the support of, say 50 percent, of the membership. In others words, the G7 would have to forge a wider alliance of members in order to pass measures. This would immediately create an incentive for the powerful members of the Board to forge alliances with the numerically large African constituencies. One obvious issue to which an extension of the decision-making rule would apply is the institutions' leadership selection (more on this below).

C. Enhancing capacity to prepare, to lobby, and to have a voice on the Board

Mustering a coalition of countries within the IMF requires extensive preparation and lobbying. For this reason the lack of capacity of many developing countries within the institution has been highlighted by many. It has several aspects. Traditionally, for each "chair" on the Board, an Alternate Director and a number of advisers is allocated and paid for by the institution. Clearly this greatly benefits to countries who have their own chair or are in a small constituency. Conversely, it means that the resources spent on supporting any chair representing a large number of countries are tiny if measured on a per country basis.

The workload imposed on many developing country representatives is unwieldy. For this reason a discussion has begun about how to enhance their capacity. In large constituencies it is also more difficult to ensure full consultation, report, and accountability to member countries. A modest recognition of this has been made in the recent decision to introduce a communication system which will enable video-conferencing and access to Bank and Fund documents from the capitals. However, the fact that there is already very little support from member country bureaucracies suggests that this will not resolve the problem. Unlike the British, American, or Dutch chairs—to name but three—who benefit from substantial back-up technical support from their home bureaucracies, several developing country chairs do not.

One possibility is for countries to shift constituencies, grouping themselves into smaller units and making the most of the fact that there are no set rules governing how countries group together within the IMF.[5] For some countries this would permit more effective and more active representation.

---

[5] See Woods and Lombardi 2006. Constituencies are not written into the IMF's Articles which provide for the membership-wide elections of 15 Directors (Schedule E), increased to 19 by a Resolution of the Board of Governors in 1992.

The "constituency system" has permitted significant change in groups within the institutions—Indonesia has shifted constituency in the IMF three times (Boughton 2003; Woods and Lombardi 2006). The Australian-led constituency began as a partnership with South Africa and other southern Africa countries, but then as members shifted, became an Asia–Pacific grouping. That said, the overall number of chairs on the Board (currently 24) has to be agreed by the membership as a whole. If African countries were to regroup in smaller constituencies, this would require either that their relative voting share be first bolstered (to meet the minimum required to form a constituency), and/or that the number of chairs on the Board be increased. The alternative is for African members to regroup with large vote-wielding countries—taking into account the necessary trade-offs implied for agenda-setting, influence, and power within the constituency. However, these trade-offs are considerable and to prevent African members in mixed constituencies from simply being drowned out would require careful power-balancing within constituency memberships.

D. Bolster and build on networks and enhance accountability

Underpinning the influence of powerful countries and groupings within the IMF is a degree of networking absent among African countries. In the G7, the EURIMF, and the Asia–Pacific groupings, countries bolster pre-existing links to one another to coordinate their policies, to share information, and to leverage their access to senior management and staff within the organization. Developing countries could initially use trade and other partnerships to attempt to build similar, albeit not-as-powerful, networks. African countries participate in the G11 (borrowers' group) of the Board but this has not proven effective (Woods and Lombardi 2006).

Further to this, the United States and Western European countries informally get to select the leader of the organization as well as to weigh in heavily on key senior management positions. This gives these countries a direct additional leash on which to hold the institution. It is for this reason that developing countries made a significant move when they nominated their own candidate to be Managing Director of the IMF in the selection which culminated in Horst Kohler's appointment. This issue has still not been satisfactorily taken forward. Crucial it is for members to recognize that it is not simply a matter of who gets to choose the leader. The selection and appointment of senior management creates a structure of accountability for the whole staff. It goes to the heart of who holds the institutions to account and how. For developing countries to have more voice in either the IMF or the World Bank requires opening up the main lines of accountability of leadership within each organization to the full membership.

Finally, the issue of developing country voice and influence within the governance of the IMF and World Bank is not just an issue of capacity and voting-power of Executive Directors. As intimated above, it also necessitates enhanced accountability of these Directors back to their members. Presently, the links between most member governments and their Directors on the Board are weak. There are few formal mechanisms of consultation, report, or account which connect that official to governments or parliaments ostensibly being represented within the group. Improvements are currently being made to the means of communication between Directors and countries. Several more robust steps could be taken. These include: (1) a closer, more formalized system of reporting to Parliament in each constituency country; (2) full transparency of positions taken by Directors on the Board and of decisions taken so as to enable a broader range of national actors to engage and monitor decision making in each of the institutions; (3) in-region offices for the African chairs (as has been proposed by a former Director); (4) a formal evaluation procedure for all Directors and staff in which constituency members participate (Woods and Lombardi 2006).

E. Leadership in the IMF

The senior management of the IMF is crucial to the overall governance of the organization. Chairing the Board and holding to account all staff within the IMF is the Managing Director who is, in theory, elected by all Executive Directors. In practice, he or she is appointed and held to account by European shareholders and the United States (which has always insisted that the second in command at the IMF be a US national acceptable to the administration in power at the time of his or her appointment). This makes the senior management directly accountable to those who appoint and can renew (or not) him or her. In turn, all staff report to the senior management and become accountable to those same preferences.

The board of the IMF has already discussed changing these arrangements. In 2001 a working group drawn from both the Fund and Bank Boards formally proposed that there should at least be clear criteria for identifying, nominating, and selecting qualified candidates and that there should be transparency in the subsequent process (IMF 2001). To a limited extent these proposals were invoked in the selection of Rodrigo de Rato as the previous head of the IMF. They were, however, comprehensively ignored when Paul Wolfowitz was appointed by the United States to head the World Bank and in the subsequent appointment of Robert Zoellick. Subsequently, in 2007 the IMF Board adopted a formal resolution opening the process to all candidates on an equal basis without regard to nationality. This was followed by the selection of yet another European as Managing Director. It remains the case that the IMF needs a leadership selection (and reappointment) process which fully engages all members, giving them an active voice in this important mechanism for ensuring the responsiveness, effectiveness, and accountability set out at the beginning of this chapter.

VI. References

Bauer, Peter. 1984. *Reality and Rhetoric: Studies in the Economics of Development*. London: Weidenfeld and Nicolson.

Bhatia, Rattan. 1985. The West African Monetary Union: An Analytical Review. *IMF Occasional Paper* No. 35. Washington, DC: IMF.

Boone, Catherine. 1991. Politics under the Specter of Deindustrialization: Structural Adjustment in Practice, in Christopher Delgado and Sidi Jammeh (eds.), *The Political Economy of Senegal under Structural Adjustment*. New York: Praeger, pp.127–49.

Boughton, James M. 2001. *Silent Revolution: The International Monetary Fund, 1979–1989*. Washington, DC: IMF.

——2003. *Governing the IMF: Issues for Asia*. Washington, DC: IMF.

Callaghy, Thomas. 1990. Lost Between State and Market: The Politics of Economic Adjustment in Ghana, Zambia, and Nigeria, in Joan Nelson (ed.), *Economic Crisis and Policy Change*. Princeton: Princeton University Press, pp.257–319.

Chakravarthi, Raghavan. 1989. South's Share in World Manufactured Exports Grows, But..., *SUNS–South–North Development Monitor: From GATT–Uruguay Round to the WTO*. (Geneva). <http://www.sunsonline.org/trade/areas/environm/> (accessed 10 December 2004).

De Macedo, J.B. 1986. Collective Pegging to a Single Currency: The West African monetary union, in S. Edwards and L. Ahamed (eds.), *Economic Adjustment and Exchange Rates in Developing Countries*. Chicago: University of Chicago Press.

Devarajan, S., and J. de Melo. 1987. Evaluating Participation in African Monetary Unions: A Statistical Analysis of the CFA Zones. *World Development* 15 (4): 483–96.

Economic Commission for Africa. 1980. *The Lagos Plan of Action*. At <http://www.uneca.org/itca/ariportal/docs/lagos_plan.PDF>.

Economic Commission for Africa. (30 April) 1982. *Declaration of Tripoli*. Tripoli: Conference of Ministers, Economic Commission for Africa.

Elbadawi, Ibrahim, and Nader Majd. 1992. Fixed Parity of the Exchange Rate and Economic Performance in the CFA Zone. *PRE Working Papers* WPS 830. Washington, DC: World Bank.

Guillaumont, P., S. Guillaumont, and P. Plane. 1988. Participating in African Monetary Unions. An Alternative Evaluation. *World Development* 16 (5): 569–76.

IMF, External Evaluation. 1998. *External Evaluation of ESAF: A Report by a Group of Independent Experts*. Washington, DC: IMF.

IMF, 2001. *Draft Joint Report of the Working Group to Review the Process for Selection of the President of the World Bank and Managing Director of the IMF*. 28 April 2001. Washington, DC: IMF. At <http://www.imf.org/external/spring/2001/imfc/select.htm>.

——2008. *Report of the Managing Director to the International Monetary and Financial Committee on IMF Quota and Voice Reform*. 8 April 2008. Washington, DC: IMF.

IMF–Senegal. 2004. *Transactions with the IMF–Senegal*. Washington, DC: IMF. At <http://www.imf.org/external/np/tre/tad/> (accessed 10 December 2004).

Independent Evaluation Office of the IMF. 2007. *The IMF and Aid to Sub-Saharan Africa*. Washington, DC: IMF/IEO.

—— 2008. *Aspects of IMF Corporate Governance: Including the Role of the Executive Board*. Washington, DC: IMF/IEO.

Ka, Samba, and Nicholas Van de Walle. 1994. Senegal: Stalled Reform in a Dominant Party System, in Stephan Haggard and Steven B. Webb (eds.), *Voting for Reform: Democracy, Political Liberalization, and Economic Adjustment*. New York: Oxford University Press.

Kapur, Devesh, John Lewis, and Richard Webb. 1997. *The World Bank: Its First Half Century. Vol. 1*. Washington, DC: Brookings Institution.

Killick, Tony. 1990a. *A Reaction Too Far: Economic Theory and the Role of the State in Developing Countries*. ODI Development Policy Studies. London: Overseas Development Institute.

—— 1990b. *Markets and Governments in Agricultural and Industrial Adjustment*. London: Overseas Development Institute.

—— 1996. *IMF Programmes in Developing Countries: Design and Impact*. London: Overseas Development Institute.

Landell-Mills, Pierre, and Brian Ngo. 1991. Creating the Basis for Long-Term Growth, in Christopher L. Delgado and Sidi Jammeh (eds.), *The Political Economy of Senegal Under Structural Adjustment*. Westport, Connecticut: Greenwood Publishing Group.

Lofchie, Michael. 1994. The New Political Economy of Africa, in David E. Apter and Carl G. Rosberg (eds.), *Political Development and the New Realism in Sub-Saharan Africa*. Charlottesville: University Press of Virginia, pp. 145–83.

Loxley, John. 1986. Alternative Approaches to Stabilization in Africa, in Gerald Helleiner (ed.), *Africa and the International Monetary Fund*. Papers presented at a symposium held in Nairobi, Kenya, 13–15 May. Washington, DC: IMF, pp. 117–47.

Mbodji, Mohamed. 1991. The Politics of Independence: 1960–86, in Christopher Delgado and Sidi Jammeh (eds.), *The Political Economy of Senegal under Structural Adjustment*. New York: Praeger.

McDonald, David A., and Eunice Njeri Sahle, eds. 2002. *The Legacies of Julius Nyerere: Influences on Development, Discourse, and Practice in Africa*. Trenton, NJ: Africa World Press.

Medhora, Rohinton. 1992. The West African Monetary Union: Institutional Arrangements and the Link with France. *Canadian Journal of Development Studies* 13 (2): 151–80.

—— 2000. "Dollarization in the Americas: Lessons from the Franc zone?" Ottawa: International Development Research Center.

Ndiaye, Abdourahmane. 2003. *Foreign Debt, Structural Adjustment Programs, and Poverty in Senegal*. ATTAC. At <http://attac.org/fra/list/doc/ndiayeen.htm>.

Rustomjee, Cyrus. 2005. Improving Southern Voice on the IMF Board: Quo Vadis Shareholders?, in Barry Carin and Angela Wood (eds), *Accountability of the International Monetary Fund*. Ashgate and IDRC.

Tucker, Robert. 1977. *The Inequality of Nations*. New York: Basic Books.

Uganda Economic Study Team. 1987. *Advisers Appointed June–July 1986, to Advise on Short and Medium Term Economic Policy in Uganda.* Ottawa: International Development Research Center.

UNCTAD. 1989. *Trade in Manufactures and Semi-manufactures of Developing Countries and Territories, 1989 Review.* Geneva: UNCTAD Secretariat (UNCTAD/TD/B/ C.2/228).

United Nations Economic Commission for Africa. 1989. The African Alternative Framework to Structural Adjustment Programs for Socio-Economic Recovery and Transformation/(AAF-SAF) (United Nations Economic Commission for Africa, Addis Ababa, 1989).

Van de Walle, Nicholas. 2001. *African Economies and the Politics of Permanent Crisis, 1979–1999.* Cambridge: Cambridge University Press.

Waterbury, John. 1999. The Long Gestation and Brief Triumph of Import-Substituting Industrialization. *World Development* 27 (2): 323–41.

Woods, Ngaire. 2006. *The Globalizers: The IMF, the World Bank, and their Borrowers.* Ithaca: Cornell University Press.

—— and Domenico Lombardi. 2006. Uneven Patterns of Governance: How Developing Countries Are Represented in the IMF, *Review of International Political Economy* 13 (3): 480–515.

World Bank. 1989a. *Adjustment Lending: An Evaluation of Ten Years of Experience.* Washington, DC: World Bank.

—— 1989b. *Sub-Saharan Africa: From Crisis to Sustainable Growth.* Washington, DC: World Bank.

—— 1989c. *Africa's Adjustment and Growth in the 1980s.* Washington, DC: World Bank.

—— 2003. *African Development Indicators.* Washington, DC: World Bank.

—— 2004. *Country Information: Senegal.* Washington, DC: World Bank. At <http://web.worldbank.org/WBSITE/EXTERNAL/COUNTRIES/AFRICAEXT/SENEGALEXTN/0,,menuPK:296308~pagePK:141159~piPK:141110~theSitePK:296303,00.html>.

13

Proposing IMF Reforms for Low-Income Countries

Bessma Momani (University of Waterloo and Centre for International Governance Innovation)

I. Introduction

In recent years, the International Monetary Fund has faced a legitimacy crisis that has spawned a debate on how to reform the institution. Currently, the concerned policy community—comprising academics, think-tanks, member states, and the IMF itself—have put forth a plethora of reform proposals that are meant to address the loss of members' faith in the institution. Throughout the history of the IMF we have seen debates on what should be the Fund's appropriate mandate, role, scope, and activities. Today, however, there is a sense that members have lost faith in the institution, particularly after a series of financial crises of the late 1990s hit Emerging Market Economies (EMEs). The EMEs lost confidence in the IMF to predict, warn, and solve the repeated financial crises. Critics charged that the roots of IMF failure were its lack of accountability and undemocratic governance structure (Stiglitz, 2003). We have since seen IMF reform debates dominated by governance reform proposals to return the faith of would-be EME borrowers. Division in members' interests has been further segmented, as the current IMF governance reform proposals are meant to return the faith of EMEs, but in the meantime LICs have received less attention.

Recently, the IMF has been engaging in a debate with the concerned policy community about the Fund's future role and structure. The resulting reform proposals have weighed heavily on issues related to governance, however, these reform proposals reflect the interests of EME and G7 countries while providing less output value to LICs. Changes to Fund governance structures may be made in the name of democratizing the institution and augmenting the relative power position of EMEs, but the net gain accrued to LICs might be minimal and lean heavily toward being more symbolic. This raises the question, how are low income countries' needs for Fund reform different from those of the EMEs and the G7? If the Fund could be reformed to reflect LIC's needs, what type of reforms should be high on their agenda? This chapter argues that low-income countries would gain more from IMF reform proposals that addressed substantive policy issues; issues that debtors have long pursued about the efficacy, application, and fundamentals of Fund advice. In other words, improving Fund function would better serve LICs. Why have functional reform issues been sidelined in current Fund reform proposals? Explaining why the IMF reform debate has taken the turn to governance reforms rather than functional reforms is further explored.

II. Why do governance reform proposals have less output value to low-income countries?

While debates on reforming international organizations are often shaped by a variety of changing international political, economic, and normative circumstances, it is important to reflect on the output value of reform proposals to various stakeholders. Dominating the current IMF reform proposals today are three governance issues: reallocating IMF quotas and votes, reconfiguring the Executive Board, and examining the selection process of the Managing Director.[1] A number of these issues have been implemented by the IMF in recent years and others continue to be debated within and outside of the Fund. This author suggests that many of these governance reforms may be less effective in meeting the needs of the IMFs low-income countries than suggested by their proponents. Governance reforms may not result in the substantive changes to Fund policies that greatly affect low-income countries.

A. Quotas and votes

Perhaps the strongest item on the agenda of Fund reformers has been the redistribution of quotas and votes. Quotas determine the amount of money members can borrow, members' voting power on the Executive Board, and the amount members contribute to IMF liquidity (IMF, 2005). The Fund has responded to numerous studies showing how many of the EME's quotas are underrepresented and in 2006 raised the quota levels of China, Turkey, South Korea, and Mexico. In 2008, the Fund also agreed to a second round of quota increases that will benefit 54 countries that are mainly emerging market economies. Clearly, quotas and votes have not matched the pace of economic

---

[1] The Managing Director's attempts to devise a new IMF income model has also been an important part of his restructuring efforts.

growth and importance of many emerging market economies (Truman, 2006). Moreover, many have suggested that enhancing the quotas and votes to economically justified levels would improve Fund accountability to its members. In 2008, the Fund also committed to tripling members' basic votes (from 250 to 750) and to a simpler and clearer quota formula that will incorporate purchasing power parity in its GDP variable (IMF, 2008).

In theory, these quota reform measures are meant also to help LICs improve their nominal and relative quota shares and improve LIC participation in Fund governance and programs. This author argues, however, that several factors cast doubt on the idea that enhancing quotas and votes will serve LIC's long-term interests. Here, several points are worth noting. Increasing members' basic votes from approximately 2 percent today toward 11 percent of its relative historical position would apply to all members, making modest relative gains for LICs. Even increasing LICs' basic votes to 750 would do little in relative terms and result in modest changes to their overall quota standings (see Woods and Lombardi, 2006: 495). One benefit of increasing basic votes, however, would be to increase members' allowable ceiling on loan access. However, as the next point argues, even this benefit is less than useful.

The relationship between a member's quota and the amount a member could borrow has already been severed. Historically under traditional stand-by agreements, a member could borrow up to 100 percent of its quota each year to a maximum of 300 percent of its quota. These technical rules have been frequently trumped since the onset of the debt crisis and the 1990s financial crises because of "exceptional circumstance". The 1997 Supplemental Reserve Facility (SRF), for example, allowed EMEs "with exceptional balance of payments problems" due to sudden loss of market confidence to borrow without a formal link to their quota. In part taking advantage of the SRF, Turkey in 2002 borrowed 2,900 percent of its actual quota (Rapkin and Strand, 2006: 315). Low-income countries have also been benefactors of trumping lending limits. For example, lending programs like the former Enhanced Structural Adjustment Facility (ESAF) allowed developing countries to bypass the technical rules with enhanced access to financing that exceeded the limits of their quota contribution. Under the ESAF's successor, the Poverty Reduction and Growth Facility (PRGF), LICs can borrow up to a maximum of 185 percent of their quota in exceptional circumstances. But, the pool of resources used to finance the PRGF facilities do not come from the quota-based subscription, which gives LICs less stake in enhancing quotas (Bird and Rowlands, 2006: 157). Simply put, quotas are no longer a *sine qua non* of loan amounts, making this reform proposal of less value to LICs than might be thought. It is therefore of little surprise that some suggest removing the quota-borrowing limitation rule all together (Kelkar et al. 2004: 738; Rapkin and Strand, 2006: 315) and reconfiguring access limits to be based on need to finance balance of payments (Bird and Rowlands, 2006: 170).

Enhancing quotas and votes, it is argued, may not result in long-term and substantive changes for most LICs; perhaps more importantly, the economic rationale for enhancing LIC quotas and shares was also arguably weak. Low-income countries' actual quotas and votes were not disproportionate to their calculated quotas. If one were to examine the low-income countries' actual quotas prior to the 2008 increases and compare these to the calculated quotas (based on the then five economic variables taken into consideration), an overwhelming number of the 78 LICs were overrepresented in their quotas (see IMF, 2004a). The technical discrepancies in developing countries' actual and calculated quotas have been a part of the institution's historical compromise, where enhancing developing countries' quotas was intended to aid their perception of having a "consequential role" in the institution (Rapkin and Strand, 2006: 311). When the Fund Executive Board commissioned the Cooper team to redesign the Fund quota formula, it should have been to no one's surprise that the report's recommendation was to *decrease* the relative share of developing countries' quotas (see IMF, 2000). The LICs could not have made the claim that they were underrepresented using the quantitative variables and indicators debated within the Fund.

Another issue worth noting is that the IMF's tradition of consensual voting may actually compensate shortcomings in quota inequalities, to the benefit of smaller and less powerful countries. Evans and Finnemore (2001: 14) argue that the IMF's Executive Board tradition of not taking votes, but reaching decisions through consensus, actually gives members with smaller quotas an opportunity to shape the Board's final decisions. It could be argued that an African Executive Director, for example, has more influence in a 24-seat Executive Board where his or her position is used in shaping a consensus position, than if he or she had only 1.4 percent of voting power. So, despite the "inegalitarian distribution of votes" based on quotas, Evans and Finnemore (2001: 27) suggest that smaller countries' voice at the consensual Executive Board is a "democratizing feature" of the IMF that counterbalances quota inequalities.

Altering the quota formulas has also been an important part of IMF reform debates. Here are a couple of points to consider though. Some have suggested using population as a variable in quota formulas. This might help developing countries more generally, but not those countries designated as LICs. Most of the 78 LIC members are not very populous—India would be a notable exception—and so the benefits of using population as a variable in quota formulas would be limited. The notion of using population as a variable, or using a "one country one vote" (Westphalian) policy for that matter, is not currently being considered. Many have also suggested double-majority voting rules, where both majority of votes and majority number of members would be required to pass many of the decisions currently using a weighted voting rule at the Executive Board (see Rapkin and Strand, 2006; Woods, 2006). This could augment the voice of the 78 LIC members as they currently constitute

42 percent of Fund membership (IMF, 2007). The problem, however, is that these proposals will be politically difficult to achieve. Changing to a double-majority rule requires an amendment to the Articles of Agreement which must pass the US veto, and more importantly it requires the US Congress to approve a US Executive Director vote to amend the Articles. Again, the idea sounds morally persuasive, but may be politically challenging.

One point often suggested in international relations literature is that state effectiveness is also measured by how much others in the forum are affected by member states' positions. It is worth noting that many studies have found a correlation between countries' United Nations voting patterns and IMF loan approval, suggesting that issue-linkages are indeed made at the Executive Board (see Thacker, 1999; Oately and Yackee, 2004; Barro and Lee, 2005; Dreher and Jensen, 2007). Issue-linkages in the broader context of international economic and political relations is seen as important to members' Executive Directors' voting power or persuasive abilities. The question then is whether changes to quotas and votes within the Fund will make a difference if unreflective of the external power balance. As the Governor of the Bank of England aptly noted, "The fact that China has a small quota now relative to its calculated quota does not mean to say that people take China less seriously now than they would 12 months from now if the quota were increased" (King, 2006: 11). Quotas and votes may be altered within the Fund, but external power balance may be just as important to understanding Board members' influence. This takes us to the issue of Executive Board reform proposals.

B. The Executive Board

Numerous reform proposals had suggested consolidating many European, specifically Euro-led, seats to make room for more directors from developing countries and LICs on the Executive Board. Truman (2006) suggests that non-European states leave from EU-led constituencies and then EU-led constituencies absorb remaining EU states (Ireland, Spain, and Poland). In this way, EU members could be consolidated into fewer EU-led seats. Others suggest one seat to represent the entire eurozone (Camdessus 2005; Bini Smaghi, 2006; Lombardi and O'Neill, 2008). These proposals are ambitious, but at first blush we are talking about the addition of perhaps one additional Executive Board seat for the LICs. Particularly if consolidating European seats is a proposal that is to be combined with US calls to reduce the Executive Board from 24 to 20 by 2012 (see Guha, 2008). The likelihood of LICs' getting more than one other seat on a reduced IMF Board may be low if US preferences for the size of the Board are realized.

Increasing the number of Executive Directors from LICs on the Board, moreover, may not address the substantive policy concerns of LICs. Take the former Managing Director's proposal, before the 2006 Singapore meeting, of adding another African seat on the Executive Board. What effect will an additional seat have on LICs overall say in IMF decision-making and policy-making? One former African director argued that adding LIC votes and voice at the Board will result in improved loan conditionality (Rustomjee, 2004). Civil society actors have also suggested that added voice at the Board would allow less powerful members to refuse to give in to the Board's "pressure to liberalize" and to recruit more staff from the South (see Birdsall, 2003: 12). Several things cast doubt on these assumptions.

First, the Executive Board does not negotiate loan agreements, but can *collectively* play a role in vetoing or denying the whole of the loan agreement. In most cases, and there have been some exceptions, it is the IMF staff who negotiate the details of loan agreements and not the Executive Directors. That said, Executive Directors often play an informal mediating-like role between the staff and the government officials. Also, directors from powerful countries have been known to interfere politically in negotiations particularly when geopolitical interests are involved (see Momani, 2004). Directors from debtor states do not, however, have the same influence and often depend on polit-icking with powerful members to get concessions on conditionality. Moreover, as a former Mexican Executive Director noted, directors from debtor states do not take it upon themselves to challenge senior staff on country loan agree-ments, for fear of damaging country–IMF relations (Buira, 2003: 232). In an IEO survey of directors from the LICs, 56 percent stated that they rarely criticize staff and Management for fear of repercussions (IEO, 2008a: 16). Second, "pressure to liberalize" does not come from the Executive Board, nor for that matter from the IMF staff; instead, several factors are at play including structural, market, and ideational forces at the global level and economic, political, and social forces at the domestic level. On the domestic factor, indeed in many LICs, governments seek out IMF loans to help bring in a reform agenda (Vreeland, 2003). The Fund may then be used as a scapegoat for unpopular policies. Finally, how the IMF determines staff recruitment is linked less to Executive Board decisions and more to constraints of the IMF's technocratic organizational culture (see Momani, 2005a).

A broader question to ask is, will a third African Executive Director make a difference to the workings of the Board? If, as Woods and Lombardi (2006) note, elected constituencies by their nature tend to lean toward technocratic individuals as opposed to political bargainers, there may be even less impact of an elected African seat than this reform proposal would suggest. Moreover, having several seats at the Executive Board is worth less than having one effective seat—the United States par excellence. How to improve the effective-ness of LICs' representation at the Executive Board, without new seats, is then a matter worthy of discussion. Woods and Lombardi (2006) have argued that developing countries (both LICs and EMEs) could improve their effectiveness at the Executive Board through coalition-building and making constituency chairs more accountable to its members. In addition to reforming decision-making rules to maximize the voting power of developing countries, the authors point to subtler forms of internal organizational reforms that will help those countries enhance their voice at the Board. Similarly, the Fund has implemented a positive step to ease the workload burden on the two African directors, who manage a large number of constituency members. This involves helping the existing African directors with added staffing and the appointment of an additional alternate Executive Director (IMF, 2008). These informal and staffing changes to the existing directors' offices are helpful initiatives.

Finally, several prominent policymakers have suggested a nonresident or "professionalized" Board which would meet infrequently over the year (See King, 2006; DeGregorio, 1999; Kenen, 2006; also see IEO, 2008a). Proponents of this view could point to how powerful members of the Executive Board have, albeit infrequently, politically interfered in the IMF staff's technocratic analysis, prompting IMF "clientism" and powerful members' interference in staff–debtor negotiations (see Stone, 2004; Momani, 2004). But, this reform proposal might enhance the authority of the IMF staff to prescribe conditionality without a political check or oversight of conditions. In the case of Africa, Stone (2004) has documented Executive Board political involvement, particularly US, French, and British, into African debtor conditionality "to prevent rigorous enforcement". Without the Executive Board checking on the technocratic staff, we might see greater theoretical advice that is insensitive to the African domestic political situation (see Woods, 2006: ch. 6). Moreover, creating an "independent" Board would not depoliticize the organization, but "further distance most countries from the institutions" (Woods, 2006: 205). One could add that LICs would have the most to lose from an independent Board, because it has fewer external forums, access points, and issue-linkages to use in influencing decisions.

C. Managing Director

One issue with strong symbolism is the continued appointment of a European to the position of Managing Director. As Ariel Buira noted, "it is neocolonial to assume that only a European is capable of becoming managing director" (Buira, 2003: 231). For many LICs and developing countries, more broadly, the symbolism of having a European in charge of an organization that is mainly used by the LICs and developing world is reminiscent of Europe's "white man's burden". Opening the selection process to include other qualified non-European candidates has been proposed from within and outside the

IMF (Kahler, 2002: 92–8; Ostry and Zettelmeyer, 2005: 17) and has become an official policy endorsed by the Executive Board.

But, how useful is this reform idea for low-income countries? Would a Managing Director from the United States or Africa, as opposed to Europe, make a difference in day-to-day IMF policies?

The theoretical literature is mixed on the importance of international organization (IO) leadership to affect outcomes. While many have argued that leaders can make a difference in international organizations (see Cox and Jacobson, 1973: 20–5), recent systematic studies suggest that perhaps individuals' influence on outcomes is more limited by structural power considerations (Moravcsik, 1999). Moreover, leaders of international organizations can have limited mandates and resources, further weakening the personal influence of an IO leader (see Kille and Scully, 2003). Indeed, the IMF's Managing Director's mandate can be limited, constrained both by power considerations at the IMF Executive Board and the intellectual dominance of the IMF staff (see Momani, 2005b). The Managing Director is but one figurehead in charge of the brains of the IMF—the IMF staff. This organ of the IMF is forgotten in reform proposals, but could be reformed to benefit the LICs.

III. What kinds of reforms would low-income countries benefit from at the IMF?

While the previous section raised questions about the long-term efficacy of governance reforms for the LICs, this section argues that LICs could benefit from many internal reforms in the IMF, but these reforms should better target improving IMF function, mandate, and performance—all related to the policy output of the IMF. The LICs are vulnerable, in need of good policy advice, and are often lacking both the expertise and the resources to accomplish economic growth. The LICs are viewed here as receptive, if not captive, learners—after all, the LICs account for 52 percent of all of the Fund's technical assistance (IMF, 2007). The issues are how to help LICs improve on the implementation of Fund advice and how to ensure that IMF staff will propose reforms that are implementable.

After many years of internal Fund discussion on ways of achieving this balance, it has been argued that LIC governments need better to own their policies to improve on implementation and that IMF staff need to streamline conditionality and to focus on key areas of Fund expertise (IMF, 2001). This two-pronged strategy is intended to improve the implementation record of debtor countries and to keep Fund staff from prescribing policies that are more traditionally in the jurisdiction of the World Bank and thereby avoid mission creep. Specifically, attention has been focused on the LICs' use of the PRGF and the accompanying Poverty Reduction Strategy Papers (PRSPs) that attempt to broaden the participation of stakeholders and civil society actors in loan and

program design. The PRSPs are intended to improve implementation by enhancing country ownership of policies. For their part, the IMF staff would limit
conditionality to their core areas of expertise and let the World Bank play the
lead role in areas such as reform of the public sector. Both the 2002
Conditionality Guidelines and the accompanying staff guidance notes were
meant to improve IMF procedures. This new arrangement between LICs and
the IMF embodied important policy shifts that were needed to renew LICs,
faith in Fund-supported programs. Evaluations of these new policies, however,
suggest that more needs to be and could be done.

The internal and independent IMF watchdog, the Independent Evaluation
Office (IEO), conducted a number of appraisals that point out the need for
Fund improvement in relation to staff relations with the LICs. In the IEO
report on structural conditionality, it found that the number of structural
conditions remained stable and that streamlining was not occurring as rapidly
as had been anticipated. In the 219 programs (agreed in 1995 to 2004) of the 94
countries that were examined, the IEO evaluation found that structural conditions were "extensive", had "little structural depth", and consequently compliance was weak (particularly in reforming the wider public sector and
privatization) (IEO, 2008b). Similar, if not more critical, findings were provided by a Eurodad study as well (Eurodad, 2008).

An IEO report assessed the Fund's role in and effectiveness with LICs' experiences with the PRGF and PRSPs. While pointing to some positive developments, the report suggested that there remained internal Fund ambiguity over
country ownership (IEO, 2004). Moreover, participation of stakeholders in
PRSPs had improved, but there was less institutionalization of the process in
domestic polities. Country ownership was hampered in some cases and LICs
would pass through the procedural requirements with weak country ownership. Finally, many Fund staff continued to operate in a "business as usual"
manner, with PRSPs conducted in similar terms to traditional program negotiations. Surveys of Fund staff suggested that this occurred because of "staff
resource constraints, the demands of the review process, or doubts about the
value added of the new approach" (IEO, 2004: 65). In a follow-up report, the
IEO studied IMF relations with its sub-Saharan African members. The findings
of this report echoed many of the previous findings but also pointed to the
issue of the staff's organizational culture. The staff remained focused on
achieving macroeconomic stability while, at times, overlooking key elements
of the PRGF agenda (IEO, 2007).

What can be learned from these evaluations and what kinds of reforms
would LICs benefit from at the IMF? The evaluations point out that despite
operational guidance to streamline conditionality and promote country ownership, there remain institutional drivers that explain Fund policy outcomes
and, at times, weak country ownership. While there are many ways of improving the outcomes of Fund programs and improving country ownership that

require changes within the LICs themselves, this chapter seeks to suggest possible ways of improvement through reform of the Fund. Again, a neglected component of IMF reform debates is the question of functional reforms at the staffing level that can improve implementation of Fund programs.

As previous studies have argued, borrowing members have at times raised concerns over the inadequate consideration of country circumstances in the design of programs and the orthodoxy of the policy advice they receive (IMF, 1999; IMF, 2004b; Momani, 2007). This chapter argues that one possible avenue of Fund reform would be to consider incorporating stronger political-economy analysis of its policies. This, however, requires some modification to Fund staffing and recruitment and to the training of staff to become more attuned to the political circumstances of LICs. In an IEO (2006) survey, it was found that the IMF's organizational culture was highly bureaucratized, hierarchical, conforming, and economistic. There are many positive outcomes to be attributed to these cultural characteristics—such as speedy internal communication, organizational cohesiveness, policy consistency, and quick deployment of needed resources in times of crisis. However, coupled with the feeling among some borrowers that Fund staff can at times be inattentive to local circumstances and that agreements are overly focused on macroeconomic stability at the expense of social and political factors, there is a potential downside to these noted cultural traits: institutional weaknesses on proposing ways of implementing policy advice. So while many Fund staff are skilled in explaining "what to do" to borrowers and hence their staff expertise is sought out by many borrowers, including LICs, Fund staff can at times find it challenging to offer ideas on "how to do it". Simply put, the political feasibility of the Fund policy advice may not always be taken into consideration, because some staff may not have policy experience themselves or are not trained in political-economy.

Some have pointed out that these bureaucratic and organizational features of the IMF can at times filter into policy challenges. With respect to Africa, for example, Woods finds that Fund missions have at times been poorly staffed, insular, and risk-averse. Consequently, Fund staff went to some African countries with "standard templates" to save time and resources and so as not to have to explain the nuances of terms and conditionality to senior Fund officials in Washington (Woods: 2006: ch. 6). But, as Woods notes: "The most difficult, irrefutable, and profoundly challenging critique for both the IMF and World Bank is that their work in fostering economic reform has ignored or wished away political realities—in Africa just as much if not more than in other countries" (2006: 161). Here, improving on the political-economy understanding of borrowers' situation would have been helpful in providing policy advice that had a better chance of being implemented.

The Fund's challenge in providing policy advice that has a political-economy component may stem from the Fund's reliance on hiring macroeconomists.

As I have argued elsewhere, perhaps the Fund should consider complementing its staff with the recruitment of political-economy specialists and increasing the number of staff on secondment (and fewer from the Economist Program) who may have more policy experience (Momani, 2007). To improve also on implementation of policy advice, others suggest enhancing local knowledge and recruiting more Fund staff from developing countries (Evans and Finnemore, 2001; Woods, 2006). Reorganizing the Fund's organizational structure could also be useful. One proposal has suggested increasing the number of IMF staff assigned to area departments where there are borrowers (Evans and Finnemore, 2001: 30). Much like the idea that African directors are overwhelmed with constituency members and can improve their performance through added staffing, the area departments with more borrowing members could benefit from more staff. Coupled by the observation that IMF staff already feel overworked in area departments with excessive travel and paperwork, it is unsurprising that many staff want to avoid working for the LIC-dominated departments like the African department.[2] Easing the workload burden on LIC-dominated area departments would be a useful reform proposal.

Fund reform proposals have emphasized governance reforms and not discussed the intellectual designers of everyday Fund work—the IMF staff. By focusing on governance reforms, the debate about how to improve the efficacy of Fund policy advice has been top heavy. For LICs, their primary concern should be on reforming the IMF to improve policy outcomes and to make it a responsive organization that serves LICs and client interests. Organizational reforms could be one avenue of improving IMF policy advice for LICs.

IV. Why the IMF reform debate is concerned more with governance than with functional reforms

There are a multitude of reasons why the current IMF reform debate turned to focus on governance reforms rather than functional reforms. First, the current push for IMF reform is coming generally from EMEs, but most importantly from these members' state capitals. The EMEs' new sense of bargaining power in the international financial system—both for being perceived by some to be "too big to fail" and for having access to private capital markets—led to these Fund debtors' interests diverging from those of LICs. The pressure for reform is state led, and less market driven, or civil society driven (as it had been in the past). We see EME states increasingly emboldened with the power of exiting the IMF altogether, either through creating regional arrangements, accumulating foreign reserves, or borrowing on private capital markets (see Helleiner and Momani, 2008). While few countries will voluntarily suspend their IMF

---

[2] Based on personal interviews with former IMF staff members on the issue of recruitment.

membership, their creating and using alternative means of financing could seriously undermine or damage the institution's reputation and authority. There is a deep recognition that the IMF's pride in being one of the few universal international organizations is at risk unless the EMEs have a renewed stake in the organization.

Moreover, officials in powerful members' capitals are unusually contributing to the reform discourse. We have seen many, such as Mervyn King, David Dodge, and Timothy Adams, speaking about IMF reforms. This type of G7 response was muted throughout the debt crisis when nongovernmental organizations were the Fund's loudest critics. Today, it is the capitals of G7 and EME states that are piping in on the need for Fund reforms. Indeed, IMF staff have observed that the G7 capitals have more recently become interested in micromanaging IMF policies and outcome, rather than delegating autonomy to their Executive Directors (Cottarelli, 2005: 8). There are four reasons suggested for why G7 capitals are more involved in IMF affairs: (1) added public attention to G7 financial contributions to IMF liquidity have raised public concern over taxpayers' money; (2) enhanced public and NGO scrutiny of IMF policy advice have pushed G7 capitals to question the IMF staff authority and legitimacy to intervene in the sovereignty of others; (3) the number of financial crises in the late 1990s prompted G7 capitals to question IMF effectiveness; and, (4) the expansion and added speed of G7 capital communication with their Executive Directors has led to less authority being delegated to them (Kenen et al., 2004: 99–100). This state-center-led reform debate, in contrast to the previous civil-society one, is speaking in traditional state-centric terms: augmenting and maintaining relative power. State capitals are focused on quota and vote redistribution because in state-centric terms these are viewed as their source of accumulating power in the organization.

Second, there has been a great fatigue factor in the debate over the utility of the IMF economic paradigm. Numerous studies have been conducted on the efficacy of conditionality and the results have almost always been contradictory. Whether the IMF economic paradigm is neoliberal, conservative, fiscal, or orthodox has become an exhausting discourse. Moreover, Fund critics who call for its demise have criticized the foundation of its ideology, but have not provided alternative economic paradigms to bring in its place. While the IMF's economic principles may have their shortcomings, viable economic alternatives are not being provided by the mainstream economic discipline. This seems to suggest that the study of economics is not near any paradigm shift, despite showing a number of recent cracks particularly at the World Bank and as reflected in the 2004 "Barcelona Consensus" (see World Bank, 2005). Perhaps this is owing to the belief that the benefits of free markets, underpinning Fund ideology, have yet to be exhausted. Those criticizing the IMF for its underlying economic philosophy have added to the burgeoning litany of complaints against the Fund for something far from IMF control.

Third, some argue that the IMF is busy debating governance reforms for the lack of a real crisis to deal with. The IMF, often depicted as a firetruck to put out the fires, now has "no cat to rescue" (as noted by *The Economist*) and so the Executive Board has time on its hands to debate ambitious governance reform. The relative respite is perhaps creating the "luxury of squabbling" for power within the upper ranks of the Fund (Weisman, 2006). Despite the long-standing tradition of not taking votes and establishing a Board consensus, Executive Directors have noted the eroding "collegial" environment of the Board and the question of members' voting power has therefore grown in importance in recent years (Woods, 2005: 1). This is coupled with the internal observation that the Executive Board has become more powerful, vis-à-vis the IMF staff and Management, since the mid-1990s. Cottarelli (2005: 8) argues that the Executive Board has increased its political oversight over the technical work of the Fund staff. This is exemplified by the increase of staff reporting to the Board, diminishing scope of allowable loan conditionality at the discretion of the staff, enhanced Board approval of lending programs that exceed members' proportion of their quotas, and new Board approval of commencing negotiations with members who have outstanding loans to the Fund (ibid.).

Fourth, for many EMEs, and developing countries more generally, IMF governance reforms have a strong symbolic component. Sidelined for much of the IMF's history, there is a greater awareness that as the 'users' of the organization, they should have a greater stake in the decision-making process. No doubt, the IMF's own "good governance" discourse, emphasizing account-ability, fairness, and participation, has rubbed off on Fund borrowers' percep-tion of their role in the Fund (see Woods, 2000). Similarly, while it may be that for many developing countries increasing quotas would not enhance their relative power position at the Board, there is an inherent institutional feeling that quotas do more than translate into votes; they also translate into "national prestige" (see Mikesell, 1994: 35).

Similarly, the normative and ideational push that international organiza-tions ought to be democratized as a measure of a good and advanced global society (David Held's cosmopolitan democracy) is appealing (see Held, 1995). But, democratizing international organizations today is unrealistic and pre-mature, notwithstanding the noble and moral arguments that can be made. As Robert Dahl aptly noted:

if it is difficult enough for ordinary citizens to exercise much influence over decisions about foreign affairs in their own countries, should we not conclude that the obstacles will be far greater in international organizations? Just as many important policy de-cisions in democratic countries are in effect delegated by citizens to the political elites, will not the citizens of countries engaged in an international association delegate effective control to the international policy elites? And will not the extent of delegation in international organizations go well beyond any acceptable threshold of democracy?

(Dahl, 1999: 32)

259

If democracy cannot be achieved, how will international organizations achieve legitimacy in an age of growing democratic consciousness? Dahl, and many functionalist theorists before him, suggests that international organizations should entrust authority to "an elite of guardians possessed of greatly superior knowledge and virtue". In other words, governments should delegate to professional international civil servants with expertise and authority to solve functional problems (see Mitrany, 1946). Barnett and Finnemore (2004) suggest that the IMF once had this noted authority to have states listen to their advice; perhaps something has gone awry. This turns the focus back again to the IMF staff. The Fund needs to consider ways of making changes at the staff level—the missing link in current Fund reform proposals (Momani, 2007).

The IMF was designed keeping creditor confidence in mind. Democratization, where debtors as users have an equal or proportionate say in Fund governance, is a dilemma. This is not to pass moral judgment on what is right or just, but to state the international political reality of Fund governance design and purpose. As some have rightly noted, diluting creditor control of the IMF will simply prompt creditor states to take key decision-making outside the Fund and into other forums (see Bird and Rowlands, 2006: 164). Rather than having debate at the Executive Board where an element of transparency among member capitals exists, the major creditors will take their discussions wholly outside the IMF to back-room settings, leaving the Board with a ceremonial role.

In conclusion, reforming an international organization like the IMF would never be an easy task. Organizations tend to be stuck in a time warp where governance structures reflect past political bargains. While many have highlighted the outdated governance structure of the IMF, we are still talking about modest tweaking of the IMF. For the LICs, the governance reform proposals suggested by the concerned policy community may have minimal effect on what matters most to them: the Fund's policy advice and conditionality. To get at these functional reforms, the IMF does not need a top-down shake-up, but a bottom-up reorganization of the Fund operators: the Fund staff. Reforming the IMF staff by reexamining Fund recruitment and organizational design are positive ways of producing policy changes. Moreover, unlike the fate of many of the governance reform proposals, bottom-up organizational reforms would not require the type of grand political bargains and engagement of the US Congress that would be required to amend the Articles of Agreement. Synergy to reform the IMF has been created, but this also needs to be channeled into achievable and beneficial ends for Fund borrowers.

V. References

Barro, R. and Lee, J. (2005) "IMF-Programs: Who Is Chosen and What are the Effects?" *Journal of Monetary Economics*, 52, 7: 1245–69.

Barnett, M. and Finnemore, M. (2004) *Rules for the World: International Organizations in Global Politics.* Ithaca: Cornell University Press.

Bini Smaghi, Lorenzo (2006) "IMF Governance and the Political Economy of a Consolidated EU Seat," in *Reforming the IMF for the 21st Century*, Edwin Truman (Ed.). Washington, DC: Institute for International Economics.

Bird, G. and Dane Rowlands (2006) "IMF quotas: Constructing an international organization using inferior building blocks," *Review of International Organizations*, 1, 2 (June): 153–71.

Birdsall, Nancy (2003) "Why it matters Who Runs the IMF and the World Bank," Working Paper Number 22, January.

Buira, Ariel (2003) "The Governance of the International Monetary Fund," Washington, DC: Group of 24. <http://www.g24.org/imfgover.pdf>.

Camdessus, Michel (2005) Lecture. "International Financial Institutions: Dealing with New Global Challenges." Washington, DC: The Per Jacobsson Foundation, September. <http://www.perjacobsson.org/lectures/092505.pdf>.

Cox, Robert and Harold Jacobson (1973) *The Anatomy of Influence: Decision-Making in International Organizations.* London: Yale University Press.

Cottarelli, Carlo (2005) *Efficiency and Legitimacy: Trade-Offs in IMF Governance.* Working Paper 05/107. June. Washington, DC: IMF. <http://www.imf.org/external/pubs/ft/wp/2005/wp05107.pdf>.

Dahl, Robert (1999) "Can International Organizations be Democratic?" in *Democracy's Edges*, Ian Shapiro and Casiano Hacker-Cordon (Eds.). Cambridge: Cambridge University Press.

De Gregorio, Jose, et al. (1999) *An Independent and Accountable IMF.* Geneva: Centre for Economic Policy Research.

De Rato, Rodrigo (2006b) "The Managing Director's Report on Implementing the Fund's Medium-Term Strategy." Washington, DC: International Monetary Fund. April 5.

Dreher, Axel and Nathan M. Jensen (2007) "Independent Actor or Agent? An Empirical Analysis of the Impact of US Interests on IMF Conditions," *The Journal of Law and Economics*, 50, 1.

Eurodad (2006) "World Bank and IMF Conditionality: A Development Injustice," Eurodad Report (June).

Evans, Peter and Martha Finnemore (2001) "Organizational Reform and the Expansion of the South's Voice at the Fund," G-24 Discussion Paper, no.15. Geneva: UNCTAD.

Guha, Krishna (2008) "IMF 'must reform to remain relevant'," *Financial Times*, February 25. <http://www.ft.com/cms/s/0/8ba0ddbe-e3ed-11dc-8799-0000779fd2ac.html>.

Held, David (1995) *Democracy and the Global Order: From the Modern State to Cosmopolitan Governance.* Oxford: Polity Press.

Helleiner, Eric and Momani, Bessma (2008) "Slipping into Obscurity: Crisis and Institutional Reform at the IMF," in *Can the World Be Governed?* Alan Alexadroff (ed.). Waterloo: WLU Press/CIGI.

Independent Evaluation Office (IEO) (2004) *Evaluation of the IMF's Role in Poverty Reduction Strategy Papers and the Poverty Reduction and Growth Facility.* Washington, DC: International Monetary Fund.

—— (2006) *Report of the External Evaluation of the Independent Evaluation Office*, 29 March. <http://www.imf.org/External/NP/pp/eng/2006/032906.pdf>.

Independent Evaluation Office (IEO) (2007) *The IMF and Aid to Sub-Saharan Africa.* Washington, DC: International Monetary Fund. <http://www.ieo-imf.org/eval/complete/pdf/03122007/report.pdf>.

—— (2008a) *Aspects of IMF Corporate Governance—Including the Role of the Executive Board* April. Washington, DC: International Monetary Fund. <http://www.ieo-imf.org/eval>.

—— (2008b) *An IEO Evaluation of Structural Conditionality in IMF-Supported Programs.* Washington, DC: International Monetary Fund. <http://www.ieo-imf.org/eval>.

International Monetary Fund (IMF) (1999) "External Evaluation of IMF Surveillance," Report by a Group of Independent Experts, Washington: International Monetary Fund, September. Available at <http://www.imf.org/external/pubs/ft/extev/surv/index.HTM>.

—— (2000) *Report to the IMF Executive Board of the Quota Formula Review Group.* Washington, DC: IMF, 12 April.

—— Policy Development and Review Department (PDR) (2001) *Conditionality in Fund-Supported Programs: Policy Issues.* Washington, DC: International Monetary Fund, 16 February.

—— (2004a) *Quotas—Updated Calculations.* Washington, DC: IMF. <http://www.imf.org/external/np/fin/2004/eng/082704.pdf>.

—— (2004b) "Biennial Review of the Fund's Surveillance—Overview; Modalities of Surveillance; Content of Surveillance; and Public Information Notice on the Executive Board Discussion." Washington, DC: International Monetary Fund. <http://www.imf.org/external/np/pdr/surv/2004/082404.htm>.

—— (2005)"A Factsheet: IMF Quotas." Washington, DC: IMF, September 2005. <http://www.imf.org>.

—— (2006) "Report of the Executive Board to the Board of Governors: Quota and Voice Reform in the International Monetary Fund." Washington, DC: IMF, 31 August. <http://www.imf.org/external/np/pp/eng/2006/083106.pdf>.

—— (2007) "How the IMF Helps Poor Countries." Finance Department. Washington, DC: IMF. <http://www.imf.org/external/np/exr/facts/poor.htm>.

—— (2008) "Reform of Quota and Voice in the International Monetary Fund—Report of the Executive Board to the Board of Governors" Washington, DC: IMF, 28 March. <http://www.imf.org/external/np/pp/eng/2008/032108.pdf>.

Kahler, Miles (1992) "External Influence, Conditionality, and the Politics of Adjustment," in *The Politics of Economic Adjustment: International Constraints, Distributive Conflicts, and the State*, Stephan Haggard and Robert R. Kaufman (eds.). Princeton: Princeton University Press.

—— (2002) *Leadership Selection in the Major Multilaterals.* Washington, DC: Institute for International Economics.

Kelkar, Vijay, Yikash Yadav, and Praveen Chaudhry (2004) "Reforming the Governance of the International Monetary Fund," *The World Economy*, 27, 5 (May): 727–43.

Kenen, Peter (2006) "Comments on the Address of the Managing Director of the IMF." Remarks made at the book release meeting "Reforming the IMF for the 21st Century," Institute for International Economics, Washington, D.C., April 20.

—— Jeffrey R. Shafer, Nigel L. Wicks, and Charles Wyplosz (2004) *The International Economic and Financial Cooperation: New Issues, New Actors, New Responses.* London: Centre for Economic Policy Research.

Kille, Kent and Roger Scully (2003) "Executive Heads and the Role of Intergovernmental Organizations: Expansionist Leadership in the United Nations and the European Union," *Political Psychology*, 24, 1: 175–98.

King, Mervyn (2006) "Reform of the International Monetary Fund." Speech at the Indian Council for Research on International Economic Relations, New Delhi, India. 20 February. <http://www.bankofengland.co.uk/publications/speeches/2006/speech267.pdf>.

Lombardi, Domenico and Jim O'Neill (2008) "How Europe can shape the Fund," *Financial Times*, April 8. <http://www.ft.com/cms/s/0/51f3ac48-0573-11dd-a9e0-0000779fd2ac.html>.

Mikesell, Raymond (1994) *The Bretton Woods Debates: A Memoir*, Essays in International Finance, 192. Princeton University, International Finance Section.

Mitrany, David (1946) *A Working Peace System. An Argument for the Functional Development of International Organization*. London: National Peace Council.

Momani, Bessma (2004) "American Politicization of the International Monetary Fund," *Review of International Political Economy*, 11, 5 (December).

—— (2005a) "Recruiting and Diversifying IMF Technocrats," *Global Society*, 19, 2 (April).

—— (2005b) "Limits of Streamlining Fund Conditionality: the IMF's Organizational Culture," *Journal of International Relations and Development*, 8, 2.

—— (2007) "IMF Staff: Missing Link in Fund Reform Proposals," *Review of International Organizations*, 2: 39–57.

Moravcsik, Andrew (1999) "A New Statecraft? Supranational Entrepreneurs and International Cooperation," *International Organization*, 53, 2 (Spring): 267–306.

Oatley, T. and J. Yackee (2004) "American interests and IMF lending" *International Politics* 41, 3: 415–29.

Ostry, Jonathan and Jeromin Zettelmeyer (2005) "Strengthening IMF Crisis Prevention," *IMF Working Paper*. Washington, DC: IMF.

Rapkin, David and Jonathan Strand (2006) "Reforming the IMF's Weighted Voting System," *World Economy*, March 29, 3.

Rustomjee, Cyrus (2004) "Why Developing Countries Need a Stronger Voice," *Finance and Development*, September, 41, 3.

—— (2005) "Improving Southern Voice on the IMF Board: Quo Vadis Shareholders," in *Enhancing Accountability in the International Monetary Fund*, Barry Carin and Angela Wood (eds). Aldershot: Ashgate.

Stiglitz, Joseph (2003) "Democratizing the International Monetary Fund and the World Bank: Governance and Accountability," *Governance: An International Journal of Policy, Administration, and Institutions*, 16, 1: 111–39.

Stone, Randall (2004) "The Political Economy of IMF Lending in Africa," *American Political Science Review*, 98: 577–91.

Thacker, S. (1999) "The High Politics of IMF Lending," *World Politics*, 52, 1, October: 38–75.

Truman, Edwin (2006) "Rearranging IMF Chairs and Shares," in *A Strategy for IMF Reform*, Edwin Truman (ed.). Washington, DC: Institute for International Economics. February.

Vreeland, James (2003) *The IMF and Economic Development*. Cambridge: Cambridge University Press.

Weisman, Steven (2006) *"U.S. Seeks Bigger China Role in I.M.F."* US Section. *New York Times*, 30 August.

Woods, Ngaire (2000) "The Challenge of Good Governance for the IMF and the World Bank Themselves," *World Development*, 28, 5: 823–41.

—— (2005) "A Note on Decision-Making Reform in the IMF" G24 Technical Meeting. Manila: Group of 24. March. <http://www.g24.org/WoodNote.pdf>.

—— (2006) *The Globalizers: The IMF, the World Bank and Their Borrowers*. Ithaca: Cornell University Press.

—— and Lombardi, Domenico (2006) "Uneven Patterns of Governance: How Developing Countries Are Represented in the IMF," *Review of International Political Economy*, 13, 3, August.

World Bank (2005) *Economic Growth in the 1990s: Learning from a Decade of Reform*. Washington, DC: World Bank Group. <http://www1.worldbank.org/prem/lessons1990s/>.

14

Rethinking the Governance of the International Monetary Fund

Abbas Mirakhor (IMF) and Iqbal Zaidi (IMF) *

I. Introduction

Just as national regulation was broadened in the nineteenth and twentieth centuries to protect workers and consumers (e.g. anti-trust legislation, health standards, corporate governance, bank supervision) from the excesses of free markets, there is now a general recognition that globalization needs a regulatory framework in the twenty-first century that is less fragmented than what exists today, and international financial institutions—in particular, the International Monetary Fund (IMF)—can be expected to have major roles in this area. In fact, the IMF has already taken steps in this direction (e.g. evaluating countries' compliance with international data standards, moving in the direction of setting a new surveillance remit, and launching a multilateral consultation on addressing global imbalances). However, for the IMF to play an important role in global governance, it is essential to enhance its credibility as an international cooperative institution: there is widespread recognition that the quotas (IMF capital shares), voting rights, and voice imbalances have become progressively worse.[1] The effectiveness of the IMF has been questioned both inside and outside the institution not only because members' quotas have become increasingly out of line with countries' economic weight (measured by GDP) in the global economy, but also because there is a growing recognition that some important aspects of members' economic weight and

---

* This chapter should not be reported as representing the views of the IMF. The views expressed in this chapter are those of the authors and do not necessarily represent those of the IMF or IMF policy. Abbas Mirakhor was Executive Director and Iqbal Zaidi was Senior Advisor to Executive Director when this chapter was written.

[1] Quotas are currently calculated according to a member's gross domestic product, current account transactions, and official reserves. The quota largely determines a member's voting power in IMF decisions and is reviewed every five years (see Section II).

other variables that should have a bearing on voting rights are not captured in the current quota formulas.

These concerns are reflected in the International Monetary and Financial Committee's communiqué of April 22, 2006, which stated that the IMF's effectiveness and credibility as a cooperative institution must be safeguarded and its governance further enhanced, and emphasized the importance of fair voice and representation for all members. The IMF adopted a two-stage process for quota and voice reform, with initial ad hoc increases for the clearly most underrepresented members in the first stage, and more fundamental reforms in the second stage.[2] Two years later, the IMFC's communiqué issued April 12, 2008 welcomed the agreement by the Executive Board on the package of quota and voice reforms as an important contribution to enhance the Fund's credibility but noted that the "Committee also looks forward to further work by the Executive Board on elements of the new quota formula that can be improved before the formula is used again."[3] The reason that the quota formula problem is still with us is that the discussion was confined to an unduly narrow area, and important issues were given short shrift. Concerted efforts were made in many quarters to validate the traditional approach of basing voting power in the IMF largely on countries' respective weight in the world economy, with the justification being provided in terms of the mandate of the institution. However, representatives from developing countries have rightly pointed out that the IMF mandate is not as narrow as some would have us believe, and history bears this out (see Sections III and IV). Furthermore, even in the discussions on the need to find ways to enhance the representation of developing countries, the discussion has been almost entirely directed to the admittedly important, but still only one area of voice reform, namely, the need to arrest the declining role of basic votes since the IMF was established, which has weakened the voice of smaller developing countries. However, the voice reform should mean much more than just ensuring that small countries, whose share in the world economy is small but for whom the IMF provides important policy advice and financing, have adequate opportunities to participate in the governance of the institution. In particular, the IMF also provides policy advice and financing to countries with large populations—and, of course, it has important regulatory and supervisory functions that affect

---

[2] A two-stage process with an ad hoc increase in the first stage was not consistent with the need for a comprehensive review, and Palaniappan Chidambaram, Finance Minister of India, was correct in saying during the IMF–World Bank Annual Meetings in Singapore in October 2006 that "[b]y definition, a comprehensive reallocation of quotas to reinforce legitimacy cannot be achieved by a short-term ad hoc approach."

[3] The reforms approved by the Board of Governors in May 2008 include a simpler quota formula; a second round of ad hoc quota increases to enhance the representation of dynamic economies; a tripling of basic votes that will increase the voice of low-income countries; and an additional Alternate Executive Director for Executive Directors elected by a large number of members, which will benefit the two African constituencies on the Executive Board.

them—and there will remain a "democracy deficit" if these countries are not adequately represented in the governance structure.

This chapter takes a forward-looking approach and attempts to set out the principal issues that need to be resolved in formulating a proposal for quotas and voice reform that could command broad support. Following John Rawls, we argue that "justice is the first virtue of social institutions," and we think that his theory of justice provides an appropriate method for understanding what should be the case, in the context of voice and voting shares, before international institutions, such as the IMF, are to be justifiable to their members. Our analysis is based on the Rawlsian notion of "justice as fairness" and, at the risk of oversimplification, our conclusion is that justice in the IMF governance structure requires a distribution of voting power that participants accept as the end-result of a fair process. The implementation of this process suggests that a major revision of the quota formulas is long overdue, and leaving this unaddressed raises serious concerns regarding the IMF's governance. Furthermore, there is no legitimate way to view these issues in isolation, and a holistic approach is required, which would entail increasing basic votes sharply—to at least restore its importance at the inception of the IMF—and revamping the quota formulas, with the latter allowing for selective quota increases for a broad group of developing countries. However, we hasten to add that this work should be regarded as advancing possible options for further discussion, and not as constituting a specific proposal. In particular, the ranges given to demand and supply variables, or for treating the democracy and Westphalian deficits, in the quota table in this chapter, are for heuristic purposes only and are not meant to be specific recommendations.

The IMF has a complex governance structure in which the constituency system attempts to reconcile the legitimacy of an almost universal membership with efficient decision making and collegiality of a not-too-large Executive Board (24 Executive Directors). In the constituency system, the five member countries with the largest quotas appoint an Executive Director, while the remaining members elect the remaining Executive Directors. Questions have been raised about the constituency system, particularly the point that the Executive Director cannot split his/her vote even though there are instances in which the countries within the constituency are divided on the issue being considered by the Board; this is especially relevant in those cases in which there are mixed constituencies, industrial and developing countries. Another governance issue has been the debate on converting the International Monetary and Finance Committee (IMFC) into a decision-making council. After long debates, this was turned down in 1999, attributed mainly to the concern that the industrial country members of the council may not show the necessary patience and willingness to work toward consensus decision making, which is necessary to protect the interests of minority groups. Yet another set of questions relates to the simple majority that applies to many decisions and the special majorities of 70 percent and 85 percent for certain key decisions. The special majorities help to protect sizeable minorities, but the 85 percent majority gives veto power to one country.

The issues raised in the preceding paragraph are just a few of the many outstanding issues in the IMF governance debate, but this chapter does not attempt to cover every conceivable area. First, it does not discuss the merits or otherwise of voting majorities, or the efficacy and representation of the constituency system. Nor does it express a view on converting the IMFC into a council. The chapter focuses on the quotas and voice debate, which is arguably the overriding issue in the larger governance debate. Second, and at least equally important, the chapter does not discuss the question of increasing the independence and accountability of the Executive Board. The Board of Governors is the highest decision-making body of the IMF but the daily business is conducted by a resident Executive Board, which exercises under delegation most of the powers. The main functions of the Executive Board include: approving all policies of the IMF; discussing consultation reports with individual countries to carry out its mandate on bilateral surveillance; discussing the *World Economic Outlook* and the *Global Financial Stability Report* for conducting multilateral surveillance; approving loans provided for adjustment programs; and reviewing the implementation of the conditions attached to those programs to decide whether to disburse the loan tranches. The question of political oversight by national capitals of the business of the IMF has garnered attention from time to time, and in particular, some rules and practices related to the appointment, election, and term duration of Executive Directors have been challenged by some observers from the point of view of strengthening the autonomy and accountability of the Executive Board. These issues are not discussed in the chapter not because they are simple and unimportant, but rather because these problems have been extensively analyzed elsewhere and because they are quite distinct from the questions raised in this chapter on quotas and voice reform.[4] Third, it should perhaps be made explicit that the chapter is not concerned with other areas, such as the desirability of further enhancing the capacity of Executive Directors' offices representing large numbers of African members and of including more transparent selection procedures for the position of Managing Director. These issues are not discussed not because they are unimportant, but because they are simple. There is no question that the challenges faced by the two African chairs, each of which represents more than 20 countries, are serious. However, this

---

[4] See Kenen (2001), King (2006), Portugal (2005), Truman (2006), Van Houtven (2002), and Woods (1998, 2001) for comprehensive discussions of these issues. See Boughton (2001) for the recent history of IMF finances, pp. 849–74.

is not an area that requires further deliberations, and it should be implemented expeditiously. The point is that the resources involved for strengthening capacity of African Executive Directors' offices are not substantial in terms of the overall budget of the IMF, and by having these problems linger on, they only serve to confuse the discussion about quotas, basic votes, legitimacy, which are issues of a different kind from some small budgetary matters; in short, a larger budget for an Executive Director's office is no substitute for underrepresentation. On the desirability of including more transparent selection procedures for the position of Managing Director of the IMF, this too should have been done some time ago because there really is no debate about it, at least ever since the discussion on the joint draft report of the IMF's Working Group to Review the Process of Selection of the Managing Director and the World Bank Working Group to Review the Process of Selection of the President. In this regard, specific procedures for ensuring this transparency should be developed soon, and there is no need to wait for the two-year program of actions on governance reform. As with strengthening capacity of African Executive Directors' offices, this issue should not be allowed to remain unaddressed because it needlessly complicates the more important issues of quotas and voice reform.

II. Quotas, voice, and Rawls

Many policymakers, not to mention researchers, have commented that trying to understand IMF quota formulas is a formidable undertaking, yet the mathematics involved is nothing worse than the simplest algebra. One reason is that, even in the very first reading when one is busy trying to understand the formulas, it is difficult not to get bogged down in disagreeing with just about everything contained in the formulas and to start arguing why a particular variable is used, why it has more weight than some other variables, or why there are five distinct formulas, and so on. That problem could be overcome, to some extent, by practicing in advance of the need, that is, the first step in understanding these formulas should be just to peruse them without any comments, and then only afterwards go about disagreeing with the formulas. Even with this practice, one may find IMF quota discussions rather confusing unless one is careful in defining the objectives. The procedure followed in this section is: first, we discuss what the IMF quota formulas are meant to achieve; second, we simply state the formulas; and, third, we take issue with several aspects of the formulas, including the choice of variables, multiple formulas, and nonlinearities in the formulas.[5]

---

[5] Readers familiar with IMF quota formulas may wish to skip subsection II.A.

A. Quota formulas

Quota subscriptions generate most of the IMF's financial resources, and they perform several functions, including delineating basic aspects of members' financial and organizational relationship with the IMF.

Subscriptions A member's quota subscription determines the maximum amount of financial resources the member is obliged to provide to the IMF. A member must pay its subscription in full upon joining the IMF: up to 25 percent must be paid in SDRs or widely accepted currencies (such as the US dollar, the euro, the yen, or the pound sterling), while the rest is paid in the member's own currency.

Voting power The quota largely determines a member's voting power in IMF decisions. Each IMF member has 250 basic votes plus one additional vote for each SDR 100,000 of quota.

Access to financing The amount of financing a member can obtain from the IMF (its access limit) is based on its quota. Under Stand-by and Extended Arrangements, for instance, a member can borrow up to 100 percent of its quota annually and 300 percent cumulatively. However, access may be higher in exceptional circumstances.

SDR allocations A members' share of general SDR allocations is established in proportion to its quota.

Since quotas serve multiple purposes, the quota formula necessarily has to balance sometimes competing considerations about what variables to include in the formulas and the weights to attach to each variable. The formulas are overburdened by the multiple roles of quotas, and there is no particular need to have a rigid relation between financial contribution, access to Fund resources, voting power, and share of SDR general allocations. A formula used in 1944 when the IMF was established has become known as the Bretton Woods formula.[6] This formula contained five variables: national income, official reserves, imports, export variability, and the ratio of exports to national income. This single formula was replaced by a multi-formula approach in the early 1960s, when the original formula was supplemented with four more formulas containing the same basic variables but with larger weights for external trade and external variability. However, this was not the end of the problem because two different datasets were used; there were in effect ten formulas.

The quota formulas were simplified in 1981–2, including the following changes: (i) eliminating five of ten formulas by focusing on only one dataset; (ii) replacing nominal income with GDP, which was viewed as a more comprehensive and readily available measure of national output; (iii) broadening the

---

[6] For a more comprehensive overview of quota formulas, see International Monetary Fund, 2001b.

measure of reserves to include holdings of SDRs, ECUs, and IMF reserve positions and calculation of the holdings as a 12-month average rather than an end-of-period total; and (iv) reducing the coefficient of variability in the four derivative formulas by 20 percent to moderate the impact of the very sharp increases in the prices of certain commodities, especially the increases in oil prices in 1973–4 and 1979. These new formulas were supposed to help the developing countries because of their vulnerabilities to terms-of-trade shocks and reliance on a narrow range of exports. However, it is interesting to note that there are several industrial countries—and one G7 country—that have calculated quotas determined by the new formulas. Also, the 60-year-old Bretton Woods formula is used for more than one-third of the members, including many developing countries.

There have been no changes in the formulas since 1983, and the current five formulas are as follows:

Reduced Bretton Woods formula:
$$(0.01Y + 0.025R + 0.05P + 0.2276VC) \times (1 + C/Y)$$

Other modified formulas:

Scheme III formula:
$$(0.0065Y + 0.0205125R + 0.078P + 0.4052VC) \times (1 + C/Y)$$

Scheme IV formula:
$$0.0045Y + 0.03896768R + 0.07P + 0.76976VC) \times (1 + C/Y)$$

Scheme M4 formula:
$$0.005Y + 0.042280464R + 0.044 (P + C) + 0.8352VC$$

Scheme M7 formula:
$$0.0045Y + 0.05281008R + 0.039 (P + C) + 1.0432VC$$

where Y = GDP at current market prices for a recent year; R = twelve-month average of gold, foreign exchange reserves, SDR holdings and reserve positions in the IMF, for a recent year; P = annual average of current payments (goods, services, income, and private transfers) for a recent five-year period; C = annual average of current receipts (goods, services, income, and private transfers) for a recent five-year period; and VC = variability of current receipts, defined as one standard deviation from the centered five-year moving average, for a recent 13-year period. For each of the four non-Bretton Woods formulas, quota calculations are multiplied by an adjustment factor so that the sum of the calculations across members equals that derived from the Bretton Woods formula. The calculated quota of a member is the higher of the Bretton Woods calculation and the average of the lowest two of the remaining four calculations (after adjustment).

Just reading the last sentence could be sufficient reason to say that something is wrong here, if only because it takes a couple of readings to understand what is said in the sentence. One is left wondering why is the calculated quota the *higher* of the Bretton Woods formula and the *lowest* of the average of the remaining four formulas, given that this is after adjustment. Indeed, one could even ask the more basic question of why is there a need for five formulas when they have basically the same set of variables. It seems that the devil is both on the surface, but also, as usual, in the details. Since there are several formulas, a major problem is the absence of uniformity of treatment. For instance, the weight of the GDP variable differs across the formulas, and since different formulas are used for different countries, it is not the case that this purported measure of economic size gets the same treatment for all countries. This measure of economic size is in itself wrong because it uses market ex-change rates to convert GDP to a common currency rather than PPP-based GDP. Nevertheless, there are problems with other variables as well, and these issues are discussed in Section III, starting with the GDP variable, but first we discuss how the Bretton Woods formula, which has been around for over sixty years, compares with some well-known ideas about social justice.

B. Original Bretton Woods formula versus original position

According to the IMF staff, the original Bretton Woods formula was "a single equation intended to provide a comprehensive measure of the relative size of a country's economy that took into account important differences in the economic structures of countries."[7] Be that as it may, its origin is dubious, to say the least. According to Raymond Mikesell, the economist in the US Treasury Department who worked out this formula, it was designed to attain a political objective, which he described in his memoirs:

In mid-April 1943, shortly after the White plan was made public, White called me to his office and asked that I prepare a formula for the ISF (original acronym for what became IMF) quotas that would be based on the members' gold and dollar holdings, national incomes, and foreign trade. He gave no instructions on the weights to be used, but I was to give the United States a quota of approximately US$2.9 billion; the United Kingdom (including its colonies), about half the U.S. quota; the Soviet Union, an amount just under that of the United Kingdom; and China, somewhat less. He also wanted the total of the quotas to be about US$10 billion. White's major concern was that our military allies (President Roosevelt's Big Four) should have the largest quotas, with a ranking on which the president and the secretary of state had agreed. I was surprised that White did not mention France, which was usually regarded as being third in economic importance among the Allied powers. He said he did not care where France ranked, and its ranking did not need to be an objective in the exercise. As was typical, White wanted something on his desk in a couple of days—it took me four, including a weekend. A modern computer would have saved several days of work on my state-of-the-art calculator and might have produced a more credible result.[8]

---

[7] See International Monetary Fund, 2005, p. 29.
[8] Mikesell (1994), p. 22.

Mikesell also noted that, for several countries, data for some variables were missing and he had to rely on crude estimates: "I confess to having exercised a certain amount of freedom in making these estimates in order to achieve predetermined quotas. I went through dozens of trials, using different weights and combinations of trade data before reaching a formula that satisfied most of White's objectives." Deriving a quota formula to achieve a political objective, but one with little or no economic sense, was perhaps the biggest problem. However, it was not the end of the story because Mikesell goes on to write about how he made the formula nonlinear in variables: "I then found that I could get even closer if I increased the quotas by the ratio of average exports (from 1935 to 1938) to national income (1940)...The final formula for determining quotas was 2 percent of national income, 5 percent of gold and dollar holdings, 10 percent of average imports, 10 percent of the maximum variation in exports, and these three percentages increased by the percentage ratio of average exports to national income." Unfortunately, by introducing the nonlinearity in the formula, White made it impossible to reach a clear economic interpretation of the formula. In particular, one cannot go from some considered judgments or agreements on what weights to give to the national income variable in the supply for quotas, and, accordingly, derive the calculated quotas for the countries because there is a multiplicative factor that increases the role of exports relative to national income in the determination of calculated quotas. In this instance, nonlinearity was introduced into the equation when there was no need for it, except to get as close as possible a fit to some precooked numbers. This is in sharp contrast to the usual procedure in which equations are linearized by Taylor series approximation to derive meaningful results, that is, when the real world is nonlinear, we make it linear via approximations to make it more tractable.

The quota formula was not distributed, and White asked me not to reveal it. Even though White wanted to suppress the formula, however, copies were circulating at the conference... After the list was distributed to the Quota Committee, more than half the delegates present strongly objected to the quotas for their countries, and several demanded to know how the quotas had been calculated. Vinson (Chairman of the Quota Committee), who had not been well briefed on the history of quotas, asked me to explain the basis for the list. I had anticipated this request and gave a rambling twenty-minute seminar on the factors taken into account in calculating the quotas, but I did not reveal the formula. I tried to make the process appear as scientific as possible, but the delegates were intelligent enough to know that the process was more political than scientific.[9]

The artificial complexity in the quota formulas or the lack of transparency reminds us of what one of the founders of the institution and Head of the British Delegation to the Bretton Woods conference, John Maynard Keynes,

---

[9] Ibid. pp. 35–6.

noted: "The Monetary Fund, in particular, has the great advantage that to the average Congressman it is extremely boring."[10] Or what an associate of Keynes and noted economist Roy Harrod wrote about the debate on the Bretton Woods institutions: "[i]n view of the need for 'good handling' the less public lucidity there is on this matter the better."[11] Contrast this with the widely accepted proposition in political philosophy that public justification should be a never-ending commitment because citizens and governments are always confronting new circumstances, as clearly articulated in the following quotation from Macedo:

> we could have no confidence in our reasons for committing ourselves to what we understand justice to be unless we keep debating it and remain open to new and better interpretations of it. We cannot honor our status as reasonable beings unless we remain open to a critical dialogue about the justifiability of our deepest political conceptions, whatever they may be . . . Public justification is not a means only but also an end in itself: being a self-critical reason giver is the best way . . . The reflective, self-critical capacities we associate with public justification must, therefore, be regarded as *permanent* and ever-developing characteristics of liberal citizens at their best.[12]

For the purposes of this chapter, we would suggest replacing "liberal citizens" with "international institutions" in the last sentence.

The reader is also asked to contrast the above discussion about the original Bretton Woods formula with what John Rawls, arguably the greatest political philosopher of the twentieth century, had called the "original position" in his theory of justice.[13] He had emphasized that, in light of their reasonable economic, philosophical, and moral disagreements, members in a cooperative institution or citizens in a society will willingly and freely support a regime only if the political conception on which it is founded can be the object of "an overlapping consensus." At the risk of oversimplification, Rawls's theory of justice has two parts. In the first part, the original position is constructed to permit a theoretically rigorous way of moving from disagreement or uncertainty about the requirements of justice to an answer that is a reflective equilibrium. The original position is formed in light of beliefs about justice that are held in the community, or on which there is agreement, and the procedure is to see if the parties in the original position would decide on definite principles of justice. The second part is devoted to establishing the principles that would be agreed upon in the original position.

The idea of the original position may be viewed as a hypothetical situation in which agents acting as trustees for the interests of concrete individuals or countries are pictured as choosing those principles of social relations under

---

[10] Moggridge (1980), p. 445.
[11] Ibid. p. 267.
[12] Macedo (1990), pp. 287–8.
[13] Rawls (1987, 1988, 1989, 1996, 1999).

which their principals would do best. Their choices are subject to certain constraints that are required to embody the specifically moral elements of original position argumentation. In particular, the trustees do not know facts about their principals which are morally irrelevant to the choice of principles of justice. This restriction in their reasoning is embodied in Rawls's so-called veil of ignorance, which screens out information, among other things, about principals' age, sex, wealth, and education when discussing individuals; population, national output, level of development, and the like, in the present case of considering countries in the IMF. Once this information is unavailable to their agents or trustees, the plurality of interested parties disappears. Accordingly, the problem of choice is rendered determinate because each individual's trustee has the same information and motivation as every other individual's trustee. Therefore, the original position is a situation of choice, not of "negotiation" between a plurality of distinct individuals. Original position argumentation is a primary example of what has come to be called contemporary contractualism in political philosophy, which involves a pure-proceduralist approach to the determination of moral principles, and is framed by reflective equilibration with widely agreed principles of justice.

Rawls argued that ordinary individuals would never be able to get a sense of the just structure of social institutions if they only behold the world from their limited perspectives. The key to social understanding does not lie in an immersion in the details of particular cases or institutions, but the precise opposite: for example, getting sufficient distance from the particulars of one's own country. To make this system work, an individual has to shed any attachment to the particular interests of his country, and, in order to guarantee their reasonableness, Rawls puts his hypothetical subjects behind a "veil of ignorance" to capture that sense of remote impartiality. The veil of ignorance removes from their sight the morally irrelevant factors that distinguish them from other trustees, which allows their choice to be fair principles for social cooperation. Specifically, Rawls posits that a just social contract is that upon which the trustees would agree if they did not know in advance what sort of position their countries would occupy in the institution they are joining. In the original position, the trustee would not know the economic size, financial situation, or other morally irrelevant facts about the country and, from behind the veil of ignorance, the trustees would be able to discern the form of a truly just international institution. Put differently, the process used in the design of institutions is of crucial importance for justice, and the original Bretton Woods formula is as far away from the Rawlsian original position as the two poles of a magnet, but there is a difference in that, unlike the opposite magnetic poles, these two "originals" are not attracted to each other.

Rawls's theory is an end-result approach insofar as choice of principles is reached behind a veil of ignorance—the choice must be based on calculations about what people are likely to end up with under the various possible sets of principles—but Nozick (1974) has provided an alternative or historical theory of justice. Nozick's entitlement theory does not require that the just distribution should be correlated with, for example, moral merit, need, or usefulness to society. In this approach, people may be entitled to things obtained by chance or as a gift. In general, any distribution, irrespective of any pattern it may or may not have, is just if it has the appropriate history, or, in other words, it has come about in accordance with the rules of acquisition, transfer, and rectification. We have worked with Rawls's theory but it should be clear that IMF quota formulas do not meet Nozick's test either.[14] These formulas determine, among other things, the distribution of voting power in the IMF. However, they were simply the numbers decided by Secretary White, and were not based on any rules of acquisition, transfer, or rectification. Treasury staff economist Mikesell was asked to come up with a formula that would justify the precooked numbers, which means that Bretton Woods formula does not have what Nozick would call "appropriate history" and there is no basis for discussing any rules of acquisition or other requirements of the entitlement theory.

III. Rawls's method

Rawls's idea of reflective equilibrium expressed his political understanding of justification but in a more complicated way than is usually thought. To justify the claim that some particular conception of justice is the appropriate one, Rawls argued that this could be done by finding that conception which is best fitted to play the role of adjudicating competing claims on scarce social resources or distribution of power. Furthermore, to judge fitness for this purpose, he emphasized that no conception of justice can play such a role unless there is widespread "up-take" of its basic principles and deliverances. Hence, we see, for each candidate conception, whether its implications can be brought into reflective equilibrium with the considered judgments of justice in a particular community. If that cannot be done, then up-take will not be secured and the conception cannot facilitate mutual benefit. This is what distinguishes principled reasoning about justice in a "pragmatic mode" from the modus vivendi argument that Rawls repudiated in no uncertain terms. Before discussing the applications of the reflective equilibrium and overlapping consensus to the

---

[14] Nozick provided an apt characterization of his approach to philosophy in his last book: "My own philosophical bent is to open possibilities for consideration. Not to close them. This book suggests new philosophical views and theses, and the reasons it produces for these are meant to launch them for exploration, not to demonstrate conclusively that they are correct...Similarly, my criticisms of some major competing theories or positions are not intended to refute them conclusively, merely to weaken them enough to clear a philosophical space in which the newly proposed views can breathe and grow." Nozick (2001), p. 3.

voice and quota debate in the IMF, it is illustrative first to discuss some aspects of the recent history of the quotas and voice reform, and next, contrast it with the Rawlsian approach.

A. Quota Formula Review Group (QFRG)

Given the concern that the quota formulas did not reflect changes in the world economy, such as the growing role of emerging markets and the increased importance of international capital flows, the IMF convened the Quota Formula Review Group (QFRG) in 1999 to provide an independent review of quota formulas.[15] The eight-member panel, chaired by Professor Richard Cooper (Harvard University), was asked to review the quota formulas with respect to "their adequacy to help determine members quotas . . . in a manner that reasonably reflects members' relative positions in the world economy as well as their relative need for and contributions to the IMF's financial resources, taking into account change in the functioning of the world economy and the international financial system in light of increasing globalization of markets." The QFRG recommended a single formula with two variables: GDP as a measure of the ability to contribute resources to the IMF and variability of current receipts and net long-term capital flows, as a measure of external vulnerability, with the GDP variable having the larger weight.

We will not comment on the obvious problem that the specific formula recommended by the panel pointed toward a greater concentration of quotas among the largest industrial countries, a result which is unacceptable because it is in the opposite direction from what are the universally acknowledged objectives of the quota reform, namely, giving more voice to: (i) the emerging countries because of their relatively faster growth rates and increasingly larger weight in the world economy, and (ii) the low-income and small countries to address the Westphalian and democracy deficits. Instead, we confine our comments to the specific variables suggested by the QFRG. They recommend the use of GDP, converted to a common base at market exchange rates, and a broader definition of variability to indicate potential vulnerability. The problem with the first variable is that the alternative PPP-based measure of GDP is superior for the task at hand (see below). The problem with the second variable is that QFRG variability measure did not reflect vulnerability to short-term capital shocks, nor did it take into account the fact that capital account disruptions in developing countries are not just different in degrees, but in kind, from those in advanced economies and, accordingly, should be measured using different metrics (see below).

---

[15] See International Monetary Fund, *External Review of Quota Formulas*, (2000a, 2000b, and 2001a).

Several difficult issues remain to be resolved, including agreeing on the precise weights of each variable, but there are major concerns among many Directors, particularly those representing the developing countries, that the voice and quota debate is being narrowed down and some important issues are not being addressed. For example, recent staff papers have noted that

[i]n June 2002, Executive Directors reached understandings on broad principles for arriving at an alternative quota formula... there was general endorsement of a simpler and more transparent approach in specifying the variables in quota formulas... that variables included in the quota formulas should be indicators of members' economic position in the world... also agreed to limit consideration to three or four variables used in existing quota formulas, but updated and modernized. These variables include GDP, a measure of openness, variability, and possibly international reserves... Board reaffirmed these broad conclusions in the July 2003 discussion on quota-related topics.[16]

The following discussion takes as a starting point the QFRG's suggested criteria for assessing proposals for changes in the formulas, notably a focus on variables that reflect changes in the world economy, consistency with the multiple functions of quotas, and simplicity and transparency, but goes further in analyzing additional variables that could be included in a revised formula. We propose a new way of looking at the quota formulas, which overcomes the main shortcomings of the present approach, and one which we think will go a long way to addressing the democracy deficit and the legitimacy problems facing the IMF.

B. Variables in the quota formulas

Economic size The advanced countries have favored using the three-year average (in lieu of the recent year) of GDP at market exchange rates as the most important variable to be included in any new formula because they view it as the best indicator of countries' economic size and of their potential either

---

[16] There has been a disappointing rush toward eliminating certain variables from further discussion and/or to downplay their possible inclusion in the quota formulas. Statements such as the following are not helpful for advancing the very contentious debate on quota reform: the possibility of using purchasing power parity rather than market exchange rates to derive GDP was discussed in October 2001 when a "majority of the Board considered that market exchange rates should be used to convert GDP to a common currency." It is disconcerting that, in this instance, little consideration was given to the fact that many Directors had very strong views on the need for PPP-based measures of GDP. In a similar vein, staff note that at the discussion in September 2005, most Directors reconfirmed that a revised formula should be based on an updating of the traditional economic and financial variables and should comprise at most four variables (see International Monetary Fund, 2006). This sentence has the same problem of not giving weight to the diversity of views expressed on alternative variables that may be included in a new quota formula but makes an even bigger mistake by pushing the discussion toward an inexorable and mistaken conclusion of sticking close to the flawed formulas. Moreover, it does not recognize that the holistic approach, in which basic votes are increased, could have other implications for the quota formulas.

to provide to or to use of IMF resources.[17] However, most economists would agree that using purchasing power parity rather than market exchange rates to derive GDP would be the more appropriate procedure. The variable is meant to capture economic size, but this cannot be done using market exchange rates because there are wide variations in common currency prices for the same commodity bundle across countries, with distortions being particularly severe in the case of developing countries. The argument that market exchange rates should be used to convert GDP to a common currency, so as to obtain the best measure of the total amount of resources generated by a country, has an irony embedded in it. If one is measuring economic size, there is no argument but that the PPP measure is clearly the right metric because the same bundle of goods gets the same measure.[18] The counter-argument would be that all bundles of goods cannot be sold in the international market, that is, economies contain two sorts of activity: tradable, that is, manufacturing and services that can be supplied at a distance; and nontradable, that is, haircuts, childcare, and so on. The irony and major weakness of this counter-argument is that nobody is possibly imagining an IMF so large that countries would have to attempt to sell their nontraded activities on the international market to come up with the financing of their quota shares; the present IMF quota of any country is a tiny share of its foreign transactions.

Openness Some countries have been strong proponents for the inclusion of an openness variable. This is specified as the absolute sum of current receipts and current payments, averaged over a five-year period, to reflect countries' integration in the world economy. There is also support for broadening the openness measure by including a variable for financial openness, although there are data difficulties that first would need to be resolved. Setting aside the problem of the correlation of openness with other variables in the formula, it is clear that this variable also suffers from a second, closely related problem, which is the treatment of trade within currency unions. In particular, given the emphasis being placed on the so-called "modernizing" of the traditional variables in the quota formulas, one would think that attention would focus on adjusting the treatment of trade within currency unions, not least in light of the fact that the European Single Market was completed in 1992, and moreover, the euro was adopted as currency by a number of these countries in 1999. There is not that much difference, say, in the trade between Belgium and Luxembourg, and between two provinces inside a country. For the

---

[17] The proposal of using a three-year average for GDP works to the advantage of the industrial countries because it postpones the incorporation into the quota formula of the catching-up effect on the GDP variable of the fast-growing emerging market economies and LICs.

[18] See McLenaghan (2005) on the progress that has been made in compiling PPP-based GDP for developing countries, which has largely taken care of the oft-repeated problem that this measure is not available for a large number of countries.

purposes of quota calculations, the IMF staff have used techniques in the past to exclude certain receipts and payments in order to avoid exaggerating the size of the external sector, such as in the case of excluding certain interest payments and entrepôt trade. However, the question of trade within the currency unions is of far greater significance for relative quota shares than the exclusions currently being practiced, but unfortunately, this debate has proceeded rather slowly. Above and beyond this consideration, the problem is that the openness variable is supposed to capture the demand for IMF resources. However, as discussed below, there are far better proxies for the demand variable in that they have far higher correlations with the actual use of IMF resources than the openness variables currently being used.[19]

Variability The inclusion of a measure of variability of current receipts and net capital flows appears to be warranted, in order to capture countries' vulnerability to balance of payments shocks in the quota formula (and the attendant potential demand for IMF resources). There is general support that variability be specified as deviations from a three-year average, which would serve to smooth trends while adequately capturing the fluctuations in capital flows. As noted below, there is a strong case for supplementing the variability variable with others that capture the demand for IMF resources.

Reserves It can be argued that reserves are a useful indicator of members' financial strength, and should be retained as a variable in the quota formula; this is also consistent with recent emphasis on adequacy of international reserves. The counter-argument would be that, for many members with access to capital markets and floating exchange rates, reserves are of declining importance and should be excluded. However, high reserves can be a useful indicator for both demand and supply of IMF resources, and it ought to be retained (see below).

C. Reflective equilibrium

Rawls noted that to facilitate the achievement of certain goals, we should understand the circumstances that make it necessary to develop and propagate the principles of justice. Suppose that scarcity of supply relative to demand for IMF quotas is characteristic of our situation, which seems reasonable because there is no price mechanism to equate supply and demand. Moreover, there is no example of any country voluntarily offering to lower its quota share. This is part of what makes the propagation of distributional principles and practices necessary: given scarcity and certain other factors, countries will not individually, or collectively, self-equilibrate to ensure demand–supply equilibrium.

---

[19] Hence when one asks *"qui bono?"* (who benefited?) from these quota formulas, the main countries (in relative terms) include the advanced countries and the countries belonging to the European Union, all of which benefit from the market-exchange-rate-based GDP and the openness variables.

However, it is exactly this fact that should be captured in the procedure applied for the development of these principles, which the trustees have to take into account if they are to achieve justice. If they just assume away the problem of distribution by presupposing, for instance, that countries will spontaneously adjust their demands and supplies to achieve an equilibrium—because there is a price variable that is adjusting—then they would have completely ignored the fact that the quotas are not traded and that there is no price variable attached to them. One can imagine the public reaction if the global leaders of a particular industry colluded to suppress the workings of the free market and arbitrarily fixed the price of their goods, or the capital subscriptions in their firms were not allowed to be traded. There would be an outrage that there was conspiracy and restraint of trade, and the corporate heads would be asked to implement reforms to improve governance. If the IMF is only a financial institution, why then are its capital shares not traded, or its lending terms arbitrarily fixed, and why does the market mechanism not play a role.[20] Given the important differences between the IMF and other financial institutions, it seems odd not to recognize the unique nature and responsibilities of the IMF, and even odder that some recognize the need for quotas and voice reform, but then insist that the variables in the quota formulas should be confined to just a couple of economic variables, which severely biases the representation of developing countries.

In what has become known as the Rawls test, policymakers should always ask themselves the question: "Would the best-off accept particular social or economic arrangements if they believed, at any moment, their fortunes were to be reversed and they were to be placed in the position of the worst off?" The present IMF structure does not fit Rawls's conception in many respects. Apply his method to the openness variable in the quota formula and ask whether we would, behind a veil of ignorance, opt for this variable, which ostensibly is meant to capture the demand for IMF resources. This would only be fair if it could be shown that the openness variable is the best metric for gauging which countries borrow from the IMF. However, some of the countries that score the highest in terms of this variable and, therefore, benefit the most in terms of quota shares, have had no need for IMF resources for the last 25 years; in fact, some of these countries have never borrowed from the IMF. As discussed below, a straightforward approach to capturing the demand for IMF resources in the quota formulas would be a variable that takes into account the history of borrowings by a member country and/or external vulnerability (e.g. credit ratings on sovereign borrowing or spreads on sovereign debt).

Since the present quota formulas have severe weaknesses and are not well designed to capture the likelihood of borrowing from the IMF, the interests of

---

[20] Unlike shares in a joint stock company, IMF quotas are not traded in a market and as such there is no market-clearing price for these quotas or share subscriptions.

debtors were not taken sufficiently into account. However, it would be wrong to stretch the "original position" argument so far that it forces one into the untenable position of defending, for example, the proposition that IMF quota formulas should be the equilibrating mechanism that balances out all other inequalities, injustices, and effects of luck so as to make members indifferent between being an advanced economy and being a developing economy. To say that the trustees are behind a "veil of ignorance" is to say that they do not know the following sorts of things: their countries' economic size, level of economic development, population, possible need for IMF resources, and so on. However, they are aware of the general types of possible situations in which countries can find themselves and the purposes of the IMF, such as multilateral and bilateral surveillance, provision of conditional liquidity (IMF-supported adjustment programs), and provision of unconditional liquidity (SDRs). The original position argument has to be used with some care, namely, to imagine a situation in which a group of individuals are brought together to agree upon the basic constitution of a society or social institution that they are about to enter, but in which, to ensure their impartiality, they are placed behind a veil of ignorance. In the present context, self-interested rational persons behind the veil of ignorance are given the task of choosing the principles that shall determine the governance structure of the IMF. In deciding what the quotas formula should be for determining, among other things, the distribution of the voting rights in the IMF, we should try to imagine what formula the representatives of the countries would choose if they didn't know what type of country they were going to represent. The veil denies them any knowledge that is morally irrelevant. With the expulsion of bias-inducing knowledge, the participants in the original position are forced, even if self-centered, into the moral point of view, which allows Rawls to claim that he has set up an inherently fair procedure, and the principles to be chosen by means of this procedure would be fair.

In sharp contrast to what the Rawlsian approach would require for justice as fairness, it is clear that creditors would mind if they swapped positions with debtors. Since this is not the case, the present quota shares do not pass the fairness test. One implication of this failure to pass the Rawls test is that the IMF programs have been overloaded with conditionality—recall the programs during the Asian financial crisis in which programs had more than a hundred performance criteria or benchmarks and the subsequent deliberations that led to the streamlining of conditionality. The following quotation from Hubert Neiss, who was Director of the Asian Department during the Asian financial crisis, gives an idea about the design of the adjustment programs and the involvement of the Executive Board.

In the end, programs had to be approved by the Fund's Executive Directors, who represent member governments and whose votes are weighted by the economic importance of the countries they represent . . . Governments' views were obtained through regular informal contacts with the Executive Board during the program negotiations (in the case of Indonesia, including two video conferences), as well as in discussions with the Paris Club members. It was amply clear that the international community required comprehensive action . . . I do not think the Board would have accepted programs which failed to dismantle the monopolies in Indonesia which were a main source of corruption; or in the case of Korea, failed to liberalize foreign ownership and take-over rules in order to attract capital into the financial sector and introduce effective competition, or to make changes in the labor laws to allow corporate restructuring. Similarly, programs failing to revise bankruptcy and foreclosure laws in Thailand and Indonesia, in order to allow effective debt restructuring, would have been considered inadequate. And in all cases, programs would not have been passed without including extensive privatization, an area that is not mentioned in the Fund's Articles.[21]

An extensive comment on whether conditionality was excessive—or on the question of mission creep that seems to be implied in the last sentence of the quotation—would take us too far from the main focus of this chapter. Accordingly, we confine our comments, first, to the point that the industrial countries have over 60 percent of the votes in the Executive Board, and this majority does matter in getting a sense of the views of the Directors and the governments they represent, and, second, refer the reader to the article by Alan Blinder, the noted economist and former Vice Chairman of the US Federal Reserve Board, in which he called for major reforms:

As I stated at the outset, the new financial architecture needs to give greater weight to developing and strengthening the social safety nets that shield innocent bystanders from the fallout of financial crises. This idea is not alien to the IMF's way of thinking. But neither is it central. The IMF pays inadequate attention to the protection of innocents— compared, say, to the protection of creditors who have made ill-conceived loans . . . A reformed IMF, working in conjunction with the World Bank and regional development banks, should ensure that foreign creditors are not bailed out while local populations drown.[22]

The Blinder quote is not about quotas but about the criteria that should be used in designing adjustment programs and then judging whether they are succeeding or failing. Whereas his paper aims to persuade people in the "high quota" countries to reform the IMF, it is relevant for the quota debate insofar as it makes clear that the design of adjustment programs needs to be improved. We discuss in the next subsection that any progress made in improving the distribution of quotas would also mean progress in addressing the problem of program ownership and the design of adjustment programs because those who approve the programs (i.e. the Executive Directors) would include a significant proportion of people whose economies are directly affected by those programs.

---

[21] Neiss (2001).   [22] Blinder (2003), pp. 59–60.

What are the implications of the original position argument for the conditionality debate and IMF governance? An answer would be that a self-interested rational person behind the veil of ignorance would not support a governance structure that gives almost no weight to the Westphalian principle of "one nation, one vote" and an exact zero weight to the democratic principle of "one person, one vote." In particular, such a person would not wish to represent either a small country that gets almost no voting power—basic votes reflect the Westphalian principle but give a mere 1/100th of 1 percent of the voting power to each country—or a country with millions of people, when the democracy principle is not even acknowledged. Another answer would be that a rational person would not want to support a governance structure in an institution to which members cede some important aspects of national sovereignty in the interest of global monetary cooperation, and whereas the institution impacts in important ways—not only when there is an IMF-supported adjustment program, but also because of IMF's surveillance, regulatory, and policy advice activities—the livelihoods of hundreds of millions of people, the governance structure does not give any weight to the population variable in the quota formula. With regard to the future, this point bears emphasis because the IMF's lending role is becoming less important relative to surveillance, technical assistance, and other activities, which would suggest larger weights for the Westphalian and democracy principles and smaller weights for the traditional creditor–debtor variables.

It has been argued by some observers that even though population is not included in the quota formulas, there is some correlation between population and some other included variables, such as GDP. There are at least three ways in which this argument fails. The first deals with the simple fact that since data are available on population, and if that is the variable we are trying to capture, then there is no need for a proxy variable. Second, the correlation coefficient between population and GDP is quite low to begin with and declines very sharply when large emerging market economies are excluded from the sample. Third, this argument is wrong because, as we have seen, GDP was meant to capture a country's economic size and ability to contribute to IMF resources. The GDP variable cannot account for our sense of ourselves as "self-interpreting" and "self-reflective" beings, or in other words, that the self (in the abstract, general sense) is prior to its ends, and it cannot be measured by some aggregate economic concept.

Despite the need to incorporate additional variables in the quota formula, the IMF Board has focused on a small set of traditional variables in the quota formula. Unfortunately, population is not one of the variables that has received much attention. Also, little progress has been made in these discussions toward agreement on a new metric to measure members' relative economic positions and capital flows. A major difficulty is a high correlation among the variables in the current quota formula and the need for further work to reduce this correlation, including the inclusion of additional variables. The correlation among variables means that the coefficients attached to each variable cannot be taken to represent the variable's relative importance in a new quota formula.[23]

The openness variable, which supposedly captures the demand for IMF resources, has generated considerable controversy. Whereas there is considerable support for the view that a capital flow volatility variable be included in the quota formula, the measures proposed by the IMF staff have major shortcomings. However, the idea to capture countries' vulnerabilities to capital account shocks in the quota formula is clearly correct, not least given the number of financial crises that many IMF members have faced since the late-1980s and during the 1990s. The idea received support in the G24 Ministers' communiqué of October 2004, which stated that enhancing the representation of developing countries requires a new quota formula and specifically mentioned the need to take into account their vulnerabilities to the volatility of capital movements. The current quota formula estimates a country's vulnerability only to current account shocks, by including variables such as trade openness and export volatility. In recent years, however, many of the balance of payments crises have been of the capital account variety, which are related to developments in financial markets and often precipitated by exogenous factors, such as contagion and "sudden stops." Although recent IMF Board discussions on quota formulas have emphasized the need for a measure of capital flows volatility, the problem with variables that have been analyzed by the staff is that they do not capture the countries' macroeconomic vulnerability to capital account shocks.[24] The capital flow variables examined by the staff are either just gross capital flows or volatility measures that have not been normalized to reflect major differences across countries. Thus, the variables under consideration are not a good measure of the amount of resources potentially required to stabilize a given country. It should be apparent that if two countries experience the same capital account shock in absolute terms, the smaller

[23] It should be emphasized that this is not an argument about some problems in econometric estimation, or more specifically that multicollinearity would reduce the precision of the estimated coefficients, because there is no econometrics involved in determining IMF quotas. Instead, our argument is against the point that has been raised by some observers that the quota formulas are an attempt to capture the weights that different properties of economies have and that are relevant for the voting power, access levels, SDR allocations, etc., and if these properties are correlated across countries, so be it—that's our choice and there is no multicollinearity problem. This argument is wrong because it is not a multicollinearity problem in the econometric sense that is being discussed, but the simple point that if two variables are very highly correlated, adding the second variable into the equation does not bring with it much additional information; even though these variables may seemingly represent different characteristics, the high correlation means that the dominant underlying factor would be the same for these variables. Put it differently, when there are many variables that are highly correlated, just a few principal components would capture most of the information.

[24] See, for example, dos Reis (2005).

economy will face a greater burden. The first step should be to measure net capital flows as a proportion of the size of the economy—by measuring volatility of capital flows as a proportion of GDP—which is the alternative evaluated in the paper by dos Reis (2005).

Furthermore, measuring volatility of capital flows as a proportion of GDP is only the first step because of the important differences between the capital flows of industrial versus developing countries that should also be addressed. Some recent open-economy theoretical models, including a few third-generation currency crisis models, have incorporated these differences. For example, a key insight from the dual liquidity models developed by Caballero and Krishnamurthy, which bears directly on the question of the capital flow variable in the quota formula, is that for many low-income countries with international liquidity shortages, there is a sharp distinction between international and domestic collateral unlike the case in industrial countries. The Caballero–Krishnamurthy model, henceforth C–K model, which emphasizes the financial constraints affecting borrowing and lending among agents within the economy—as distinct from those constraints affecting borrowing from foreign lenders—also points to the need for substantial international liquidity in emerging and low-income countries.[25] In the C–K model, international liquidity constraint is defined as a situation in which domestic agents have sufficient collateral to borrow from other domestic agents, but cannot borrow from foreigners because of the country's shortage of international collateral.[26]

Another major difference between the capital flows of industrial versus emerging and low-income countries is that, in the latter case, external debt is overwhelmingly denominated in foreign currency, which has its own problems apart from those relating to the dollarization of liabilities in the banking system. One explanation for why emerging and low-income countries have not been able to borrow abroad in their own currency is that they have pursued financial policies that have resulted in high inflation rates and depreciating exchange rates. Another explanation is that they have not built the social institutions required for policy credibility, which makes investors reluctant to invest in domestic currency assets. Furthermore, if these countries were

[25] Caballero and Krishnamurthy (2001).

[26] The Caballero–Krishnamurthy model focuses on two distinct situations, which have sharply divergent implications for the conduct of monetary policy. In the horizontal view, the distressed firms are constrained in meeting their financing needs because they have limited collateral, that is, their total liquidity is insufficient to meet the higher financing needs due to the production shock. This situation is termed horizontal, because the international financial constraint is not binding for intact firms, and the interest rate they charge against domestic collateral is equal to the international interest rate. In contrast, the vertical view is the situation where the international supply of funds is vertical, because there is a shortage of country-wide international liquidity. In the vertical framework, international reserves are an important component of liquidity, because here the supply of international liquidity is inelastic, with foreign investors unwilling to provide additional funds and domestic agents resorting to hoarding of whatever little they have of international liquidity.

to issue debt in their own currencies, there is the risk that even those that had hitherto pursued sound financial policies might be tempted to pursue more inflationary policies as a way of eroding the real value of their external debt. However, even emerging and low-income countries with low inflation, balanced budgets, and good governance have not acquired immunity against this problem. It is not clear what these countries have done to bring this problem upon themselves and because foreign currency debt is the source of many other problems, it is referred to as "original sin" in the literature.[27]

These considerations suggest that the capital flow variable for developing countries cannot be put in the same basket as that for the industrial countries because that would be mixing apples and oranges together. One promising approach would be to attempt to assess the demand for IMF resources by emerging and low-income countries by examining the ratings assigned to these countries by major rating agencies. Yaqub, Mohammed, and Zaidi (henceforth YMZ) proposed in the context of SDR allocations that one should start with the group of countries that received concessional financing from the Poverty Reduction and Growth Facility (PRGF), and broaden this group by including other emerging-market countries that have not received investment grades by credit rating agencies, such as Moody's and Standard and Poor's Investor Services. It seems quite straightforward to use a modified YMZ approach in the quota formulas, and it would be a more appropriate measure for the demand for IMF resources than gross capital flows that have garnered most of the attention in the quota formula debate.

Without getting involved in a debate about the credit rating agencies, it may be mentioned that the scheme just mentioned relies heavily on the credit rating agencies for the determination of quotas, which could be a source of concern for some observers. There has been some controversy about the reliability of the ratings and the lack of transparency, particularly in light of the rating agencies' failure to warn investors about the impending bankruptcy of some major companies in the past couple of years. In light of the foregoing discussion, it would be useful to modify somewhat the YMZ approach and replace their second criterion based on ratios of reserves to imports with a broader set of indicators. The new method would have the advantage of bringing more continuity in the variables by using a wider information base. In addition, it would be more of a hybrid approach because, instead of relying on ratings assigned by the major agencies or reserve–import ratios, one would start with three or four variables, which could include reserves to short-term debt, financing gaps, and monetary base (or money supply) ratios. Including reserves to short-term debt would follow the suggestions of Guidotti and Greenspan regarding self-protection policies and because empirical crisis-prediction models have shown that this ratio is an important factor in determining a

---

[27] See Eichengreen and Hausmann (1999), p. 11.

country's vulnerability to financial crisis.[28] The reason for including the ratio of monetary base (or money supply) to reserves is that, as discussed in the Chang–Velasco and Dooley models, the size of a country's monetary base (or money supply) in relation to its reserve holdings is an important indicator of the country's potential exposure to the withdrawal of assets and, hence, a country's vulnerability to crisis.[29] One could also use sovereign bond spreads to measure the likely need for IMF-supported adjustment programs. Needless to say, several of these variables would have high correlation, and one could either eliminate those variables with the highest correlations, or the demand variable in the formula could be a weighted average of several of these variables, but, as emphasized in the Rawlsian approach, the total weight of the demand variable in the formula would be agreed upon at the outset.

The foregoing discussion shows that simple variables do not always perform the task assigned to them because there are cases in which the situation could seemingly be classified in a known type through a particular variable, but one would not be comfortable with the implementation of the simple "ready-made variable." We know that judgment according to that variable involves a certain amount of misfit between the general rule and the particular situation at hand. Even if we were to assume, for the sake of argument, that there is no misfit and we attempt to act according to a simple rule and a simple variable, we should be open to the point that we are still not dealing with the situation in which we stand, but that we are dealing with a certain type of situation under which we class it. For example, if a particular variable in a quota formula may appear at first glance to be similar to the general concept we are trying to measure, it is nonetheless true that, although the general concept provides us with a handle with which to grasp the particular situation, we still have to recognize that the generality of the rule interferes with the specific aspects of the situation we are trying to grasp. In other words, for all of the reasons mentioned above for the special and unusual aspects of the capital account variable, it is clear that the difference between the capital flows of developing countries and those of the industrial countries is not just a difference in degree but a difference in kind, between the generality of the capital account variable and the specific situation at hand. Therefore, insight and careful deliberation are required in the decision-making process of quota formulas, and we can not say that 100 percent of decisions about variables in these formulas could be easily determined by a strict application of the rule that the same variable applies to both advanced and developing countries. It is for these reasons that the quota formula should treat some variables differently for industrial and developing countries, and, while simplicity of the

---

[28] See Radelet and Sachs (1998) and Berg et al. (1999).
[29] See Calvo (1996).

formula is important, it needs to be balanced with the need to capture the main objective of the exercise. These considerations suggest that the quota formulas should have moral and economic underpinnings, not just political underpinnings; two secondary conclusions are that the formulas are worse than useless unless they are designed properly and, with apologies to Albert Einstein, quota formulas should be made as simple as possible but not simpler.[30]

In the Rawlsian approach—specifically in achieving an overlapping consensus—the aim is not to have a regulative device, and in particular, it is not as though the principles of justice are adjusted to the claims of the dominant political and social interests. It is important to distinguish between the two stages in justice as fairness, and to be clear that the idea of an overlapping consensus is used only in the second stage. In the first stage, justice as fairness is seen as a free-standing political conception that articulates the values applicable to the special domain of the political, as marked out by the basic structure of the society or the institution under consideration. In the second stage, an account of the stability of justice as fairness is formulated, which provides the basis—in view of the content of its principles and ideals as formulated in the first stage—to generate its own support. In other words, the idea of an overlapping consensus is introduced only in the second stage to explain that despite the plurality of conflicting comprehensive philosophical, economic, and moral doctrines, free institutions may gain the allegiance needed to endure over time.[31]

From Rawls's method, it could be argued that rational individuals will adopt two principles for IMF governance, which would be ordered lexicographically. The first principle would state that each country is to have an equal right to a meaningful percentage of total quotas (Westphalian principle) and that population would be a determinant of a certain percentage of the voting power (democracy principle) compatible with the purposes of the IMF. The second principle would have the remaining amount of the quota apportioned among members based on two different sets of variables: (i) those that would reflect a country's economic size and ability to contribute to IMF resources; and (ii) those that would reflect a country's need to borrow IMF resources, which would include external vulnerability and other variables that would capture possible borrowings from the IMF.

These considerations suggest that the IMF should build what Rawls calls an "infrastructure of justice" that ensures every country some reasonable level of voting power and the opportunity to influence decisions, thereby giving it a proper chance to achieve full membership of this global institution. Moreover, the creditor countries should recognize that, whereas they have certain voting

---

[30] Albert Einstein, "Everything should be made as simple as possible but not simpler."
[31] See Rawls (1989).

powers that come from the weights in the quota formula for the supply of capital variables, such as GDP, the interests of the debtor countries should be taken into account with variables that are the best predictors of future IMF borrowings. When debtor country interests are taken into account and, moreover, the broad mandate of the IMF acknowledged, the argument that safeguarding the use of IMF resources trumps all other considerations would be seen to be vacuous. In contrast, original position argumentation requires that the position of the debtors should be the best possible after taking into account the creditors' interests, so that, were the positions to be swapped, the creditors would accept their new position as fair.

D. Basic votes

At the Bretton Woods conference that founded the IMF and World Bank, a compromise was reached between the Westphalian principle of the legal equality of states, which called for one country, one vote, and the economic argument for basing votes solely on capital contributions or capacity to lend to the IMF. The compromise was to allocate 250 "basic votes" to each member country, which meant that every country had a voice because after all each was affected by the institution's regulatory work, even if it did not approach it for conditional loans. The economic argument for the supply of resources to the IMF and the need to safeguard creditor countrys' interests was reflected in the agreement that countries would have one vote for every US$100,000 of IMF quota subscribed and, in turn, the quotas took account of the capacity to lend to the IMF.[32] The balance achieved in this compromise has been lost over time because whereas basic votes have remained unchanged, there has been a 37-fold increase in IMF quotas, which has resulted in a sharp reduction of basic votes as a proportion of the total voting power, and therefore severely reduced the participation of small countries in decision making. Thus, the basic votes have declined from 11.3 percent to 2.1 percent, and for the original members of the IMF to 0.5 percent. The 0.5 percent is the appropriate measure for the relative decline of the Westphalian principle because the 2.1 percent includes new members, whereas the metric is for one nation, one vote.[33]

---

[32] The basis for calculating voting power—and the role of basic votes—is set out in Article XII, Section 5(a) of the Fund's Articles of Agreement. It provides that "[E]ach member shall have two hundred and fifty votes plus one additional vote for each part of its quota equivalent to one hundred thousand special drawing rights." The two hundred and fifty votes specified in this provision are generally referred to as "basic votes."

[33] Some observers have argued that the relevant point of comparison is 11.3 percent to 2.1 percent rather than to 0.5 percent because even under a pure "one country one vote" principle, the voting share of each country would be diluted with the entry of new members, and that the 0.5 percent for the original members is merely reflecting the fact that, in all elections, the larger the electorate, the smaller the relative weight of each individual's voice. This argument is valid for individual members in an electorate but it does not carry over to the comparison done here, which is not for individual members but between different

The issue of restoration of the basic vote to the original 11.3 percent, or the maximum of 15.8 percent (reached in 1958), is of the utmost importance if the institution is to gain legitimacy, but the reform package accepted by the Board of Governors stipulated only a tripling of the basic votes. However, there is still some uncertainty because the restoration of basic votes requires an amendment of the Articles of Agreement, which hinges on the question of the strength of commitment of major shareholders to the timing and implementation of the second stage reforms. Even if commitments have been made, the track record is not exactly solid. The membership recalls disappointingly the strong commitment of major shareholders to the Fourth Amendment, which is yet to be ratified a decade after it was approved by the Board of Governors.

As the Rawlsian approach makes abundantly clear, ways to ensure that low-income countries (LICs) have adequate opportunity to participate in governance of the institution should be one the top priorities of efforts aimed at enhancing the IMF's legitimacy. The LICs' share in the world economy is small, but the IMF has a far larger role in these economies in terms of policy advice, financing, conditions attached to IMF-supported adjustment programs, and the like. The LICs are not effectively represented in the IMF—although the institution is spending a disproportionately larger amount of resources in work on these countries relative to their quota, mainly because of the adjustment programs and the need for more intensive technical assistance. Addressing the quota problems of LICs would also help in attenuating the problem of ownership: if those who design the adjustment programs for the IMF (i.e. staff members) and those who approve the program (i.e. the Executive Directors) included a significant proportion of people whose economies are directly affected by those programs, then this would be a direct way to give meaning to the concept of ownership.[34] Thus, if there is going to be a new Washington Consensus of best-practice economic policies (e.g. the analytical backdrop for IMF-supported adjustment programs, provision of technical assistance, role of the IMF in LICs), or if the IMF is going to have a bigger role in international surveillance—as envisaged in its medium-term strategy—the countries that are most affected by the these reforms should also be given the opportunity to provide important inputs in these areas. Such steps to enhance the legitimacy of the IMF would make its conditional financing,

characteristics (economic size and potential demand and supply for IMF credit, creditor versus debtor interests, Westphalian principle, democracy principle, etc.). Our point is not about what happens to individual members as the group size increases but what would be the appropriate weights for these variables in the quota formulas.

[34] In the present governance structure, the LICs have an almost negligible proportion of total quotas, which means that in the approval process for IMF-supported adjustment programs, they have virtually no say. With regard to the design of programs, the LICs share of total staff positions in the IMF is very small, because the staffing is based on merit but it does take into account geographical representation and IMF quotas.

regulatory, and other roles more credible, thereby potentially shortening financial crises and raising global welfare.

IV. The way forward

The issue of voice and representation and its importance for the good governance of the IMF cannot be overemphasized. Unless this issue is addressed in its totality, the risks to the IMF will only increase, including those relating to the perceived weaknesses of the IMF's role in multilateral surveillance and in influencing the policies of advanced countries. There is a need for multilateral consultations to strengthen the surveillance of the world economy, thereby addressing the growing global economic imbalances, which, in turn, would enable its members to address vulnerabilities that affect individual countries and the global financial system. Even more worrisome is the disquieting trend, which could affect the core mission of the IMF and runs the risk of marginalizing the institution, of huge and rising foreign currency stockpiles in Asia and other developing countries that come at high financial and opportunity costs. These countries are self-insuring against future shocks and vulnerabilities through the build-up of reserves far in excess of the levels required by the fundamentals of their economies.[35] It is difficult not to infer from this behavior that, in the views of these countries, there are shortcomings in the IMF's role in crisis prevention and resolution. As discussed earlier, the IMF was heavily criticized in Asia for attaching excessive loan conditions on Indonesia and others in the region during the 1997–8 Asian financial crisis. Some commentators have noted that one reason for the subsequent build-up of reserves in Asia has been to avoid a repeat of such experiences with the IMF. If this trend is not urgently and appropriately addressed through the adaptation of IMF's facilities to the insurance-type need of the membership, and moreover, through voice and quotas reform, it could develop into a core mission risk and jeopardize the relevance of the institution.[36]

[35] If international reserves are held for a rainy day, then some of the emerging market and low-income countries must be saving for Noah's Ark, as noted by the former IMF Chief Economist Kenneth Rogoff.

[36] As discussed above, the quotas for many fast-growing market countries are way out of line with their economic weights, and these countries, unhappy about their lack of representation on the IMF Board, have in a way already started leaving the fold of the institution insofar as they have been accumulating vast reserves to lower markedly the probability of any return to the IMF-supported adjustment programs. Furthermore, if these countries conclude that they will not be getting adequate representation and sufficient influence in the IMF, they are likely to continue on the path of larger reserves and even bolstering the regional arrangements such as the Chiang Mai Initiative in east Asia, which is an ambitious effort to create a regional financing facility, including a network of currency swap lines launched by the ASEAN + 3 group in 2000.

A. Adjusting voting power and quotas

The democracy and Westphalian principles should be seen in tandem, with one reinforcing the other. The point can be expressed most clearly in terms of its converse, namely, what are the implications of giving no weight to the democracy principle in the governance structure, but a very large weight to the Westphalian principle? Supposing the share of basic votes were increased not to the 11.3 percent observed at the inception of the IMF, but to a significantly larger number. That would create a tension because the movement along this path would make the governance structure more and more indifferent between, say, Maldives and Palau, on the one hand, and China and India, on the other hand, which would not meet Rawls's test. In this regard, as the concerns relating to the Westphalian principle are addressed, it becomes all the more important to address the democracy deficit and incorporate the population variable either in the quota formula, or alternatively, by instituting two classes of basic votes, one based on the Westphalian principle and the other based on the democracy deficit or population principle. The following table on basic votes and variables for the quota formula is set up according to the idea of two types of basic votes, but it should be reiterated that the listed variables and voting shares are for heuristic purposes and not a specific proposal (Table 14.1). Indeed, our view is that the basic votes should be much larger than 6 percent, but we decided to start the range at that low level because that is the number in the recent Resolution of the Board of Governors.

Table 14.1. Basic Votes and Variables for Quota Formula

		Percentage votes
Basic vote I	Westphalian principle	6–15
Basic vote II	Democracy principle	6–10
Variables for the quota formula (Supply and demand for IMF resources)		
Supply variables		45–55
PPP-based GDP		
International reserves		
Demand variables		25–35
Current payments or receipts and capital flows		
Variability of current receipts and capital flows		
Past IMF-supported programs		
Capital flows/GDP		
Subinvestment grade credit rating		
Sovereign bond spreads		
Reserves/short-term debt		
Reserves/financing gap		
Reserves/monetary base		

The main message to deduce from the table, or from this chapter, is that instead of deciding arbitrarily (and by just one man, former US Treasury Secretary White) what the voting shares of each country should be in the IMF, and then come up with a formula that delivers those numbers, the trustees are to visualize themselves in the Rawlsian original position whereby they are all self-interested rational persons motivated to select whatever seems advantageous for their countries, but, because they stand behind the veil of ignorance, they will decide in an informed and enlightened way. There are many different concepts of the IMF that the trustees in the original position could design, but the important point is that since they do not know what their country is in the real world, they should be prepared to end up representing anyone. Therefore, each trustee would want to pick the one IMF that offers the least bad alternative, meaning, they will pick the IMF with the least fortunate country in the least unfortunate situation. In particular, a self-interested rational person would not want to belong to an institution in which the least fortunate, who in fact is most affected by the workings of the institution, ends up with the least voting power. For this reason, before a decision is made about what variables to insert in the quota formula, there should be a broad agreement about what the voting shares ought to be for the Westphalian and democracy principles, as well as the demand and supply variables. An agreement on the shares for the demand and supply variables will be an important step in ensuring that the interests of debtors and creditors are adequately taken into account in the overlapping consensus.

Among the supply variables, we have put PPP-based GDP for the reasons given in the earlier section of this chapter. We are aware, however, of the suggestion that a weighted average of the PPP- and market-exchange-rate-GDP could be used in the spirit of a compromise. In our view, the first best option would be to agree on what is the right metric for the supply of resources behind the veil of ignorance, and, as pointed out earlier, it is hard to perceive why PPP-based GDP would not be chosen.[37] The other supply variable is international reserves, although this variable could also have been put among the demand variables because it serves both purposes. This has been done just for ease of presentation, but one should not belabor this point because it is clear that the GDP variable would take up the bulk of the weight in the supply variable. Alternatively, one could include international reserves in the demand and supply variables just to emphasize that it is a determinant of both variables, but in any event, the weight of the sum of these two variables would simply be equal to the weight given to the reserves variable when shown only in the demand side.

---

[37] The reforms adopted by the Board of Governors in May 2008 include a simpler quota formula that has a blended GDP variable.

Among the demand variables, those in the current quota formulas (open-ness and export variability) are included, but needless to say, they could be dropped altogether or could be given low weight because the other (new) demand variables are superior predictors of the use of IMF resources. The new demand variables included in the table are: those that capture past use of IMF resources; subinvestment grade credit rating; sovereign bond spreads; reserves/short-term debt; reserves/financing gap; reserves/monetary base. Although these new variables are good predictors of the demand for IMF resources, there is correlation among them. As noted earlier, one approach would be to work with a subset of these variables with the lowest correlation. An alternative approach would be to use most or all of these variables, but assign low weights to the individual ones. Yet another approach would be to use a hybrid variable, which uses information from each to construct a new variable; this approach would also take care of the problem of the missing data in some countries.

Some observers have noted that a couple of the variables that have been included in the demand side suffer from the problem of moral hazard, namely, there is a problem of hidden action which leads to increased likelihood of undesirable outcomes: countries will be rewarded with higher quotas if they pursue policies that increase their economic vulnerabilities, which cause lower credit ratings, higher sovereign bond spreads, and so on. The answer to this charge is that whereas it should be recognized that moral hazard exists and it can be an important consideration in some policy measures, it should not be oversold. In those situations such as when banks (or governments) are shielded from the consequences of their actions and take imprudent risks because of expectations of bail outs, policymakers must devise ways of dealing with this problem. However, it is hard to understand how this might be a problem in the present context, namely, that governments will implement risky policies because even when things go wrong, they benefit from a higher IMF quota. As argued in this chapter, IMF quotas are important, but it is certainly not the case that they are *so totally important* as to cause negative incentive effects in the implementation of financial policies. In any event, the moral hazard argument would also apply to the traditional variables such as international reserves because countries that self-insure (e.g. have higher international reserve holdings) will have a lower need for IMF-supported adjustment programs. In other words, to the extent that they are less likely to borrow from the IMF because of a greater ability to respond to external shocks, this would be reflected in a lower quota. To the contrary, it could be argued that international reserves should be given a higher weight in the quota formula because this variable is a determinant of a country's ability to provide resources to the IMF, which is the traditional view, but it is also a determinant of the need for borrowing because a country that is subjected to terms of trade and other external shocks will also hold higher reserves, *ceteris paribus*.

B. Aligning quotas and basic votes with justice as fairness

It might be argued that Rawls's principles are easier to apply abstractly in a general setting than to specific complex circumstances, such as the IMF governance structure. In particular, we cannot know for sure what quota formulas would be chosen by rational actors in the original position. However, this should not stop us from doing our best to imagine what the outcome of an original position negotiation might be, even while recognizing that reasonable people can disagree. The issue of IMF quota formulas seems particularly complicated, because the political reality is that, if certain principles of democratic equality (one nation one vote, or one person one vote) are pressed too far, the countries with strong economic power will simply refuse to be part of the arrangement. Indeed, one could argue that the industrial countries will never agree to any formula that is "fair" in the Rawlsian sense. More generally, as noted earlier, there is a high probability that the industrial countries will not be borrowers, but this does not mean that the IMF should follow the Golden Rule: "whoever has the gold makes the rules." As mentioned earlier in the chapter, the IMF is not a mere lending institution; its remit is far broader than what some observers claim to be the case, and this broad mandate is here to stay. Also, developing countries are creditors in the IMF as well, and moreover, they would like to have a larger role as creditors.

Another point that bears emphasis and one that is of particular importance in the original position is the question of how much deviation from pure democratic principles would be acceptable in order to secure participation of all countries. This is analogous to the widespread debate in political/economic/philosophical circles concerning how much economic inequality would be allowable in a society deemed just via Rawlsian principles. Rawls theoretically allowed for such inequality because it is conceivable that the least well off could, nevertheless, have more absolute wealth if the economy allowed for the entrepreneurial incentives that create winners and losers. Of course, stating this theoretically doesn't resolve the debate about how much inequality is acceptable. In effect, liberals and conservatives debate this question endlessly. That said, it is much easier to demonstrate what does not satisfy Rawlsian principles than what does, and that has been a major aim of this chapter. The quota formulas and the governance structure prevailing at present in the IMF do not even come close to justice as fairness.

We wish to emphasize that we are not trying to downplay what economists would call efficiency criteria (does this contribute toward the furtherance of the IMF's goals, and does it do so at low cost?) because surely these considerations should be given appropriate weights when designing quota formulas and the governance structure. In fact, we have argued that even these efficiency criteria are not always met in the IMF's governance structure, such as the mixed industrial–developing country constituencies in the Executive Board, the special majorities required for certain decisions, and the selection of the management team. With regard to the quota formulas, the efficiency considerations are taken up in the debate on the appropriate variables for measuring a member's ability to contribute to the IMF's financial base (e.g. GDP converted to a common base at market exchange rates versus the alternative PPP-based measure of GDP, openness variables versus international reserve holdings). Put differently, the aim has not been to emphasize equity criteria over efficiency criteria, but rather to point out that Rawls's framework provides important insights for judging competing proposals.

A number of important issues relevant to the revamping of the quota formulas and basic votes have been identified and recognized for quite some time but remain unresolved. Despite the claims of some who view the IMF as a financial institution, with little or no implications for global governance, the fact of the matter is that the IMF is *sui generis*. The IMF is the focal point of the international monetary system and provides a unique framework for international monetary cooperation. The IMF never was, and it is impossible to envisage it as, being transformed into a narrowly defined monetary institution. For example, the IMF has developed a number of elaborate reporting systems for member countries, including the Financial Sector Stability Assessments (FSSA) to report on the member countries' financial sectors and the Reports on the Observance of Standards and Codes (ROSCs) to assess their adherence to certain standards. These reports are important to the IMF's surveillance activities, as are the bi-annual World Economic Outlook (WEO), the Global Financial Stability Report (GFSR), and most importantly, the annual Article IV consultations with members. The surveillance activities take up more than one-quarter of the IMF's administrative budget. Since the IMF produces these and other public goods that are not subject to market discipline or even have a price attached to them, how can it possibly be engaged in mere financial transactions and be narrowly defined as a pure financial institution?

At the risk of repetition, we wish to stress that since quotas serve multiple purposes, the quota formulas have necessarily to balance sometimes competing considerations, and it can be argued that they are overburdened. Moreover, whereas the different roles of quotas provide guidance as to the variables that should enter the quota formulas, it is unfortunately true that several of the traditional variables do not meet the efficiency criteria of being the best proxy for the characteristic that the formulas are trying to capture. In particular, the demand variables that reflect a member's potential need to borrow from the IMF have severe shortcomings. At the same time, there has been an unfortunate tendency to focus on a member's ability to contribute usable resources to the IMF, but as noted earlier, the supply of credit to the IMF is not a market-clearing phenomenon. A large number of countries would be more than willing to provide all the resources needed by the institution, and indeed many small groups of developing countries can meet the financing requirements without any difficulty. Therefore, the argument that the use of quotas as a basis for calculating voting power derives from the role of quotas in determining the amount of a member's financial contribution to the IMF is misleading. There is little basis for arguing that many decisions taken by the IMF relate directly to how its financial resources are used, and hence voting power should be linked to members' roles as contributors of financial resources. The more important consideration is that quotas should determine voting power in relation to the IMF's broader responsibilities, including bilateral and multilateral surveillance, as well as capacity building, and the institution would be better equipped to discharge these broader responsibilities if there were to be the active engagement of all its members. The argument that there is a close link between these activities and IMF financing is not very convincing. For example, the point that effective surveillance will reduce the risk that members will demand IMF financial resources is stretching the point quite a bit because that demand depends on many things other than policy slippages.

The selection of variables in the quota formulas is a challenging task but one would expect that they should capture, at a minimum, a member's capacity to contribute financial resources to the IMF and the potential need to use its resources; we set aside for the moment the broader issues that were stressed above, including the Westphalian and democratic principles. Regarding the capacity to contribute financial resources, we have pointed out that GDP converted at market exchange rates should not be viewed as the more relevant measure of a member's ability to contribute resources, because the argument that it reflects the international market value of resources generated by an economy misses the point that there will never be a need to convert nontraded goods and services at market exchange rates to pay for IMF quotas. Quotas are a small fraction of GDP or exports and one cannot imagine an IMF that would be so large that countries will become strapped for cash and have to sell nontradables to pay for their quotas. Therefore, PPP-based GDP is the more relevant indicator for measuring potential contributions to the IMF because the larger the volume of goods and services produced by an economy, the greater its size and role in the world economy. In this respect, since the quota formulas are based on GDP converted at market exchange rates, and even the recent resolution of the Board of Governors gives more weight to the market-based GDP than the PPP-based GDP in the hybrid variable, the supply variable is barking up the wrong tree. It may be worth emphasizing that the two different measures of GDP make a big difference in the calculations of quotas: the share in global totals of advanced economies of GDP converted at market exchange rates is over 75 percent of the global total but declines to about 50 percent for PPP-based GDP. The situation with the demand variables is worse. The openness variable is based on the argument that relatively more open economies are more vulnerable to external shocks, and therefore will be more likely to use IMF resources. The biggest irony is that the advanced economies have 70 percent of the share in global totals of current payments and receipts, which means that the bulk of the share in calculated quotas from the demand variable is eaten up by the countries that have not borrowed in decades and are not expected to borrow in the foreseeable future. Variability of current receipts, which is the other demand variable in the quota formulas, is not much better because the advanced economies' share is over 60 percent. If these variables are supposedly capturing the demand for IMF resources, then why is it that their correlation with actual use of IMF resources is so low and has been on a downward path toward zero when calculated with rolling windows over the last thirty years. The bottom line is that it is high time to look for new demand variables in the quota formulas, and the variables discussed in Table 14.1 would appear to be prime candidates. In particular, the traditional openness and variability variables in the quota formulas need to be replaced with new variables that have at least some correlation with actual use of IMF resources.

V. Conclusion

There is no disagreement that a major strength of the IMF is that it is a cooperative institution—bringing together 185 countries with diverse conditions and needs—that has provided some of the most valuable public goods available to the international community, nor is one challenging the account that some efforts have been made to assure members that their voice is heard and that they have an appropriate weight in decision making. However, these efforts are insufficient and much remains to be done. Legitimate concerns have been raised on the voice and quotas issue in various parts of the developing-country membership and, unless comprehensive solutions are found, it should be clear that the IMF quotas will remain a contested terrain, both within the IMF and in the public domain. Developing countries have long pushed for changes in the IMF's voting structure to reflect better their international economic weight and to give a stronger voice and representation to LICs, arguing that the current system undermines the legitimacy of the institution. There is the concern that unless the matter is addressed, some developing countries, especially in Asia, would start moving away from the IMF's fold.

The Rawlsian approach suggests a more fundamental review of the governance issue than is implied from the state of the discussion in the Executive

Board. Some areas of quota and voice reform that require a good deal of further work either are not discussed or are presented by the IMF staff as if the discussions are in the final stages, namely, the selection of variables for a new quota formula. In particular, the possibility of using purchasing power parity rather than market exchange rates to derive GDP receives only a cursory mention, and possible other variables for external volatility and demand for IMF resources are not discussed at all. Suffice it to say that the quota formulas require a major rethink, and it does not make much sense to confine the discussion by imposing unreasonably tight boundaries. There is also the concern that once the current already protracted reform effort is completed without fundamental corrections, some countries will say that now we are done with the reform and we don't have to go back to this subject for several decades. Recall that the utterly flawed Bretton Woods formula has been with us for over six decades.

Justice as fairness is—to use the IMF's own language—a continuous performance criterion that must be observed by all those who would strive for a well-functioning IMF. The method that Rawls developed in *A Theory of Justice* (1999) and refined in numerous other publications, of postulating an original position—a hypothetical situation in which individuals behind a veil of ignorance decide to agree on principles of social cooperation—and the work on overlapping consensus that is discussed in detail in *Political Liberalism* (1996) provide a framework for overcoming the impasse on the quota formulas. Giving voice to just principles is a *sine qua non*, and this requires the willingness to pay the costs necessary for their realization, which means reaching an acceptable outcome that will no doubt require tough political decisions by the IMF's major shareholders. As Rawls puts it in the famous last sentence of his first book, "[p]urity of heart, if one could attain it, would be to see clearly and to act with grace and self-command from this point of view."

VI. References

Berg, Andrew, Eduardo Borensztein, Gian Maria Milesi-Ferretti, and Catherine Pattillo, 1999, "Anticipating Balance of Payments Crises: The Role of Early Warning Systems," Occasional Paper No. 186 (Washington, D.C.: International Monetary Fund).

Blinder, Alan, 2003, "A New Global Financial Order: The Art of the Possible," in D. Das (ed.) *An International Finance Reader* (London: Routledge), pp. 104–13 (an update and revision of "Eight Steps to a New Financial Order," *Foreign Affairs*, September/October 1999).

Boughton, James M., 2001, *Silent Revolution: The International Monetary Fund, 1979–1989* (Washington: International Monetary Fund).

Buira, Ariel, 2003, "The Governance of the International Monetary Fund," *Challenges to the World Bank and the IMF—Developing Country Perspectives*, Buira, Ariel (ed.), pp. 13–36 (New York: Anthem Press).

Caballero, Ricardo, and Arvind Krishnamurthy, 2001, "International and Domestic Collateral Constraints in a Model of Emerging Market Crises," *Journal of Monetary Economics*, 48, pp. 513–48.

Calvo, Guillermo, 1996, "Capital Flows and Macroeconomic Management: Tequilla Lessons," *International Journal of Finance and Economics*, July.

—— and Carmen Reinhart, 2000, "Fear of Floating," *Quarterly Journal of Economics*, May, pp. 379–408.

Chang, Roberto, and Andres Velasco, 1998, "Financial Crises in Emerging Markets: A Canonical Model," NBER Working Paper W6606. <http://papers.nber.org/papers/W6606.pdf>.

—— 2000, "Financial Fragility and the Exchange Rate Regime," *Journal of Economic Theory*, XCII, pp. 1–34.

dos Reis, Laura, 2005, "Measuring Vulnerability: Capital Flows Volatility in the Quota Formula," *Reforming the Governance of the IMF and the World Bank*, Buira, Ariel (ed.), pp. 195–212 (New York: Anthem Press).

Eichengreen, Barry, and Ricardo Hausmann, 1999, "Exchange Rates and Financial Fragility," NBER Working Paper W7418, <http://papers.nber.org/papers/W7418.pdf>.

Feldstein, M., 1998, "Refocusing the IMF," *Foreign Affairs*, March–April.

International Monetary Fund, 2000a, *External Review of Quota Formulas* (EBAP/00/52, 5/1/00, Supplements 1 and 2, 5/1/00 and Supplement 3, 5/2/00) <http://www.imf.org/external/np/tre/quota/2000/eng/qfrg/appb/index.htm>.

—— 2000b, *Staff Commentary on the External Review of Quota Formulas* (EBAP/00/66, 6/7/00) <http://www.imf.org/external/np/tre/quota/2000/eng/qfrg/comment/index.htm>.

—— 2001a, *IMF Executive Board Informally Discusses Quota Formulas*, PIN No. 01/118, November 7, <http://www.imf.org/external/np/sec/pn/2001/pn01118.htm>.

—— 2001b, *Alternative Quota Formulas—Considerations*, Annex II, (SM/01/293, 9/27/01) <http://www.imf.org/external/np/tre/quota/2001/eng/aqfc.htm>.

—— 2002, *Executive Board Discusses Further Considerations in the Twelfth General Review of Quotas*, PIN No. 02/105, September 20, <http://www.imf.org/external/np/sec/pn/2002/pn02105.htm>.

—— 2005, "Quotas and Voice—Further Considerations," SM/05/341, September 2, p. 29, <http://www.imf.org/external/np/pp/eng/2005/090205a.pdf >.

—— 2006, "Quotas—Updated Calculations," August 4, <http://www.imf.org/external/np/pp/eng/2006/080406.pdf>.

Kelkar, L. Vijay, Praveen K. Chaudhry, Marta Vanduzer-Snow, and V. Bhaskar, 2005, "Reforming the International Monetary Fund: Towards Enhanced Accountability and Legitimacy," *Reforming the Governance of the IMF and the World Bank*, Buira, Ariel (ed.), pp. 45–74 (New York: Anthem Press).

Kenen, Peter B., 2001, *The International Financial Architecture: What's New? What's Missing?*, (Washington: Institute for International Economics) <http://bookstore.petersoninstitute.org/merchant.mvc?Screen=PROD&Product_Code=335>.

King, Mervyn, 2006, "Reform of the International Monetary Fund," speech given at the Indian Council for Research on International Economic Relations (ICRIER) in New Delhi, India on February 20, 2006. Available at <http://www.bankofengland.co.uk/publications/speeches/2006/speech267.pdf>.

Krugman, Paul, 1979, "A Model of Balance of Payments Crises," *Journal of Money, Credit and Banking*, XI, pp. 311–25.

—— 1999, "Balance Sheets, the Transfer Problem, and Financial Crises," in *International Finance and Financial Crises: Essays in Honor of Robert P. Flood, Jr.* (Washington, D.C.: International Monetary Fund).

Le Fort, Guillermo, 2005, "Issues on IMF Governance and Representation: An Evaluation of Alternative Options," *Reforming the Governance of the IMF and the World Bank*, Buira, Ariel (ed.), pp. 107–48 (New York: Anthem Press).

Macedo, Stephen, 1990, "The Politics of Justification," *Political Theory*, 18/2, pp. 280–304.

McLenaghan, John B., 2005, "Purchasing Power Parities and Comparisons of GDP in IMF Quota Calculations." *Reforming the Governance of the IMF and the World Bank*, Buira, Ariel (ed.), pp. 171–94 (New York: Anthem Press).

Mikesell, R., 1994, "The Bretton Woods Debates: a Memoir," *Essays in International Finance* (Department of Economics, Princeton University), March, no. 192.

Moggridge, Donald (ed.), 1980, *The Collected Writings of John Maynard Keynes, Activities 1940–1944, Shaping the Post-War World: The Clearing Union*. Volume XXV (Macmillan Cambridge University Press for the Royal Economic Society).

Neiss, Hubert, 2001, "Conditionality and Program Ownership", Written Remarks during IMF Seminar on Conditionality, Tokyo, July 10, 2001.

Nozick, Robert, 1974, *Anarchy, State, and Utopia* (New York: Basic Books, Inc.).

—— 2001, *Invariances: The Structure of the Objective World* (Cambridge, Massachusetts: Harvard University Press).

Portugal, Murilo, 2005, "Improving IMF Governance and Increasing the Influence of Developing Countries in IMF Decision-Making." *Reforming the Governance of the IMF and the World*, Buira, Ariel (ed.), pp. 75–106 (New York: Anthem Press).

Radelet, Steven and Jeffrey Sachs, 1998, "The Onset of the East Asian Financial Crisis," Chapter 20 in National Bureau of Economic Research, *Asian Crisis and International Solutions*.

Rawls, John, 1987, "The Idea of an Overlapping Consensus," *Oxford Journal of Legal Studies* 7 (Spring): pp.1–25.

—— 1988, "The Priority of Right and Ideas of the Good," *Philosophy and Public Affairs* 17 (Fall): pp. 251–76.

—— 1989, "The Domain of the Political and Overlapping Consensus," *New York University Law Review* 64 (May): pp. 233–55.

—— 1996, *Political Liberalism*, Paperback edition, with new Introduction (New York: Columbia University Press).

—— 1999, *A Theory of Justice*, revised edition (Cambridge, Mass.: Harvard University Press).

Truman, Edwin M., 2006, *A Strategy for IMF Reform*, Policy Analyses in International Economics, Number 77 (Washington: Institute for International Economics) <http://bookstore.petersoninstitute.org/merchant.mvc?Screen=PROD&Product_Code=3985>.

Van Houtven, Leo, 2002, *Governance of the IMF* (Washington, DC: International Monetary Fund).

Woods, N., 1998, "Governance in International Organizations: The Case of Reform in the Bretton Woods Institutions," *International Monetary and Financial Issues for the 1990*, Geneva: UNCTAD, Vol. IX.

——2001, "Making the IMF and the World Bank More Accountable," *International Affairs*, 77/1.

Yaqub, Muhammad, Azizali Mohammed, and Iqbal Zaidi, 1996, "A Focused SDR Allocation," in Mussa, Michael, Boughton, James M., and Isard, Peter (eds.), *The Future of the SDR in Light of Changes in the International Financial System*, pp. 202–16 (Washington, DC: International Monetary Fund).

Index

Index

Bretton Woods (*cont.*)
 and American political power 32
 collapse of classical system 28
 collapse of 116, 175
 development issues 15–19
 formula 270, 271–6, 300
 opposing ideas 19–23
 poor country borrowing 34
 ratification debate 35
 and universal rules 31
 and Westphalian principle 290
Boughton, James 158
budget development 200–1
buffer stocks 45
Bureau of Statistics 31
Burkina Faso 91, 193, 196
Burundi 91

C

Caballero-Krishnamurthy (C-K) model 286
Camdessus, Michel 56
Cameroon 91, 179, 180
Canada 65, 70
Canadian International Development Research
 Centre 233
Cape Verde 142
capital
 account shocks 285
 diminishing marginal productivity of 122
 flow 30, 286, 287
 inflows and debt 177
 markets access 17, 72–3, 257
 productivity and debt 177
 shares 265
 and stabilization 36
 US markets 33
Central African Republic 91
Central Banking Service 31
CFA (African Financial Community) 237,
 238, 239
CFF (Compensatory Financing Facility) 53–4,
 55, 113, 142
Chad 91
Chang-Velasco model 288
Chase National Bank 32, 33
Chenery, Hollis 29
Chicago boys 46
Chile 36, 46, 70, 71
China 65, 70, 73, 248, 251, 272
Citibank 64
C-K (Caballero-Krishnamurthy) model 286
classification of countries 70, 72–4, 138–9
Colombia 40, 70, 71
commodities 42–3, 234
commodity prices 17, 19, 20, 27, 45
Compensatory Financing Facility (CFF) 237,
 238, 239

concessional lending 87–90, 137, 151
conditionality
 and adjustment 116
 for Africa 232–3
 credibility of 131
 efficacy of 258
 excessive 283
 and IMF 126, 131, 212, 284
 and LIC votes 252
 and ownership in PRGF program 96–9
 program 167–8
 and realistic estimates 169–70
 and signals 168
 upper-credit-tranche 66
Conditionality Guidelines 98, 168, 255
Congo 91, 179, 180
constituency system 242, 267
Conway, Patrick 9
cooperative equilibrium 164
Cooper, Richard 23, 122, 277
cosmopolitan democracy 259
Côte D'Ivoire 179
CPIA (World Bank Country Policy and
 Institutional Assessment) 143, 150
credit 54
credit expansion 38–9, 47
creditors 70, 71, 73
credit rating agencies 287
currency
 composition and debt 180
 convertibility 16, 32
 devaluation 21, 38, 46, 124, 238
 instability 43
 reform 28
 in Senegal 236–9
current account
 adjustment 195
 deficits 29, 36, 118, 119, 120, 140, 195
current receipt variability 299
Czech Republic 65

D

Dahl, Robert 259–60
Dawson, Thomas C. 204
debt
 1982 crisis 116
 additionality 184–7
 bilateral claims 181
 build up 179–80
 burden 180
 burden indicators 149
 and capital inflows 177
 concessional 151, 152, 155
 currency composition 180
 default 151, 177, 178, 183, 233
 and discipline 152
 distress 149, 150, 180